MVFOL

UNORTHODOX MARXISM

UnOrthodox Marxism

An Essay On Capitalism, Socialism and Revolution

Michael Albert
Robin Hahnel

Copyright ©1978 by South End Press
First Edition

Printed in the U.S.A. Copyrights are still required for book production in the United States. However, in our case it is a disliked necessity. Thus, any properly footnoted quotation of up to 500 sequential words may be used without permission, so long as the total number of words quoted doesn't exceed 2,000. For longer quotations or for a greater volume of total words quoted, authors should write for permission to South End Press.

Library of Congress Catalog Card Number: 78-53575
ISBN 0-89608-004-8 (paper)
ISBN 0-89608-005-6 (cloth)

South End Press, Box 68, Astor Station
Boston, Ma. 02123

DEDICATION

In Vietnam there is a myth of creation which glorifies resistance. A woman gives birth to a strange little child, Holy Giong, who is silent for three years until messengers come asking for volunteers to resist the country's enemies. Holy Giong's first words are, "I will fight the enemy," and she goes forth.

This book is dedicated to the women and men of Vietnam and to our own children here in the United States that they should have the same dignity and will to resist as Holy Giong, and that their children will live in a world where such militance will be unnecessary.

> The Wheel of law turns
> without pause
>
> After the rain good weather
> In the wink of an eye
>
> The universe throws off
> its muddy clothes
>
> For ten thousand miles
> the landscape
>
> Spreads out like a beautiful brocade
> Light breezes. Smiling flowers.
>
> High in the trees amongst
> the sparkling leaves
>
> All the birds sing at once
> People and animals rise up reborn
>
> What could be more natural?
> After sorrow, comes joy.
>
> Ho Chi Minh

ACKNOWLEDGMENTS

Any book is a collective product: a result of the distillation of many ideas and experiences involving contributions from many individuals, social movements, organizations, and the like. It is impossible to precisely enumerate such sources. But for their contributions, and especially for the knowledge we gained through our participation in the New Left we are forever indebted.

But more specifically we also wish to thank Stanley Aronowitz for his comments on our treatment of Marx in chapters one and two, Sam Bowles and Herb Gintis for their comments on an early draft of part one, Ronald Meek for his considerable suggestions on our treatment of orthodox Marxism—both the presentation and the critique, Steve Shalom for his general help with the whole manuscript and especially for suggestions concerning the content of chapter three, Lydia Sargent for suggestions concerning the four foci of the core characteristic presentation in chapter three, Peter Bohmer for his comments on the whole manuscript and especially for help with the ideas in chapter seven and eight, Melvin Albert for critical comments and editing on chapters five, six and especially seven, Vickie Sansalone for editorial work and suggestions concerning chapters one through five, and John Schall for suggestions concerning chapters one through three and for his help on all matters of production and design. We'd also like to thank the many students who gave valuable suggestions, comments, and criticisms concerning all the materials in this book as they were presented to courses we have taught at the University of Maryland, American University, and the University of Massachusetts in Amherst. Finally, we'd like to thank Michael Prokosch for his design and development of the cover of this book.

TABLE OF CONTENTS

INTRODUCTION

The spectre of reality haunts orthodox Marxist theory.

The orthodoxy emphasizes material conditions, the economic sphere, the contradiction between forces and relations of production, and the proletariat and the bourgeoisie. Reality, however, presents a different set of critical relations. Orthodox Marxism says one thing, but reality, it would seem, marches to the beat of a different drummer.

In the United States and throughout the world, the past two decades have been a time of rich political development. There is now a fundamental critique of the dominant orthodox Marxist theory, a critique based in action and rooted in real historical experiences. But this critique has not yet become solidified in new political organization or theory. It is there, in the events of the two decades, for all to see, but most refuse to pay it any attention.

In the United States hippies and other counter-cultural activists have made culture and daily-life experience a central socialist concern. Blacks, Chicanos, and other Third World people have shown the critical importance of racism and the need for autonomous Third World organizations. Women have revealed a "new" realm of oppression and resistance. They have shown the interrelatedness of the personal and the political. Blacks, Chicanos, women, and youth have all demonstrated that proletarians won't be alone in the struggle for a new society.

In May of 1968, French students and workers rebelled against alienation and authoritarianism; they tried to redefine the very contours of daily-life. They showed that advanced capitalist societies are not invulnerable to revolutionary upheaval. The Hungarian revolutionaries in '56 and the Czechs in '68 demonstrated both the inhumanity of their own "socialist" societies and that of the Russian "fatherland" as well. And however dubious its final outcome, the Chinese Cultural Revolution propelled many to reconsider the relations between society's economy and its culture and politics.

5

For two decades people's struggles have made evident that orthodox ideas are insufficient. Yet, however strongly this case has been made, the ironic truth is that now, with the smoke of the sixties cleared, the old ideas are back in the theoretical saddle again, or, in any case half way up the side of the horse. But the people have need for something new.

*****

In one of his early writings, Karl Marx remarked that "religion is the sigh of an oppressed creature, the heart of a heartless world, as it is the spirit of spiritless conditions,"[1] and yet now, ironically, orthodox Marxism has itself become little more than a religion. There is scripture. There is exegesis. But there is no revolutionary spirit.

Orthodox Marxism pervades left thought. It shapes what we think by providing the very tools we most often think with Yet the orthodoxy is mechanical and lacking in wisdom. Its concepts are a mental straight jacket impeding socialist revolution. They are a barrier between revolutionaries and a rich understanding of society, between revolutionaries and effective action.

The orthodox theory does little to explain the complex dynamics of human behavior and personality. Historical materialism, the orthodox theory of history and social change, focuses our attention on too few needs, makes a fetish of production, and overlooks too many aspects of capitalist everyday life. It seeks fundamental contradictions where none are to be found. It misses the complex dynamics of how societies maintain their stability, and of how revolution occurs as well

The biblical orthodox Marxism which is still quite prevalent and at the root of almost all socialist organizational activity, insufficiently recognizes the multiplicity of groups and issues central to social change. Economic aspects continually exclude concerns of a more social and cultural nature; ownership relations exclude more complex sex, race, and authority relations. In short, orthodox Marxism is vulgar. It clings to so-called fundamentals and in so doing misses the broader picture. The modern orthodox Marxist sees reality through a set of insufficient concepts. Reality's fullness is obscured. Facts are made to conform with the theory rather than the reverse. The person as subject/object of history is lost to view.

The Labor Theory Of Value, perhaps the cornerstone of the orthodox Marxist economic analysis of capitalism, is simply wrong. It is built upon a set of suppositions about economic life which have likely never been good approximations of the real world, and certainly aren't now. Chief among these are the assertions that capitalism is competitive so that capitalists and workers can freely move about from industry to industry, and that consciousness is but a simple reflection of material interests. The theory virtually ignores the roles of racism and sexism. It misunderstands the effect of economic activity upon its human agents. It overlooks the full complexity of economic production and consumption—how each activity produces and consumes not only goods but also social relations, consciousness, and personalities. The Labor Theory Of Value mistakenly takes insufficient account of the fact that society molds its own economy, just as the economy molds society.

Orthodox Marxism has degenerated to the point where it conceals as much as it exposes. It has lost touch with day-to-day life and people's needs. Yet it still reigns unparalleled as the underlying basis of most left thought. Certainly there are many innovative and creative contributions being made by socialists, but how many more could there be? To what extent are even the most productive Marxist intellectual workers still crippled by the degree to which the concepts of historical materialism and the Labor Theory Of Value guide their thought? Why is this theory so resilient despite its weaknesses? Indeed why will many readers find this introductory list of criticisms so unthinkable as to make them want to close this book without proceeding?

*****

Old ideas die very hard.

In the face of an immensely powerful capitalist enemy one does not easily relinquish a time-honored theory which promises socialist victory.

In the face of a world, most of whose socialists still call themselves Marxists, it is very difficult to even entertain the notion of condemning orthodox Marxism.

In opposition to orthodox believers who have answers for everything, it is difficult to assert incomplete new ideas—yet without the new ideas, the criticisms are simply dismissed as destructive and anti-Marxist.

In a world where most people who attack the orthodoxy do so from the right, it is easier for leftists to line up in its defense. It is common as well for all critics to be immediately labeled "anti-communist", "bourgeois", "reactionary", or worse as the case may be. Such sectarian name-calling is very potent. Lumping all critics of the orthodoxy with those whose purposes are indeed reactionary, this reverse baiting effectively intimidates most leftist critics. It asserts that there can be no justifiable criticism, only ill-motivated anti-communism, so that those that venture critical analysis run the risk of stimultaneously losing all "revolutionary credibility". The orthodoxy is sacrosanct and disbelievers are heretics, beholden, one way or another, to the capitalist devil.

But giving in to these pressures does not serve the socialist movement. To be sure we should not seek newness for its own sake. That which is of value in the Marxist heritage—and there is much that is—ought to be preserved. But that which is outmoded or even wrong from the beginning must be replaced. This is a task which should be imperative to all who are concerned with making a revolution, no matter what the counter pressures.

*****

T.S. Kuhn, a historian of science and a thinker about thoughts, has suggested that knowledge frequently comes in bundles which he calls "paradigms."[2] These bundles include a way of looking at the world, organizing perceptions and thinking about them, and an analysis of the world or some aspect of it based on these methods. In physics, for example, Newtonian mechanics was and remains a paradigm.

A paradigm tells about any particular field what's important and what isn't, what questions we should ask, and what answers we should expect. When a paradigm begins suggesting unimportant questions, overlooking others that are important, or making false predictions, it comes into question itself.

While a particular paradigm is in favor, most intellectual workers follow its dictates and extend its analyses. When it begins to be doubted, some workers take up the task of uncovering its weaknesses and developing a new paradigm to take its place.

In science the transition between paradigms is very slow. People are never eager to admit that a system which has given them excellent service is no longer sufficient. In politics the situation is even more extreme. Here similar allegiances are at work, but in addition there are material, psychological, and institutional "vested interests" as well. Political paradigms give people roles in society, sometimes power and wealth, and always a self-image. Overturning a well-rooted political paradigm is a difficult task. The paradigm's adherents usually defend their "science" with a vengeance.

This is the current situation of orthodox Marxism. Practice has put many of its basic tenets in question. The most conservative of the "religious adherents" simply ignore this fact claiming that the theory has no problems at all. The more enlightened adherents admit the difficulties but claim they are far from insurmountable. All that is necessary to amend the orthodoxy is to take the new lessons into account. But this is an endless patch-up job, and there are new leaks spouting all the time— who knows what holes still lay unseen? Both types of adherent receive criticisms of the orthodoxy with hostility. Their goal is to preserve the old view, not to alter or replace it.

But there is another way to relate to the period of demise of an outmoded paradigm. Rather than struggling to preserve what was, one can freely critisize it, and then move from the criticisms to new ideas and finally to a whole new paradigm, with roots in what went before, preserving its strengths, but superceding it as well.

Our contention is that the problems of orthodox Marxism are beyond patching up. The paradigm is unsuited to the tasks now at hand. There is a word in Hegelian philosophy which, in our understanding, summarizes the task at hand. It is "aufheben"—to destroy but preserve the strength of what was destroyed as part of a new and higher synthesis.

What are the concrete conditions we socialists are trying to overcome? What is the socialist goal we are seeking? How can we link it to our everyday struggles in the here and now? What are the links between race, sex, class, and authority oppressions? How can revolutionaries address all these oppressions simultaneously while also respecting the integrity of Third World, womens', workers', and other movements? What are the organizational vehicles best suited to our struggle to create a new society?

We need to know the agents, organizational forms, issues, arenas of struggle, goals, and character of the socialist revolution we wish to bring about here in the United States. The orthodox Marxists, however, tell us about non-existent crises of the falling rate of profit, the immiserated proletariat, and the philosophical intricacies of "dialectical thinking". And even these ideas are examined in ways we can't understand and certainly can't apply to our life situations. Without a revolutionary understanding accessible to people and developed by people out of their own experiences, there will be no revolutionary movement. Socialist intellectuals should contribute tools and other means for developing such a popular understanding. Instead they most often obscure reality behind the densest rhetoric and academic debate.

Marx himself saw revolution as a way by which history would once again become the province of people themselves. People are social beings of praxis; the revolution puts people at stage center, determining their own future in accord with their own needs and capabilities. Marx was relentless in pursuit of socialism—he was concerned to overthrow, not to preserve the past. It is this Marx to whom we look, not as a prophet, but as a useful teacher from whom we can learn a great deal. We critique orthodox Marxism precisely so as to reclaim and expand upon many of Marx's own most profound and important insights.

In the first chapter of this book we present a summary of the orthodox Marxist paradigm. In Chapter Two we present a full critique. We discuss methodology, historical materialism, and the Labor Theory

Of Value. We use what is best in the heritage of Marxism, as well as many lessons from modern experience, to critisize what is worst.

But it is not enough to just attack what is outmoded—we must, however tentatively, put forward something to stand in its place. This we do in Part Two. In Chapter Three we seek a Marxist understanding of history more useful than the historical materialist views we dismissed in Part One. In Chapter Four we seek to develop a "political economy of praxis" to replace the orthodox Marxist economic theory as based on the Labor Theory of Value.

In Part Three we apply our new theory to an analysis of the United States. Chapter Five offers a view of the "human center" and Chapter Six of the "institutional boundary" of U.S. society. These chapters are an overview, a first step. They provide an illustration of our theory in use and they enable us to develop a hypothesis concerning the character of our society. But the final proof of their assertions is a major task far beyond the scope of any single book such as this.

Part Four contains our vision of socialism (Chapter Seven) and some ideas on how to get there (Chapter Eight). We criticize centrist socialist theory and the market socialist alternative, and develop in their place a decentralized participatory planning model. Similarly we criticize Marxist Leninist strategy as well as feminism, anarchism, nationalism, and a number of other approaches as all being only partial and thus insufficient to understanding current United States conditions. We develop a new councilist orientation consistent with our theoretical analysis and very much in tune with the potentials of our time.

In the face of orthodox Marxism, our purpose is to outline the contours of a new view of socialist revolution, one consistent with the dictates of modern circumstances. We inject a human orientation into economics and an economic orientation into humanism. We elaborate a theory and vision—a hypothesis—which recognizes itself as not the world itself, but rather only the world exposed to our particular methods of questioning. It is but a rough map which must always be improved according to the dual criteria of internal consistency and a positive relation to concrete practice. All our own efforts must be aimed toward just such a practice—toward socialist revolution.

FOOTNOTES: INTRODUCTION

1. Karl Marx quoted in *Karl Marx: His Life and Thought,* by David McClellan, Harper and Row, Page 88-89.
2. See Thomas Kuhn, *Structure of Scientific Revolutions,* Chicago, 1962.

PART ONE
LAYING THE ORTHODOXY
TO REST

Marxism, after drawing us to it as the moon draws the tides, after transforming all of our ideas, after liquidating the categories of our bourgeois thought, abruptly left us stranded... it no longer had anything new to teach us, because it had come to a stop. Marxism stopped.... Marxism possesses the theoretical bases, it embraces all human activities; but it no longer knows anything.

> Jean Paul Sartre
> *Search For A Method*

CHAPTER ONE
ORTHODOX MARXISM

He, who before was the money owner, now strides in front as
capitalist; the possessor of labor power follows as his laborer.
The one with an air of importance; the other hesitant, like one
who is bringing his own hide to market and has nothing to
expect but—a hiding.

Karl Marx
Capital

In this chapter we present the current orthodox Marxist paradigm.
By "orthodox Marxism" we mean the interpretation of Marx which was
initiated by Kautsky and Plekhenov, pursued by Lenin and Trotsky,
codified by Stalin, and currently reproduced immaculate by Cornforth,
compellingly by Mattick, and subtly excised by Althusser. We
intentionally exclude the "unorthodox Marxists" (e.g. Korsch, Gramsci,
Pannekoek, Kollantai, de Beauvoir, Sartre, Castoriadus, Gorz, etc.)
from this diverse "family" not because they were immune to the sway of
orthodox notions, but because even immersed in orthodox waves they
have established many new ideas and the heritage we now seek to extend.

But to the questions "what is the true Marxist economic theory?"
and "to what extent is the theory you put forward true to Marx?", we
reply:

1-There is no single Marxist theory, no one true Marxist theory,
and there is no way to know what theory Marx would hold were
he alive today. However, we can confidently assert that the
orthodox theory we present is at the core of the worldview of
most currently active Marxists.
2-The most important question about orthodox Marxism is not
who held what thoughts, but rather, what is the value of the
thoughts themselves in the context of our current needs and
possibilities? What can we retain from the orthodoxy? What
can we learn through analyzing its weaknesses?

13

THE DIALECTICAL METHOD

Almost all Marxists regard the dialectical method as an important foundation of their perspective. They feel that the prevalent ways of perceiving and thinking about the world are largely metaphysical, and, with Engels, they see these metaphysical approaches as "exhibiting natural objects and natural processes in their isolation, detached from the whole vast interconnection of things; and therefore not in their motion, but in their repose: not as essentially changing but as fixed constants, not in their life, but in their death."[2]

For orthodox Marxists, the dominant "bourgeois", "metaphysical" way of seeing things gives analysts a disjointed, static, and cause-effect understanding of interrelations. The capitalist appears to exist separately from the worker and from the relations of production. The capitalist is viewed as if he has always been and always will be just as he is now. He is understood as an entity which can be pushed and pulled all about, changing this or that minor aspect, but remaining permanently the same in all that really matters. This way of seeing may be powerful for some purposes but it is not well suited to understanding societies and social change, precisely because it is ahistorical and assumes a permanent status quo.

As a counter view, dialecticians say we should see social systems in their motions and relations, not in some fictitious, static isolation. Dialecticians argue the need for a methodology that sees each entity as involved interactively with all others. According to this way of thinking, to separate something from this worldly "web" is to reduce that thing to less than it really is. Such simplification is often necessary, but it should be undertaken with great care. For the most part, we should train ourselves to see any particular event, institution, idea, or product in its social context. For example, viewing "money" we must see those who exchange it as well as the reasons why they exchange it. Viewing workers we must see their employers and the relations between employees and employers as well.

But beyond seeing things "relationally", dialecticians enjoin us to be highly aware of development through time, that is, to see things "historically". Not only must workers be seen in relation to their employers, but the historical transformation that separated independent producers from their means of production and created a class of workers separate from a class of employers must be kept in mind as well.

Orthodox dialectics is an attempt to translate these injunctions, these desired ways of seeing things, into a formal methodological framework. Orthodox dialectics begins with the assertion that all things constantly change, and that the ultimate source of this perpetual change is internal, and proceeds to elaborate three general submethods for analyzing the change that goes on within all things: the law of transformation of quantity into quality, the law of the unity of opposites, and the law of the negation of the negation.[3]

All things undergo continual small quantitative changes, but eventually the accumulation of quantitative changes leads to a major, qualitative transformation. Ice changes temperature a degree at a time, but suddenly it becomes water, and later steam. In young capitalism firms grow larger and larger initially retaining their competitive relations with one another, but suddenly monopoly emerges and the relations have changed. Or, as we will see later, the rate of profit slowly falls, but suddenly there is a qualitative disruption—a crisis. As a means to discover potentials for change, orthodox dialecticians continually keep watch for quantitative trends that hold potential for qualitative ruptures.

Every system engenders its opposite. In all things and their motions there is a "unity of opposites". To search out these opposites that conflict but are necessary to each other's existence, even in systems that seem internally "calm" is a major task for dialecticians. For example, capitalist production and "free market" exchange relations, which seem so natural and permanent, are found to be in contradiction with the development of productive potential and therefore generate their opposite, socialist relations.

Capitalism negates feudalism. And then socialism negates capitalism. Each negation is itself negated in turn. History, and all relations, move by way of this spiral. When one unity of opposites is transformed, another takes its place.

One particular way of implementing the "dialectical injunction" is often attributed to Mao Tse Tung and especially to his essay, *On Contradiction*.[4] Though Maoist, this approach is also prevalent in most orthodox Marxist presentations.[5] The submethod of the "unity of opposites" is elevated to a central position. Analysts search for the contradictions in all things. One contradiction is singled out as *primary*. It is the one (and there is always only one) whose influence dominates the rest, whose resolution is most critical to the definition of the whole system and the dynamics of all its lesser, secondary contradictions. Moreover, in each contradiction, a distinction is made between the opposing aspects: the aspect which is temporarily dominant is called "principal", the other is called "secondary". The search for contradictions, the determination of the primary contradiction and secondary contradictions, their principal and secondary aspects, and all their interrelations, becomes the central methodology for understanding historical dynamics.

The three submethods and the Maoist elaboration are basically components of the orthodox dialectical viewpoint. They are separate only as tools by which we can guide ourselves. As Lenin described, dialectics is a way of understanding a reality which moves in spirals and not straight lines, repeating past phases but only at new higher levels, by the steady accumulation of quantitative phenomena until finally a qualitative revolutionary leap occurs by the resolution of contradictory forces and tendencies acting within history and in context of forces from within as well as without.[6] The dialectical approach teaches one to view any thing in its relations with all others and in its motion, as a process rather than as an object. It focuses on possibilities for change and exposes us to the complexity of worldly interactions.

THE MATERIALIST OUTLOOK

Extreme idealism says that the world is an imposition of an absolute idea. History is just the development of this idea in the material world. The world of material objects, if there is such a world at all, is but a reflection of the world of ideas and especially of The Idea. Less extremely, what Marxists would call an "idealist deviation" is seeing ideas with a life of their own, separated from their material context, and exerting pressure upon the world independently of the dictates of that context.

In opposition to idealism of all kinds, the orthodox materialist outlook focuses on objective material conditions as the root of all subjective ideas, feelings, and desires. To explain historical events it is necessary to look first at the real material conditions, and only then at what people say or feel about those conditions. Ideas reflect material reality and not vice-versa.

The materialist outlook directs us to the realm of economic relations and particularly to production as the bedrock of any society. Economic relations are at the root of survival and growth, and indeed underlie all social activities. In the materialist view, people need food and shelter first. Economic activity provides these and in so doing it also largely governs how people will perceive and act on their world. The materialist interpretation of history rests on this point.

As but one example, the history of education must be studied not as the history of an idea or series of ideas affecting methods of schooling, but rather in terms of the history of concrete material relations between people, and of the role of schooling in upholding or otherwise affecting these relations. Rather than first examining what John Dewey or Horace Mann said, one should examine the role of schools in the economy—to supply acculturated workers, to teach required skills, etc.—and then study how historical changes in the economy were the basis for alterations in teaching philosophies and the structure of schooling.

THE METHOD OF HISTORICAL ABSTRACTION

Even armed with the dialectical method and the materialist outlook, no one could analyze a whole society or historical epoch in all its detail. To understand social systems one must focus instead on only those aspects most critical to one's own concerns.

Looking at only some of its aspects, in an effort to understand a whole, is the "method of abstraction". The aim is to isolate the central features to study them in an "abstract model". To the extent this model excludes only the peripheral, it allows for the possibility of a powerful approximate understanding of reality. To the extent that we progressively lower the model's level of abstraction by adding more details, our knowledge can approach a fuller understanding of real world relations.

The orthodox dialectical materialist method (especially with its Maoist injunction to distinguish between primary and secondary contradictions) is particularly well-suited to the constraint imposed by our need to abstract. First, it helps us make abstractions which keep track of material relations and history; and, second, it provides a good clue to which aspects we should retain in our most abstract model of any society—that is, the internal contradiction most crucial to the definition and development of that society. In fact, the most prevalent way that the dialectical method is used to understand social systems is called the "corrected history" or "successive approximations" approach.[7] Once we have our model based on the primary contradiction we attempt to explain historical events based on this analysis. Then we add features to our model, making it correspond ever more closely to the complex society we actually live in. We'll elaborate this procedure more fully, showing both its strengths and weaknesses, when we later discuss the orthodox Marxist economic analysis of capitalist societies.

HISTORICAL MATERIALISM

The orthodox Marxist applies the method of abstraction, the dialectical theory of things and their motions, and the materialist outlook to the problem of understanding human societies. The result is historical materialism, the orthodox Marxist theory of history. This theory then acts as a general guide to concrete investigations of any particular historical epoch or society. Understanding historical materialism is thus a prerequisite to understanding the orthodox Marxist economic theory of capitalism. Similarly, later, criticizing historical materialism will aid us in criticizing orthodox Marxist economic theory.

Historical materialism begins with the awareness that people must produce to survive, and that in the act of production they enter into social relations with one another, and use tools, science, and their own insights to create their social means of survival and growth.

All societies have at their core a *mode of production* around which daily-life activities develop. This mode of production is characterized by:

> 1-*the forces of production* which consist of the tools, buildings, and other physical means of carrying out production, as well as the relevant knowledge, skills, and techniques of all sectors of society's work force.
> 2-*the social relations of production* which consist of all the kinds of interrelations people establish in carrying out their work: landlord to tenant, lord to serf, capitalist to worker, supervisor to subordinate, etc.

In very early societies the level of productive forces was only sufficient to produce a *subsistence* equal to the materials required to reproduce the work force, that is, to feed, house, and care for all workers at an historically determined subsistence level. But at some point the forces of production developed to the point where a *social surplus*, or a material product above and beyond the subsistence, was produced. This gave rise to the possibility that some people might live off the efforts of others. In such societies the most crucial social relations of production are between those who produce society's product and those who appropriate the surplus.

In any society citizens are first affected by the requirement to create their own means of survival. In order to do this individuals must enter into the social relations of production that exist in their society, thereby subjecting themselves to their powerful influence. It is in this sense that production is necessary and central. It affects different people differently depending upon what social relationships they enter in the production process. People who share essentially the same relation to the mode of production are similarly affected by it, and, because of this commonality, historical materialists look upon them as well defined groups called *classes*. For in the view of the historical materialists, people are largely a product of their economic situations because these govern well-being, determine the nature of one's economic interests, and simply involve the greatest part of one's waking efforts. Thus which class one is in has a tremendous impact upon what one can do, how one perceives the world, what one's material interests are, and what one thinks about life and history.

In the historical materialist view, to understand a society it is necessary to first understand its mode of production and class structure. But, in accord with the dialectical viewpoint, one must view the mode of production and class structure historically, uncovering the society's past history and also its tendencies toward future alteration.

According to historical materialism, the central point in achieving this understanding is realizing that any society's productive forces continually develop while its social relations of production are relatively fixed. Eventually the continuing advancement of the forces of production brings them into contradiction with the social relations of production. There is a unity of opposites—the two features depend for their existence one upon the other, and together they make up the mode of production; yet they are also in contradiction.

In any society's early days its relations of production contribute to the fullest use of its productive forces, but as the society reaches maturity the situation alters. The mature relations of production begin to "fetter" the steadily enlarging forces of production. For example, under feudalism the relations of production impeded the fullest use of the developing capitalist technology and technical organization of labor. Classes with an interest in preserving a society's social relations of production—the classes whose position allows them to appropriate the surplus—struggle to preserve the status-quo despite its growing irrationality. But other classes with interests in economic growth and development—the classes consigned to a subsistence existence, or those who will be the beneficiaries of a new social organization—seek to undermine the status-quo and to free society's productive capabilities. The latter classes struggle with the former ones to institute revolutionary changes in the society's mode of production.

Historical materialism tells us that 1-production is centrally important, 2-class structure is critical, 3-differences in class motivations arising from differing positions in the mode of production generate class struggle, and finally 4-the contradiction between the forces and the relations of production and the ensuing class struggles are crucial to social change and thus to any society's particular laws of motion. Historical materialism also suggests a methodological search for the unity of opposites which must exist at any society's economic core, and which must hold the key to understanding its class structure, its general economic dynamics, and its potentials for revolutionary change.

THE HISTORICAL MATERIALIST ANALYSIS OF CAPITALISM

The historical materialist analysis of capitalism applies these abstract categories to the concrete capitalist context. The result is a rough description of capitalism's mode of production, class structure, class struggles, and propensities for social change, particularly for a revolution to socialism.

The analysis emphasizes the scientifically advanced character of the productive forces, and the private, individual, and backward character of the social relations of production and appropriation. It focuses attention on the bourgeoisie, which owns the means of production and controls the social surplus; and on the proletariat, which owns only its own labor power, but creates the social surplus. It finds that the bourgeoisie and the proletariat struggle over the creation and appropriation of the economic surplus—that is, around the length of the workday, the intensity of the work process, and wage levels. It finds that this struggle is engendered automatically by the motivations and requirements capitalism imposes upon each class, and that it is thus the human form of the contradiction in the central mode of production. The social character of production and the private character of appropriation is the actual content of this contradiction. Revolution is the final outcome. The state, church, and schools are institutions evolving out of historical requirements and struggles. They serve essentially to reproduce capitalism's class relations while simultaneously expanding the bourgeoisie's power and wealth. The fine details of all these various relations are explicable only through more intensive economic analysis—that is historical materialism's practical injunction—and thus we arrive at the central task of orthodox Marxist economics.[8]

THE LABOR THEORY OF VALUE

Theories of value have as their subject matter the ways in which goods are produced in certain fixed amounts and then exchanged according to definite ratios. Why do apples and oranges, or beaver pelts and deer skins, exchange in the proportions they do? What is it that makes an economy produce 100 million instead of 200 million tons of steel a year, or 700 thousand instead of 500 thousand pairs of shoes?[9]

SIMPLE COMMODITY PRODUCTION MODEL

Marxists start their analysis in an abstract society of "simple commodity production" where separate individuals produce commodities to be exchanged for other commodities they wish to consume. Each producer is assumed to either own the tools necessary for producing the commodities he/she makes or to be capable of making any necessary implements as part of the process of producing the commodities themselves. The society is characterized by a division of labor—some people do one kind of work, others do another—so people must trade with one another. For example, the only way a beaver trapper can consume deer skins is by trading pelts for skins. It is in this sense that the social division of labor necessitates exchange which is the sign that each individual works for all others and therefore that labor is social regardless of how individually it may be carried out.

The system functions according to the prescription C^1—M—C^2. Each individual produces commodities, C^1, and exchanges them for money with which to buy other commodities, C^2. Commodities have use-value because they meet needs, and have exchange-value because they trade for one another in definite proportions. For the materialist the important question is "how do the relations of production determine the relations of exchange?"[10]

Some producers trap beaver and others hunt deer. At some point they each wish to exchange part of their product for some of the other product. How many beaver pelts will go for one deer skin? More generally, what is there about a certain number of beaver pelts that can be compared to a certain number of deer skins? According to orthodox Marxist economics, the only reasonable answer is that what is quantifiably equalized is the "socially necessary labor time" embodied in the production of each.[11] According to the Labor Theory Of Value, if we assume that producers can freely change work activities, commodities will come to exchange one hour of necessary labor time for one hour of necessary labor time. For if this were not the case, producers of commodities exchanging below their necessary labor time would do well to switch to the production of commodities exchanging above their necessary labor time thereby being in a position to obtain more of either commodity with an hour's worth of work. For example, if beaver pelts and deer skins are exchanging one-for-one, but it takes two hours to trap and skin a beaver and only one hour to slay and clean a deer, then beaver trappers should become deer hunters since a deer hunter with two hours work can have either two deer or two beaver (through exchange) whereas a beaver trapper with two hours work can only obtain one beaver or one deer (through exchange). By decreasing the supply of the commodity selling below its labor time and increasing the supply of the commodity selling above its labor time, this movement of producers would act precisely so as to drive the commodity exchange ratios toward the ratio of their embodied labor time.[12]

But how many people will end up hunting deer and how many trapping beaver? This depends on how many people have use for the two commodities and how great their need is. Not only is labor "socially necessary" only if it is performed with average efficiency, but it must also be applied to the production of what people want. If there are too many beaver trappers and too few deer hunters as judged by the number of pelts and skins that people want, then the excess supply of beaver pelts and the insufficient supply of deer skin will drive the exchange rate for pelts in terms of skins below the ratio of their embodied labor times. But we have already seen in this case that trappers would do well to turn into hunters, thereby bringing about an adjustment in work activities so as to conform to the use-value that people have for the two commodities.[13]

So, for the orthodox Marxist, embodied socially necessary labor time determines exchange value, while use-value determines how much of society's labor capability is allocated to the production of different commodities. Exchange-value is quantifiable—measured in labor-hours—and can be observed in the ratios in which commodities exchange. Use-value is not quantifiable but can be inferred from the fact that people want a particular commodity. Through market operations the two together determine:[14] 1-the proportions in which commodities exchange, 2-the amount of society's labor devoted to each kind of production, and 3-the amount of each commodity produced. This is the core of the Labor Theory Of Value as applied to simple commodity production economies.

Now suppose that technical knowledge of productive techniques has improved in a simple commodity production economy to the point that the producers can produce more commodities than are needed for the basic subsistence of the working population. As we have already seen, this allows for the possibility that some people could live without working if they could somehow manage to appropriate the "surplus" from others' production.[15] If, through some historical process, the producers of a simple commodity production economy should become separated from the means of producing their commodities, that is, if one class of people should come to own and control the means of production while another class of people have no means of gaining their subsistence but to go to work for the owners of the means of production, this possibility becomes a reality.[16]

THE CAPITALIST MODEL

The orthodox Marxist analysis of capitalism begins by identifying two classes: one which does no labor itself but which instead owns capital, that is, the means of production, and buys the labor power of others; and another class which owns no capital but instead must sell its labor power if it is to obtain its means of subsistence. This economy is still characterized by production in separate units coordinated through market exchanges, but the exchanges in capitalism have ceased to be simple C^1—M—C^2 exchanges and have become syntheses of two opposite processes.

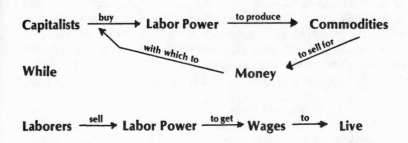

The workers exchange their labor power, which is a commodity, for money, and then exchange that money for other commodities which they need in order to live; this is represented as C^1—M—C^2. In essence it is still one commodity for another, with money as an intermediary just as it was in exchanges in simple commodity production. It is, however, a new type of commodity—the worker's own labor power—which was not exchangeable in the simple commodity system where only the products of one's labor were exchanged.[17]

The capitalists, on the other hand, follow a new and different prescription: money for commodities for a different amount of money (M—C—M'). The capitalists exchange money as wages for the workers' labor power and various other non-labor inputs of the production process (raw materials, machinery), combine these to produce new goods, and then in turn exchange these commodities for more money, M'. Laborers are still motivated to seek commodities for their use-value, but capitalists are motivated only to obtain the surplus for themselves. That is, they seek to accumulate profit in the form of the difference between M' and M.

The worker takes a commodity, exchanges it for money, and then buys another commodity which fills some pressing need. The process is complete. The capitalist takes some money and buys a worker's labor power and other resources, combines these in a new commodity, and sells the new commodity thereby acquiring a greater sum of money than he held in the first place. The money is then exchanged again, the single process is never-ending. In short, the general circulation of commodities now embodies a unity of opposites, $M—C—M'$ and $C^1—M—C^2$, the unity of circulation for profit and circulation for use, within the same set of market transations. And it does this precisely because each circulated commodity also embodies a unity of opposites, exchange-value and use-value, the former sought by the capitalist, the latter by the worker.

But how is it that in this class model the bourgeoisie manages to live off the proletariat's labor? That is, how is it that the fruit of the worker's activities winds up largely in Moneybag's pockets in the form of profit?

Profit, Labor, and Labor Power

To find the answer the orthodox Marxist turns to the realm of production.[18] The capitalist gives money, M, for labor power and non-labor inputs, C. He then exchanges the results of consuming the labor power and non-labor inputs, C', for a sum of money, M'. In other words the capitalist's operation should be represented as $M—C—C'—M'$ indicating not only that the original sum of money M is different from the resulting sum, M', but that the commodities the capitalist buys as inputs to production, C, are different than the commodities he sells as outputs of production, C'. But what commodity is such that its consumption in the production process leads to a greater exchange-value than it was originally purchased for? "In order to be able to abstract value from the consumption of a commodity, our friend, Moneybags, must be so lucky as to find, within the sphere of circulation, in the market, a commodity whose value possesses the peculiar property of being a source of value, whose actual consumption, therefore, is itself an embodiment of labor and, consequently, a creation of value. The possessor of money does find on the market such a special commodity in capacity for labor or labor power."[19]

For the orthodox Marxist the search for the origin of profit ends with recognition of a unique characteristic of the commodity, labor power. Like any other commodity, labor power has an exchange-value equal to the number of labor-hours necessary to produce it, or embodied in it. In this case that means the number of labor-hours required to produce the food, clothes, and shelter needed to keep the worker alive for a day.[20] The exchange-value of labor power is the labor time needed to produce a day's subsistence. But in all non-subsistence economies, in all economies capable of producing a social surplus, it takes *less* than a full work day to produce this subsistence. What the capitalist obtains when he pays the exchange value of labor power is the same as what any buyer gets when he or she purchases any commodity—the use-value of the commodity. But what is the use-value of labor power for the capitalist? It is the labor time embodied in the commodities produced during the production process, or a full day's labor time. The difference between the amount of labor time needed to produce the worker's subsistence and the amount of labor time in the work day is the surplus value that arises in the production process as the quantifiable difference between the use-value and exchange-value of labor power.[21] It is the process of extraction of this surplus which is called *exploitation*.

In a capitalist economy where all commodities exchange in accord with the amount of labor time embodied in them, that is, if we assume "equal exchange", labor power is the only conceivable input to the production process that has this capacity of generating surplus value for the capitalist. It is the only exploitable input. The labor time embodied in the non-labor inputs to the production process will also be embodied in the commodities produced, so when the capitalist sells his products at their values he will obtain an exchange-value that includes the amount of labor time embodied in the non-labor inputs to the product as well as the amount of direct labor time it took to transform these inputs into outputs. But since the capitalist must pay for the non-labor inputs at their value as well, and since the same amount of labor is embodied in the non-labor inputs when purchased as is conferred by them to the product to be sold, there is no opportunity for the capitalist to realize a surplus through their use.

So according to orthodox Marxist economists, the surplus does not derive from paying less for materials or machines than their embodied labor time values, or paying labor power less than its exchange-value for that matter. It comes from the fact that the exchange-value of a day's labor power is less than a day's labor. "It is the subtle distinction between the exchange-value and use-value of labor power that becomes the basis of the Marxist theory of surplus value, the chief contribution made by Marx to the development of economic science."[22]

In other words the source (and the only source under normal equilibrium conditions) of profits at the level of the individual firm is that by paying its living laborers according to the exchange-value of their labor power, the firm pays them less than the value they impart to the commodities they produce. This is true because it takes less than a day's work to produce the amount of food, shelter, and clothing needed to keep a worker alive and working (at her or his accustomed level) for a whole day. Maurice Dobb explicates these orthodox points very clearly.

Hence the emergence of profit was to be attributed, not to any procreative quality of capital per se, but to the historically conditioned fact that labor in action was able to realize a product of greater value (depending upon the quantum of labor involved) than the labor power itself as a commodity was valued at. Hence the exchange between labor and capitalist both was and was not an exchange of equivalents. Given the social basis which constituted labor power as a commodity, an exchange of equivalents took place which satisfied the requirements of the law of value—the capitalist advanced subsistence to the workers and acquired labor power of equivalent market value in return. The capitalist acquired the labor power of the worker; the worker obtained in exchange sufficient to replace in his own person the physical wear and tear that working for the capitalist entailed. Economic justice was satisfied. But without the historical circumstance that a class existed which had the sale of its labor power as a commodity for its only livelihood to confront the capitalist with the possibility of this remunerative transaction, the capitalist would not have been in a position to annex this surplus value to himself.[23]

So we have both equal exchange and exploitation. Equal exchange (all commodities including labor power exchanging in accord with their labor time values) generates some ideological stability for the system in the illusion that all is as it should be, just and natural. But this only masks the fundamental struggle going on between capitalist and worker. It is in the capitalist's interest to make the surplus value as large as possible, whereas it is in the workers' interests to achieve just the opposite. The result is a daily battle between the worker and the boss over the length of the work day, the pace of work, and the wage rate.[24] This is class struggle on a local level. So beneath the serene surface of equal exchange we find, in capitalism, where labor power is a commodity, a unity of opposites, exchange-value and use-value, that generates class struggle and basic contradictions which tend to undermine the system.[25] To see this in more detail, however, it is necessary to follow the Labor Theory Of Value analysis of capitalism somewhat further.

Some Key Variables

The total exchange-value of any given commodity, Q, is the number of socially necessary labor hours embodied in it. This equals the number of hours of direct labor (V+S or wages plus the surplus value) plus the hours of indirect labor, that is, the labor that went into that portion of the machinery and raw materials used up in production—which are called constant capital, or C. So we can write:

$$Q=C+V+S$$

Q is the value of a commodity produced under capitalism expressed in terms of direct and indirect labor, the latter including a wage and surplus component. The system is exploitative in the sense that a part of the worker's labor goes directly to the capitalist. A measure of this relation is the *rate of exploitation* (S'), defined to be $S'=S/V$. Another useful concept is that of the *organic composition of capital* which is a measure of the relative balance between living and "past" labor employed in the production process. The organic composition of capital, q, is defined to be $q=C/(C+V)$. Finally, the rate of profit, P, is defined to be $P=S/(C+V)$, the ratio of surplus value to the capitalist's total outlay—that is, the rate of return on capitalist's investments. Rewriting and making algebraic substitutions for the variables in this equation we find:

$$P = S/(C+V) = (S)[1/(C+V)] = (S/V)[V/(C+V)]$$
$$P = (S/V)[(C+V-C)/(C+V)] = (S/V)[(C+V)/(C+V)-C/(C+V)]$$
$$P = S'(1-q)$$

With these variables (measured in labor hours or in ratios of labor hours) and this equation in hand, orthodox Marxists are equipped to analyze their abstract model of capitalism.

Price and Value

The first task is to determine whether or not exchange in this model really occurs in accord with the dictates of the Labor Theory Of Value as was the case in simple commodity production. In the case of capitalist economies it proves necessary to be somewhat more careful about the assumptions made in analyzing this question than was necessary in simple commodity production.

In simple commodity production whether there was "simple reproduction" (replacement of the means of production each time period without any additions) or "expanded reproduction" (additions to the means of production through accumulation) was irrelevant to the question of whether exchange would take place in accord with embodied labor times. Furthermore, it was of no consequence whether the ratio of "direct" to "indirect" labor was the same or different for producers in different sectors since each producer was assumed to make her or his own means of production as part of making the commodities exchanged, eliminating any distinction between "living" and "dead" labor for simple commodity producers. These considerations cannot, however, be ignored in capitalism, and orthodox Marxists therefore proceed by beginning at a high level of abstraction which can be subsequently reduced by dropping assumptions. So we begin by analyzing a model of capitalism characterized by simple reproduction and equal organic compositions of capital throughout.

Moreover, where it was only necessary to assume complete mobility of producers in simple commodity production models, there are no longer simply producers but capitalists and workers, and orthodox Marxists assume complete mobility of both groups. That is, there is complete mobility of financial capital between sectors where capitalists will presumably seek the highest available rate of profit, and there is complete mobility of labor between different sectors where workers will presumably seek the highest wage for the shortest work day, or the lowest available rate of exploitation. So the question becomes, in a capitalist economy characterized by simple reproduction, equal organic compositions of capital in all sectors, and complete mobility of capital and labor between sectors, will commodities exchange in accord with their embodied labor hours? The orthodox Marxist answer is yes.

To develop a better feeling for how this equilibrium comes about and for its actual structure, consider a simple economy with two sectors, sector 1 in which means of production are produced, and sector 2 in which consumption goods are produced. Then, in the aggregate, we have:

$$C^1+V^1+S^1=Q^1 \quad \text{for sector 1, and}$$
$$C^2+V^2+S^2=Q^2 \quad \text{for sector 2}$$

where all variables, including the values of outputs of each sector, are measured in terms of embodied labor times.

If there is to be only simple reproduction, that is, if the society in each period is only to replace used capital (C^1 and C^2) and consume the rest of the output in the form of surplus and wages (V^1, S^1, V^2, and S^2), that is, if there is to be no accumulation and growth, we must have:

$$Q^1=C^1+C^2 \text{ and } Q^2=V^1+S^1+V^2+S^2, \text{ or,}$$
$$C^1+V^1+S^1=C^1+C^2 \text{ and}$$
$$C^2+V^2+S^2=V^1+S^1+V^2+S^2$$

But these last two equations each reduce to:

$$C^2=V^1+S^1$$

And this is the condition which must hold if there is to be simple reproduction. Sector 1 must create a new supply of means of production, Q^1, and sector 2 a new supply of consumption goods, Q^2, each sufficient to keep the economy operating at a constant level of output period after period. This will be the case if and only if $C^2=V^1+S^1$ *and* if all commodities exchange in accord with their labor time values. Otherwise either sector 1 or sector 2 would not have enough exchange-value in its "net supply" to obtain its necessary "net demand". If means of production exchanged below their value capitalists in sector 1 would not realize enough by the sale of their product to simultaneously replace their equipment, purchase new labor power, and consume at their expected level. Similarly, if consumption goods exchanged below their value, the capitalists in sector 2 would realize too little for them to carry through the requirements of simple reproduction. In either case there would be an "imbalance" and simple reproduction would be precluded. But can this situation prevail under conditions of capital and labor mobility?

If there is complete mobility of labor then no worker need accept employment in a sector with a rate of exploitation higher than any other.[26] And if there is complete mobility of capital no capitalist need provide his funds to any sector with a profit rate lower than any other. So to allow an equilibrium, any set of relative prices must allow for equal rates of exploitation and equal rates of profit in the two sectors. This means that if labor time prices are to be equilibrium prices S^1/V^1, or $S^{1\prime}$, must be equal to S^2/V^2, or $S^{2\prime}$. And $S^1/(C^1+V^1)$, or P^1, must be equal to $S^2/(C^2+V^2)$, or P^2. But this will be precisely the case if all commodities exchange according to their labor values.

S^2/V^2 is the number of hours per day the average worker in sector 2 works for his or her employer's benefit divided by the number of hours per day the average worker in sector 2 needs to produce enough consumption goods for his or her own daily subsistence.[27] S^1/V^1 is the number of hours per day the average worker in sector 1 works for his or her employer's benefit divided by the number of hours per day the average worker in sector 1 works for his or her own benefit in the sense of being paid an exchange value of this number of hours. But if the exchange value of labor power is determined in accord with the Labor Theory Of Value, this means it is determined in sector 2 alone, and if labor power is exchanged everywhere for its "labor value", then the number of hours the worker in sector 1 works for his or her own benefit must be equal to the number of hours needed to produce his or her subsistence in sector 2. If the length of the work day is the same in both sectors, the number of hours the average worker works for the capitalist's benefit must be the same in both sectors as well. Hence $S^{1\prime}=S^{2\prime}$. But we have already seen that:

$$S^1/(C^1+V^1)=P^1=S^{1\prime}(1-q^1) \text{ and}$$
$$S^2/(C^2+V^2)=P^2=S^{2\prime}(1-q^2)$$

So since with labor value exchange rates $S^{1\prime}=S^{2\prime}$, and since we have assumed that $q^1=q^2$, P^1 must equal P^2 as well, and labor value prices do produce equal rates of exploitation and equal rates of profit in the two sectors.

THE TRANSFORMATION PROBLEM

The assumption of capital and labor mobility, and the assumption that the forces of supply and demand bring about an equilibrium price in the markets for all commodities, are, while by no means unquestionable, potentially realistic enough so as to make this model interesting.[28] That is, there would seem to be some purpose in analyzing an equilibrium model of competitive capitalism. But what justification is there for the assumption of equal organic composition in all sectors?

Not only is the organic composition of capital, q, not the same throughout actual capitalist economies, but there are no forces one could identify that would tend to make it so. After all, the wage and profit rates in different sectors of real world capitalist economies are not the same either, but at least one can identify a tendency for them to become so in the mobility of labor and capital. On the other hand, there is no reason to expect labor or capital mobility to equalize the organic compositions between sectors. The ratio of labor costs to capital costs is simply different from industry to industry as is quite evident by thinking about the production of oil and shoes, or steel and goat-herding, as but two clear cut examples; and there is no reason to expect them to become less so. So any theory of value that must assume equal organic composition of capital simply becomes uninteresting.

If we assume capital mobility, the rate of profit must be the same from industry to industry, for otherwise capitalists would simply move their investments until such equality existed. And similarly, if we assume labor mobility, the rate of exploitation must be the same throughout—or else workers would refuse to work where it was worse and flock to where it was better.[29] So P and S', the rate of profit and the rate of exploitation, must not vary throughout the economy. However, we earlier demonstrated that if all commodities exchange at their "values":

$$P = S'(1-q)$$

So then if P is the same from one industry to another, and if S' is the same from one industry to another, and if q is just a function of P and S', that is if $q = 1 - P/S'$, then q must also be constant from industry to industry and throughout the whole economy.

But then what is the effect upon this Labor Theory Of Value analysis if we drop the assumption of equal organic compositions of capital? Must we have unequal profit rates or rates of exploitation from sector to sector? Do commodities still exchange according to embodied labor time ratios? Consider the following case where a capital intensive sector 1 produces oil and a labor intensive sector 2 produces shoes:

	C	+	V	+	S	=	Q	S/V	q	P
1:	90		10		10		110	1	.9	=10%
2:	10		90		90		190	1	.1	=90%

To say that the oil and shoes exchange according to their hours of embodied socially necessary labor (that is in the ratio of 110 to 190) is to arrive at the inconsistency of unequal profit rates—for sector 1 we would have P=S/(C+V) equal to 10%, and for sector 2, P would be equal to 90%. To allow for unequal organic compositions of capital, there are only two ways to continue to get equal profit rates: 1-one can assert that in fact the rates of exploitation, S', vary from sector to sector in a manner precisely offsetting the variations in organic composition, or 2-one can drop the assertion that commodities exchange in proportion to their socially embodied labor-hours showing instead a set of exchange prices consistent with all our other assertions.

The first choice is unacceptable. Even if we drop the assumption of labor mobility and thereby allow for varying rates of exploitation, there is no way to make a case that these variations would precisely offset variations in the organic composition of capital. That is, with q in sector 1 and 2 different, for there to be equal profit rates with commodities exchanging at their labor-values, S' would have to vary from sector 1 to 2 in an exactly offsetting fashion: $S^{1'}/S^{2'}=(1-q^1)/(1-q^2)$. There is simply no mechanism which can explain such a precise relation between the organic composition and the rate of exploitation.[30]

So this leaves the second choice: The solution to the seeming inconsistency is that commodities no longer sell at their labor embodied exchange values. There is now a new set of relative prices which tells in what ratios commodities exchange. Finding these "prices of production" and calculating the exact degree by which they differ from labor values is the famous "transformation problem".[31] While we leave the mathematical solution of the transformation problem to an appendix to this chapter, it is helpful to indicate the direction of the deviations.

In the example above the oil industry is relatively capital intensive, or has a relatively high organic composition of capital and a relatively low rate of profit, while the shoe industry is relatively labor intensive, or has a relatively low organic composition of capital and relatively high rate of profit. The reason for this is that the rate of profit is calculated on the basis of the entire amount of capital outlay, that is as a percentage return on the sum total of exchange value in the form of money, M, used to purchase both constant capital and variable capital; whereas, according to the Labor Theory Of Value, only living labor is exploitable. So an industry like the oil industry, with a relatively high organic composition must use a relatively large proportion of M to obtain the constant capital necessary for oil production and is left only a relatively small proportion of M with which to hire labor power, the only exploitable input, or "value creating" commodity. On the other hand, an industry like the shoe industry with a relatively low organic composition of capital spends a relatively large proportion of its total financial outlay on living labor, the exploitable input to production. So labor value prices give us relatively high profit rates in sectors with low organic compositions and relatively low profit rates in sectors with high organic compositions.

If the profit rates are to be equalized the prices received for their products by sectors with high organic compositions would therefore have to be higher than the labor value prices, and the prices received for their products by sectors with low organic compositions would have to be lower than the labor time embodied in them. Calculating the degree to which the "prices of production" must be higher than labor values for goods produced by sectors of high organic composition, and the degree to which the "prices of production" must be lower than labor values for goods of sectors of low organic composition is the solution to the transformation problem we have left for the appendix.

But if prices must diverge from labor values, what consequence can all the prior value analysis retain. How can we continue to use such variables as C, V, and S, all measured in labor-hours, when such measurements no longer correspond to what is going on in the economy itself?

According to Marx's argument in *Volume III of Capital,* this seeming contradiction can only be resolved by admitting that in the unequal organic composition model equilibrium prices will deviate from embodied labor-time prices. Although this is a matter of undeniable importance with respect to the determination of the relative prices that can be expected in a capitalist economy, orthodox Marxists argue: 1-It is not a refutation of the Labor Theory Of Value since the deviations from labor value prices are determinant and calculable by the very series of transformation equations presented in our appendix. 2-The correct relative prices can be derived from the Labor Theory Of Value. 3-The "transformation problem" in no way undermines the theory's explanation for the origin of profits in a competitive capitalist economy. 4-The impact of the alterations on the laws of motion of capitalism can be shown to be negligible (assuming the value framework was legitimate in the first place). And, therefore, 5-little is to be gained by working with the transformed prices rather than the more graphic labor values in all analytic tasks with the exception of relative price determination. In other words, once the transformation problem has been solved the Labor Theory Of Value explains relative prices, and for all other concerns the transformation problem is merely a technical complexity which can be by-passed for purposes of clarity.

ACCUMULATION

Historical materialism tells orthodox Marxists that a class's relation to the means of production largely determines its consciousness and needs. Thus capitalists, who function in the economy simply to enlarge their wealth via the accumulation of profit, $M'-M$, should always want to enlarge their activities. They should want to invest the surplus they extract rather than always consuming it. Furthermore, as we shall discuss, competition enforces this tendency toward investment rather than consumption. So to bring the model closer to reality we must incorporate the fact that capitalists use their surplus in part to accumulate ever greater amounts of capital, and the assumption of "simple reproduction" must be dropped for "expanded reproduction" as there was nothing more central to Marx's view of capitalism than its dynamism.[32] The most important question for the orthodox Marxists is where this dynamism leads.

THEORY OF INVESTMENT

The orthodox theory of investment is essentially a study of the interaction between firms under conditions of capitalist competition. The individual capitalist must constantly compete lest he be left behind by his fellow capitalists. The one way of competing and of staying ahead of the game is through technological innovation. That is, the individual capitalist seeks to incorporate new technologies which lower his plant costs relative to those of other capitalists in the industry (who are still stuck with the old technology). The society wide exchange-values haven't changed since they are based on "average" necessary labor-time. So the innovative capitalist is able to make "super profits" by selling his more cheaply produced goods at the same price as everyone else.

But the innovative capitalist's higher profit rate is only temporary. It vanishes as soon as the innovation is generalized throughout the industry, thereby bringing the labor value of the goods into line with their cost of production in his individual plant. Thus the pursuit of "super profits" by the individual capitalist, and the forces of competition that compel other capitalists to follow suit, lead to a perpetual incorporation of new technologies throughout the economy. A very important corollary of this theory is Marx's prediction of a constant tendency toward ever greater concentration of capitalist industry. During the period of innovation it is often the case that inefficient capitalists who either can't afford new technologies or who under-estimate their importance fail to make this kind of investment and are driven out of business as a result. This adds to the steady concentration of industries. But our principal concern here is with the effects of the technological changes when they become generalized. Is there a tendency for the rate of profit or employment levels to change in any particular direction? At first it might seem that one could draw some definite conclusions, but this is not necessarily the case.

The individual capitalist would not have introduced the new technology unless it increased his profits. But he makes the calculations in terms of the reigning prices, not in terms of what the prices will become once the new technology is generalized. In effect his competitive condition reduces him to this near-sighted view. For this reason it is *not* possible to conclude that the final effect of introducing new technology will be to increase the rate of profit even though the initial effect for the

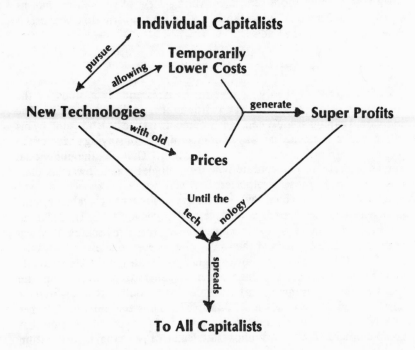

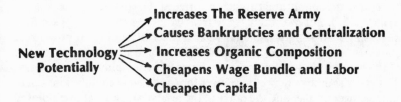

New Technology
Potentially

Increases The Reserve Army
Causes Bankruptcies and Centralization
Increases Organic Composition
Cheapens Wage Bundle and Labor
Cheapens Capital

innovating capitalist is to do so. In other words, we know that the new technology reduces C+V in the industry where it is introduced, otherwise it would not have reduced the innovative capitalist's costs below that of his competitors. However, whether the rate of profit will rise when the lower C+V for all firms brings about a fall in the price of the industry's product due to the fall in average necessary labor-time depends upon other particulars and is indeterminant for the general case we're discussing. Similarly, whether the incorporation of any particular new technology is relatively labor saving (raises q) or relatively capital saving (lowers q) is equally indeterminant at this point. And the question of whether a given sum of financial capital will employ more or less labor after the generalization of some technological change depends upon further factors as well.

But of course not all investment takes the form of implementing new productive techniques. As a matter of fact, during normal periods most investment is simply an expansion of production through use of previous profits using the same techniques as before. That means that more financial capital is used to purchase more constant capital and more labor power in the proportions that they had been previously used. The increased purchase of constant capital can be supplied by an increase in production of the means of production in sector 1. And the increased demand for wage goods by workers that would come about if more labor power were hired can be supplied by increased output in sector 2. But where will the increase in supply of labor power itself come from? Marx repudiated Malthus' theory of population whereby the working class increases its rate of reproduction and/or infant survival whenever there is an increase in capitalists' willingness to pay means of subsistence in exchange for labor power as a libel on the human race. Instead Marx turned to the "reserve army of the unemployed", and in the process provided a theory of the "business cycle".[33]

THE BUSINESS CYCLE

Accumulation in the form of "normal" investment increases the demand for labor power. When the demand for any other commodity rises, its price rises temporarily above its value until capitalists move into the industry producing the good in response to the higher profits, thereby increasing the supply and driving the price of the commodity back down to its "value". But Marx refused to treat women as some sort of sector 3, increasing their supply of babies whenever the price of labor power rose above its "value". Instead, he introduced the concept of the reserve army of the unemployed which is simply a pool of unemployed workers that provides a source of new labor power for capitalist accumulation. But as expansion continues and the ranks of the reserve army of the unemployed are depleted, there is nothing to keep wages from rising above the value of labor power. This leads to a fall in the rate of exploitation, S', and consequently a fall in the capitalists' rate of profit. When the profit rate dips below its normal level, expansion is choked off as individual capitalists await more auspicious times. The fall in investment leads to lay-offs, thereby replenishing the ranks of the reserve army. This "corrects" the situation that led to the rise in V, drop in S', and drop in P in the first place, and establishes the necessary conditions for new expansion. Thus we have a theory that predicts a business cycle based on capitalists' attempts at steady accumulation and expansion.

CRISES

What is a crisis? Suppose we have a society of simple commodity producers where money is used so that all exchanges take the form C^1—M—C^2. Then if a particular producer sells a commodity but fails to buy one, a second producer will not have sold his or her commodity and won't be able to buy from a third, and so on. There is a potential crisis, a potential disruption of the circulation process leaving individuals unable to function as they had intended. But since production is for consumption or for trade leading to consumption, and since consumption is a generally continuous process, there is little reason to expect individuals to sell and then not to buy in simple commodity production economies. In other words, as long as circulation is characterized by exchange in pursuit of use-value, there is little reason to expect a disruption of circulation that can snowball into a crisis. However, no such statement can be made about a system in which production is for profit, and exchange incorporates a unity of opposites in which workers pursue C^1—M—C^2 but capitalists pursue M—C—M'. In this case capitalists might sell their products but refrain from trying to buy more constant capital and labor power to produce again if the profit just realized was below their expectations.

In capitalism the owner's dynamic is M—C—M' and so, whenever $(M'-M)/M$ is less than it is expected to be in the future,[34] capitalists will likely withold their investments and cut back production and employment. Then, on the assumption that the capitalists withdraw the non-invested surplus from circulation there will be a disruption of the entire circulation process and eventually what appears to be a crisis of overproduction. According to orthodox Marxist analysis, this crisis will then act to recreate new conditions again favorable to capitalist expansion. There are two general ways in which the situation confronting the capitalist can induce his withdrawal from the sphere of production. First, the profit rate as calculated in labor values can fall, either due to a falling rate of surplus value or due to a rising organic composition of capital. Second, though the profit rate in terms of labor values might be high, the capitalist might be unable to sell his products at their values so as to realize that high rate—a realization crisis. This could come about either through market disproportions of an anarchic type or through a more general tendency to underconsumption. Let us consider these possibilities in turn.[35]

We have just seen how "normal" investment or expansion leads to a depletion of the ranks of the reserve army of the unemployed and consequently a rise in wages above their value and a fall in the rate of exploitation, S'. What our analysis of crisis in capitalist economies elaborates is the mechanism whereby the fall in the rate of profit can lead to a recession or even snowball into a depression. The second kind of crisis in orthodox Marxist theory also involves a falling rate of profit but one that comes from a secular trend in investment in new technology. According to this scenario, there is a long-run tendency for investment in new technology to be more labor-saving than capital saving. That is, over the long haul new technology tends to increase the organic composition of capital. While these new techniques will certainly increase the rate of exploitation as well by diminishing the number of hours needed to produce workers' means of subsistence and thereby lowering the value of labor power, Marx, at least as Sweezy interprets him, seemed to think that the rise in q would outstrip the rise in S'. This is the famous law of the falling rate of profit of orthodox Marxism.[36]

Of course when properly stated it is "a tendency for the rate of profit to fall" rather than a "law of the falling rate of profit". Sweezy makes this clear in his presentation by enumerating a number of so-called "counter-acting" tendencies beginning with the tendency for new technology to cheapen constant capital by reducing the necessary labor time for making any particular piece of machinery.[37] But rather than complete the list of counter-acting tendencies which always left us with the question why they were labeled "counter-acting" instead of "main" and why the rising organic composition was labeled "main" instead of "counter-acting", we will present a rather simple argument for why one might expect an upward drift in the organic composition of capital.

Although we have not come across this explanation in any orthodox Marxist treatment of the falling rate of profit, it might be argued that while the tendencies for individual capitalists to implement labor-saving technologies during periods of expansion might be equally matched by tendencies to emphasize capital saving technologies during periods of contraction, since the bulk of investment on average takes place during expansions there would be a secular tendency for the organic composition of capital to rise. Capitalists would be anxious to implement labor saving changes during expansion because wages would be their most rapidly rising costs according to Marx's theory of the business cycle. Although labor costs would be the least troublesome input during contractions, the volume of investment that occurs during these periods is not as great. At any rate, the long-run tendency for the rate of profit to fall due to a rising organic composition of capital can also, in the orthodox view, trigger a failure of capitalists to buy after selling and hence a crisis.

The third kind of crisis tendency that orthodox Marxist economics posits is that of a disproportionate distribution of capital and labor. Capitalism is an essentially anarchic system where prices only fluctuate around their values. When capitalists calculate based on incorrect expectations about these price fluctuations, there is the possibility that firms will overproduce relative to the demand they confront in one sector and underproduce in another. When this happens the firms in the sector that has overproduced will be unable to "realize" the value embodied in their products and will cut back production. This, through the layoffs it implies and the consequent cuts in consumption expenditure, at least implies the possibility of a crisis.[38]

The fourth kind of crisis is one of underconsumption. Every individual capitalist seeks to increase profits by reducing wages, and out of profits to maximize the part going to accumulation.[39] Thus the demand for output in the form of workers' demand for consumption goods and capitalists' demand for consumption goods should be falling relative to demand for investment goods. But the more investment goods purchased this period, the higher still the output will be next period, and businessmen cannot be counted on to continue to expand their investment demand just to keep aggregate demand apace of potential supply. Even though it might be in their class interests to do so, individual capitalists competing with one another will only increase their investment demand if they perceive sufficient consumption demand for the products these new investment goods would produce, and the problem arises from the tendency for this consumption demand to diminish relative to the potential supply over time. As before, this leads to an inability to realize the value embodied in products and consequently the possibility of crisis.

And again there are a number of counter-acting factors such as epoch-making discoveries stimulating waves of investment demand, expanding export markets, etc.

In conclusion, the four different kinds of crisis identifiable in orthodox Marxist theory are not to be interpreted as alternative explanations for crises in general. Rather each one is a potential cause of a disruption of the circulation process that can snowball into a fullblown crisis. Moreover, both the secular tendency for the rate of profit to fall and the trend toward insufficient consumption demand can be thought of as problems that would aggravate any crises starting from disproportionality or a falling rate of exploitation. Although we do not have time to explore the matter further, it is interesting to note that there are well-known state policies that can be interpreted as being aimed at solving each of the four tendencies toward crisis. Incomes policies can be used to prevent the rate of exploitation or the rate of profit from falling. Expansionary fiscal policy, or deficit spending, can be used to combat underconsumption. And indicative planning is directly aimed at reducing the "anarchy" of capitalist markets thereby decreasing the probability of disproportionality crises. So in the last analysis, the likely impact of each of the tendencies toward crisis must be judged in light of conscious state counter-actions.

SUMMARIZING THE ROLE OF THE LABOR THEORY OF VALUE

Historical materialism is a general theory of the laws of motion of history from mode of production to mode of production, and also of change within any one mode. For any mode there is a contradiction between forces and relations of production, and normal societal functioning exacerbates that contradiction as production relations act as fetters on productive forces. Moreover, in all societies there are classes, defined by their positions with respect to the society's mode of production, whose normal desires as dictated by their social functions bring them into conflict with one another.

The orthodox Labor Theory Of Value results from an application of historical materialism to the capitalist mode of production. It shows how in capitalism the contradiction between forces and relations of production is essentially the contradiction between commodity use-value and commodity exchange-value, or what is the same thing, between production for use and production for profit, and how under capitalism the class struggle is between the proletariat and the bourgeoisie.

The Labor Theory Of Value, therefore, brings the historical materialist framework, applicable to all modes of production, into direct contact with the capitalist mode and the political economy of capitalism.

The aim of the Labor Theory Of Value is not random, exhaustive study for its own sake, but rather specifically to discover the laws of capitalist motion and the forces which can propel its revolutionary alteration. To conclude our presentation of the orthodox Marxist perspective we will briefly discuss this more practical aspect of the approach.

THEORY, SOCIALISM, AND REVOLUTION

Marxists understand theory and practice to be dialectically related, each influencing and being influenced by the other in an on-going spiral of change. The theory is applied and the results either verify the theory or demonstrate its weakness. When practice illuminates theoretical failures the theory is altered. The new theory then guides a changed practice. This is the orthodox view: there is an endless progression as knowledge increases and its application comes to correspond ever more closely to the contours and requirements of the real world.

However, despite this encouraging view, the relationship between orthodox Marxist theory and Marxist revolutionary strategy has not been quite so simple. First, the theory has taken on varying qualities in the hands of different practitioners, and second, its alteration over time has been very slow. Nonetheless, in all interpretations the theory provides a critique of capitalism, an indication of capitalism's historical nature and thus of the possibility of revolution, a theory of the forces favoring revolution and of the classes who would oppose and favor it, a theory of the long and short run tendencies of the capitalist economy which can aid in the formulation of strategy, and finally some insights into the character of the society which will replace capitalism—i.e., socialism.

For pedagogic purposes and to avoid controversy about "who really said what," we shall describe four *hypothetical* revolutionary applications. Although each is modeled on historical precedent, our purpose is simply to give an overview of how orthodox Marxist economic theory can lead to a variety of revolutionary perspectives.

In the first instance we have a revolutionary who accepts the orthodox Marxist analysis of exploitation and of labor as the root of profit, and who also sees in the falling rate of profit the possibility of crisis conditions that can foster either revolutionary upheaval or chaos. There is no view that capitalism in crisis must crumble and automatically be replaced, but instead there is only a vision of an arena for struggle, made favorable by the workings of the capitalist laws of motion. There is recognition that the proletariat, because of its place in the economy, is the social group with an interest in revolution and with the power to bring it about, but there is no worship of the class, there is no presumption that it will spontaneously have either the organization or the insight necessary to accomplish its historically dictated task. To carry out its appointed leadership role in the revolution the proletariat requires guidance from a revolutionary party specially suited to the tasks of analyzing capitalist society and organizing for an assault upon the heights of the capitalist economy. There is here a voluntarist approach to revolution wherein the motion of the capitalist economy defines the arenas and contours of struggle as well as the most propitious moments for a full revolutionary upsurge, while the activities of the revolutionary party ensure that the working class is able to take advantage of all the opportunities that material crises provide.[40]

In a second perspective, crisis theory is viewed as "breakdown" theory. The onset of crisis over and over, in an ever-worsening spiral, eventually leads to the literal dissolution of the old system. In the chaos workers either spontaneously organize themselves into revolutionary councils and seize power, or the moment passes and barbarism is the result. Further, the attempt to create revolutionary organizations prior to the actual revolutionary moment is either futile, or worse, counter-revolutionary. For all such organizations, created under the sway of capitalism, inevitably incorporate the dynamic features and social relations of capitalism and thus impede rather than foster revolutionary potentials. So in this second view, before the revolution itself there is a contradiction between desiring revolution and carrying out an organized revolutionary program—the tension is resolved in the spontaneity of the revolutionary upsurge.

In the third view, we have a kind of synthesis of the first two positions: voluntarism and breakdown, the role of prior organization and the role of spontaneity temper one another in a more dialectical formulation. This view asserts that voluntarism is an insufficient force for revolution, while "last minute" spontaneity is a ridiculous myth. It sees the requisites of capitalist production in concert with the dynamics of class struggle engendering the impossibility of capitalist prolongation. It sees that there is an objective and subjective aspect to all historical revolutions—the material laws provide the setting, and revolutionary practice fosters the consciousness. Further, revolution comes not because of technical breakdown but because the system becomes unbearable for the workers and they revolt: not as a reflex action but as a result of overcoming past consciousness and developing the new insights needed for revolutionary struggle. And these insights, in this third perspective, cannot come by way of participation in capitalistically structured movements, nor by way of teaching from "experts," but only through concrete experience and struggle over a long period prior to the actual revolutionary moment.[41]

In a final view, we have a reformist approach based on either of two perspectives. In one case, the activist views the problems of capitalism as being rooted entirely in disproportions. He or she comes to disavow revolution entirely; all that is needed is a sequence of reforms allowing the system to rediscover stability through capitalist planning. In the other case the activist sees capitalism's collapse as inevitable, so that all that can be done in the meantime is to temper the injustices of the present situation. Revolution will take care of itself, in the long run.[42]

So coming out of one analytic framework we can have a host of political perspectives. Orthodox Marxist economics is an incomplete theory of social change. Depending upon how activists interpret it, and depending upon what additional insights they append to it, different revolutionary orientations emerge. Collapse and a party; collapse and no party; no collapse and no party, or no collapse and a party; reform or revolution; voluntarism or mechanism. The additional insights which help to engender these alternative perspectives are most often views about consciousness and its impact on economic and organizational dynamics.

With reference to the development of a socialist society the lessons of orthodox Marxist analysis are again vague. Since all orthodox Marxists focus their criticisms on capitalist exploitation and the misdirected nature of capitalist production, they all also see socialism as a means of overcoming these failings. However, in one view the failings derive solely from the nature of the capital-labor relation, while in another they also derive in part from the nature of market exchange dynamics. Thus one perspective sees a socialism that retains free market exchange while the other sees socialism with a central planning agent, though both agree on the need to eliminate private ownership of the means of production and income earned from property ownership. Little is said about the actual organization of separate production units under socialism by orthodox Marxist economic theory and what views there are vary widely with different practitioners. The one consistency is that those who emphasize the party form also most often argue for a rather traditional factory arrangement, while those who favor some variant of spontaneity often favor an arrangement along the lines of worker management. Here again, as in the strategic instance, the differences seem to derive from different perceptions of the way in which social relations affect consciousness: according to one tendency it is only through the material interests they impose, while according to the other it is also through the role activities they require.[43]

We might here add that the relation between Marxism and practice is not by any means one directional. Historically, revolutionary activists have often added to the body of the theory by way of lessons from practice and recently this has taken a turn in tune with some of the main points of the rest of this essay. Further, much of the reason why Marxist economics is interpreted in a "vulgar" manner stems from the victory of the Bolshevik Marxists and the enshrinement of their particular interpretation of Marxism during the sway of Lenin and then even more destructively of Stalin. The roots of the present orthodox Marxist economic theory, it is true, are certainly there in Marx's own work, but as we shall show, so are the roots of a much more powerful and relevant political economic theory better suited to our own revolutionary needs and in no way compatible with the kind of inhumane and mechanistic thinking that has characterized socialist activism for all too long.

In the next chapter we will elaborate our criticisms of the Marxist orthodoxy. We conclude this one with a list of the theory's main strengths, features we'll have to preserve in any new interpretation.

THE STRENGTHS OF ORTHODOX MARXIST THEORY

The key lessons from our analysis of orthodox Marxism should be the importance of methodology, the priority of a general historical theory, and the importance of class struggle.

The orthodox methodology teaches us the need to understand social systems in their relations and in their motions. It correctly combats all forms of mystical idealism, and it accurately recognizes the need for abstraction as a tool of analysis.

The historical materialist view of history teaches the importance of production, of economic relations in general, and of class struggle. It uncovers the existence of the surplus and explains the importance of the social relations of appropriation.

The Labor Theory Of Value teaches the primacy of social relations in the determination of exchange relations and the fact that commodities are not entities unto themselves but instead achieve their character as relational entities whose aspects are functions of the entire dynamics of circulation and production.

The orthodox Marxist analysis of capitalism's laws of motion explains better than any other prevalent approach the dynamics of 1-the qualitative distinction between labor and labor power, 2-the nature of exploitation and the origins of profit, 3-the nature of the capitalist accumulation process, its general laws, and its tendencies to crisis, 4-the role of the reserve army of labor and the roots of the "business cycle," 5-the various forms of capitalist crisis and their causes and counter-acting tendencies, 6-the forces promoting centralization and monopoly, and finally 7-the nature of the contradiction which generates class struggle and creates conditions that can potentially foster societal revolution.

Even in its orthodox interpretation the Marxian framework represents a damning critique of capitalism which holds considerable appeal for all those who have come to feel capitalism's oppressions and who have sought a set of tools suitable to understanding those oppressions and then guiding a practice aimed at their elimination. The sad fact is that despite its many adherents and its prevalence among radical perspectives, the orthodox Marxist framework is now as much a hindrance—for what it says incorrectly and leaves unsaid—as it is an aide.

FOOTNOTES: CHAPTER ONE

1. R.L. Meek, *Studies in the Labor Theory of Value*. Lawrence and Wishart, London. 1973. Paul Sweezy, *The Theory of Capitalist Development*. Monthly Review Press, New York. 1942.
2. Frederick Engels, quoted by Vernon Venable, *Human Nature: The Marxian View*. Meridian Books, Cleveland, Ohio. 1946.
3. See V.I. Lenin, *Karl Marx*. Foreign Language Press, Peking, 1967.
4. Mao Tse Tung, "On Contradiction", *Selected Works, Volume One*. Foreign Language Press, Peking, 1971.
5. For more on these matters see *What Is To Be Undone*, Michael Albert, Porter Sargent Publisher, Boston. 1974.
6. Lenin, op. cit. Page 12.
7. Meek, op, cit.
8. In the next three sections we follow Sweezy, *The Theory of Capitalist Development*, and Meek, *Studies in the Labor Theory of Value*, op. cit.
9. There are many Marxists who deny that the Labor Theory Of Value is concerned with "prices" at all, claiming rather that it is meant to explicate only matters of exploitation and surplus value or profit—i.e. the distribution of society's product. The genesis of this view was no doubt the desire to preserve the theory (paradigm) in face of its obvious weaknesses (anomalies)—if you're worried that the theory can't explain prices, why not claim that the matter was never of any importance anyway?

But this view flies in the face of two critical points: 1-the obvious emphasis in almost every presentation of the theory including Marx's own, on exchange ratios, and even more importantly, 2-the fact that there can be no theory of society's surplus or of its income distribution in the absense of a theory of real wages, which in itself requires a theory of almost all commodity exchange ratios as well as of how much is produced to then be distributed.
10. See I.I. Rubin, *Essays on Marx's Theory of Value*. Black and Red, Detroit. 1972.
11. Karl Marx, *Capital, Volume One*. International Publishers, Page 37-38.
12. Many Marxists underestimate the importance of supply and demand pressures to the functioning of the Labor Theory Of Value. These pressures are not determinant but they are the mechanism by which embodied labor time exchange values are arrived at.
13. See footnote 12.
14. R.L. Meek, *Economics and Ideology*. Cambridge University Press, London. 1967. Page 97.
15. This could obviously occur in a number of ways in different modes of production, for example, in feudalism, slavery, or capitalism.

16. For Marx, of course, this transition is not a theoretical matter of a few sentences, but rather a historical process of centuries requiring careful description and analysis. Note also that without the appearance of merchant capital there is no accumulation of surplus, while with its appearance there is such an accumulation—occurring in exchange due to unequal exchange and not in production due to exploitation of a "capitalistic type".

17. In the *Communist Manifesto*, Marx and Engels write, "Laborers...must sell themselves piecemeal, are a commodity like every other article of commerce," they spell out the analysis in greater detail throughout their economic works, *Capital*, in particular. But the orthodox formulation may well owe the most to Marx's short simplified monograph, *Wage Labor and Capital*, International Publishers, 1933, which discusses not only what constitutes the commodity, labor power, but also what determines its exchange-value, the wage the worker receives for his or her day's labor.

18. Karl Marx, *Capital, Volume One.* op. cit. Page 175-176.

19. Karl Marx, *Capital, Volume One.* International Publishers, New York. 1975. Page 167.

20. What actually determines the real wage, or wage bundle—what the money wage can actually buy—is somewhat ambiguous in orthodox Marxism. On the one hand it's asserted to be the exchange-value of labor power, i.e. the amount of goods, measured in hours of embodied labor, necessary to recreate the worker him or herself. On the other, however, its seen to be a function of culture and past history, particularly the class struggle. The first assertion confirms the Labor Theory Of Value as an explanation for the exchange-value of all commodities under capitalism. The second, however, is more compatible with the idea that the wage rate has more to do with the relative powers of capitalists and laborers than with some notion of embodied hours of labor in labor power. Regretably most interpretors gravitate to the second approach only in their verbal discussions, while retaining the first interpretation in all their formal, theoretical renditions. As we shall see in chapter two this is a cause for considerable confusion and weakness in the orthodox approach.

21. Karl Marx, op. cit. Page 186-198.

22. Paul Sweezy, op. cit. Page 83.

23. Maurice Dobb quoted in David Horowitz, *Marx and Modern Economics.* Monthly Review Press, 1968. Page 54.

24. For a brief exposition of these relations see *Wage Labor and Capital,* op. cit.

25. This is the notion of there being an essence behind the appearance which the system itself presents to our senses. We see commodities with the characteristics of people, almost animate, exchanging for one another—but at a deeper level there lie the true human interrelationships governing this appearance and determining its actual laws of motion. Indeed, many orthodox Marxists use this sort of argument to explain the need for Marxist "science" in the first place.

26. This is not because workers are necessarily consciously opposed to exploitation as we have defined it. It is rather that workers seek the best possible

conditions of employment. The rate of exploitation, S/V, is a ratio of hours of labor to hours of labor, not of outputs. If S/V is higher in one sector than in another, either the workday lengths or the salaries per equal workday must differ. In either instance the workers will move to the sector with lower S/V, i.e. to the sector with either a shorter workday (and the same wages) or with higher wages.

27. The analysis could easily be extended to include the notion of a family subsistence wage, rather than merely a single worker's subsistence wage, and indeed efforts in this direction are not unusual.

28. It is a very fine line between an interesting or a useful abstraction, and a misleading one. Here, we are not employing hindsight, but rather adopting the stance of the originators of these theories.

29. See footnote 26.

30. No one has actually pursued this choice in a serious fashion. We present its logic and refutation here simply for purposes of further clarifying the issues involved in the transformation problem.

31. Karl Marx, *Capital, Volume Three.* International Publishers, Page 154-172.

32. "Accumulate, accumulate, that is Moses and the Prophets", Karl Marx *Capital, Volume One.* op. cit. Page 595.

33. For discussions of the Reserve Army of Labor and the Business Cycle see Karl Marx, op. cit. Page 628-640.

34. Sweezy's discussion in *Theory of Capitalist Development* addresses the idea of "less than normal" as well as "lower than the rate of interest" as cutoff points for capitalist investment. We think that "less than expected in the future" is the most compelling formulation, though even it seems a little dubious as long as there are profits to be garnered at all.

35. Perhaps the clearest discussion of a variety of perspectives on crisis theory in one article is Eric Olin Wright's "Alternative Perspectives in Marxian Crisis Theory". Insurgent Sociologist.

36. The expression for the rate of profit, remember, is $P=S'(1-q)$. If q continually rises approaching 1 as an upper limit, the expression in parenthesis approaches zero. S', the rate of exploitation can certainly rise at the same time, as its denominator, V, declines with growing productivity, but, according to Marxists the rise in S' will eventually fall behind the decline in $(1-q)$ as the determinant factor in the trend in the rate of profit, P, itself. For an especially insightful analysis of the political, strategic implications of this theory see Russell Jacoby's "The Politics of Crisis Theory—Towards A Critique of Automatic Marxism" in Telos, no 10, Winter, 1971; and "Toward the Critique of Automatic Marxism II" in Telos, no 23, Spring, 1975.

37. The notion of "capital cheapening" is especially important to any full analysis of the tendency for the organic composition of capital to rise and thus for the rate of profit to fall. As productivity increases any particular machine, and thus the sum total of machines as well, can be produced in a smaller number of hours than previously. The exchange-value of constant capital declines as the number of hours required to produce machines declines. Therefore, though there may be

a steady aquisition of more and more machinery, there may still be no rise in the organic composition of capital due to the fall in value of constant capital.

38. A discussion of market dynamics, especially interesting in context of an understanding of disproportionality crises, is in *On Keynesian Economics and the Economics of Keynes*, Axel Leijonhufvud, Oxford University Press, New York, 1968. Pages 49-109.

39. See Paul Sweezy, op. cit. Page 162-186.

40. This view is "Bolshevist"—for further analysis see Albert, op. cit.

41. If the reader likes, this can be considered a kind of composite approach of Luxemburg and Pannekoek.

42. Hilferding is a fine example of the former politics, and many Communist Parties of the latter.

43. See Albert, op. cit. and also Chapter Seven of this work for more on these topics.

CHAPTER TWO
THE ORTHODOXY'S
DECLINING RATE
OF RELEVANCE

...The struggle against religion was indirectly the struggle against the world whose spiritual aroma was religion.... The criticism of religion is thus in embryo a criticism of the veil of tears whose halo is religion.... The demand to give up our illusions about conditions is the demand to give up conditions which require illusions.... Criticism has plucked the imaginary flowers from the chains not so that people will wear the chain without any fantasy, but so that they will shake off the chain and cull the living flower.

Karl Marx
Critique of Hegel's Philosophy of Right

The critique of orthodox Marxism is most often really only a critique of its pedigree—"You are not Marxists; your reading demolishes all that was important in Marx." The defense is a citing of quotations to demonstrate—"Marx himself was an orthodox Marxist." We feel that Marx was anything but an orthodox Marxist though it is indeed easy to misinterpret his work into an orthodox mold. But we are *not* concerned to prove this point. We want to critique the orthodox ideas, not claims about their lineage. We relegate to footnotes a few brief asides concerning Marx's own views. We spend this chapter criticizing only the dominant "posthumous interpretation" of Marx's work. Why?

The current Marxist orthodoxy exerts a profound influence on modern socialists. Its concepts have deeply influenced our language and thought. Due to them we understand our world better than we would armed with bourgeois social science alone but the orthodoxy has limited the fullness and depth of our understanding as well. Indeed, as much as the Marxist orthodoxy has contributed, it has become a fetter on further theoretical progress.

In this chapter we critique orthodox Marxist theory both to challenge its near universal influence on the left and to lay groundwork for the development of an alternative, richer interpretation of Marxist thought. Many Marxists will join us in calling the orthodox theory "vulgar". In fact, many will prefer to call the object of our attack "vulgar Marxism" than "the current Marxist orthodoxy". Yet even a brief survey of socialist texts and journals shows that the vulgar theory we have described is also the dominant theory among those who practice Marxist analysis. Of course there are variations, but the main concepts we criticize are quite prevalent. Indeed, upon investigation, most Marxists would likely find that they use a close facsimile of this theory we call "vulgar".

The name calling, line quoting, Marx preservationists are unlikely to even read a work daring to question their time-honored truths. But the rest of us should recognize the need to take a clear look at our "Marxist" methods, concepts, theories, and all that depends upon them, to determine if really the whole edifice hasn't long since sunk beneath the actual ground we must walk and act upon. We should welcome this critique and put our energies to it, hoping it will bear original ideas rather than fearing its outcome.[1]

ORTHODOX DIALECTICS

We could not agree more with the perceived need for a general methodology that pushes us to see the whole rather than only individual parts, and that teaches us to see the process of system development. But in spite of its proponents' frequent claims that orthodox dialectics helps us to think relationally and historically, there is very little in the actual methodology that does this, though much that prevents us from understanding the process of system reproduction and the qualitative differences between human and non-human systems.

THE SO-CALLED LAWS OF DIALECTICS
APRIORI CAUSE AND PREDICTION

The three dialectical submethods are mechanical, and even more important, knowledge of them somehow seems to induce practitioners to mistakenly think there is a Dialectic which itself generates events and thereby allows us, through our abstract knowledge of it, to predict things.

The pejorative term, "mechanical", could hardly be better placed than at the feet of those who scurry about looking for unified opposites, qualitative quantities, and negating negations—and yet there is little else one can do with these submethods. There is no definition of what constitutes a "unity of opposites". There is no clear statement of what kinds of quantitative change engender qualitative changes, much less when this abrupt leap occurs. Nor is there any discussion of why a new systemic quality should be labelled the "negation" of that which had prevailed before. In general the laws of the unity of opposites, the transformation of quantity into quality, and the negation of the negation are unsupported as either ontological truths—statements about the nature of reality—or useful epistemological devices—assertions about useful ways to understand reality. Worse still, the concepts aren't even clearly defined! It's no wonder that the associated practice is usually simple-minded and then defensively enshrined as "gospel".

The Maoist extension concerning the universality and particularity of contradiction—adding the concepts primary and secondary contradiction, and principal and secondary aspect—is little improvement. Maoist dialecticians never offer any reason why contradictions must have exactly two aspects, or why there must always be one primary contradiction that is somehow more critical than all others, much less how we can determine this primary contradiction in advance of its resolution.[2] Aspects of things such as waterishness and iciness are described as "struggling" with one another when only people struggle. We are left no recourse but to conclude that the Maoist elaboration is largely mechanistic didacticism and fetishistic.[3]

Yet these criticisms are minor compared to the fact that many orthodox Marxists fall into the trap of "using the dialectic" not just to investigate, but also to draw conclusions about historical events: "My knowledge of the dialectic tells me that capitalism is a dying system soon to be replaced by socialism." "The natural dialectic ensures that the development of man parallels the development of nature and that the latter eventually becomes subordinate to the former." "The unity of opposites at the center of the capitalist mode of production is of such character that we can predict that capitalism by its very motion necessarily overthrows itself." Orthodox Marxists continually derive truths about the world from dialectical laws.[4]

Since what we do is a reflection of what our economic objective situations require us to do, it is the motion of these "situations" and of them alone that is critical. The human aspect is reduced to the moved, rather than the mover. The Dialectic is the mover. The Contradiction is the mover. It is by this remarkable dynamic that the orthodox Marxists virtually abstract themselves out of the historical picture, and then refuse to glance toward the mirror for evidence of their error. With this particular step the system becomes determinist, the outcome of history is written in the very fabric of apriori dynamics. History is subjectless.[5]

Although not all orthodox Marxists are guilty of this fundamental confusion between ontology and epistemology the confusion is common enough in major texts and among activist practitioners that it has become a major problem.[6] If some of the notions of dialectics are to be of use, they must be clearly understood as epistemological methodology and not ontology. Otherwise the need for concrete investigation disappears, and the role of human will and activity evaporates.

A UNIVERSAL METHODOLOGY?

If human beings are qualitatively different from other living and non-living entities, then it would seem likely that an appropriate methodology for understanding human systems would have to go beyond the most appropriate methodology for understanding other living creatures and inanimate objects. This is not to suggest that human beings are not subject to the laws of physics and chemistry that apply to all matter, or the laws of evolution that apply to all living things. But since human beings are unique in their conscious analytic abilities, since only we are capable of conceiving our activities in advance, analyzing their probable effects, and modifying our actions in light of this evaluation, it would seem that some additional methodological directives might be helpful.[7]

Orthodox dialectics obscures this crucial awareness that the human and non-human worlds are fundamentally asymmetrical. The very title of Engels' text, *The Dialectics of Nature,* indicates his concern to apply the same methodology to social and natural phenomena alike.[8] The more recent popular essay by Mao-Tse-Tung, *On Contradiction,* contributes to the same confusion by the frequent use of such explanatory examples as eggs hatching into chickens and water freezing into ice.[9] There is nothing particularly wrong with developing a general methodology but this must not mask the greater richness of historical dynamics and human systems nor obscure the need to have a qualitatively different framework for viewing these phenomena. The whole flavor of orthodox dialectics impedes development of such a framework.

THE MYSTERIOUS "DIALECTICAL RELATION"

What are "dialectics"? With no single answer the debate among disagreeing Marxist camps often revolves around just this question. The orthodox Marxists lay claim to the most mechanical approach. Whether formulated in terms of the three submethods already discussed, or in terms of the "spiralling motion" of two "dialectically related" aspects (e.g. base and superstructure or capital and labor), the orthodox dialectic is in fact indistinguishable from complex cause/effect relations. Orthodox dialecticians have never been able to indicate exactly how they see dialectical relations as different from any of the more complicated combinations of simple cause/effect relations such as co-causality, cumulative causation, or simultaneous determination of a many variable system where no variables are identified as dependent or independent in advance.

The tremendous mystique surrounding the word "dialectic" has a twofold root: first, there is the fact that for the orthodox practitioners there is only the word and a lot of "hand-waving" about its importance and uniqueness—but no clear indication of how and why. Second, among the Marxist/Hegelian critics of the orthodox approach though there is clearly something more from which we in fact take our lead, it is formulated in a language so complex that it's out of most activists' reach.[10] The dialectic is at the center of attention and debate, but what is the dialectic—and if I don't know, then what's wrong with me? Perhaps I should hand-wave too.

We say that ontologically "dialectic" should simply communicate an awareness that the world is a whole, every aspect dependent for its character on every other, so that no single aspect may be examined outside the whole except as an abstraction. When the system changes qualitatively it's because in its regular motion it has for some reason "thrown up" a possibility contrary to its own on-going character, a possibility which becomes manifest through qualitative change.[11] The motion of the aspects is thus merely one feature of the motion of the whole. Looking at "things" separately as if they had some self-definition exclusive of their exact place and function in the whole and exclusive of the motion of the whole is an abstraction from reality.

Epistemologically, on the other hand, "dialectical thinking" should connote a way of looking at the world that can allow us to be sensitive to its "wholeness" and motion at the same time that we seek to understand and deal with particular aspects in ways suitable to our own needs. However, experience suggests that people are only capable of conceiving the relations between entities as separate entities affecting one another or as entities which define one another and are "one" and therefore not separable at all. Even if this isn't a permanently myopic condition, there is nothing concrete in the orthodox references to dialectical relations that moves us beyond these two modes of thought. So, in our view, after making the ontological point, instead of incantations about the mysterious powers of dialectical relations, what is needed is some powerful methodological way of combining our understanding of cause/effect and defining relations into a dialectical mode of thought which can sensitize us to the whole and simultaneously help us make the most effective abstractions possible in studying those aspects of greatest concern to our particular ends. This requires specific techniques, but if the orthodoxy's three submethods are attempts in this direction, they fail miserably, obscuring more than they reveal.

Our own views on dialectical relations and thinking derive from the Hegelian Marxist tradition of Marx, Lukacs, and more recently Marcuse and Ollman, but we will speak of these more next chapter. An additional point to address here, however, is that none of the generally applicable dialectical approaches can possibly be the "qualitatively different and more complex approach" needed to understand human systems. Neither the orthodox dialectical approach nor our own version can highlight the specifically *human dimension* of historical relationships. The very generality of these approaches precludes them from either describing or helping us to analyze the specifically human relations we wish to understand in history. The road to developing an appropriate methodology for analyzing human systems lies in recognizing a qualitatively new sphere in human systems that complicates their motion considerably, the sphere of consciousness.

People have *consciousness* of their own history and of the history of their environments, both of their pasts and of their potential futures. People have the power to understand not only the effects of their actions on the physical and social environment, but the effects of that environment on themselves as well. This knowledge plays a considerable part in people's decisions about their actions. A person evaluates past experiences to gauge the relative merits of current alternatives. Last time the effect was such and such, which was favorable, so I'll act similarly now. Or a person calculates possible future conditions—how is the economy likely to look, what am I likely to be capable of or interested in—and decides today's course in order to conform with or suitably alter the expected future environment. People have *creative capabilities* with respect to themselves and their environments which allow them to step beyond their particular immediate conditions, and to try to change those conditions.

In other words, human societies are characterized not only by a sphere of activity that responds to the sphere of the physical and social environment, but by a sphere of consciousness as well, allowing for the possibility that activity will be directed toward changing the environment. In a sense, the uniqueness of the additional sphere of consciousness in human systems can be summarized by recognizing that both the past *and* the calculated or projected future can affect the present. It is not that the relations between the spheres of environment, consciousness, and activity are qualitatively different from cause and effect and mutual definition, but that the addition of the sphere of consciousness produces a qualitative change in the outcome of the operation of cause and effect and mutual definition in human systems.

The situation is analogous to the difference between systems of living things and systems of inanimate objects. It is not that cause and effect are any less applicable to the relations between the parts of systems of living organisms than to the relations between physical objects. The difference is that the characteristic of species reproduction with the possibility of genetic mutation gives rise to the *more complex* "composite" dynamic of evolutionary adaptation to the environment in systems of living things. We recognize this by making "evolutionary adaptation" a dynamic concept which we can use without always refering back to the prior and more general cause/effect and defining approaches. Similarly, the sphere of consciousness providing for the possibility of planned changes in the environment itself gives rise to the even more complex dynamics of human history.[12] Unfortunately, there is nothing in orthodox dialectics that points to consciousness as the source of the uniqueness of human systems, and much in the mystique attached to "dialectical relations" that serves to obscure it.

THE PROBLEM OF REPRODUCTION

Another problem of the orthodox approach is its unnecessary extension of a justified critique of ahistoricism into a disdain for attempts to understand historical continuity. As much as one may be interested in revolution and concerned to promote historical "leaps", it is a fact that long periods of relative quiescence and evolutionary continuity are more common conditions. Asking why societies sometimes undergo revolutionary transformations is important, but it is also important to ask why they more often do not. We need a method which helps us understand tendencies toward *reproduction* as well as revolution. Why do ideas often persist long after they have been logically refuted, even long after they serve anyone's objective material interests? Why and how do economies reproduce during the long periods of their relative stability? When reproductive tendencies clash with revolutionary forces which will "win"? Surely we need an approach which can help answer these questions.

It is true that all things change, and yet for many systems this very change has a reproductive quality preserving the main characteristics of the system for years, decades, and even centuries. To label people "ahistorical" or "anti-dialectical" because they see such continuities merely reveals the one-sidedness of one's own orientation. Such attacks are rightfully perceived as defensive and as indicating religious or sectarian faith. The only counter to misplaced notions of permanency is an explanation of historical reproduction that clarifies *both* the long continuity of observed relations as well as their historical contingency. We will not convince people of the historical contingency of oppressive conditions by simply asserting that all things must change, but by showing how these *particular conditions* are historically contingent and therefore how they can change. Dialectics focuses only on contradictions whose resolutions demand qualitative change, and in so doing gives us a tool we need, but it also overlooks another need awaiting another theoretical tool: i.e. the need to understand historical continuity requiring the theoretical tool of reproduction.

CONCLUSION

It is profoundly true, as the Marxist orthodoxy tells us, that we need a powerful method to guide our theoretical analyses. But we have demonstrated four main objections to choosing the orthodox dialectical method as that approach:

1-The three submethods are arbitrary, ill-defined, and mislead practitioners into the notion that the Dialectic allows predictions or itself generates changes.

2-The approach obscures the critical distinctions between human and non-human relations and systems.

3-The approach's intense focus on tendencies to change largely overlooks important tendencies to continuity.

4-As practical aides to make us sensitive to the "wholeness" of real world systems, as tools for thinking systemically and historically, the three submethods are simply insufficient.

THE MATERIALIST OUTLOOK

As a counter to extreme idealism, the orthodox materialist outlook represents a great improvement. But as a theory of ideas being reflections of material relations, or as an argument against the need to seriously study the subjective world, or as an a priori assertion of the importance of production over all other forms of human activity, orthodox materialism is an impediment to an effective analysis of the world around us.

THE REFLECTIVE THEORY OF CONSCICUSNESS

Our consciousnesses are not mechanical reflections of our material environments. They are affected by our whole life histories, by the accumulation of our past thoughts and feelings, and by the thoughts and feelings of other people as well. Furthermore, people are not blank slates upon which appears a reflected imprint of their life histories called consciousness. Rather, we are complex entities whose *internal characteristics* (how could orthodox dialecticians ignore these?) play a crucial role in how our social situations become translated into social world views.

Thus, one major problem with orthodox materialism is that its righteous indignation against extreme idealism is mechanically translated into a twofold downgrading of the importance of the subjective world. The orthodox theory asserts first, that the subjective is a mere reflection of the material world and second, that the subjective element plays no critical role in determining historical events. It is created, it does not create.

Both these assertions are false. Our subjective consciousness is an outgrowth of a complex historical interplay between our own internal aspects and the aspects of the environment. Part of our internal aspects is the power to realize how our environment molds us, and molds our consciousness as well, and to respond to that understanding with creative activity designed to remold our environment more to our liking. Sometimes consciousness is indeed molded rather pliably by social conditions. Each individual is confronted by the expectations of others crystallized into social roles and institutions as "alien objects external and opposed to him" to use the language of the young Marx. They are a "material force" that molds individuals' consciousness because these roles and institutions are taken as givens during the relatively lengthy periods of social stability. But sometimes it is we who mold social conditions, doing away with old institutions and replacing them with new ones that more adequately serve our desires and plans. It is especially during these periods of revolutionary practice that ideas (people's consciousness) become a "material force" and the subjective side of human beings (never a mere reflection of previous material conditions) becomes the creator. Changes might very well stem from the acts or thoughts of only a small group of people, spreading to others not through "material relations", but rather by way of human interaction, for example, by books or stories.

Certainly ideas always have a relation to material conditions—at least insofar as they are useful for affecting the real world. But just as surely historical conditions always have a relation to human ideas. Which came first is simply a misplaced question. What matters is that ideas, like material conditions, have the power to influence the flow of history. Therefore, each must be studied and understood. Neither can exist in isolation from the other, and neither should be understood except in relation to the other; certainly one should not be viewed as prior, and the other mere reflection. The orthodox view denies all this, explicitly in its most vulgar formulations, and implicitly, by exclusion, in its more subtle renditions. It therefore fails to properly reflect the subject/object duality of the human condition and the complexity of their interplay that produces human history. By reducing the sphere of human consciousness to an object of material conditions it succumbs to a mechanistic materialist determination even while protesting otherwise. Daniel Guerin, the French "Marxist anarchist" has a telling passage on this matter:

> Some people believe themselves very "Marxist" and very "materialist" when they neglect human factors and only concern themselves with material and economic facts. They

accumulate figures, statistics, percentages. They study with extreme precision the deep causes of social phenomena. But because they don't study with similar precision how these causes are reflected in human consciousness, living reality eludes them. Because they are only interested in material factors, they understand nothing about how the deprivations endured by the masses are converted into aspirations of a religious type.[13]

THE APRIORI PRIMACY OF PRODUCTION RELATIONS

But orthodox materialism doesn't stop at downgrading the importance of the creative aspect of human consciousness and the role it plays in historical development. According to the orthodox materialists, of all the different objective material conditions, those having to do with production are always most critical. Production is the prerequisite of human existence. Productive activity is the basis for all other activity. Therefore, consciousness rests primarily on the nature of the objective production relations. Cut to the bone, this is the essence of the orthodox materialist argument.

But what is the theoretical significance of the fact that production of the material means of subsistence is a necessary condition for society's survival? Without sexual activity and the activities of rearing children society would cease to exist as well. And what of consumption? The orthodox materialist is surely right to argue that without production there can be no consumption, but without consumption there can be no production either. The argument for the primacy of production cannot rest on the grounds that it is the sole necessary condition for societal reproduction. After all, breathing is necessary as well.

The only legitimate argument for the primacy of production is that the necessary function of material production can only be fulfilled through social activity engaging a large proportion of society's citizens' time. In this way it would require elaborate social relations (not being a function fulfillable through individual activity), and those relations, manifested institutionally, would have a dominant impact since people would fall under their influence so frequently. It would be helpful if orthodox materialists stated this as the reason for the primacy of production relations rather than the more frequent allusion to production's "necessity", but when so stated the contingency of the conclusion is clearer.

What about societies where production is largely carried out by individual family units engaged in subsistence farming? If economic activities are largely individual, but cultural or religious activities, for example, were social, would they be deemed primary as well, or even dominant? Or if the time element is more significant than the status of social activity, doesn't the individual consumption activity of housewives in modern capitalism take up much of these citizen's time? After all, orthodox Marxism does not honor housework with the status of production activity, and this leaves a large segment of the population presumably under the influence of the material conditions of consumption. And if we started to seriously investigate the amount of time devoted to the "necessary" activity of sexual reproduction, being careful to include time spent in any particular society's courting and child-rearing activities, and if we made empirical efforts to establish the comparative degree of "sociality" versus "individuality" of these activities, we might well develop a strong argument for considering these relations just as centrally as production relations.

Or what if a society allocates a large proportion of its activities to defending itself through guerrilla war or waging wars or aggression against its neighbors? And what about a "post-scarcity" society where a great deal of time is leisure time devoted to the social activity of play?

Our purpose is not to deny the likelihood that productive relations will be highly significant, or conceivably dominant in many actual settings. But once the actual reason for this is clearly understood, the possibility that other kinds of activities and relations can be quite significant, or even dominant in certain situations, can be recognized. Most societies engage in many social activities that are not aimed at producing the means of subsistence, and many people in these societies devote a great deal of their time to these activities. In addition to economic activities (including production, consumption, and exchange), sexual activities (including child rearing), decision making activities, and activities aimed at conducting whatever kind of relations a society maintains with its neighbors, are all equally "necessary" functions for societal reproduction. There is every bit as much reason to expect these latter kinds of activities and relations to play a significant role in molding individuals' consciousness and personalities as there is to expect production to do so. As a matter of fact, whether these activities are deemed "necessary" functions by some outside observer has absolutely no bearing on whether or not they will be significant or dominant in a particular society. The social activity of group prayer to make the sun rise could be more significant than economic activity in a society where food fell from trees. The criteria for dominance are frequency and sociality, as these make their impact upon human development, not abstract necessity, and certainly not some apriori presumption of the dominance of production relations.

The orthodox reflective view emphasizes "objective" to the almost complete exclusion of "subjective"—and this is labeled materialism. All who do not prescribe to this view are termed bourgeois, "idealist", both or even worse. Production is emphasized to the virtual exclusion of understanding the totality of other daily activities people engage in. Institutional conditions are emphasized to the virtual exclusion of the dynamics of human personality and psychology. The alternative to this one-sided objectivist materialism is not idealism, but rather an intelligent *synthesis* of materialism and humanism: we should recognize both the objective and the subjective aspect as each influences the other and as they together govern daily societal outcomes. In fact, as we shall see shortly, the orthodox materialist's emphasis on objective over subjective leads directly to a value theory which emphasizes quantitative aspects over qualitative ones.

The orthodox view takes people to be mere "bearers" of societal dictates—creatures or objects of history. This leads one to say there is no such thing as human nature or that it is totally malleable. The environment is everything. The idealist approach sees people as totally free to act according to their own independent wills—creators or subjects of history. Human nature determines everything and the environment is a malleable reflection. What is necessary is a view recognizing that people are free to act and be creative beings, but only within the constraining circumstances they historically encounter. We mold and we are molded. We are creators and creatures, subjects and objects of history. Human nature and historical impositions are both important. Marx certainly knew this, even if most orthodox Marxists take little account of it.[14]

HISTORICAL MATERIALISM

Historical materialism, or what is sometimes referred to as dialectical historical materialism, is the overall orthodox Marxist social theory derived by combining the techniques of dialectics and the materialist outlook. Although our criticism of historical materialism is based on our critique of its parts, some objections are best understood in the context of the complete view.

EXIT HUMAN BEINGS!

The central flaw in historical materialism's view of human activity is its constricted view of human nature and its misinterpretation of the role of consciousness. When the "laws of dialectics" are applied to this false starting point the result is a materialistic determinism that virtually abstracts people out of the historical picture despite all protestations to the contrary.

Orthodox materialists frequently argue "that Marx wholly denied any abstract human nature. Instead he is supposed to have held that human beings are totally malleable and derive whatever nature they possess from their concrete socio-historical environment."[15] But as we have seen, the orthodox argument for production as prime cause implicitly admits that human needs for the material means of survival and powers to create material goods are unconditional, a fixed point in all societies. It is for this reason that we say the error is in a constricted view of human nature rather than a denial of any intrinsic human nature. After all, were we to take historical materialists at their word and accept "the total plasticity of human nature",[16] what grounds would remain for insisting that "fettering" the productive forces generates a contradiction? If people could be molded not to need material goods and not to exercise their productive powers, there would be no basis for asserting a materialist dialectic. No, the lynch pin of the materialist dialectic is not the complete denial of human nature, but the abstraction from or denial of anything intrinsic in human nature other than material needs and productive powers.

That is the first mistake because in addition to economic needs and powers we have instrinsic needs for sexual fulfillment, community with others, self-awareness, and self-management over our own activities as well as the intrinsic powers to pursue these needs. Just as no amount of social conditioning could eliminate a person's need for food, shelter, and clothing, no amount of conditioning can eliminate his/her needs for sexual activity, interaction with others, a favorable interpretation and justification for his/her behavior, and the capability to manage his/her own efforts. This is not to say that the forms in which these needs and powers manifest themselves are not subject to wide variation depending on socio-historical environments, or that these needs are always fulfilled and these powers always exercised equally in all settings. This is no more the case than it is that economic needs are met and productive powers exercised in the same way in all economies. When plasticity is interpreted as the recognition that sexual needs can be manifested in the form of sadomasochism as well as equal love relations, or that self-management needs can manifest themselves as decision-making power over others' activity as well as one's own, or that economic needs, for that matter, can be in the form of mink stoles and caviar as well as wool overcoats and soup, then it is helpful. But even the malleability of plastic is limited by the innate characteristics of the material itself, and the malleability of human beings is limited by more than their economic needs and powers. No matter how distorted the form of the needs for sex, community, self-awareness, and self-management, and no matter how debilitated the power to attain them, these innate needs will be pursued by people in all societies just as economic needs will be.

Whereas the first error lies in a constricted view of human nature that leads to a single, materialist dialectic, the second error lies in underestimating the creative capacity of human consciousness and the complications this implies in the mutual molding relation between people and their socio-historical settings. While recognizing the greater complexity of human nature allows for more than one "primary" dialectic, recognizing the subject side of the subject/object duality of the human condition reflects the greater complexity of the dynamic interplay between people and conditions in any one of these processes, as well as the greater complexity of the processes' interrelations. It is this recognition that can rescue us from the determinist characteristic of historical materialism and reinsert people into the historical picture.

By simply expanding our list of intrinsic human needs and powers we would still be in a framework where people are viewed as mere reflections, or objects, of their societal settings. People and their settings would be seen as multi-faceted, to be sure, but as long as people were seen as automatic reflections of their social settings, no matter in how many different respects, contradictions would necessarily lie within the sphere of the social settings rather than between those settings and people's needs, powers, and characteristics. In other words, contradictions would arise only because different aspects of the social setting conditioned people to behave in contradictory ways, or the social setting conditioned people to want something it was incapable of providing, rather than because the social setting was oppressive in obstructing the fulfillment and development of people's needs. The motion of the social setting would still assume the sole critical role. The human aspect would remain reduced to the moved rather than the mover. And we would still have a framework whose remarkable logic abstracted people out of history.

As we argued previously, the remedy for this lies not in appealing to the mysterious power of "dialectical relations" as an exorcism against mechanical determinism, but in carefully applying the notions of cause/effect and defining relations to the three spheres of environment, activity, *and* consciousness, and in recognizing that subjective consciousness is an outgrowth of a complex historical interplay between our own internal aspects and the aspects of our environment.

ABSTRACTING FROM WHAT?

To understand complex systems it is certainly necessary to abstract. We neither want to, nor are capable of explaining every dynamic interrelation.

But the pitfalls of careless abstraction are immense. It is not true that the error of leaving things out that are really important is always caught later. The world we examine is very complex and the interplay between us and it adds still another dimension. Once we decide a certain factor is relatively unimportant and ignore it temporarily, it is possible that we will also ignore all contradictory evidence, excluding it from our perception as we have excluded the feature from our abstract theory.

Historical materialism asserts the primacy of material needs abstracting from everything else intrinsic to human nature. From there it is a short step to the conclusions that: 1-The economy can be usefully analyzed in isolation from the rest of society, with other factors analyzed as secondary aspects at a later time. 2-Classes are the sole critical social grouping of human agents. 3-Since consciousness is a reflection, the mode of production is analyzable separately from the wills of human agents and any central contradiction must be at the level of material conditions first and manifested in human relations only thereafter. 4-The principal contradiction of any society, in isolation from other societies, must be between the forces and relations of production.

But in fact, all these seemingly logical steps are in error. People are not homo-economi. The economy can only be understood in the context of society as a whole. Classes are not the sole important collective agents of history. And the only unbridgeable contradictions are those between social institutions and human nature. We will develop all these points throughout the remainder of the book but the effects of relegating race, sex, and authority relations to a secondary status bear some elaboration here.

Historical materialism can only understand racism and sexism as peripheral to class issues. Whether little or immense importance is attributed to them, race and sex divisions receive attention only insofar as they inhibit class solidarity, as secondary contradictions, never as central parts of society's structure, with a primary reproductive dynamic of their own, and on equal footing with class dynamics. This makes it impossible to see, as we will argue later, that active anti-racist and anti-sexist consciousnesses are critical to overcoming reactionary relations in the United States. The orthodox Marxist misses the fact that people arrive at revolutionary consciousness via different routes due not only to class, but to racial and sexual differences as well. This contributes to his/her inability to clarify the content of a full revolutionary consciousness.

With no focus on hierarchy and the dynamics of power in their own right, orthodox Marxism does not understand the effects of authoritarianism and hierarchy on people's well-being, personalities, and propensities toward revolutionary or reactionary behavior. Thus there is no understanding of how authoritarian social relations and consciousness contribute to the reproduction of the United States status quo, and of how anti-authoritarian programs, practice, and consciousness are essential to a revolution that can overcome U.S. hegemony and institute socialism in its place.

The problem is not just that orthodox Marxism, like any theory, is capable of making mistaken abstractions and subject to the self-justifying dynamics that impede the corrective function of "practice", but that the dialectical tool of principal and secondary contradictions, and the ever-present suspicion of critics' counter-revolutionary motivations aggravate the tendency toward blind dogmatism. For example, in the thirties, many viewed state ownership of the means of production as removing all obstacles to the development of society's productive forces. Since all other contradictions were deemed secondary and under the sway of the principal contradiction, further development of the forces of production was deemed the cure-all for the ills of Soviet society.[17] When the most heinous crimes of the Stalin period were pointed out to these people the evidence was either dismissed on the grounds that such anti-Soviet propaganda could only come from bourgeois sources (such as Trotskyists, anarchists, independent radicals,etc.), or attributed to the temporary lack of development of Soviet forces of production. That fundamental contradictions were still operative or that the revolutionary party was mis-managing the revolutionary process was unthinkable for many dedicated revolutionaries. The psychological force obscuring Stalin's crimes was the desire to have a successful socialism to point to; it was the need to see good fruit come from the only revolution led by socialists. But the theoretical rationalizations were nonetheless instructive about the ills of incorrect abstractions enthroned as "scientific truths".[18] If the choice of focus is initially poor, later analysis may or may not reveal this to the practitioner. It all depends on the extent to which the narrowness of his or her theory is forced into perceptability.

Orthodox Marxism is supposed to be a "growth science". It is supposed to continually expand and alter to fit new conditions, and moreover to better explain what was earlier only partially understood. The theory is that this should happen more or less automatically as a result of the "dialectical interplay" between theory and practical experience, the latter continually correcting and expanding the former. However, the dynamics of false abstractions tending to enforce their own legitimacy (and various psychological factors as well) greatly impede this progression. So does the sectarianism of developing a vested interest in a particular set of fixed explanations. For these reasons, in addition to the weaknesses of method and of analysis we have discussed, orthodox Marxism also suffers from being *fixed in time,* written in stone it would seem, and almost completely immune to progressive alteration.[19]

THE PROBLEM OF SCALE

The last problem with historical materialism is quite practical: it has little to offer political activists that can be applied to the actual problems of day-to-day organizing.

In the first place, finding people infinitely malleable by their social settings, historical materialism looks for contradictions first within the technical relations of society and in what society *makes* people do. Contradictions derive only from our being structurally compelled to pursue pleasure through commodity consumption and then being denied the income and time to do it with. This ignores the reality that social breakdown comes because people are *not* infinitely malleable and because their needs and capacities come into contradiction with oppressive social constraints. Being determinist in the sense of seeing classes as "agents of inevitable forces", historical materialism enforces the image of humans as mere pawns—the oppressed are but victims. The role of creativity and will, the need for responsibility, and the power of human initiative are all underestimated.[20]

But beyond its mistreatment of the role of consciousness and neglect of the totality of human needs, there is another reason why historical materialism has little of practical import to offer activists. The theory abstracts from all stabilizing forces and tendencies to societal reproduction. Offering no insights into why people don't rebel, the theory is of little help to activists attempting to help people overcome these barriers. How should activists talk, what issues should be raised, how should old views be uprooted and new ones expressed, what tactics best mobilize different groups of people? None of these questions is addressed by the epic scale of historical materialism. Instead they are addressed on a rather ad hoc basis by a variety of strategic designs that are not at all closely tied to the over riding social theory. The blame for the fact that most Orthodox Marxists pay little heed to what kind of new order their pragmatic strategies and tactics designed for overthrowing the old order are likely to produce should not be laid entirely at the feet of the strategists. For the theory of historical materialism had very little to say about such matters in the first place.

We conclude our critique of orthodox Marxist social theory with a quotation from Jean Paul Sartre that expresses our feelings about orthodox Marxism though not about Marx himself.

> Marxism, after drawing us to it as the moon draws the tides, after transforming all of our ideas, after liquidating the categories of our bourgeois thought, abruptly left us stranded... it no longer had anything new to teach us, because it had come to a stop. Marxism stopped.... Marxism possesses

theoretical bases, it embraces all human activities; but it no longer knows anything.[21]

It is always true that the only compelling criticism of an intellectual system is the presentation of a superior alternative. In the next chapter we will propose an alternative approach for understanding society and history, in contrast to historical materialism, but in tune with the goals and insights of the original Marxian project, through a focus on people at the center of society and institutions at the boundary. We will show the necessity of understanding any society's centrally defining features, their mechanisms of reproduction, the social groupings (based on their members' similar life situations) which arise, and all the day-to-day contradictions offering opportunities for effective revolutionary organizing. Instead of the mechanistic view of totally malleable people and of revolution through societal "crises", we will develop an awareness that what people seek is in part socialized but in part given, and that revolution thus arises from a host of needs, not just those which society compels us to have. At this point, however, we would like to extend our criticisms of historical materialism to a critique of orthodox Marxist economics.

ORTHODOX MARXIST ECONOMIC THEORY

Orthodox Marxists claim that the Labor Theory Of Value clarifies both how capitalist production reproduces the social relations of capitalism and how exchange relations between commodities are the products and expressors of production relations between people. Furthermore, the Labor Theory Of Value is touted as revealing the origins of capitalists' profits and laying the groundwork for an understanding of the laws of capitalist motion and tendencies toward crisis. In part our critique is an explanation of how orthodox Marxist economics fails to accomplish these important tasks. But in part our critique is also an argument that orthodox Marxist economics has set its tasks too narrowly leaving out much of importance to current analytic and practical needs. We criticize the orthodox theory for insufficiently clarifying how people are created in and through their economic activities and how societal reproduction takes place. We show that orthodox Marxist economics inadequately addresses the process whereby people's consciousness and personalities are brought into conformity with capitalist institutions. We also criticize the continuing insistence on abstracting from important "economic" and "non-economic" relations of inequality other than class in a way that belies not only the degree to which the "economic" and "non-economic" spheres are entwined but misrepresents the totality of reproductive dynamics operating within the economic sphere itself. In other words, we criticize orthodox Marxist economics for reflecting the errors of historical materialism.

NOT AN ECONOMIC THEORY OF PRAXIS

The notion that people *both* create themselves *and* are created by social conditions is Marx's view of human beings as creatures of praxis. In our view an understanding of praxis lies at the center of Marx's social theory, and the idea that people create not only commodities but themselves as well through their economic activities should be central to a Marxist economic theory. Unfortunately this is not the case with orthodox Marxist economic theory whose concepts fail to reflect the view of humans as beings of praxis.

Human Outputs of Production Ignored

Marx said that by acting on the external world and changing it, people change themselves at the same time. When we labor we create material products and we also create human characteristics and degrees of fulfillment or oppression. We reinforce old personality traits or create new ones. We develop talents or we smother them. We fulfill or aggravate needs. In general people's personalities, skills, and consciousness as well as levels of need fulfillment are functions of their working activities, and it is perfectly possible for people to become aware of this and act upon the knowledge. Suppose you and a potential trademate meet in the market place in a simple commodity production economy. She spends four hours picking a bale of cotton and you work four hours forging an iron cooking pot. Whereas the Labor Theory Of Value concludes that she will be willing to trade 1 bale of cotton for 1 cooking pot there are two important reasons this may not be so. She might say she is only willing to give up 1 bale for 2 pots because bending over in the hot sun is more burdensome than forging iron. Or she might say that irrespective of relative irksomeness, trudging in a field does little to develop her understanding of the environment and ability to manipulate it, whereas forging a cast iron cooking pot generates an understanding of the nature of metals and effective ways of rendering them more useful. Or perhaps she would argue that cotton picking generates a relatively undesirable lackadasical personality making future fulfillment less likely whereas forging creates a self-confident purposeful spirit. Variations upon this kind of reasoning would abound in a simple commodity producing economy where producers recognized the human outputs of production activities as well as the material outputs that were exchanged. Nor is there any reason to expect that similar factors would not be taken into account in exchanges in capitalist economies, although we will argue that there is every reason to expect the weighing process to become greatly distorted by the capitalist institution of private enterprise. So not only does the Labor Theory Of Value abstract from the different use-values that different work activities have for the laborer, it abstracts from the human characteristic-producing effects of work activities as well.

Use-Value As A Social Relation Is Ignored

Whereas the above example of neglecting the human outputs of productive activity leads to the relatively minor error of misestimating the exchange ratios of commodities in simple commodity production (or capitalist) economies, it points to a more fundamental problem with the Labor Theory Of Value. If productive activity affects our personalities, skills, and consciousness, then doesn't it also affect what has use-value for us? While we are perfectly willing to grant that some human needs are innate, both the specific form these needs assume, as well as a host of derived needs are influenced by the personalities, skills, and consciousness that an individual has developed. Since these characteristics are at least in part products of previous production activities, use-value cannot be an innate human disposition but must be, at least in part, a social relation deriving from the productive activities society imposes upon its citizenry.

Suppose we find that in capitalist societies there are few opportunities for self-managed productive activities—that the institution of private ownership of the means of production implies an inherent bias toward under supply of this particular economic good. Then whatever the human effects of engaging in productive activity directed by others, and whatever the effects of those human characteristics on the forms in which needs will be expressed, those derived aspects of use-value must be treated as partially a product of the social relations of capitalist production. If motorcycles have use-value because they meet needs for freedom that are unrealizable in work activities, then their use-value is in part a product of the social relations of production. More importantly still, if self-managed work activity were a scarce commodity in capitalist societies, citizens of such societies would quite sensibly try to mold their characteristics as much as possible away from personality and consciousness traits that place a high use-value on self-managed work. In this case the use-value of a good is directly influenced by the expected exchange-value of the commodity itself, which is in turn largely a product of the social relations of production.[22]

The Social Relations of Consumption and Exchange Are Ignored

But the weakness of ignoring both the human outputs of production activity and the consequent effect of social relations of production on the development of use-value are more pervasive still when we remove the blinders of the materialist outlook. Economic activity includes consumption and exchange activity in addition to production activity, and specific social relations of consumption and exchange are potentially as important as production relations in their influence on use-value. The fact that *all* economic activities transform human characteristics as well as material objects, and that *all* the social relations governing the economic activities can therefore exert a molding effect on what holds use-value for people is totally unreflected in the concepts and analysis of orthodox Marxist economics. Whereas the orthodox view of human consciousness as a mechanical reflection of material interests implicitly admits that production activity and the social relations of production exert some effect on people, in the case of consumption and exchange activities and relations there is no such acknowledgement. Consumption activity generates changes in personality, skills, and consciousness just as production activity does. Ignoring this fact leads to misestimation of relative exchange-values just as ignoring the human molding effects of production activity does. The roles of buyer and seller that govern the relations of capitalist exchange influence the development of personality traits and consciousness just as the roles of employer and employee do. So there is every reason to expect these relations to affect the development of use-value as well. Finally, should we find that market institutions create an inherent bias in the relative availabilities of different kinds of goods—that they are more receptive to the expression of individual needs than collective needs—then the specific consumption relations of capitalism would influence the development of use-value just as we found that capitalist production relations would. All this is not only absent from, but disguised by the production-oriented material flows approach of orthodox Marxist economics.[23]

Inability to Clarify the Mechanisms of Societal Reproduction

How important is the criticism that the Labor Theory Of Value of orthodox Marxism ignores the human creating aspect of economic activities, and mistreats use-value as separable from exchange value? After all, all theories must abstract from some features in order to focus upon others. Orthodox Marxists might argue that the complex nature of use-value and the human molding effect of economic activity are of little consequence to the "laws of motion" and the "inevitable tendencies toward crisis" of capitalist economies. While most of our reasons for not concurring with this judgement must await the remaining sections of this chapter, we can point out here that the abstraction from human outputs and the mistreatment of use-value is critically debilitating to orthodox Marxist economists' ability to help clarify the nature of capitalist societal reproduction.

Marx said, "Capitalist production, therefore, under its aspect of continuous connected process, of a process of reproduction, produces not only commodities, not only surplus value, but it also produces and reproduces the capitalist relations—on the one side, the capitalists, on the other the wage laborers."[24] But these wage laborers are not insensate. What if their "reproduction" imparts consciousness and needs not fitted to the roles they are expected to play? What if they are made to have solidarity with one another, to have skills that can't be employed, or expectations that can't be met? What if they are not given tastes that will push them into the market to spend their wages on the commodities capitalism makes available, or are not imbued with the desire to work to get those wages in the first place?

Reproduction obviously entails more than just the production of replacements for constant capital and subsistance bundles of wage goods. It also requires the reproduction of consciousness and needs in workers compatible with the roles they must play if capitalism is to persist. The question is whether or not orthodox Marxist economics helps us understand the means by which this comes about not to speak of providing some hints for why it might fail to occur. Alfredo Medio points out that a theory of value should direct our attention "both to the mechanism of capitalism itself and to the way in which capitalists maintain this basis. Not only are they maximizing their profits but they also strive to preserve the social framework which makes profits possible at all."[25] But the "social framework which makes profits possible" consists of much more than the condition in which the worker has need for material subsistence and nothing but his/her labor power to sell whereas the capitalist possesses the means of producing commodities. After all, on the "morning" of a socialist revolution this condition prevails but it is insufficient to save the capitalist relations of production. A lack of critical consciousness concerning the social relations of capitalism and more desireable alternatives, a lack of solidarity among oppressed groups, a lack of knowledge of the processes of production and distribution, obedient personality traits—a whole host of individual and group human characteristics must be produced and reproduced if capitalist social relations are to be preserved. Do capitalists consciously plan for these human outputs or do they come about automatically as by-products of other decisions? If they are planned must this be a conspiracy of "class conscious" capitalists or is the process largely conducted through individual capitalist initiative? Does the reproduction of system stabilizing human characteristics coincide with individual profit max-imizing or is there sometimes a conflict in which some potential profit must be sacrificed? And what are the implications for reproductive dynamics when a society is also pervasively racist and sexist?

The problem is that by neglecting the human outputs of economic activity, and by ignoring the complicated process by which commodities come to have use-value, orthodox Marxism forfeits the ability to address these questions. The question of societal reproduction is a qualitative matter of the molding of personality, skill, and consciousness traits as well as perceived need or use-value to conform with societal role and commodity availabilities. The quantitative reproductive schemes of orthodox Marxism ignore how economic activities create, modify, and develop human needs and thus the use-values people come to have, and how the context of capitalist production, exchange, and consumption institutions, by providing specific structures within which economic relations will take place, influence the kind of human characteristics and use-values that result. In short, orthodox Marxist economic theory fails to reflect the subject side of human praxis—the fact that humans evaluate the human outputs of the productive activities—and the object side of praxis as well—the fact that institutional roles dictate economic activities that mold use-values in a way that conforms to societal requisites. Not surprisingly, the failure to incorporate praxis into their economic theory prevents orthodox Marxists from understanding societal reproduction.

The Embarassing Attachment to the Subsistence Wage

What is the reason given for why the worker will receive V and no more or less in exchange for his or her labor power? One can make V the value of labor power by defining the value of any commodity as the quantity of labor time necessary for its production. But that is not an argument for why labor power will exchange for its "value". The argument behind the Labor Theory Of Value for commodity exchanges under capitalism is that competition between capitalist producers will bring about relative prices proportional to embodied labor times. But even if we assume, for the moment, that this reasoning is justifiable for commodities produced in factories under capitalist relations of production, the argument involving competition between capitalist producers is obviously inapplicable to a commodity like labor power that is produced (if one cares to think this way) in households under familial relations of production. Having rejected the Malthusian notion that working class familial relations of production would always raise the supply of labor power to meet the demand at a subsistence wage as a "libel on the human race", Marx must have had another explanation in mind.[26] To answer no more than that labor power sells for V because that is its "value" without an explanation behind the assertion similar to the argument for produced commodities is the worst form of metaphysical clap-trap, although it is not an unknown response in orthodox Marxist circles.[27]

The alternative argument for the subsistence wage comes from the Labor Theory Of Value understood as a theory of productive relations determining the relative bargaining strength between capitalists and workers. We are much more sympathetic with this kind of reasoning and are frankly amazed that it is so seldom presented explicitly by orthodox Marxists unencumbered by references to the "value" of labor power.[28]

The fact that capitalists possess the means of production as well as a stock of goods more than sufficient for meeting their personal needs while workers have no stocks and must obtain their subsistence with only their labor power to sell, obviously enhances the bargaining strength of capitalists over workers when they negotiate the wage rate. Furthermore, the reserve army of the unemployed waiting in the wings can be expected to diminish the workers' leverage still further. But as significant as these "material" relations might be, they are not sufficient to determine a subsistence wage any more than they were sufficient to guarentee the reproduction of capitalist social relations. Much more goes into determining the relative bargaining strengths of workers and capitalists over the wage rate and there are many more possible outcomes than a subsistence wage. Intra-capitalist and intra-working class social relations as well as the human characteristics of workers we referred to in the previous section are also critical in determining the wage rate.[29] Moreover, we have taken care to point out that these "subjective" relations are created and reproduced in large part through the economic activities people engage in. So the point is that these qualitative factors cannot be ignored, as orthodox theory does in deducing a "subsistence" wage. These factors which are foreign to orthodox Marxist economic theory are nonetheless to a great extent determinant of the bargaining strength of workers vis-a-vis capitalists and this, rather than the labor time necessary to produce the subsistence wage bundle or property ownership relations alone, is what determines the wage rate. At the very least recognition of the importance of the qualitative factors opens the way for explaining the obvious reality of non-subsistence wage rates other than as entirely the results of working class political power within the capitalist state. Non-subsistence wages are not only obvious realities in most capitalist societies but they are primarily won through working class power within the economic sphere, a most important albeit complex phenomenon whose analysis Marxist economists should not want to shirk.

The True Uniqueness of Labor Power Is Ignored

In the rush to establish the quantitative uniqueness of labor power as the only commodity whose use generates more value than is embodied in its production, orthodox Marxists pass by the qualitative uniqueness of labor power as a commodity that cannot be totally alienated.

There is nothing quantitatively unique about labor power that is not common to any commodities exchanged by owners of unequal bargaining strengths. If a monopolistic manufacturer purchases an input from a competitive supplier, its use will generate a profit just as the use of labor power generates a profit if the worker is in a disadvantageous bargaining position and unable to negotiate a wage equal to the full net product of production. On the other hand, if workers' bargaining strength was great enough to erase the inequality in their relations with capitalists, use of labor power in production would no more generate profits than does a material input to production purchased from a fellow capitalist of equal bargaining strength.[30]

What gives the impression of quantitative uniqueness to the commodity labor power is the *definition* of value as embodied labor time. In a non-subsistence economy people produce more than enough to meet their subsistence needs in a day's work. If "value" is defined as embodied labor time then any part of the surplus gained by exploiting the unequal relation between a capitalist and worker must be seen as taking place through the supposedly "normal" process of "equal exchange", whereas any surplus gained by exploiting any other unequal relation must be attributed to the transitory phenomenon of "unequal exchange". In other words, the value creating uniqueness of labor power is the tautological result of the Labor Theory Of Value's definition of "value". What we principally object to however, is the fact that this approach serves to bestow the quantiative uniqueness label on labor power *rather than* focusing attention on the quantitative implications of the unequal social relation between capitalist and laborer, and the fact that the theory demeans the quantitative significance of all other social relations of inequality. Worse still, the qualitative uniqueness of the commodity labor power is lost in the shuffle.

When a worker sells her commodity, labor power, to the capitalist she purportedly sells her "capacity to work", her powers of "expenditure of brain and muscle."[31] But these powers cannot be separated from the worker's consciousness and will. It is not as if the worker can direct her labor power to leave her being at 8 AM, enslave itself to the consciousness and will of the capitalist until 5 PM, and then return to its night time owner. The worker accompanies her labor power and hence arises the inevitability of the clash of wills over its use in the production process. The capitalist of course insists that he paid for a commodity that was to be subject to his will and attempts to make use of it as such, but the worker is not only incapable of selling her birth right (her labor power dragged her through the factory gate at 8 AM with it) but quickly discovers that it is not to her advantage to accept the capitalist's interpretation of the labor exchange in any case. The worker's view of the exchange becomes that she sold the capitalist the chance to try and make use of her labor power. We will develop this line of reasoning further in chapter four using it as a starting point for a theory of the capitalist firm that can analyze the contradictory forces influencing the nature of the human outputs of production. But for now it is sufficient to note that orthodox Marxist economic theory, for all its pretense of clarifying the uniqueness of the commodity labor power, proclaims a false quantitative uniqueness, and misses the true qualitative uniqueness of labor power being inalienable for creatures of praxis.

VALUE AS MORE THAN METAPHYSIC

In *An Essay On Marxian Economics* Joan Robinson comments: "The concept of value seems to me to be a remarkable example of how a metaphysical notion can inspire original thought, though in itself it is quite devoid of operational meaning."[32] And in a more eloquent formulation she states that:

> ...no point in the substance of Marx's argument depends upon the labor theory of value. Voltaire remarked that it is possible to kill a flock of sheep by witchcraft if you give them plenty of arsenic at the same time. The sheep, in this figure, may well stand for the complacent apologists of capitalism; Marx's penetrating insight and hatred of oppression supply the arsenic, while the labor theory of value provides the incantations.[33]

The traditional Marxist response to Robinson seems to be indignation over her inability to understand the subtleties of the theory. However, the arguments supporting this indignation prove not so compelling. On the one hand, it is asserted that Robinson misses the fact that the theory is a method; on the other, that she misses that value is a relation and not merely a thing. Both these points are true—the problem is that they are irrelevant to Robinson's critique; for that critique argues simply that the whole edifice of Marxist analysis need not have as its foundation the Labor Theory Of Value. According to her, it can stand well enough on its own. The notion of value can be jettisoned at no loss—it is metaphysical, an "incantation" which inspired original thought but no more.

We agree and we do not. Robinson and the other neo-Ricardians are right that the Marxist theories of prices of production, investment, the business cycle, and most of the theories about crisis, could all be expressed and defended without reference to the Labor Theory Of Value. And it is true enough that these arguments are what constitute the substance of the theory according to many orthodox Marxists. But in our view they are not the essential part. Rather it is something about value that the neo-Ricardians and their technically oriented price equations are blind to that is central—the idea that exchange value is a social relation. The title of Piero Sraffa's book, *Production of Commodities by Means of Commodities,* foreshadows his insight that technological relations—

expressing what commodities must be employed to produce other commodities—influence the relative prices of different goods. But beyond this insight lies the more profound insight that social relations— the relations people must enter into in order to engage in the activities of production, exchange, and consumption—influence the relative prices of commodities as well. From the perspective of an engineering science Sraffa's insight might be critical, but from the perspective of the social sciences the view of commodity prices as the expressors of all the social relations operative in the economy is what is significant.

NOT A SOCIAL RELATIONS THEORY OF VALUE

Marx tried to penetrate the fetishism of commodities whereby people lost sight of the social relations between people in the exchange relations between things. He thought he had succeeded in bringing social relations to the fore through the Labor Theory Of Value. We will argue here that this, unfortunately, was not the case: that the Labor Theory Of Value is not a social relations theory of value for capitalist economies. Moreover, when Marxists mistook the labor time accounting framework for the heart of the theory, enshrining it as the methodological barrier against fetishism in Marxist economic thought, they created a new labor time fetishism ironically acting as a fetter on the development of a true social relations approach to value theory.

Ignoring All Unequal Social Relations But One

The first problem is that the Labor Theory Of Value presumes that the relations between owners and non-owners of the means of production are the *only* important social relations reflected in the relative prices of commodities when they are not. Relations between different groups of capitalists in which some have greater monopoly power than others, as well as relations between different groups of workers in which some possess more skills than others, or some are organized into stronger unions than others are all social relations that influence the relative prices of commodities. Moreover, unequal relations between different races or ethnic groups and between males and females, that are treated by orthodox Marxists as social relations from the "non-economic" sphere, are also reflected in different wage rates and the prices of different commodities. Perhaps orthodox Marxism's most vehement condemnation of neoclassical economists is that they fail to recognize the fundamental asymmetry in the relation between capitalists and laborers. Orthodox Marxists argue that while capitalists can move their investments freely from one sector to another, and workers can sell their labor power to whichever capitalists they like, capitalists do not become workers (by choice) and workers are simply unable to become capitalists.

This lack of free mobility is the basis of the structural inequality in the relations between capitalists and workers that prevents the scheme of workers selling their labor power to get money for other commodities (C^1-M-C^2) and capitalists buying labor power to be able to sell the commodities workers produce (M-C-M') from degenerating back into the less complex (C^1-M-C^2) scheme of Simple Commodity Production. But the orthodox Marxist accusation that neoclassical economic theory disguises unequal social relations between capitalist employers and employees as well as the effect these have on the exchange values of different commodities can be extended to the Labor Theory Of Value itself with respect to all other unequal social relations and their effects on exchange values. Whether or not we can conceive of a uniracial, one sex society with completely free mobility of all laborers and capitalists *within* their respective classes but no mobility between classes is no more the question than whether we can conceive, along with neoclassical economists, of a society with complete mobility of all people between all roles! The question is whether or not there *are* significant barriers to movement between the roles of worker and capitalist and whether or not there are significant barriers to movement between roles for capitalists with different monopoly powers, workers of different skill levels, degrees of organization, races, and sexes in any particular society. And the point is that the appropriate value theory must reflect all important social relations.

Ronald Meek allows that "the conditions of monopoly are the setting within which the problem of the reapplication of the Marxian theory of value to present day conditions must be considered."[34] But why only "present day conditions" and why not conditions of sexual and racial inequality and of inequality between different categories of labor as well? We could not agree more with Michael Kalecki when he said:

> To abstract from all semi-monopolistic and monopolistic factors, ie. to assume so-called perfect competition, is a most unrealistic assumption not only for the present phase of capitalism but even for the so-called competitive capitalist economy of past centuries; surely this competition was always in general very imperfect. Perfect competition when its actual status as a hand model is forgotten becomes a dangerous myth.[35]

As for different categories of labor, orthodox Marxist economists have gone to elaborate lengths to demonstrate that all skilled or "complex" labor can be reduced to multiples of abstract labor. This is a hypothetical intellectual task whose ultimate feasibility we don't doubt for a minute. But the argument for why skilled labor would in fact exchange in accordance with the amount of unskilled labor time it took to produce the skills in the first place is not so fully explained. Again, as in the case of the wage to be expected for labor power, the argument for "equal exchange" elaborated for produced commodities (in a simple commodity production society with no attention given to human inputs and outputs no less!) is implied to cover this case as well. If any doubts are voiced, they are silenced by reference to the "fact" that labor equalization occurs in the marketplace in exchanges all the time. That is the essence of the proof. But all things are equalized in the market place in the sence that they are reduced to comparable quantities of money! The question is whether the relative wages of different categories of labor will be in proportion to their embodied labor time. Again, we have every reason to expect that there are barriers to free mobility—for purposes here qualitatively no different than barriers to mobility between the working class and the capitalist class—and that "equal exchange" is here also a figment of mind and not a fact of productive life. However, we will leave further discussion of the general importance of these other unequal economic relations, as well as unequal racial and sexual relations to chapters three and four, and arguments for the primacy of a number of specific unequal relations in the case of the United States for chapters five and six.

In any case we can conclude here that the common something which commodities share is a set of "roots" in the complex of social relationships which govern the bargaining power of their traders. And in our opinion orthodox Marxist economic theory has been operating in a rarefied world without monopoly, unions, skill differentials, and racial and sexual differences far too long under the *presumption* that monopoly and intra-labor differences are insignificant, and racial and sexual relations of secondary importance.

Failure of the Labor Theory Of Value on Its Own Terms

Our principle criticism of the Labor Theory Of Value as a quantitative theory of relative prices has been its presumption that the only significant unequal social relation is that between capitalists and laborers. While this remains our most important substantive objection, there remains a more technical problem that orthodox Marxist value theory does not even accomplish the limited tasks it poses for itself. If the Labor Theory Of Value were the appropriate social relations theory of value for the most rarified world of a unisexual, uniracial, perfectly competitive capitalism with homogeneous labor, then at least the errors could be dismissed as operating at too high a level of abstraction for useful purposes. But unfortunately, this is not the case. In addition to the problem of ignoring the impact of the production and reproduction of human characteristics upon both use and exchange values, the Labor

Theory Of Value also fails to express the orthodox Marxist assumption of equal relations between capitalists and unequal relations between capitalists and workers in the case where the organic composition of capital varies in different sectors of the economy. Moreover, the orthodox Marxist resolution of this difficulty through the "solution" of the transformation problem is unacceptable. Instead, it turns out that the neo-Ricardian theory of relative prices as developed by Piero Sraffa is the appropriate theory of value for expressing the social relations specified in the orthodox Marxist model of competitive capitalism, and that the essence of the Labor Theory Of Value as applied to capitalism—the assertion that only living labor is exploitable—must be discarded. Since the justification of these conclusions is rather lengthy and technical we have relegated the argument to the appendix entitled "The Problem with the Transformation Problem." The interested reader will find that the argument serves to demonstrate one further way in which the Labor Theory Of Value fails to be the appropriate social relations theory of value for capitalist economies. However, our major criticism of orthodox Marxist value theory—the exclusion of important unequal social relations other than those between employers and employees—stands irrespective of the argument offered in the appendix. Moreover, this criticism is equally applicable to Sraffa's neo-Ricardian theory of value even though that theory does finally succeed in solving the overly abstract problem posed by orthodox Marxism.

A TECHNICAL VIEW OF CAPITALIST CRISIS

We have argued that orthodox Marxist economic theory emphasizes quantitative, material reproduction at the expense of qualitative social reproduction, and material expansion at the expense of societal evolution within a capitalist framework. Therefore it should come as no surprise that such a theory would neglect the possibilities of a disruption in the process of societal reproduction whereby people's personalities, skills, consciousnesses, needs, and expectations fail to conform to the role requirements of capitalist institutions, and emphasize the possibilities of disruption in the process of material reproduction and expansion. It is in this sense we find orthodox Marxist crisis theory one-sidedly "technical". In some cases we find that the supposed tendencies toward crisis are deduced from incorrect premises in orthodox value theory and do not operate in the real world but only confuse and mislead those in constant search of their appearance. But in other cases we find the analysis of technical crises illuminating in that they have proved real possibilities and disrupted the operation of numerous capitalist systems. We in no way wish to detract from the power and practical importance of these latter insights. Yet even in these instances the technical nature of the crises allows for the possibility of technical remedies within the structure of capitalist social relations. In our view the replacement of capitalist social relations themselves will be in large part propelled by a general recognition of their oppressiveness, and it is this possibility of consciousness development incompatible with societal reproduction that orthodox Marxist crisis theory says nothing about.

THE EMBARRASSING PREDICTION OF A FALLING RATE OF PROFIT

Of all of Marx's important writings on crisis theory, the theory of the falling rate of profit has long stood out as a sore thumb, an embarrasment to all but the most dogmatic defenders of orthodox Marxism. The theory has been showered with ridicule by bourgeois critics as empirically unsupported, but stubbornly defended by the devout who draw no small solace from the implied inevitability of capitalism's demise. But once it is recognized that a neo-Ricardian theory of value is the appropriate theory for the orthodox Marxist model of capitalism and that profit is generated by cost-plus mark ups on all components of cost rather than through the exploitation of labor power alone, it is obvious that even should there be a tendency for labor costs to fall as a proportion of total costs that this would not imply that the profit rate must fall as well. In fact, once one's mind is cleared of the Labor Theory Of Value, it becomes obvious that only two forces could possibly cause a long-run tendency for the rate of profit to fall: 1-If the social surplus were to diminish in size while the bargaining strength between capitalists and laborers remained constant, the rate of profit would fall. Aside from the unlikely events of a destruction of society's tools or general amnesia among the labor force concerning productive technology, the depletion of natural resources is the only possible cause of a reduction in society's net product. 2-If the bargaining strength of workers vis-a-vis capitalists were to rise faster than the rate of growth of the net product itself, the rate of profit would decline. In this case the change is clearly the result of a qualitative trend in social relations. That technological change which reduces the necessary labor time to make goods and services embodies a tendency to diminish the rate of profit in and of itself, is just plain fantasy.

TECHNICAL CRISES AND CAPITALIST SYSTEM REFORMS

Marx made crystal clear the possibility of deflationary crises in any monetary exchange economy where the possibility of deferring buying with the proceeds of selling existed. As a refutation of Say's Law it stands unsurpassed. Moreover, he clarified the greater liklihood of interruption in the process of exchange inherent in a system where important actors were motivated by expectations of the difference between M and M' being more than zero rather than the pursuit of use-value. Finally Marx's analysis of the capitalist business cycle and the possibilities of disproportionality in a system where sectoral production plans are only coordinated after the fact are invaluable contributions to our understanding of possible beginnings of deflationary crises.

We find no fault with these contributions from orthodox Marxist economics, but merely wish to point out: 1-that Joan Robinson is correct in saying that these accomplishments do not require the Labor Theory Of Value, and 2-that these technical problems have been precisely the objects of major capitalist system reforms reducing the probability of their disruptiveness. Keynesian stabilization policies allow for a tremendous diminution of the amplitude of the business cycle without any disruptive increase in labor's bargaining strength when accompanied by "appropriate" incomes policies. Indicative planning can go a long way to reducing the liklihood of disproportionality crises. And government underwriting of banks and major corporations can immunize the exchange system against deflationary snow-balling to a great extent. The point is not that any existing capitalist economy has succeeded completely in eliminating the possibility of the types of crises that are the subject of orthodox Marxist analysis, but that the potential exists and there has been a general movement in that direction. But these are not the only possible sources of capitalist crises; they are not the only ways in which capitalism is irrational from the point of view of promoting human fulfillment and development and might come to be perceived as such by its inhabitants. No system reform can make capitalism capable of providing non-alienated work opportunities where people can exercise self-management. No system reform can make capitalism receptive to the expression of social consumption needs. No system reform can make capitalism promote solidarity rather than competition or variety rather than conformity among its inhabitants. Only a change of system can accomplish these ends. An increasing awareness of this in people's consciousness generates the kind of crisis no "Keynesian reform" can remedy.

IGNORING PERCEIVED OPPRESSION

We mentioned earlier that orthodox Marxists might try to justify their abstractions from the complex nature of use-value and the human molding effect of economic activity on the grounds that they were of little consequence in revealing the "laws of motion" and "inevitable tendencies toward crisis" of capitalist economies. This is certainly the case for the kinds of crises emphasized by orthodox Marxist economics. But we have just seen that these are not the only kinds of crises, that in addition to contradictions between capitalist institutions there can be contradictions between those institutions and human needs and potentials. Moreover, whereas the former can in most cases be ameliorated, if not resolved, by new capitalist institutions in the form of the reforms we mentioned above, crucial contradictions between particular human needs and potentials and capitalist institutions—with or without reforms—cannot be bridged.

Through its emphasis on the total plasticity of human nature, orthodox Marxism exhibits an extreme bias toward underestimating the possibility of a crisis deriving from contradictions between people's needs or perceptions of well being, and the opportunities offered by social institutions. Any disconformity is accidental, in a sense, and remediable by a more thorough molding of human characteristics. But we see humans as having some needs, beyond material subsistence, such as the needs for self-management and solidarity, that cannot be entirely "molded away". For this reason they imply a permanent possibility of crisis for any system that is incapable of satisfying them, whenever this should become understood. On the other hand, we take a more flexible attitude toward capitalist institutions than orthodox Marxists. Without denying the possibility of contradictions within capitalist institutions themselves, we see no "inevitable" falling rate of profit, and we can envision the possibility of system reforms that diminish the chances of the other kind of contradictions discussed by orthodox Marxists. In a sense we see capitalist institutions as potentially moldable to the point where all the contradictions emphasized in orthodox crisis theory can be perpetually postponed. But this is a fundamental dividing line between an historical materialist intepretation of Marxism and a praxis oriented interpretation and will become much clearer in the following chapters.

WHAT IS ECONOMICS?

Ironically, perhaps the most severe failing of orthodox Marxist economics is its ahistoricism. The concepts of the theory focus entirely upon quantitative, class-defined economic relations. But in the real world biological reproduction of the race, the socialization of young people, the development of community relations both internally and between communities, and the necessity of coordinating disparate activities and making social decisions—just like the necessity for production and consumption—each require complex social relationships. Further the relations necessitated by each of these aspects of living will be important to the definition of any society's main contours, and finally the historical development of the social relations associated with each of these areas of human activity will likely affect the development of all the others. This entwinement may even be so thorough that defining an "economic sphere" where the other social relations would be at most of peripheral importance would be horribly misleading.[36] For example, in many societies economic relations may not be determined by only class alone. The impact of sexual kinship relations or community racial relations could also be defining even in the determination of production and exchange relations themselves. In this case the orthodox Marxist mode of analysis could persist only insofar as practitioners were guilty of the analytic failing Marx attributed to Proudhon—seeing the world in terms of fixed concepts, mystically transposing the order of determination between concept and referent.[37] Indeed, this will be our contention in chapter four of this book about our own society, the United States. There also we will finally complete our critique of orthodox Marxist economics by offering a positive alternative to take its place.

A CLARIFYING DIALOGUE

In this and a number of coming chapters we are going to conclude with a fictitious dialogue demonstrating or elaborating a variety of our assertions in a debater's framework. These discussions are modeled on actual experiences, though they are also obviously constructed to serve our own particular pedagogic purposes. Every attempt has been made to avoid "straw" positions. In this first instance, the discussion is between an almost orthodox Marxist (AOM) and a critic of orthodox Marxism (COM) who accepts the arguments of this past chapter.

AOM: I guess I like many of your criticisms but I've got two problems. You're awful paranoid about the influence of what you call the "orthodoxy." Isn't it pretty much dead as a theory, and certainly not dominant. Almost all Marxists are more subtle and sophisticated than the way you describe them. And it also seems to me that you go a little too far with your critique: attacking mechanistic thinking is one thing; entirely chucking the Labor Theory Of Value and Historical Materialism is another.

COM: You just don't agree with my critique. We probably don't even mean the same thing when we use the label "orthodox Marxism".

You must mean some inconsistent, vulgarly mechanical fragment of a theory, where I mean precisely Historical Materialism and the Labor Theory Of Value, as well as the analysis of capitalism that their careful application generates. No wonder you think I'm paranoid. Sure, only the most ridiculous "Marxists" are orthodox in your sense. But most socialists—including you and me—have been immensely influenced by the orthodoxy in the sense that I mean it.

AOM: Well, it's true that I do think largely in terms of Historical Materialist and Labor Theory Of Value Concepts, but...

COM: But nothing—you do, and you're not alone. Even the so-called experts, people like Sweezy, Bettelheim, and Mandel, use theories related if not almost identical to those we criticize. Of course what they say diverges from our rendition at a great many points, but nonetheless, most of their central concepts come from the orthodoxy and much of their work is subject to the same criticisms as those we make of the orthodoxy itself. These are the people newcomers to socialism study imbibing variants upon orthodox thought and never developing original ideas at all. And most readings of the classics—*Capital* included—are so guided by the time-honored orthodox interpretations that they also don't yield much beyond the notions we've already critiqued. The situation gets even worse as soon as we start to consider the approaches of various Marxist Leninist organizations. Most use theories that are weaker—more mechanical, more economistic, and less consistent—than the ones we have critiqued.

AOM: Since I'm not in such a group I don't know about that, but aren't there people who use the orthodox models as only an approximation to real world conditions and thus in a way less subject to some of the criticisms you raise?

COM: The most sophisticated use of the orthodox Marxist model is to argue that it exists in history only as an approximation to one part, albeit the most critical part, of any modern capitalist "social formations." For within such formations there are residues of other previous modes of production, and precursors of modes to come. The orthodox capitalist mode, in this line of analysis, exists only in context of these others, affected by them, but in the end dominant. It's clear that though the approach is more sophisticated our critiques are still applicable—they apply to the analysis of the central mode of the social formation, and now to the analysis of the rest as well.

AOM: But look, at least all the folks you've mentioned and no doubt the adherents of this last approach too, concern themselves with real events and real problems of capitalism and socialism?

COM: So what? The question is what issues do they address and by what means? Look, in many ways Sweezy is the best of the bunch, and in the United States also probably the most studied by people trying to understand Marxism. Yet where are his essays dealing with racism and sexism? Where does he discuss how consciousness in the United States is formed, how it changes over time, and how it reproduces? So how can he claim to be a theorist of modern society? What is the effect on people who study Sweezy or one of the other much worse "experts" on Marxism? Can they possibly come away with anything more than a fuzzy orthodox view? Sweezy has been a most significant figure in keeping alive socialist thought in the United States, but still, how does his *Theory of Capitalist Development* differ from what we have called orthodox Marxism? Only marginally. But at least Sweezy is clear thinking and intelligent about what problems he chooses to address. Look at the Marxist Leninist sects and organizations in the United States and tell me they don't function precisely with muddled interpretations of the orthodox paradigm.

AOM: I guess there's something in what you say, but you're still not talking about the real Marxist left—at least not since the lessons of the sixties have been learned. Now people who have shared a number of new experiences are much more sensitive to matters of race, sex, and consciousness.

COM: But such people are always on the defensive! The orthodox Marxist "scientist" ridicules them for being opportunist, ahistorical, or especially idealist, and the battles are almost always one-sided. Since there is no clear alternative to Historical Materialism and the Labor Theory Of Value, even the enlightened veterans of the sixties continually return to those theories for basic concepts and methods. This leaves them hopelessly weak before orthodox criticisms, and it really limits their abilities to concretize their new intuitions and practical lessons into original analyses that movements can effectively use. Mostly the movements wind up looking for clearly expressed theory (and strategy) and find only orthodox Marxism (and Leninism). Fighting a rearguard battle and in the absence of supportive movements, those who learned from the sixties are now slowly falling back to variants upon the orthodox views themselves. This is is not wisdom finally surfacing; it is rather, insight being submerged under the weight of ideological tradition.

Until there is a full, generally-accepted critique of the orthodoxy, and a powerful, well-formulated alternative to it, its impact on socialist potentials will remain deadening.

Just saying the orthodoxy is wrong or vulgar, which I agree many have done, is a different thing than escaping from the orthodox intellectual framework, much less diminishing its influence on socialist thought.

But how about if we first have a chance to present our own alternative ideas, and then perhaps we can talk again about the orthodoxy, our critique, and our own new notions.

FOOTNOTES: CHAPTER TWO

1. Sectarian, "my line is the only line", political approaches attach tactical sureness, give (blind) confidence in the future, and usually bestow moral superiority on their beholders. That there is a resurgence of Stalinist orientations among U.S. socialists is a sorry commentary on the state of our society. Even its rebelliousness is distorted. Like the rise in religious fanaticism—Hare Krishna movements, Jesus movements, etc.—the growth of U.S. Stalinism indicates the degree to which certain sectors have been robbed of their creative/critical faculties and of their ability to admit ɔ confusion and recognize the existence of "open questions." Moreover, like the religious flowering, the new Stalinism can do considerable harm. Their practice can turn people away from the left. Their hostility and "pugnaciousness" (with independent leftists) can hurt other movements. Their intellectual narrowness can stifle thought in others. Worst by far, their uncomradely approach to anyone with a different view can diffuse to others who should know better. This phenomenon has a long history—its repitition in the present would be a tragedy.

2. For a further discussion of the weaknesses in the orthodox dialectical approach see *What Is To Be Undone,* Michael Albert, Porter Sargent, Publisher.

3. The one truly positive attribute of the Maoist approach is its considerable popularity. This points clearly to the need people feel for workable methodologies applicable to daily life and political practice. But to make a methodology accessible one need not destroy its complexity and true power; one need only define it, describe it, and give examples of its use which don't presuppose that the reader has read all of Hegel, Spinoza, Kant, or whoever else.

4. See Maurice Cornforth, *Historical Materialism*, London, 1954.

5. Louis Althusser is the main current proponent of this type of view. See *For Marx,* Vintage Books, 1970.

6. See Engels, *The Dialectics of Nature,* International Publishers, Stalin, *The History of The Bolshevik Party,* International Publishers, and Mao Tse Tung, *On Contradiction,* Peking Press.

7. We will make this argument in more detail in the next few pages and will put forward our own positive approach next chapter.

8. Frederick Engels, *Dialectics of Nature,* International Publishers, 1940.

9. Mao Tse Tung, *On Contradiction,* in *Selected Readings From the Works of Mao,* Peking, 1971.

10. See Georg Lukacs, *History and Class Consciousness,* M.I.T. Press, 1971, and Herbert Marcuse, "On the Problem of the Dialectic", Telos, no. 27, Spring, 1976.

11. This is a succinct expression of our understanding of "contradiction". It includes nothing about opposites, primary and secondary, etc. It is just a way of seeing how a system can simultaneously have tendencies to reproduction and to dissolution of its defining contours, and how the contradiction(s) defined by these opposed tendencies can be important to the system's future development.

12. It is for this reason that Veblen's call for an "evolutionary economics" to replace the neoclassical methodology borrowed from the physical sciences did not go far enough. An evolutionary methodology does not give sufficient recognition to the sphere of human consciousness, and it is largely for this reason that Veblen's economics underestimates the role of human will and falls far short of what we require.

13. Daniel Guerin, *Fascism and Big Business,* Monad Press, 1973, Page 76.

14. Marx's whole discussion of praxis, of the creation of new needs, and of the role of human plans in productive activity are in tune with our approach. Consider this quotation from *Capital* as but one example: "Labor is first a process between people and nature in which people mediate, regulate, and control their interchange with nature through their own act....People develop the powers slumbering within them and subjugate the play of their powers to their own domination." *Volume One*, International Publishers, Page 177.

15. Richard Lichtman, "Marx and Freud, Part Three, Marx's Theory of Human Nature", Socialist Revolution, no. 36, Vol. 7 Nov.-Dec. 1977, Page 45.

16. Ibid. Page 46.

17. Charles Bettelheim, *Class Struggles in the Soviet Union, 1917-1923,* Monthly Review Press, has a presentation and self-critique of this view.

18. See Svetozar Stojanovic, *Between Ideals and Reality,* for a good analysis of Stalinism. Oxford University Press, 1973.

19. Naturally, another reason for this dormancy is the influence of Stalinism on creative thought—an influence that still prevails in many quarters.

20. There are a number of interesting related points made in *Conversations in Maine,* Freddy and Lyman Paine, and James and Grace Lee Boggs, South End Press, 1978.

21. Jean Paul Sartre, *Search for a Method,* Vintage Books, N.Y., 1968, Page 21.

22. We will have much more to say about this in a positive way in chapter four.

23. Again, these arguments will be more fully elaborated in chapters three and four.

24. Karl Marx, in *Critique of Economic Theory,* Hunt and Sherman, Penguin, London, 1972, Page 327.

25. Alfredo Medio, "Profits and Surplus Value", in Hunt and Sherman, op. cit. Page 327.

26. Karl Marx, Letter to Schweitzer, *Marx and Engels Correspondence, 1846-1895,* International Publishers, New York, p. 170.

27. Even Paul Sweezy is guilty of this sort of formulation sometimes, for example, on page 49-62 of *Theory of Capitalist Development,* op. cit. though later in the same work he takes a more reasonable stance, pages 87-88.

28. Paul Sweezy, op. cit. chapters four and five.

29. We will discuss this in greater detail in the section on factories in chapter four.

30. This is a hypothetical argument. We think that long before such a state of equality, capitalism as a whole would cease to be tolerated.

31. Paul Sweezy, op. cit. p. 59.

32. Joan Robinson, *An Essay On Marxian Economics,* MacMillan, Page, 22.

33. Ibid.

34. Ronald Meek, *Essays on the Labor Theory of Value,* London, Page 286.

35. Michael Kalecki, "The Class Struggle in the Distribution of National Income", Kylos, 1971.

36. Consider for example, that in Mandel's, Sweezy's, and Mattick's major renditions of Marxist economic theory there is a total of less than thirty pages devoted to understanding matters of racism and sexism.

37. Karl Marx, *The Poverty of Philosophy,* Moscow.

PART TWO
A THEORY OF PRAXIS
HISTORY AND ECONOMICS

The weapon of criticism cannot, of course, supplant the criticism of weapons, material force must be overthrown by material force. But theory too, will become a material force as soon as it seizes the masses. Theory is capable of seizing the masses as soon as its proofs are ad hominem and its proofs are ad hominem as soon as it is radical. To be radical is to grasp the matter by the root. But for people the root is people themselves. The manifest proof of the radicalism of German theory and its practical energy is that it starts from the decisive and positive abolition of religion. The criticism of religion ends with the doctrine that people are the highest beings for people, that is, with the categorical imperative to overthrow all circumstances in which people are humiliated, enslaved, abandoned, and despised.

Karl Marx
The Civil War In France

CHAPTER THREE
A SOCIAL THEORY OF PRAXIS

...a structural model envisaging only the maintenance of a system is inadequate. It is the simultaneous existence of stabilizing and disruptive elements which such a model must reflect. And it is this which the Marxist model—though not the vulgar-Marxist versions of if—has been based on.

Eric Hobsbawn
"Karl Marx's Contribution to Historiography"

Theories of history, as compared to theories of physical objects, cannot provide exhaustive explanations and certainly not comprehensive predictions. It is not now possible, and it will never be possible to have a comprehensive theory of even a single human actor, much less of a whole community or society.

A useful theory of history can only be a product of history itself. It can only derive from the combined practical and analytic efforts of all of history's actors. It can only be a product of the collective unfolding of human self-consciousness.

The task is to develop some concepts that help that collective unfolding—frameworks for interpreting the main contours of historical development and for predicting the probable outcomes of current activities.

Historical materialism and orthodox Marxist political economy are attempts to do just this, but as we've seen, they contain numerous errors and omissions. The current task is therefore to generate some new ideas and theoretical fragments which hold greater promise. The first step is methodological.

METHODOLOGY

A society is like a complex tapestry made up of all kinds of people, jobs, customs, habits, ideas, institutions, and even physical structures. Each of these "threads" is entwined with every other and takes on meaning only in relation with the others, much as a single thread in a tapestry means little by itself. The full character of each aspect of a society is dependent on the qualities of all the others and upon its interaction with them. Moreover, society is a tapestry of highly interactive threads. Because people have consciousness and the ability to plan, these threads are connected not only across space at each moment in time, but across time as well. In human systems the past and potential futures both help determine the present.[1]

To unravel the tapestry and isolate the most important threads and to understand these threads and their interactions, and through them to understand the whole tapestry as well, is an ambitious task. Which strands should we examine first? What questions should we ask and what kinds of answers should we anticipate? Useful theory should provide answers to these questions.

THINKING RELATIONALLY

We usually see things separately as if they were independent of one another. We regard them simply as they appear at the moment. A tree is a tree is a tree. It is itself, separate from other trees, the ground, the sky, the birds; so tall, so wide, with so many branches, and of such and such a color. Similarly a job is a job. It involves particular actions for particular durations, remunerated by particular wages, repeated for a particular number of days, weeks, and years. It is separate. It is as it is. We buy a car and it is a car, nothing more and nothing less. It is a vehicle: so big, red, a vinyl roof, and "four on the floor". Furthermore, when we think about the things in our world, we see them as pushing and pulling one another, each outside and separate from the other. Separate entities constantly colliding—this is the world we conceptualize.

But this conceptualization is misleading. Movement through time is lost to the moment eternalized. The whole is lost to a countless enumeration of the parts. Independent push-pull analyses obscure more complex interrelations. To understand society and history our commonsense, everyday approach to seeing and thinking is insufficient.

True there is a need to separately identify various strands from the whole tapestry of society—people, institutions, social groups, the state, the economy, etc.—but we must remember that such independent identifications are oversimplifications. Any one strand or concept is really always entwined with all others. It does not actually exist separately as a thing-in-itself. The apparent independence of each thing we name is really a feature imposed by our act of separate identification. To minimize the problems our abstractions create, we must learn to conceptualize "separate strands" relationally and also historically.[2]

Consider the tree we spoke of earlier. What about the carbon dioxide it breathes from the air? What about the soil and the plant and animal life which provide the tree with its nutrients? What about the sunlight and the climate? What about the people—gardeners, tree climbing kids, or strip miners whose activities are involved with the tree? Are all these separate from the tree, pushing it and pulling it, or mightn't it sometimes be more useful to think of the tree as both itself and also all these other things? For certainly if these relations were to alter, the tree would be even more different than if its height or number of branches changed.

What about a job? Isn't a job related to its product, to the market on which its product is sold, to the uses to which people can put the product, and to the subsequent gains or losses in their lives? If we make steel isn't our job related to the use of steel in making automobiles? And isn't it related to the kind of technologies employed in making steel, and thus to the criteria the owner of the plant applies in choosing between alternative technologies, and to the forces on the owner molding these criteria? And if any of these many relations significantly changed wouldn't our job change as well, as much, or even more than if our wage went up or down 2%? These relations are internal. They define a whole network apart from which the separately designated elements can be known only abstractly. The job *is* the whole network, though at any moment we may usefully choose to abstract and examine only a part of the whole.

And is a car really just a car? Yes and no. To really understand a car, don't we have to see it as more than its momentary physical appearance? When we see a car, when we think with the concept "car", can't we include roads, pollution, and safety as well? Aren't these aspects all entwined— each involved in the full character of the others?

This is what we mean by conceptualizing relationally. We extract things from the whole society and give them names—inputs, products, jobs, individual people, government, theatre, ideas, etc.—but we then conceptualize each as "itself" and also all the rest to which it is most intimately related. In a sense, the boundaries between "things" become fuzzy; we may bend and even cross those boundaries as we see fit. Conceptualizing this way forces recognition of the complexity of society against the otherwise narrowing impact of our abstractions. Conceptualizing relationally, viewing and thinking of "things" as network, is a useful tool to get past momentary appearances toward a more systematic understanding of reality.

PROCESS: THINKING HISTORICALLY

But the relational technique alone is too static to meet all our needs. It helps us get a snapshot with links intact rather than severed, but this is still only a snapshot. To set it in motion we must become sensitive to history.

Let's consider our three examples one more time. Is a tree just what it seems at this moment, even relationally? What about the seed long ago? What about its growth over time, the nutrients used, and the birds that have nested in its branches? What about the cycles it has been through? What about when it is cut down, processed, and becomes a cardboard package, a newspaper, or a beam in a house? The tree is certainly just what we see there in front of us, but it is also what we see relationally, and it must further become what we see historically if we are to gain a full understanding.

A job has a past and a future "itself" as well as a history and future of relations with other jobs. Aren't these historical entwinements important to understand also? For the job of making steel shouldn't we understand the full history of development of the technology, of the different job roles and relations of work? What about the roles and relations of blacksmith and apprentice, skilled craftsman and his hired hands, or work-team member and elected team leader? Aren't these past and future roles part of the roles of union worker, management supervisor, and majority stockholder that define steel production in the present? Moreover, the relation of steel producers to coal producers and final consumers were different in the past and will be different in the future than they are at present. In a sense we must understand all these factors to complete the meaning of the present relations between steel producers and other actors in the economy.

Things are entwined with the whole and we can only understand them non-superficially through their relations with the whole. They are those relations. To be alert to this we must learn to define and use our concepts relationally. But things also have histories. All things move from past through present and into future. At any instant they are what they are, but also what they were in the past and what they can be in the future. To be alert to process we must learn to define and use our concepts historically. It is not that we should never refer to a car or job meaning just the "separate entity", but rather that we should often also be aware of the entire associated network and process integral to the job or car. One of the consequences of thinking relationally and historically that will seem awkward at first is that our concepts will overlap. Consumption and production, for example, refer to the same complex phenomenon, but they do so from two different viewpoints, thus giving us two perspectives on that same phenomenon. In general when defining and working with any concept we may extend its network and process as narrowly or as extensively as we like, depending upon our own particular analytic purposes. The narrowness or extensiveness chosen is a tactical question, but the common error we wish to correct is the choice of overly independent and ahistorical views of important social and economic concepts.

REPRODUCTION: THINKING STRUCTURALLY

As a last general methodological tool we also want to increase our awareness of reproduction via the technique of thinking structurally.[3]

Reproduction is just a particular kind of motion through time. It is not cosmic permanency or a priori stagnation, because there is no such thing. Reality is always characterized by change, but sometimes the particular character of change is to reproduce certain aspects over and over again. These aspects are then largely invariant, and for the period of their invariance we call them a structure. Viewed historically as process, a structure appears to be changeless, at least for some period of time, but it is in fact a result of continual reproductive changes. Keying ourselves to be especially attentive to the existence of structures and to recognize that their seeming permanence is really just motion of a particular reproductive type, is very useful. It forces us to admit tendencies to permanency or reproduction and then to investigate and understand the contingent, interactive reasons for such tendencies.

THINKING DIALECTICALLY

The world is a whole. Each aspect "is what it is" only relationally and historically. Pulled out of context, aspects become abstractions. We perceive the whole; we impose divisions and give names to the separately demarcated aspects. We then see in terms of those imposed aspects or concepts—people, nature, cars, lakes, iron, factories, government, etc.

We can make these divisions along any "lines"; we may define the concepts as we like. But whenever we do it, it is an abstraction. Our understanding is approximate, but it is the most we can achieve, and is most often sufficient to our ends. Indeed, our practical ends are the criteria we must employ in defining concepts and judging their worth.

Once we impose a dividing line on either side of it we have a separate aspect. According to our above methodological discussion, we should conceptualize these relationally and historically, as network and as process. Sometimes we can treat the dividing line as if it were "given in the world" and not imposed on it by us, and then guard against possible attendant errors by viewing each of the two separated aspects relationally and historically. We take this approach, basically, whenever it is sufficient to our analytic and practical needs. Other times, however, the "mutually defining, entwined character" of the two abstractly separated aspects is particularly crucial to our immediate purposes. In addition to viewing each aspect as network and process, we would also be wise to develop a concept to denote the two parts together without any dividing line, as one whole.

For example, the most mechanical Marxists might draw a line in every society between economic base and ideological superstructure. They might then treat each of these two aspects as a separate "given" which interacts with the other and assign the economic base a dominant position with respect to their cause and effect interaction. Other Marxists might make the same initial demarcation, but then treat each aspect relationally and historically. Finally a third camp of Marxists might make the abstraction, the labelling of the two aspects, and then develop an encompassing concept as well which forces them to analyze with the dividing line present as well as not present.[4] What provokes these different approaches? It should be different estimates of what is the most effective way to conceptualize whole societies in order to understand and change them in desirous ways.

The process of "dialectical thinking" is a practical strategy for knowing the world in order to change it: 1-Take the whole and divide it into aspects of particular concern. 2-Determine how well these separate concepts suit one's needs, develop them relationally and historically, keep some, eliminate some, alter some. Develop a "total" view which can inform the elaboration of each concept and be informed by their elaboration as well. 3-Determine which aspects are so entwined in ways relevant to one's purposes that while they should be viewed in turn, they should also be taken together as an encompassing whole. 4-Examine the different dynamics of the system with an eye to tendencies toward reproduction as well as dissolution of the defining contours. Flexibly following such a sequence, thinking relationally, historically, structurally, and wholeistically, and occillating over and over from the total view to each concept and back is what we call "thinking dialectically".

In the next pages we follow a "dialectical approach". We look at societies in light of our desire to change them. We demarcate certain aspects for special attention and analyze these relationally and historically, in light of our total view and so as to inform it as well. We develop encompassing concepts. We use the entire framework to develop a theoretical view and a strategy for political intervention.

HUMAN BEINGS

To understand society and history we must surely have some understanding of what a person is. The question of whether people are totally determined, partially determined, or not at all determined by their environment is basic to our understandings of how societies function. Whether people are innately "good", "bad", or "neutral" and how people's activities affect their understanding of these concepts is crucial to how we judge any society, and to what we consider to be the "best" society.

But to discuss human beings per se, out of a social historical context, the subject estranged from the object, is of course an abstraction, but one which is useful in light of our purposes. However, we'll also see that the precise manner in which individuals and human groups are entwined to their social setting is so intense and so critical to our purposes, that while we must develop an analysis of the abstractly separated aspect, "human being", we must also develop concepts which encompass humans and societal environments together in one whole.

We humans are not just what we eat. The human result is not merely an imprint upon a blank slate. If we were totally a product of our worldly situations, we would be perfectly and infinitely moldable. Treated to "proper socialization" we would be as at home living in isolation as in community; as at home repeating mindless tasks as employing creative intelligence; as at home hating and being hated as loving and being loved. The only cause for us to feel uncomfortable or oppressed would be a disparity between what we had been molded to desire and what we had actually achieved. As long as we were socialized to expect what was coming and to desire and appreciate it, we would be as happy and fulfilled in any one set of circumstances as in any other. This is the behavioral, Skinnerian notion—we are what we are "reinforced" to be; we want what we have previously been "programmed" to want—a notion well suited to rationalizing the most barbaric social institutions and policies but a totally incorrect assessment of what we human beings are.[5]

Behaviorism is simply wrong. People have an inner complex of innate characteristics that distinguish us from other organic things. Succinctly, humans are not pigeons and no amount of conditioning can bring about an equivilance. This much is so obvious that to contest it is a mindless diversion for people seeking academic makework, or for people seeking rationalizations for various sorts of oppressive goals they wish to impose upon others.

All people, simply by virtue of being human, have various needs, capacities and powers. Some of these, like the needs for food, sex, and shelter, or the powers to eat and copulate, are shared with other living creatures. These are our natural needs and powers. Others, however, such as the needs for creative activity, love, or knowledge, and the powers to conceptualize, plan ahead, evaluate complex activities, and feel various emotions are more distinctly human. These are our species needs and powers. And finally, most of our needs and powers, like the needs for particular stereo records, or to share feelings with a particular loved one, or for a certain kind of knowledge, or the ability to play the guitar, repair a roof, please a particular person, or solve certain kinds of mathematical problems, we develop over the course of our lives. These are derived needs and powers.

People have needs and powers similar to those of other animals, needs and powers shared only by other humans, and needs and powers developed only in their own particular life experiences. What we are at any moment in time is partially a matter of biology, partially a matter of human evolution, and partially a matter of social and personal history.

People engage in activities which change the world, as do all other animals. But human activity is distinguishable in two very important ways: First it is conscious, and second, it changes the agent as well as the agent's environment.

"Conscious life activity distinguishes people immediately from animal life activity."[6] Human activity is potentially preplanned. Like animal activity it is often aimed at survival or at other instinctual ends; but unlike animal activity, it is also often aimed at beauty, experimentation, social interaction, or other humanly defined ends. It is conceived before it is enacted. Human activity also changes not only the world but the person acting upon the world. For example, "labor produces not only commodities; it produces itself and the worker" as well.[7] In working we fulfill or stifle present needs, create particular kinds of new needs, enlarge or erode skills, enhance or diminish knowledge, and generally mold our personalities and consciousness. Moreover, we have the capacity to recognize this phenomenon and to seek an ever-increasing understanding not only of how the material world is changed by human activity, but of how we humans are changed by the same activity.[8]

Indeed, while we know that all humans have certain innate characteristics; first, the precise forms in which these manifest themselves are always historically mediated (we need food but what we eat and how is historically determined); second, the derived needs and powers developed as a result of human praxis are again historical; and third, the interrelations between all these needs and potentials—how meeting any one affects the others—is also a matter of specific social historical mediation and not some sort of "innate given".

All this is relatively straightforward. The theoretical controversy enters when we try to determine 1-the natural and species nature we all share, 2-the processes by which we derive new needs and powers and develop our own consciousness and personalities, and 3-precisely how the innate and the derived aspects interact in the human species.[9]

HUMAN NATURE

In discussing human nature we wish to focus on a very few of our species needs and powers, specifically the fact that we are by nature social beings and beings of "praxis", and to define the useful evaluative concepts of fulfillment, oppression, and alienation.

Human Species Needs and Powers

As humans we have a need and a power to know the world around us and in particular our own situation and relations in that world. That is, we have a natural disposition and inclination to seek to understand our involvement and we also have accompanying intellectual tools with which to carry out that task.

As humans we have a need for freedom, a choice over our activities, and the accompanying capacity to exercise such choices in accord with our understanding. In other words, we have both the need and power to engage in creative, self-managed activity.

We not only have the need to choose our own activities and the power to understand their effects, but we have a need to regard our life activities as worthwhile; the need for a "positive self-image".

We have needs for love, community, and general social involvement with others. We are capable of being lonely. Moreover, our need for self-respect is inextricably tied to our need to have others regard us as worthy actors in the social nexus.

Finally, we have a need for variety in our lives that accompanies our capacity to distinguish differences and appreciate their implications. The breadth of human needs requires a variety of activities for their exercise and fulfillment and beyond this for change and originality. It is a particularly human characteristic to become "bored".[10]

These needs and powers are *innate to all humans.* We have them by virtue of our genetic-biological make-up. They reproduce with each new birth and are with each of us throughout our lives—though they may become more or less operative and active in different ways depending upon our actual worldly involvements.[11]

Social Beings

An important implication of our "individual" needs and powers is that people are social beings.[12] We do not exist in isolation from the human community. It is not possible to fulfill our needs and employ our powers independently of other people. Moreover, we cannot even define ourselves save in social interaction. We must use social products. We must love other people, build communities with other people, work creatively with others, and know a social world. What we are derives largely from past human history and depends upon possible future human relations. In a sense this is even more true for a person than it is for other entities. For beyond being "one with the world" and existing only in its context, we have a special social entwinement with the world. It is not only that we sometimes need others for advancement of our own ends. Rather, we have a directly social aspect. We are capable of empathy. We feel through and by the feelings of others. We are social beings in the sense of human solidarity and sharing as well as in the sense of needing or using. Humans are especially relational.

Beings of Praxis

Finally humans become more than they start out as at birth. As we live, we alter and develop. We are beings of praxis. When we use things from the surrounding world, when we engage our powers to change the world either alone or in concert with others, we also change ourselves. This notion of praxis is what we take to be the chief Marxian contribution to the theory of human nature. Human beings are self-productive. Praxis is worldly activity which alters the environment and also the human agents and which is consciously chosen and elaborated. In this view humans are capable of developing their own natures as they see fit. We are both subject and object of history. We are in a position, in a non-constricting society, to develop our own beings in accord with our own criteria and experiences. And in our view this is not only a possibility, it is a requirement if an individual is to be fully human.[13] We have both a need and a power to elaborate our own beings, and this is our deepest human creativity. Our future is part of our present.

Moreover, when it serves our purposes we extend the concept "praxis" so it refers to the human agent, the activity, and the focal material or social "recipient" of that activity. It is the changing human, the activity, and the changing focus of that activity. The "subject", "verb", and "object" become a single historical network. Used this way, the concept "praxis" erases the line between humans and their environments. It compels us to recognize the whole .

Fulfillment, Alienation, and Oppression

Fulfillment is satisfaction of our human needs and capacities. It is getting the food we need; knowing our world; having community, emotional sustenance and a full sex life; and employing and developing our creative potentials. Oppression is the opposite. We are oppressed when our needs are denied or our capabilites are undeveloped or unused.

To be completely fulfilled is obviously a social phenomenon because we are social beings. It is a condition in which we and others are simultaneously fulfilled. Complete fulfillment is impossible outside of society, or, to put it another way, fulfillment is relational.

Fulfillment is also a historical phenomenon because we are beings of praxis. It is a condition of becoming as well as of being. It is a condition wherein we are in control of our own further development.

We are oppressed, on the other hand, when we do not get all that we need, or when we are restrained from exercising our full powers. Oppression is obviously a social and historical concept as well, in that it is derived from our social relations and historical interactions. As we shall see oppressions also tend to be structural, often persisting for long periods of time.

We say that a social decision or outcome of a social choice is alienated if it is aimed at some goal other than human fulfillment and development.[14] If a product is made for the purpose of advancing profits or meeting some abstract quota rather than for fulfilling consciously elaborated human needs, it is alienated. If health care is provided to earn profits or to maintain a functional workforce and not to enhance human well-being and development then, even if the care produces health, it is still alienated. Finally if an individual's personality were developed via a process aimed at achieving conformity or rationalization rather than the individual's well-being and development, then it too would be alienated.

In sum our definitions of oppression and alienation are such that the former applies to actual effects, while the latter applies to prior purpose or intent.

HUMAN DEVELOPMENT

We have argued that people have species needs and powers that are perhaps best conceived as defining the range of human potential. But people have derived needs and powers as well, and these needs and powers change over the course of our lives. Music we once found appealing now sounds dull, and music we once found harsh and empty comes to be appreciated as profound and moving. Seeking friendship we work and play with other people and thereby develop ever increasing capacities for specific forms of social involvement. We come to need people as companions in ever more varied and concrete ways, becoming more and more immersed in and indistinguishable from our social relations, and more acutely aware of any absence of such community. How are we to explain this phenomenon of activity aimed at need fulfillment leading to need development as well? The answer lies in recognizing the role of some intervening structures.

Personality, Skills, and Consciousness

People are more than their constantly developing needs and powers. At any moment we are characterized by certain personality traits, specific skills and abilities, and a collection of memories, ideas, and attitudes referred to as consciousness. These structural characteristics play a crucial mediating role. On the one hand they largely determine the activities we will select by defining the goals of those activities—our present needs. On the other hand the structures themselves are merely the cumulative imprint of our past activities. The important point is to neither underestimate nor overestimate their permanence. Although we have emphasized that people have the capacity to make themselves, they are not free to do so however they might like. They are always constrained by the personality, skill, and consciousness traits they have previously developed. But even though these structures may persist over long periods of time, they are not totally invariant. Any change in the nature of our activities can lead to changes in our personalities, skills, and consciousness. In this case the new structural characteristics lead to new needs as well.

A full theory of human development would have to explain how personality, skills, and consciousness form, why they ordinarily persist but occasionally change, what purposes they serve, and the relation between these structures and people's needs and powers. No such theory exists or is visible on the horizon, but fortunately a few simple insights are sufficient for our present purposes.

The Relation of Consciousness to Activity

The fact that our knowledge and values influence our choice of activities is readily understood. The manner in which our activities influence our consciousness and the importance of this relation is not so apparent to our "common sense." As discussed above, one of our human powers is the ability to consciously plan our own activities. But just as all human powers imply the need for their exercise, the power to act knowledgeably implies the need to act knowledgeably. When combined with the need to have a positive self-image, this implies a need to have an explanation for our activities which not only shows the intelligence of our plans in effectively meeting our needs, but their ethical worth as well.[15] It is this need that creates the subtle duality to the relationship between thought and action, each influencing the other, rather than a unidirectional causality. And it is for this reason that in fulfilling needs through particular activities we are induced to mold our thoughts to justify or rationalize the logic as well as the merit of those activities, thereby generating consciousness-personality structures that have a permanence beyond that of the activities that formed them.

The Possibility of Detrimental Personality and Consciousness Traits

We have argued that an individual's ability to mold his or her needs and powers at any moment is constrained by their previously developed personality, skills, and consciousness. But these characteristics were not always "givens" that must be worked with; they are the products of previously chosen activities. So why would anyone choose to engage in activities that resulted in characteristics detrimental to future need fulfillment and the maximum development of future powers? In part we might find the answer in the individual's failure to recognize the structure-producing effects of activities aimed primarily at fulfilling pressing current needs. But mistakes are not the most important factor.

At any moment we have a host of active needs and powers. Depending on our physical and social environment it is not always possible to fulfill and develop them all simultaneously. In many situations it is only possible to meet some needs by acting and thinking in ways that are detrimental to meeting others. Moreover, the ways of behaving and thinking that we adopt under restrictive conditions can survive long after we have escaped those conditions in the personality and consciousness traits they produced. In acting upon the world to meet needs and exercise powers we develop our consciousness and personality. These are initially rooted in particular human purposes but in time, due to the complex ways in which we need to justify ourselves and in which we develop new needs and powers by fulfilling and exercising old ones, they can develop a structural life of their own. We become what we once were not. That was what we meant by saying that ways of behaving and thinking can become structural and take on a life of their own. But a far more serious problem is that in alienated environments there is no escaping the conditions that generate the detrimental structures in the first place. In the continuing context of particular combinations of institutional roles there can be a permanent condition wherein individuals can only achieve fulfillment along one axis by accepting oppression along another.

Some Clarifying Examples

As children, in order to meet our needs for affection and approval, we must often behave in accord with certain roles defined by our parents' expectations such as behaving like "daddy's little girl" or a "rough and tumble little boy". This patterned behavior not only leads to derived needs for protective paternalism or aggressive outlets through simple repetition, but the fact that we must explain this behavior to ourselves in a manner upholding both the logic and merit of our decision also creates a personality-consciousness structure that perpetuates the effects of the behavior long beyond childhood.

As teenagers, in order to meet our needs for friendship and peer recognition, we may have to behave in accord with the rules of small cliques. Through the process of consciousness conforming to actions discussed above this may lead to a consciousness that interprets cliquish behavior as the best way to gain comradeship and social recognition and personality traits that dictate needs to downgrade the value of all outsiders and uncritically support the actions of the close acquaintances of the moment. The result may well be adult perceptions of "we" versus "they" and justifications for treating "them" differently from "us" regardless of the rather obvious barriers such attitudes pose to achieving friendship and mutual respect.

Or suppose a man works in an office setting where his fellow male workers all expect him to require his secretary to brew his morning coffee, do his shopping errands on her lunch hour, and be visibly pleased by his flirting gestures. To advance his career and obtain the respect of his male co-workers, he will behave in a sexist way. But this behavior could only be legitimate if his, and all the other secretaries in the office, were indeed inferior and incapable of anything but "women's" work and serving as sexual objects. The notions follow from the required activity— they are not separable, at least not if the man is to have a positive self-image. Ironically, his self-respect hinges on his developing a sexist consciousness and personality to accompany his sexist behavior on the job. But this comes to have important implications for many of his other life activities. His sexist traits entail new needs and may well impede development of precisely the powers necessary to achieving a true love relationship even though this might be what he wants above all else.[16]

And how is a white person to rationalize his or her participation in efforts to keep blacks out of the local trade union, neighborhood, or school? People require a self-explanation for why they act as they do toward people of other races. The simplest is that blacks are not as skilled workers, as neat and tidy neighbors, or as intelligent students, and therefore would reduce the quality of the work, living, or educational activities they were permitted to join. In other words, the most self-serving explanation is that "those people" deserve the treatment we give "them". Again, it is ironic that the need to explain our actions as sensible and praiseworthy creates a racist consciousness capable of long outliving the "external" causes of our racist behavior should those ever dissipate or disappear.

In sum, people are self-creative within the limits defined by human nature, but this must be interpreted very carefully. At any moment each individual is constrained by his or her previously developed personality, skills, and consciousness. Moreover, *as individuals* we are powerless to change the social roles defined by society's major institutions within which most of our activity must take place. So that as individuals we are to a great extent powerless to effect the kind of behavior that will largely mold future personality structures. Hence, they remain beyond our reach as well, and our power of self-generation is effectively constrained by the social situations in which we find ourselves. But in the sense that these social situations are people's creations, and that our individual characteristics are products of our own activities, the potential for collective and individual self-creation is preserved. Even though people have the capacity to make themselves they are in fact not free to do so however they might like. Instead we are constrained by the actual social situations we find ourselves in, as well as by the personality and consciousness traits we have previously developed in the context of previous social situations. Consciousness is a result of needs and powers acting in particular social settings and it often leads to praxis generating new needs and powers in new social settings. But the praxis, the needs, the powers, and the settings are all social and historical. To explore this phenomenon further we must turn to an analysis of society.

SOCIETY

In trying to understand societies and their histories, people frequently begin from one of two poles: 1-society is a function of human tendencies; it reflects these tendencies and moves through time according to laws derivable from them. Or, 2-human beings are a function of social forces which evolve according to objective laws of motion of their own. We are the mere bearers of historical injunctions. In each of these approaches society is demarcated into two critical aspects and one of them is pronounced "dominant" with respect to the other.

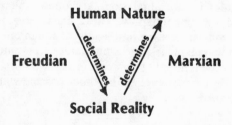

Vulgar Freudians are in the first camp. They assert that people are innately given in all their particulars, and that society and history are merely the representation of a host of individual givens in interaction. As we have seen, the orthodox historical materialists are in the second camp.

They assert that there is no significant intrinsic human nature, that we are what society compels us to be, and that societies evolve according to the objective laws of motion of their economies. But in fact, for all their claims to comprehensiveness and depth, both these approaches are one-sided and narrow.

Society and people must be conceived of as a single system. Society is formed by people in action and people become themselves in ways largely governed by their societies. People create societies, and by the settings they present for human activity, societies also create people. We can examine each as an aspect only insofar as we remain clear that for some purposes they must be taken together as one.

That people create society becomes obvious once it is recognized that neither slavery, feudalism, capitalism, or socialism are eternal and that there is no god who is guiding the process of transition from one form to the other. Although particular societal forms might weigh upon us as if they were eternal, and though they may appear impervious to change, it is still the case that people make societies and can transform them as well.

Societies create people because people growing up in different societies confront different sets of possibilities and constraints. A person in a materially poor society and a person in a wealthy society have different objects they can appropriate, different courses of action open to them, develop different needs and powers, and fulfill their common needs and powers to different extents. Similarly, the roles available to people in different societies vary greatly. The roles of slaveowner and slave, capitalist and worker, father and mother, black person and white person, and socialist citizen each give rise to different kinds of people since they permit and prohibit different kinds of human interaction.[17]

Of course there can be similar differences in life possibilities for different people in the same society as well. The possibilities and constraints, roles and social relations, and opportunites for fulfillments of needs and development of powers are quite different for serf and lord, slave and slaveowner, peasant and landlord, and in our own society for capitalist and worker, black and white, mother and father, order giver and order taker. This needn't be the case in all societies, as it probably was not in the earliest subsistence "tribal" societies and will not be again in advanced socialism.

HUMAN CENTER AND INSTITUTIONAL BOUNDARY

In analyzing societies we find it useful to create a dividing line demarcating a *human center* and an *institutional boundary*, which are dynamically interrelated and determine one another. The center is the collection of people who live within the society including all their needs, powers, personalities, skills, and consciousness as discussed above. The boundary is the society's particular institutional framework of interconnected roles that serve to coordinate social activity as well as the material objects that exist within the society.[18]

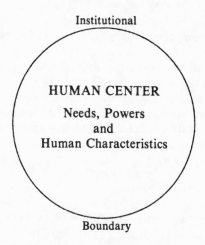

Institutional

HUMAN CENTER

Needs, Powers
and
Human Characteristics

Boundary

People produce themselves, but only in very closely defined settings which place considerable limitations on their options. Beyond the natural environment, these settings are made up of objects and institutions—both products of previous human activity. The objects delimit what tools people can use in their activities. But even more importantly, the institutions establish the patterns of expectation within which most human activity must occur.

Institutions and Roles

Institutions are simply conglomerations of interrelated roles. If we consider a modern capitalist factory, the buildings, assembly lines, raw materials, and material products are objects. Ruth, Joe, Helen, and Sam, the people who work in, or own the factory, are people and part of society's center. The institution is the roles and the relationships between those roles: assembly line worker, maintenance worker, foreman, supervisor, plant manager, pay clerk, union steward, minority stockholder, majority stockholder, member of the board of directors, etc. The market institution consists of the roles of buyers and sellers. It is not the real live people who carry out these activities—they are part of society's center. It is not even the actual behavior of buying and selling (or for the factory, riveting, accounting, managing, deciding, etc.). The actual behavior belongs in the sphere of human activity, or history itself, and is certainly not the same as the institutional boundary that produces that history in interaction with the human center. Rather the market institution is the commonly held *expectation* (and associated rules)that the social activity of exchange will take place through the patterned activities of "freely" agreed to buying and selling. Note that the objects in society are often very much in conformity with the institutions—stores, check out counters, etc. are compatible with the roles of market relations, and assembly lines, with the role of worker in an auto plant. Though we'll focus most of our discussion on the institutions and particular roles, the relevance of the analysis to "objects" should be kept in mind, in particular to the analysis of technologies.

We wish to be careful to define roles and institutions apart from whether they are actually fulfilled. To think of roles or conglomerations of roles as fulfilled expectations/rules lends them a permanence they do not deserve. Obviously a social institution only achieves a structural continuity if the commonly held expectations about behavior patterns are confirmed by actual behavior patterns. And obviously the dominant force in establishing the expectations or institutions themselves is repeated activity in conformity with these expectations. But if institutions are defined as fulfilled expectations about behavior patterns, it becomes difficult to understand how institutions might change. We want to be very careful not to prejudge the structural continuity of any particular institutions or the stability of a society's center-boundary conformity, so we define institutions as commonly held expectations and leave the question of whether or not these expectations are fulfilled—that is whether or not the particular institutions will maintain their structural continuity or be transformed—as an open question.

But why do institutions exist? Why must we add to the spheres of activity and consciousness, a sphere of rules and commonly held expectations concerning collective behavior patterns? If we were all mind readers, or if we had infinite consultative time, or if deciding time were infinitely fast in comparison with acting time, human societies might not require mediating institutions. But if there is a division of labor, and if we are not mind readers or blessed with infinite consultative time, people must have expectations about others' behavior in order to even have a conception of what they are doing themselves. If I am screwing the bolts on a fender because I think I am helping to make a car, then I am expecting someone farther down the assembly line to attach the fender to the chassis. If a collective believes it is contributing to social well-being by producing books, then they must have expectations concerning the distribution and reading of those books. If I make a pair of shoes in order to sell them and pay a dentist to fill my daughter's cavities, I am expecting others to play the role of shoe buyer, and dentists to render their service in exchange for a fee. I can neither read the shoe-buyer's and dentist's minds, nor take the time to arrange and confirm all these coordinated activities before proceeding to make the shoes, so I must act on the basis of expectations about others' behavior, and if these expectations are unfulfilled my individual efforts will not achieve the results I had planned. For there to be any conscious change there must be considerable, predictable regularity. Only with considerable regularity can people coordinate their lives and consciously determine them. The shared expectations and regular rules of behavior of institutions provide this regularity. So the relevant question about institutions is not whether they should exist, but whether they impose oppressive limits upon us, or are tools of our development alterable as we require?

SOCIAL STABILITY

It is evident that if society is to be stable people must generally fit the role slots they are going to fill; actual behavior must generally conform to the expected patterns of behavior defined by society's major social institutions. People must actually choose activities in accord with the finite number of role offerings available and this requires that people's personalities, skills, and consciousness be such that they do so. We must be capable and willing to do what is required of us. For stability:

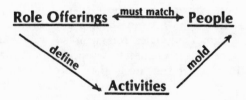

In our terms, there must be conformity between society's human center and its institutional boundary. Suppose that this were not the case. For example suppose that people came not to have racist consciousness in the United States while the racist characteristics of all white brick layer's unions and all black hod-carrier's unions, all white Elks clubs and country clubs, segregated schools and neighborhoods and all the attendant role expectations remained. This would be an unstable situation. Unless the nature of the institutional roles were changed, the rationalization of continued participation in all white clubs, segregated schools and neighborhoods, and exclusionary unions would eventually regenerate racist consciousness. Or suppose that one professor eliminates grades, no longer requires papers but makes them optional, no longer dictates the course curriculum of lectures during class time but awaits student initiatives. If the students arrived conditioned to respond to material incentives alone, wanting to be led if not entertained by the instructor, then the elimination of authoritarianism in the institutional structures of the classroom in the context of highly authoritarian characteristics in the student body, would result in very little if any learning at all.

But why should any individual choose to act so as to fit society's roles, especially in cases where these roles are oppressive? The basic "incentive" is negative: the high cost of exclusion. A great preponderance of our needs can only be filled through social activity, and to participate in social activity one must behave in patterns coincident with the expectations of the others involved in that activity. If one chooses not to behave as a buyer and seller, one is excluded from the process of exchange of material goods in a market society. If one chooses not to be a husband or wife, one is excluded from the process of sexual activity and rearing children in a society where the nuclear family is not a disintegrating institution. If one wants the income and material security that goes with being a worker at General Motors one has to fulfill the institutional expectations of the role of worker there. Even when we reject a particular role, the freedom from institutional restraints is most often only temporary. Having decided to quit her job, a woman might act very differently on the last day than she has previously. Or when a man or woman decides to get a divorce, he or she might stop fulfilling the role of husband or wife. But from one job we step into another, and from marriage we step into the singles role with its well-defined dating expectations. Only hermits (more or less) escape the restraining influence of social institutions, which they do at the cost of foregoing the need fulfillment and development that come only from engaging in social activities.

The conformity between center and boundary in any society comes about precisely because people create themselves, but only in historically given circumstances. We are not merely passive pawns of external historical circumstances, but at the same time the past has a powerful influence on present possibilities.[19]

We are born into an institutional setting which is a product of past human activity. If we are to become a part of this setting we must fulfill its role expectations. We must elaborate our activities within certain prescribed limits. Families, schools, the media, places of work, and markets all involve roles we must fill if we are to belong, and in filling them we create ourselves to "conform". Society's stability is a historical outcome.

CORE CHARACTERISTICS

When we examine a society we first distinguish the two aspects center and boundary. We examine these relationally and historically and determine that they are usually in a reasonable conformity due to 1-the strong pressures for individuals to conform to institutional role expectations, and 2-the fact that these institutions are themselves in turn a product of human praxis. Since this conformity and interrelatedness is of special importance for our concerns with how societies reproduce and change, we recognize the need to conceptualize the *social formation* as encompassing the center and boundary together, the "two" for this purpose seen as one.

But when we think about either the center or boundary, we see that it's also possible and useful to demarcate a relatively small number of important characteristics that predominate and have a defining effect on all human possibilities. For example, if racism and authoritarianism were a part of society's center and boundary, they would most likely be what we call *core characteristics*—characteristics that determine the major contours of what people are and can be in a particular society, of what fulfillments they can attain, of what oppressions they will endure, and of how they may develop themselves.

To know the core characteristics, their manifestation and interactions in any particular society, one must undertake a concrete investigation. All that we know in advance (to this point in our analysis) is that *every* society has a center and boundary which interact in the mutually co-causal ways we have indicated, and that the nature of both center and boundary is dominated by a particular set of core characteristics. However, we can now also assert that at a minimum, these core characteristics have to be mutually compatible. That is, demarcating each characteristic as an aspect of society, the relations between them must at least be non-conflicting.[20] For example, if racism and authoritarianism were the two characteristics, it couldn't be that the role requirements of one placed whites above blacks, while that of the other placed blacks above whites. If a society's core characteristics were not at least minimally compatible (they could be highly entwined or otherwise related) the society would be unstable, and in one way or another there would eventually develop a new compatible set of core characteristics within a new historical, social formation.

While recognizing that determining the list of core characteristics for any particular society is a matter of empirical investigation, it is helpful to point toward the most probable possibilities. Whereas orthodox historical materialists focus exclusively on the fact that societies must produce their means of material subsistence, we wish to broaden the list of things human societies *must* do, and therefore the list of likely candidates for core characteristics.

First, people have material needs and productive capacities. To fulfill these people must enter into *economic relationships*, and though we know that such relations will necessarily appear in all societies even before investigating these societies concretely, we cannot know in advance the precise form they will take. The form—feudal, capitalist, socialist, ...—is historical and must be discerned empirically. Second, people must engage in sexual reproduction and somehow rear the new generation. People have diverse sexual needs and capacities. In societies there must be a set of institutional relationships, kinship relations, into which people enter to more or less fulfill these functions. That kinship relations will exist in all societies to give some form of continuity to sexual and child rearing processes, we know simply by our understanding of human nature and social praxis. But what form these kinship relations will take, whether matriarchal, patriarchal, androgynous, or otherwise, is again a historical result and a matter for concrete investigation.[21] Third, people are beings who plan their activities, and in societies, to bring such plans to fruition, people must coordinate them socially. In all societies there will always be decision-making institutions or *authority relations*. This much is known even prior to investigation just from our knowledge that all societies are agglomerations of humans, but whether the authority relations will be monarchical, bureaucratic, bourgeois democratic, dictatorial, or participatory self-managing is only comprehensible via concrete study. Finally, fourth, people are social beings who need human interrelations, who can empathize, and who require respect and self-respect. In history humans inevitably enter communities with shared customs, cultures, and often a shared language. Further, these communities necessarily develop both internal relations of intra-communal life, and external relations of inter-communal life, or of interaction between communities. We know this much will occur, but the lines on which these demarcations will be defined, ethnic, national, religious, racial and the character of the internal and external *community relations* can only be known through specific historical analyses.

Each of these four types of relations—economic, kinship, authority, and community—are abstractions. We demarcate them from the whole precisely as we think it likely that their separate examination will prove useful for our own analytic and practical purposes. In some societies one or more might prove relatively inconsequential for our ends. In other societies all four might be important, and the entwinement of the four might be so relevant that we require an encompassing concept as well. But why single out these four characteristics in particular? What makes all four of these functional prerequisites to societal reproduction so important is that each function requires rather elaborate forms of *social activity* and therefore has the potential to give rise to important social institutional characteristics. After all, it's true that people in societies must also breathe if the society is to successfully reproduce itself, but the value of focusing on this necessary function is dubious in that it is accomplished by individual activity so that studying how it is carried out is not likely to reveal much about the functioning of a society. Moreover, important "we-they" distinctions can easily develop around each function we mentioned: class distinctions, sex-role distinctions, authority distinctions, and racial, national, religious, or ethnic distinctions, any one of which can become the basis for divergences in power and wealth, or more generally, life-possibilities, between different groups in a society. In other words, concrete investigations will often likely show that the particular forms economic, kinship, authority, and community relations take in a society sharply delimit and define human possibilities in that society—making these relations core characteristics.

So while not wishing to prejudge the core characteristics of any particular society, much less the forms of their actual manifestation and interrelation, this list of four possibilities is certainly a good one to investigate. Ruling out any one of these four possibilities on apriori grounds— as orthodox Marxism, radical feminism, radical nationalism, and individualist anarchism do for three of the four—would seem particularly limiting.

SOCIAL CHANGE, REVOLUTION, AND HISTORY

People act thereby creating themselves and history. "Religion, family, state, law, morality, science, art, etc. are all only particular modes of production."[22] Each involves activity which produces the world and its inhabitants. All activity is production, and all production produces objects, ideas, social relations, services, institutions, and people.

But all activity occurs in societies and in the context of their centers and boundaries. Our activity is free and yet not totally free. It is conditioned by all the other human activity which has preceded it and which is now presented to us in the form of institutions, objects, and other people at certain levels of fulfillment, with certain powers, and with certain personalities and consciousnesses. At any moment of time all history faces us as these concretized results which cannot be willed away in the present.

History is a progression of societal formations that are both molded by and also mold people's activities. In social life people apply their powers to meet human ends and even to determine the character of human development. In the process of developing ever more advanced means of meeting particular active needs, those needs may themselves be altered, others may be unleashed or aggravated, and still others created. But historically, this unfolding process is most often alienated. It is skewed to narrow ends, controlled by only a few agents, or more likely yet, almost completely out of human control and rather dominated by the constraints of institutional relations and previously determined human acts. The human actors are nonetheless always both subject and object of the process, as is society itself. The development of this type of historical process we call evolution. It is sufficiently constrained by the status-quo arena in which it occurs to largely reproduce at least the main contours of that arena. There is a progression of regular alterations occurring within the context of society's core characteristics and moreover often even reinforcing them and therefore also the general character of everyday life in the society. Details alter, but with this type of change the basic structural contours remain essentially invariant.

But when any of a society's core characteristics do change, the society is altered throughout. It is no longer "basically the same". A new social formation stands in the place of the old. There has been a revolution. What people can and will become is not what they previously could and did become.

But since in any society there are strong tendencies toward relative conformity between center and boundary, and since most alterations are influenced by their environment precisely to reproduce that environment's defining contours, why should there ever be revolutions?

There is a revolution when there is a contradiction within society which can't and won't be overcome short of the alteration of one or more of society's core characteristics, and which is overcome, through human activity, by exactly such an alteration of one or more of society's core characteristics.

So there are two issues: first, *the presence of a deep contradiction,* and second, *the translation of that contradiction into human activity which overthrows one or more of society's core characteristics.*

The kinds of contradictions which are deep enough to cause a revolution are those which involve the center and boundary and one or more of the core characteristics. Even in the unfolding, constrained application of alienated human powers to the task of meeting skewed human ends, it is possible for new outcomes to be in contradiction with the maintenance of prior core characteristics. It is this situation which augers the possibility of a revolution.

The fact of people's innate human nature being in contradiction with oppressive impositions means further, that any evolutionary alteration which allows that nature fuller expression also brings us closer to active contradictions between oppressive core characteristics and groups of people at society's center. Obviously alterations which cause diminution of the ideological rationalizations of oppressions also contribute significantly to these revolutionary potentials. For example, if the boundary requires a certain form of consciousness which is becoming undermined at the center, there is a contradiction. Or if the boundary through its roles and activity requirements causes people to act in ways which aggravate needs which then can't be met within society, there is a contradiction. If the steady evolutionary alteration of the center and boundary progressively undercuts the roots of a certain consciousness which is essential to center-boundary conformity, then there is a steadily unfolding and worsening contradiction. When it is a core related consciousness that is being weakened, or a core characteristic which is denying aroused needs, we call the involved characteristic "active". It becomes a felt limit upon people's possibilities. The related contradiction may be resolvable only through a revolutionary change. But on the other hand, when there are contradictions in which the core characteristics aren't so centrally involved, they will most likely be resolved by evolutionary changes reproducing the contours of the old society.

We will later give examples to clarify these points, but for now let us go on to the second condition, that the contradictions are translated into human activity which overthrows one or more of society's core characteristics.

In any society we can distinguish people from each other by the roles they come to fill and also by the different ways they affect themselves pursuing those roles. That is, we can distinguish people by the ways they are affected by and manifest society's core characteristics.

For example, if racism is a societal core characteristic in some country, then people of different races will have different life options and different values, ideas, skills, and consciousnesses. Similarly, in those societies where class characteristics are part of the core, what class a person belongs to will tell us a good deal about his or her life situation, needs, and powers. This is true because in societies where class is core, people of similar class position share in having to fulfill certain role definitions, and thereby also share the effects of fulfilling those role definitions.

Contradictions get translated into social activity by groups of people who share similar positions in society with respect to the aspects in contradiction. Revolutions result from active contradictions involving one or more of society's core characteristics. Revolutions are carried out by people who share *similar positions with respect to these active core characteristics.*

In a particular society revolution might be carried out through class struggle. In another society women might constitute the social group which takes the lead in creating a revolution carried out through sexual struggle. Or perhaps both women and classes are active in bringing about a revolution in two core characteristics. Just as which characteristics are core to a society is contingent and to be empirically verified, so which social groups will become revolutionary is not determinable in an apriori manner—only through investigation of the society.

Note that the existence of a contradiction involving one or more of society's core characteristics, and of social groups demarcated by having different positions with respect to the active core characteristic(s), are not alone sufficient conditions for a revolution. There must also be a translation of the contradictory situation into effective action against the old characteristic(s) and an elaboration of new ones in their place.

The revolution Marx envisioned was to be aimed against the core characteristics of capitalist society so as to produce a new socialist society. This would certainly involve class struggle as even the one-sided historical materialist analysis makes evident; but in any particular country it might also involve other dynamics as well, as our own analysis in coming chapters will reveal. But in any case, the goal of this revolution remains much like what Marx was concerned to achieve—a step from "prehistory" in which the development of humans was beyond their own wills, into real history, where human development would in fact be a result of freely determined, collective human praxis. As he put it, the goal is "the reappropriation of the *human essence* by and for humans, ...the complete return of people to themselves as social beings, ...the true resolution of the strife between existence and essence, between objectification and self-confirmation, between freedom and necessity, between the individual and the species."[23] The determination of socialist institutions and social relations becomes precisely the determination of an arena in which people can freely elaborate their own destinies. "A being only considers herself independent when she stands on her own feet, and she only stands on her own feet when she owes her existence to herself."[24]

We are social beings of praxis who exist only in a perpetual process of development. Socialism worthy of the name is a condition allowing accord between our social and developmental aspects and in which we are in control of each. The process of being human becomes the development of the human community.

CORE CHARACTERISTICS IN HISTORY

In a truly human community institutions and consciousnesses would stress the fullest possible development of human needs, capabilities, and variety. But in all historical societies this potential human community has been little more than a vague hope. There have always been antagonistic divisions with one or more sectors having power and advantage over all the others, most frequently along lines of race, class, sex, or hierarchical position.

We have already described how all societies have necessarily had economic, kinship, authority, and community relations—the fact is that each of these have virtually always assumed divisive forms. Economic relations have throughout history been almost without exception class relations wherein antagonistic economic dynamics define roles—serf, proletarian, capitalist, peasant, etc.—which by their activity requirements put severe limits upon human possibilities. The social mediation of sexual needs and potentials through kinship relations has virtually always been sexually unequal and usually patriarchal. This has had an immense attendant impact on the lives of women and men as they have filled their historic roles—e.g. mother, father, uncle, brother, sister, wife. Authority relations have generally been hierarchical and non self-managing.[25] We have had to become ruler and ruled in a host of different forms. Community relations have very often involved one group excluding and limiting another along "racial lines". This has *created* racial, ethnic, national, and religious roles, all historically contingent, which have then sharply circumscribed human social possibilities. Why and how these human functions were initially socially elaborated in ways which later developed into oppressive forms is quite problematic. Perhaps under scarcity conditions there developed a variety of we-they relations, first between tribes vying for food and space.[26] The ensuing conflicts might have led to on-going racial divisions—each group defining the other as inferior and labeling it "different". Similarly, perhaps sexual divisions of labor, hunting versus farming and child rearing, caused skill and disposition differences giving men material and particularly military advantages over women which became manifest in the structure of later kinship forms. The development of surpluses coupled with unequal divisions of prior wealth, knowledge, and power, might have generated class economic relations. In decision-making, hierarchical affiliations to religious, military, or other political organizations could also have become bases for divergences in power and wealth.[27]

In any case, once all these forms come into existence, each has the capacity to influence the others, sometimes aggravating one or more, and sometimes even altering the form of another to achieve greater compatibility.

While the specific content and order of this story is certainly debatable, it can't be denied that such divisions often exist in social formations and that they often severely limit the general quality of daily life relations and the possibilities of human fulfillment and development in these formations. In other words they frequently exist as core characteristics.

Each of these necessary social relations has taken a variety of historical forms in different epochs and social formations. As just a few examples, community divisions have existed between different geographically separated groups who have defined themselves (or been defined by others) to be different—ethnically, racially, religiously, or nationally—in the forms of slavery, exclusion, colonization, neo-colonization, or legalized inequality. Though racial distinctions are imposed and not innate, and only one form of community and inter-community definition, in our society they are perhaps most important so henceforth we will frequently oversimplify community relations to refer predominantly to race relations. Class relations have been historically manifested in feudal, capitalist, and various state capitalist and state socialist forms. Kinship relations have been according to gender and preference and institutionalized in such *contingent* forms as tribes, extended and nuclear families, by laws and by a multitude of sexual and psychological morals and habits. Hierarchical divisions in which decision-making authority over social activities is disproportionately shared among actors have existed in a wide variety of organizational forms.

In each case there has been continuity within change. The basic class, authority, race, and sex divisions have prevailed though with changing forms and intensities. Whenever one or more of these characteristics has structurally altered its form, a society has undergone what we define to be a revolution. The elimination of a colonizing country from one's society is a revolution most often altering at least the form of the community core characteristic. A transformation of the mode of production is invariably a class revolution and could involve other core characteristics as well. The Civil War in the United States, according to our formulation, whatever its varying motivations, was objectively a revolution altering the social formation via the alteration of the form of the racial core characteristic.

Whether the effect of a revolution upon people's lives is significant and even whether the effect is positive or negative is a matter for empirical determination. Similarly the number of core characteristics that change is determinable only by concrete analysis. All we know in advance is that the society enters its revolutionary period with a set of core characteristics, one or more of which have become active, and that when the "smoke clears", either things have settled back to their prior norm, or one or more characteristics have at least changed their form, and there is a new mix in a new social formation.

Not all the characteristics need change in a revolution. The existence of patriarchy in essentially unaltered forms both before and after any number of class and anti-colonialist revolutions illustrates this point. Similarly, even though a revolution against race, sex, class, or authority succeeds, it does not necessarily eliminate the division, as the case of the U.S. Civil War or the Bolshevik revolution in Russia demonstrate. Revolutions in fact most often merely alter the oppressive form their core relations are organized in, sometimes weakening the negative impact on human potentials, but not often eliminating that impact entirely.

Just as the form of these core characteristics can alter from society to society and over time, so too can the relations between them. For example, in one society there can be an uneasy co-existence between sexual and class divisions, each moving according to its own laws of development, and even occasionally coming into conflict with one another.[28] But in another instance it is possible that class and sexual divisions feed upon or reproduce one another. The two might be so reproductive of one another that for either to change both would have to. There are also possibilities between these two extremes. For example the two characteristics we took as examples could as easily have been any of the others, or we could have discussed them three, four, or more at a time uncovering a more complex totality of interrelations.

History is not a simple thing. It is not simply an unfolding economic pattern. Instead social formations are complex entities with a number of components that can be interrelated in a variety of ways, and which can also alter in a variety of different manners.

An analyst seeking to understand how a particular society operates and how it affects its citizens would seek to understand its totality of core characteristics and their manifestations in center and boundary. Which of the four, or any others, are present? In what forms and mix? What is their effect upon daily life and especially human fulfillment and development?

If this analyst wanted to help foster a revolution in the society in question, he or she would focus on the active core characteristics, their interrelations, and the nature of opposition to their on-going reproduction. What groups are opposed and why? What are the potentials for further opposition?

The historical materialist asserts that for all known societies a great part of this work is already complete. Human history is such that class division is the only core characteristic, the active core struggle is limited to class struggle, and the roots of this struggle are always in the contradiction between forces and relations of production within the mode of production. Our assertion is that while this picture represents a simplified expression of *one possibility*, it is by no means the only one, it has not been the most prevalent one, and it is not now the situation in our own country, the United States.[29]

But to get at the situation in any particular society it is necessary to do a more concrete analysis. One part of this task, and not even necessarily the most important part, is to examine the society's political economy. In the next chapter, as an extension of our theory which most usefully shows its differences from orthodox Marxism, we will develop an economic approach and apply it to understanding something about the United States.

Our argument, which we shall pursue throughout the rest of the book, will be that in the United States the active core characteristics are racism, sexism, classism, and a specific extension of hierarchical dynamics we call authoritarianism, and that they interact in such a way that only a "totalist revolutionary movement" stands a chance of really succeeding.

TWO MARXISMS OR ONE?

Continuing with our series of dialogues, we here present a hypothetical discussion between an orthodox Marxist (OM) and a "social relations" Marxist (SM) who accepts the arguments of this past chapter.

OM: Why do you spread bourgeois notions like this idea of 'structures'? Won't it just feed people's sense that reality is fixed and that human concern with change is futile?

SM: Used improperly I suppose it might, but it's more likely that it will help people get over their a-historicism by giving a powerful explanation of why basic conditions are often stable for long periods, even though there is constant activity and change going on. It will help people see that apparent stagnancy is false, and that what's really happening is a very dynamic reproduction with the important features largely invariant because they are continually reproduced. The advantage of having a method specifically addressing this task is that otherwise there is a strong tendency to minimize these matters. Activists frequently seem afraid to address questions of historical continuity because they might find that revolution is actually a pipe-dream. This ostrich tactic doesn't serve anyone. The truth is much more powerful and useful. And the truth is that in history there are invariant structures that last for long periods of time, structures whose reproductive dynamics we must understand if we are to intervene to alter them.

OM: Well, then, why do you bother with all the human nature stuff? Since you see that what's important is that people change historically, why do you assert an innate human nature? Certainly you know how the notion of innateness is almost always used to show that evil is a permanent feature of human existence?

SM: We begin by asserting human nature because we believe that it is there, and we persist in using the concept because it proves so useful in understanding society. The danger that the idea of an innate human nature can be used to justify the status-quo is very real, but there is an equally real danger that the reverse view—that there is no innate human nature—can lead to a complete lack of human concern. The intellectual's justification for bombing peasants in Vietnam was not that the peasants were innately evil, nor that they innately enjoyed being bombed, but rather that it was justified to give them negative reinforcements to influence them to act as we felt they should.

OM: All right, I agree that there are dangers either way. But I still don't see where you get your description from. What possible proof can you have for your particular listing of needs, powers, and the rest? They are unreal. Since humans are social and only exist socially, how can you take one out and say this is his or her human nature, and everyone else shares it as well?

SM: I can't do it, save as an abstraction, an approximation. There is no such thing as any separate thing, and certainly not a human outside a social context. This is true and basic to our methodological approach. But we still recognize that for certain purposes one can abstract things from the whole web, define them separately, and investigate their attributes. Since our concern is with people in history, if we can locate attributes that are relevant in all historical contexts, and are usefully regarded as general, we should cautiously do so, and in doing so, if we discover that the separateness of our description can also get in the way, we should then develop additional concepts which are broader and can force us to go beyond narrow thinking. So we do think about the individual human subject, but we also think about praxis, social groups, social formations, and so on.

OM: But you assert that people are good. You want to have socialism written into human geneology, but that is determinist and flies in the face of the oppressive details of human history. We're at least consistent in saying that human nature is neutral and in explaining oppression through the concept of class struggle.

SM: I suppose that in a sense you do explain oppression, but in our view incorrectly. It isn't true that there are only two options: All life is prescribed at birth, or there is no prescription at all, only a blank slate. We assert a human nature wired into a social being which can only take form in a social context. Human nature is only manifest in socially historically determined forms. But it is real, nonetheless. Understanding that people's needs and power exert themselves in hostile environments, we go on to demonstrate how oppressions persist, how they can become part of people's consciousness and personalities. And because we have a view of human nature and a theory which says that what people are is an outcome of the interaction between their nature and social settings, we're in a position to intelligently discuss the full complexity of human development and consciousness. On the other hand, because you largely have a simple reflection theory—the environment totally molds us—you get a very oversimplified vision of human development, and no framework for evaluating one society versus another, except as to their relative stabilities.

OM: Not at all. We see that people are a product of historical forces, which they then in turn contribute to. And we also see that major changes in human nature come about because of major changes in modes of production and that they in turn alter due to their own internal contradictions...

SM: But that's our first major disagreement and it comes directly out of the issue of human nature. You see contradictions arising only from discontinuities within the institutional framework itself. The mode of production sets people off in two directions which are incompatible. And while we agree that such contradictions occur, and that they are important, we also recognize the possibility of more basic contradictions between people themselves and the environments they encounter. Where you see revolutions emerging precisely because people do what society tells them to do—for example, workers pursuing ever greater incomes to buy commodities, and also ever more time to enjoy them—we feel that it is more often critical that people break from what society imposes upon them.

OM: Again you talk as if there is some fixed quality in all people which pushes forward to socialism. Your view of human nature seems totally at odds with all your earlier concerns to be relational and historical.

SM: Look, there is no inconsistency in asserting 1-that people have innate species natures, 2-that people exist only socially, and 3-that people exist only historically. We might even say that in the last instance there is human nature, and yet the last instance is never reached. Our abstract nature is there, at root, but our concrete being is social and historical, a product of social development, the interaction of our given nature with society. Even our innate needs express themselves only in historically conditioned ways. Hunger for raw meat and hunger for a vegetable pie are two different hungers. Nonetheless, the abstraction, hunger for food, seen as an innate human need, is useful and has a real if never finally alone-perceptible referent. Again, the alternatives are not "tabula rasa" or "instinct determined". Human needs will only be fulfilled and human potential freely elaborated under socialism but there is no end to this, it is not fixed, nor is it inevitable. The implications for revolutionary strategy and even for what socialism is are something we should discuss later though.

OM: Alright, I'm certainly happy enough to stick to theory for now. But I just can't see where you're pushing Marxism forward. It seems rather that you are diluting it into nothing more than a snapshot, or maybe a motion picture. Where we focus on the important economic aspect you babble on about everything—that's really not very helpful for practitioners who need to know where best to focus their attentions rather than being told that everything is equally important. So we have the mode of production and you seem to have the whole society. We have base and superstructure with the former more critical than the latter, and you have center and boundary with both of equal importance. We have production and you have the vague notion of activity...

SM: Why vague? Look, you choose production on the grounds that it has the most significant effect on people, creating classes that determine history. But the supporting argument has to be that something about production translates into class demarcations and contradictory class interests leading classes to become the agents of history—and indeed, you do argue that both the activity of production, which engenders certain socializing and other direct effects upon workers, and also the results stemming from one's position in production, especially with respect to one's form of income and material interests, both determine contradictory class locations. We don't disagree so much as we elaborate this analysis further. We recognize that humans are produced through their own activity in historically given settings. Production is certainly one such activity, but it is not the only one. Surely people also invest intellectual and emotional energies into their family lives, as but one obvious example. Further, it is not necessarily the case that only class divisions are key to how one lives in a society. Sometimes racial, sexual, and other divisions prove to be exceptionally important. In these cases, variations in people's positions with respect to race or sex or other modes of activity also affect their consciousnesses and their material and psychological interests. This being the case, we recognize that the question of which groups move any society and for what reasons is not to be answered on an a priori basis. Rather it requires concrete analysis of the particular society's consciousnesses and institutions—its center and boundary. In short, taking practice of all kinds and not just production as our starting point, we see the need to look at more than just the mode of production as society's determinant aspect. That this leads to more inclusiveness and complexity isn't a function of our merely taking a 'motion picture'. It's rather due to our desire to not over-abstract even for the worthy reason of trying to find a key link upon which to most effectively exert one's energies.

OM: But then you are forced into this discussion of roles. It is overly sociological and psychological. And even worse, it suggests that people just fit like worms into predug holes. It is functionalist. You have no motion in your view, at least nothing as clear as an unfolding accumulation process simultaneously required for society's maintenance and also pushing it toward dissolution.

SM: Your first point is an ironic one. I don't really mind at all being sociological or psychological—the whole point is that economics, particularly narrow economistic economics, isn't everything. As to people being worms, it is the historical materialist approach that argues that people are infinitely malleable. We merely describe the mechanisms by which people are in fact partially governed by their settings, but we also make clear the limits of this dynamic, the fact that people's underlying natures are prior and always present, and the conditions under which a variety of different types of contradiction can cause ruptures in any society's stability.

Indeed, this is one of the main strengths of our approach. It is neither instrumentalist nor voluntarist. People are neither reduced to the part of unthinking bearers of the dictates of their environment, nor are they elevated to the plane of complete autonomous freedom. Their subjective and their objective aspects are both analyzed. Society's reproductive and disruptive potentials are both opened to investigation. This was certainly Marx's approach, but history has seen Marxists in turn produce two vulgar misinterpretations. On the one hand, they sometimes have developed a stabile, functionalist approach, and on the other, sometimes a 'revolutionary rupture' approach. But what is interesting about Marx, and what we try to return to, is the attempt to capture both these tendencies simultaneously in one theory. The future is not to be reduced to the past—inherent in our fixed nature—nor is it independent, as if we had the capacity to act independently of the requisites of our fixed nature. And this has relevance to your second point as well. We don't deny accumulation, we simply understand it less economistically as one part of the whole process by which human powers are continuously applied and reapplied to accomplishing various human ends. This process of social praxis is at the center of the motion we see in society but it is not as divorced from human attributes as you describe it, nor as apolitical, acultural, and asocial...

OM: But with this approach you get a dump-everything-in-it-soup, rich in detail, but useless as a theory precisely because it doesn't locate causes and explain history in terms of them. Your core characteristics—race, sex, class, and even authority—are the clearest instance. They just aren't theoretically developed, yours is not a theoretical presentation. It doesn't hold together. How do you even determine what is core and what isn't? And anyway, if everything is so entwined why can't we understand society by way of a full analysis of its economy?

SM: If you were omniscient you probably could understand our whole society via a full analysis of just its economy, or culture, or government, etc. But you're not. To get a grasp upon the whole, in light of the difficulties that dialectical thinking presents to us, and in light of our human failings—the fact that we are historically bound and ourselves often racist, sexist, or otherwise narrow in our thinking—it's necessary to have concepts that bring us at the whole from a variety of directions and that discipline our perceptions and thoughts to make them as effective as possible. As to our view not being theoretical, you confuse theory with simplicity and determinateness. For us, dialectical thinking requires a continual development and redevelopment of concepts—one must be comfortable with unanswered questions, with a constantly growing theory. We say that to know any particular society one must investigate it. To concretely determine any society's core characteristics one has to examine center and boundary to find which features reproduce structurally, and of those which are crucial to the character of the society's daily-life relations. None of this is a priori, but that doesn't make it wrong.

OM: But isn't it just opportunism to have race, sex, and authority alongside class? Aren't you just trying to suck the nationalists, feminists, and anarchists into your movement?

SM: Again, this charge is all too ironic. What is opportunist is having a theory which says clearly that class is central and then making believe that one also considers matters of race or sex "central", knowing full-well that this lip-service will be dropped at the first opportunity. We have learned from the experiences of the various autonomous movements of the sixties and realize that these lessons have to be incorporated into the very roots of our theoretical framework. It is no longer enough to tack on slogans mentioning women or blacks, describing them as doubly or triply oppressed workers. But we cannot fully present our case until after our analysis of the interaction of the core characteristics in the United States.

OM: But what difference can any of this really make? Class is still most important to all revolutionary concerns.

SM: Not necessarily. It could be that class is secondary in some cases, for example, in certain anti-colonialist struggles, or perhaps in the struggle against apartheid in South Africa. Or it may be that while class is critical, it is so only in conjunction with other aspects, as we'll argue is the case in the United States.

OM: I think that is ridiculous, but I'll hold my criticisms until after you've fully presented your case. But regarding something you've already argued, surely you'll admit that you description of the origins of these so-called core characteristics is absurd.

SM: No. Our description isn't absurd, nor is it anything more than a sketch of one hypothesized possibility. What it intended to suggest was that class divisions need not even have been the first ones to appear in human history. In general, though, I think the importance of this issue is often exaggerated. We may never be able to answer these origin questions and a lot of energy we invest in the effort is likely misplaced. But more importantly, the first or 'original division', is not necessarily the most important now anyway. Relative importance of core characteristics now is so tenuously related to their order of origin that the latter is of little practical importance. For example, it is conceivable that your orthodox view is correct that sexual divisions, racial divisions, and authority divisions grew from prior class divisions (though we certainly doubt it) and yet even if this were true, so what? It would tell us nothing concrete about the form or mix of these core characteristics in some current social formation—for example, whether they are independent, entwined, or equally co-causal.

We believe that we have the beginnings of a theory which can explain society as an unfolding process in ways which are suited to aiding revolutionary activists. This is because it focuses on people, explains why people act and think as they do at least at the level of major social groups, and because it can help us identify the sets of relationships critical to societal reproduction and revolution. To see all this, however, we'll have to apply our approach to an analysis of the United States, and to discussions of socialism and revolution. But before going on, I would like to leave you with a question. When you ask yourself whether some new approach is a truer and more powerful extension of Marxism than orthodox historical materialism, do you want it to be an improvement or do you hope it will prove useless? Is your interest "making revolution" or "preserving a scripture" and thereby your own self-esteem as well? Just as families can involve people as much or even more than workplaces, so too can political organizations. Not only bourgeois politicians, but also Marxist Leninists can have their interests and consciousness largely molded by their political acitivities. This is not bad, except when it orients people toward organizational and self-preservation rather than revolution but this is regrettably quite frequently the case. Although you haven't criticized our theory for being similarly susceptable, it certainly is. Marx never envisioned a finished theory—but all too often we on the

Left act as if there is one. One of our priorities should be trying to build into the very terms, concepts and methods of our theory and of our practice a disposition toward continual change rather than toward stagnation. I'm just wondering, is that your disposition?

FOOTNOTES: CHAPTER THREE

1. Throughout this chapter we will further elaborate the special relations between the human and the non-human world. These are of relevance at all but the most abstract levels of analysis. They are especially important to the study of history and human societies.

2. Our methodology is quite similar to that developed by Bertell Ollman in *Alienation*, Cambridge University Press, London, and further elaborated by him in his forthcoming work on Marx and Reich to be published by South End Press. We believe, as Ollman does, that this methodology is Marx's as well. Herbert Marcuse's essay, "On the Problem of the Dialectic", Telos, no. 27, Spring, 1976 makes the argument quite powerfully.

3. For us, the concept "structure" is a methodological tool. We abstract some aspect from a complex system and call it a structure if it has certain properties *with respect to the ends we are pursuing*. We are not saying that the world is structural or that societies are structural or composites of structures in any absolute sense. We are saying that to the degree of analysis relevant to our purposes, and for the characteristics relevant to our purposes, and over the time frames relevant to our purposes, we can abstract aspects which are usefully classified and analyzed as "structures".

4. Georg Lukacs, for example, has the concept "totality", though used somewhat differently than we will use it ourselves. He also argues that Marx was sensitive to the need for encompassing concepts of this nature and that Marx understood the necessity to understand "wholes" as more than a simple sum of parts.

> It is not the primacy of economic motives in historical explanation that constitutes the decisive difference between Marxism and bourgeois thought, but the point of view of totality. The category of totality, the all-pervasive supremacy of the whole over the parts, is the essence of the method which Marx took over from Hegel and brilliantly transformed into the foundations of a wholly new science.... The revolutionary principle inherent in Hegel's dialectic was able to come to the surface less because of that (the materialist twist) but because of the validity of the method itself, viz, the concept of totality, the subordination of every part to the whole unity of history and thought. In Marx, the dialectical method aims at understanding society as a whole. Bourgeois thought concerns itself with objects that arise either from the process of studying phenomena in isolation, or from the division of labor and specialization in the different disciplines.

Georg Lukacs, *History and Class Consciousness*, M.I.T. Press, Cambridge, Mass. Page 27-28. 1971.

Note that our entire discussion of methodology has the tone of "what is easiest" or "what is most effective". But this is natural since we are discussing the choice and purposes of a particular set of tools. They should be well-fitted to our needs. However, it does make evident the *fact* that intellectual work—even perception—is never divorced from subjective ends. These ends enter precisely in our definition of concepts and in the questions we ask about these concepts, whether we are conscious of this phenomenon or not. We do not necessarily bend or distort perceptions to fit preconceived molds, but we do always necessarily see only a part of the whole in terms of a mold which we carry with us. It is still a priority to strive for accuracy and to keep our desires from warping our perceptions or analyses, but the point must be made that theories of society are inextricably linked to the interests of their holders. They are still testable through practice, they still may be judged "objective" or "subjective" in the sense of corresponding to something in the world or to something we wish were in the world, but they are not and can never be "completely value-free". Our interest is in human fulfillment and development through the collective self-management of human praxis. We want to help achieve this condition. It is the end which guides the definition of our concepts and delimits the set of questions we ask.

5. For a critique of Skinnarian approaches to psychology and policy making, see *Psychologists on Psychology*, David Cohen, ed. Taplinger, 1977.

6. Karl Marx quoted in *The Twilight of Capitalism*, Michael Harrington, Simon and Schuster, Page 167.

7. Karl Marx, *Capital, Volume One*, New World Paperbacks.

Helmut Fleischer has excellent discussions of Marx's understanding of history and of the many interpretations they have received in his work, *Marxism and History*, Harper Torchbooks, New York, 1973. Relevant to the discussion in this part of our text he quotes Marx positively asserting: "Produce with consciousness as human beings, not as separate atoms without consciousness of your species, and you will have elevated yourself above all...artificial conflicts." Fleischer, op. cit. Page 19.

8. Herb Gintis has studied a number of ramifications of this point for the study of the political economy of capitalism. See "Alienation and Power: Toward a Radical Welfare Economics", unpublished Ph.D. dissertation, Harvard University, May, 1969.

9. For further discussions of "knowing human nature" see Noam Chomsky, *Reflections on Language*, Pantheon, New York, 1975.

10. The recognition that we are an ecological species in the sense of requiring variety, and the understanding of the relation between the need for a degree of ecological balance and the need for a degree of situational variety is quite important to our own understanding of what a good socialist system should be like. For relevant discussions of ecological problems and possibilities see Barry Commoner, *The Closing Circle*, Bantam, 1971, and Murray Bookchin, *The Limits of the City*, Harper Colophon, 1974.

11. We mean "innate" in the strong, genetic sense. Certain attributes are literally "wired in". These distinguish us from all other living things as a species to ourselves, and they include much more than simply our physical appearance. In

this there is nothing mystical or idealist, it is material biological processes which insure that with human reproduction certain wired in attributes remain essentially invariant over long periods of time. It is, on the other hand, social/historical processes which reproduce structural personality and consciousness forms as well as institutional relationships from generation to generation.

12. This theme, that people are social beings, runs throughout the Marxist heritage we subscribe to. Consider Marx's own formulation:

> The individual is *the social being.* His life, even if it may not appear in the direct form of a *communal* life in association with others—is therefore as expression and confirmation of *social life.* Man's individual and species life are not *different,* however much—and this is inevitable—the mode of existence of the individual is a more *particular* or more *general* mode of the life of the species, or the life of the species is a more *particular* or more *general* individual life.

Karl Marx, *The Economic and Philosophic Manuscripts,* New World Paperbacks, 1969. Page 138.

13. See footnote 7.

14. To our knowledge, the original formulation of this approach was in Herb Gintis, op. cit., though he has since disavowed it in favor of a definition stressing "who is in control".

15. Readers with some background in psychology might compare our discussion to the common theoretical treatment of the concept "cognitive dissonance".

16. In the example here, we have placed the worker's desire to keep his position in the firm foremost. It might thus be called a "materialist" explanation in the orthodox sense of the term. Later we will discuss the dynamics of this type of interaction, whereby class relations exacerbate sexual differentiations, but we will also discuss reverse dynamics as well. We will, for example, argue that in the United States factory, role definitions are governed by patriarchal kinship requirements as well as by class requirements so that the motives behind male sexist behavior are not always correlated to job advancement, but often simply to the gains that accrue from male bonding which excludes women, etc.

17. See Ollman, op. cit., for a similar approach.

18. We will emphasize institutions and roles in our discussion of societal boundaries, but the "objects" are of considerable importance as well. What objects are available in any society has a tremendous impact upon what people are able to do. For example, capitalist technology makes some activities possible while precluding others. Ollman, op. cit., discusses this point in some detail. But since the constraints imposed by the character of any society's existent store of objects are very similar to those imposed by the society's role structures, we leave the matter for another time. Here, we should simply point out the most important instance of the store of objects attaining an importance on their own—that is, when the objects are of such complexity to use or replace, or when they impose such complex intellectual and orientational dictates upon people that they delimit role possibilities as much as the roles delimit them. The prime current example may well be the proliferation of computers in the United States. See Joseph Weizenbaum, *Computer Power and Human Reason,* W. H. Freeman and Company, 1976.

19. This is the way in which we comply with the kernal of truth in the orthodox Marxist notion that human nature is historical, at the same time that we preserve recognition that there is a human nature which is invariant over historical time spans.

20. Later we will discuss other possibilities in considerable detail.

The reader may have already noticed that a number of theoretical/political traditions emerge as soon as one determines that either race, sex, authority, or class relations are core to historical processes. We will discuss these traditions and compare them to our own views theoretically and strategically as we proceed.

21. See Gayle Rubin, "The Traffic In Women", in *Toward An Anthropology of Women,* edited by Rayna Reiter, Monthly Review Press, 1975. This article is particularly good not only for its discussion of kinship relations but as a paradigm example of how to criticize the orthodox Marxist approach and then develop a more comprehensive alternative.

22. Karl Marx, *Economic and Philosophic Manuscripts,* op. cit. Page 136.

23. Ibid. Page 185.

24. Ibid. Page 144. Here again we have taken the liberty to do a "free" translation in tune with modern anti-sexist usage.

25. For discussion of kinship relations see Rubin, op. cit. and Batya Weinbaum's forthcoming work, *The Curious Courtship of Women's Liberation and Socialism,* South End Press. For discussions of authority relations see the anarchist writers, for example, Alexander Berkman, *What Is Communist Anarchism,* Dover Books, 1972.

26. Numerous authors have written on such "origin problems", many stressing the importance of the concept "scarcity". See Jean Paul Sartre, *Critique of Dialectical Reason,* New Left Books, 1977, or Joan Robinson, *Freedom and Necessity,* Vintage Books, 1971.

27. See footnote 25.

28. We will discuss this view and its strategic implications in later chapters.

29. We will make this argument in chapters five and six.

CHAPTER FOUR
A POLITICAL ECONOMY OF PRAXIS

As it happens, there are no columns in standard double-entry
bookeeping to keep track of satisfaction and demoralization.
There is no credit entry for feelings of self-worth and confidence, no debit column for feelings of uselessness and worthlessness. There are no monthly, quarterly, or even annual
statements of pride and no closing statement of bankruptcy
when the worker finely comes to feel that after all he couldn't do
anything else, and doesn't deserve anything better.

Barbara Garson
All The Livelong Day

In this chapter we present the beginnings of a theory of political
economy compatible with the methodology and social/historical theory
developed earlier.

First we address the problem of "economism" in hopes of avoiding
this error ourselves. Then we present a model suited to analyzing the
reproduction of the social relations of capitalism, that is, a model
appropriate to the qualitative analysis of how capitalist social roles and
human consciousnesses are reproduced in the economy. In that context
we discuss the genesis of use-value, a new theory of the market and of
consumption under capitalism, the consequences of the uniqueness of
human labor in the production process, and a new theory of the capitalist
firm. Finally, we conclude by presenting a model suited to analyzing
the reproduction of the material flows of goods and services in capitalist
economies, that is, a quantitative model explaining the determination of
relative prices, wages, and profits as the consequences of the social
relations, or relative bargaining strengths of different groups in a modern
capitalist economy.

We have tried to minimize our use of mathematics and have
relegated the most complicated parts to appendices. Some readers will
probably feel that too much still remains in the body of the text; however,
they should know in advance that the main points of the chapter are
perfectly understandable without following the mathematical details,
and that the mathematical demonstrations are peripheral to the rest of
the book.

ECONOMISM IN ECONOMIC THEORY

What is economism? Some would define it as a condition of political practice in which there is an overemphasis on economic or material issues at the expense of considerations of social change. Others use the term to refer to political practice where the strategic emphasis is only at the shopfloor level, excluding the national political scene.[1] These are useful definitions but we prefer another.

For us economism means viewing capitalism "pristinely", as if it were a "pure economic system" drawn full-blown from some mental exercise, evolving independently from and governing the development of all other non-economic variables it encounters. Economism is a view which proceeds from the *apriori* assumption that the totality which governs and reproduces the character of society's daily life is the capitalist accumulation process, class relationships, and these forces alone. It is an approach which fails to remember that historically there is no such thing as the capitalism of the orthodox reproduction schemes.

In these respects economism is like those variants of feminism, which see a "pure dialectic" of sex, apriori dominant and above all else, molding and pushing everything through history; or the variants of nationalism that see only a "pure dialectic" of race. Economism is just one of a number of myopic views which dissects one aspect of society isolating it from the totality it in fact does not exist without, and declares it to be singularly important—or, at least, dominant. All else follows suit as if the unfolding of a society's daily life were a bridge game with either the factory (vulgar Marxism), the bedroom (extreme feminism), the ghetto (extreme nationalism), or the state (extreme anarchism), continuously determining trump.

Economism suggests that to understand any society we need only understand the economy in great detail; the rest is a matter of peripheral "mopping up". Further we can understand the economy by analyzing only class relationships, and we should do this by studying the determination of quantitative variables like wages, prices, and profits or the surplus.

We disagree at every turn. We see that studying the economy is just one of many crucial analytic steps, and that one can approach the analysis of any particular economy in a variety of ways, depending precisely upon the nature of the society's core characteristics and their mix. For us, all these core aspects can, and often do exist in interpenetration not only in society as a whole but within the economic institutions themselves.

If the only core characteristic in a society were class, the orthodox Marxist approach would be somewhat justifiable, though still incorrect because of its narrow conception of human development and interaction and the failure of the Labor Theory Of Value to properly express the social relations of even this "pure capitalist model". But, for example, if sexist kinship relations were also core, it would be necessary when studying economic relations to take sexual dynamics into account. If the relations between sex and class dynamics were just a parallel motion, it would be sufficient to approach the factory and market as essentially class arenas, appending analyses of the way men and women relate within them, and to analyze the family as essentially a sexual arena appending the effect of class demarcations. However, if the relation between the sexual and class core characteristics is more involved, if each characteristic helps reproduce the structural form of the other, if their dynamics are entwined rather than parallel, then our analytic tasks are more complicated. In this case the factory is not a vulgar place where class relations determine everything, with the minor theoretical annoyances of intra-class sexual divisions. Instead the factory becomes a place where sex and class reproductive dynamics together constitute a *totality* which governs both the social relations and the consciousnesses that dominate people's lives in their daily work activities.

Therefore, in the case when sex and class divisions were core and entwined, the roles of the factory and family would not only be compatible, they would each be totalistically determined. The factory roles would embody class as well as familial kinds of expectation (father, mother, brother, sister, behaviors and consciousnesses), and similarly the roles of the family would also be class defined. But we should admit that this theoretical view is largely untried—our hypothesis is that looking at the organization of U.S. factories and markets with sexual kinship categories will show them to be more complex than a "simple" class analysis suggests.

In any case, in analyzing a complex society with entwined core characteristics, we only blind ourselves by labelling some institutions "economic" and some "sexual". We lose track of the reality that class dynamics as well as sexual (or racial or authority) reproductive dynamics take place in factories and markets, just as sexual reproductive dynamics and class (race and authority) reproductive dynamics take place in families. More generally, even though the distinction between economic, social, and cultural institutions is sometimes useful, it also often serves to obscure the fact that all three of these "functions" generally occur in all major social institutions.

In short, there really is no such thing as a "pure economics" or a "pure science of class relations". Every step away from a totalist view, especially in analyzing some societies with very entwined core characteristics, is a severe abstraction which can easily distort our perceptions. As such, these steps must be carried through with great care, and never as a substitute for fuller analysis.

In this chapter our own approach will regretably necessarily be "less totalist" than we would like, but the relative emphasis on class relations is only an indication that this aspect of our analysis is further developed, not that we find it "more important" or a "better starting place".

In a sense we have more in the way of answers concerning authority and class dynamics in economic institutions, and more in the way of questions and hypotheses concerning race and sex dynamics in these same institutions. But in this chapter, since we only mean to present a theoretical approach applicable to understanding the economies of societies with varying core characteristics and core characteristic mixes, these problems of the fullness of our current analysis are not crucial. Later when discussing consciousness and institutions in the United States itself, all these concerns will be raised again, and we will give more time to the problems of sex, race, and authority as well as class.

THE QUALITATIVE MODEL

Any economy can be thought of as groups of people engaging in economic activities which constitute a collection of economic processes. At any point in time, t, each process is characterized by the complete list of inputs entering the process and outputs generated by the process, the extent to which the various needs of the people involved are being fulfilled or aggravated by the activity, and an identification of the agents who decided how the activity would be done. However the list of inputs and outputs is more extensive than has usually been recognized. Not only are there material goods entering and exiting in every process at every moment of time—i.e. natural resources, R^1, R^2, ..., and goods produced by human economic processes, X^1, X^2, ...—but there are a host of *human* inputs and outputs as well.[2] Every process is a set of activities engaged in by a particular group of humans, h, and both the individual human characteristics of the people in the group as well as the collective, group characteristics are potentially important as inputs or outputs of the process. Different individuals' personality traits, P^1, P^2, ..., the skills and talents of the people in the group, T^1, T^2, ..., the various components of people's knowledge or understanding of how the world works, U^1, U^2, ..., and the different attitudes people have toward their understanding of how the world works, or people's values, V^1, V^2, ..., as well as the social relations, S^1, S^2, ..., between the people in the group are all potentially important in defining the nature of the group's activity and can all potentially be changed to some extent by the activity itself.[3] We can keep track of this phenomenon by thinking of all these human characteristics as both inputs and outputs of economic processes, any one of which might have a different "value" as an output than it did as an input.

For example, in the modern steel making process natural resources such as coal and previously produced goods such as iron enter as material inputs. But the personality traits of male and female workers, the skills of bricklayers, the administrative attitudes of engineers, the class consciousness of organized workers and of management employees, the patriarchal social relations between male and female assembly workers, and the racial relations between black workers in the blast furnaces and white workers in the rolling mills, all enter as human inputs as well. And not only is steel of various qualities and dimensions generated as a material output, but reinforced or modified personality structures, increased or decreased skill levels, and reproduced or altered consciousnesses and social relations constitute outputs of the modern steel-making process as well. Finally, various needs are fulfilled or aggravated by the activities that the different kinds of workers and managers engage in.

So any group of people, h, at time, t, can be thought of as engaging in a particular economic activity, a_h^t, where a_h^t is some element of the set A_h^t of all possible economic activities group h could have engaged in at time t. A full description of any a_h^t for any group h includes the natural resources, material products, and human or social characteristics that are inputs and outputs of that process:

$$a_h^t = \left[\begin{pmatrix} R_r \\ X_x \\ P_p \\ T_t \\ U_u \\ V_v \\ S_s \end{pmatrix}^i \rightarrow \begin{pmatrix} R_r \\ X_x \\ P_p \\ T_t \\ U_u \\ V_v \\ S_s \end{pmatrix}^o \right]_h^t$$

Where R_r is a shorthand for the complete list of natural resources (R^1, R^2, ...); X_x shorthand for (X^1, X^2, ...) and so on for the other entries as well, and where the superscript i stands for inputs and the superscript o stands for outputs.

This way of looking at a particular process is easily extended to a view of the whole economy at any moment in time and a view of the development of the economy over time. At any time, t, the whole economy consists of the activities engaged in by all the different groups: a_1^t, a_2^t, ... a_H^t, where the groups are h=1, 2, ... h. The development of the economy is seen by observing the activities of all the groups over the appropriate time periods: a_1^0,... a_H^0; a_1^1,... a_H^1; ...a_1^t, ... a_H^t.... a_1^T,...a_H^T where t runs over the periods 0, 1, ... T. So the entire economy's development is seen as:

$$
\left[\begin{pmatrix} R_r \\ X_x \\ P_p \\ T_t \\ U_u \\ V_v \\ S_s \end{pmatrix}^i \rightarrow \begin{pmatrix} R_r \\ X_x \\ P_p \\ T_t \\ U_u \\ V_v \\ S_s \end{pmatrix}^o \right]_{\substack{t=0 \\ h=1,...H}}
\quad {}_{t=1,...T} \quad
\left[\begin{pmatrix} R_r \\ X_x \\ P_p \\ T_t \\ U_u \\ V_v \\ S_s \end{pmatrix} \rightarrow \begin{pmatrix} R_r \\ X_x \\ P_p \\ T_t \\ U_u \\ V_v \\ S_s \end{pmatrix}^o \right]_{\substack{t=T \\ h=1,...H}}
$$

$$
\| \qquad\qquad\qquad\qquad \|
$$

$$
a_h^0 \quad {}_{h=1\,...H} \qquad\qquad a_h^T \quad {}_{h=1,\,...H}
$$

We should reassert that this notation is merely a kind of shorthand. It is a succinct way of setting down a host of attributes in one easily manipulable array.[4]

Although the advantages of this choice of a descriptive model will become apparent as we apply it to the analysis of use-value, consumption, markets, human labor, and the capitalist firm, it is helpful to point out some of the key features at this point.

1-The essence of the concept of praxis, whereby humans create themselves, in part, while creating their means of material survival, was unfortunately unreflected in orthodox Marxist economic theory. The new theory highlights this phemonemon and places the transformation and creation of human characteristics at center stage. Not only do the theory's categories provide for a vivid record of the development of both individual and group characteristics over time as a result of economic activities, but they remind us that the "possibility set" of activities that any group, h, could engage in at any time t is delimited precisely by the individual and human characteristics at the end of the prior period, t minus 1, a set of human characteristics inclusive of, but also much more extensive than technological knowledge of production. In other words all the group's previously accumulated human characteristics determine A_h^t. We shall see that the pattern of development of the human characteristics is of great concern to employees and employers alike, as well as a matter of principal interest in evaluating the performance of particular economic institutions.

2-By focusing attention on the qualitative as well as quantitative aspects of economic activity, our approach remains open to the inclusion of race, sex, authority, and class dynamics in all their dimensions. If our social theory says that in some societies patriarchy will be a core characteristic so that economic roles will be defined in part by male-female kinship requisites, our economic approach is certainly able to accommodate this. Such characteristics are simply incorporated in our definition of economic activities in these societies and in our analysis of their motion through time. In this sense the economic theory is flexible and achieves its full conceptual development only in the on-going process of its application. Applied to the United States, for example, we feel that it will finally embody a fourfold totality of core characteristics and an analysis of their entwined motion throughout the economy.

3-The new theory breaks down false distinctions between economic and non-economic processes and so-called "production" and "consumption" processes. It becomes obvious that all forms of human activity are analyzable, whether they take place in a factory, office, home, school, church, theatre, or informal club, and that in all instances material objects, human characteristics, and human consciousness are integral to the processes and transformed by them. Recognition of this symmetry between all forms of activity helps undermine the tendency toward economism discussed above. Furthermore, the fundamental symmetry of production and consumption activity is re-asserted by the model. We call certain processes "production" processes because we are focusing on the material outputs, whereas other processes are called "consumption" processes because we focus on the material inputs. The distinction can be dangerous if it leads us to ignore the human outputs of consumption and production processes. Our descriptive theory provides a constant safeguard against this forgetfulness.

4-Finally the problem of exhaustable resources as well as material wastes (or pollution) has long been ignored by political economic theory and orthodox Marxist value theory in particular. Regardless of whether or not this was justifiable in the 19th century, it clearly is not today. So in at least some economic processes we expect to find non-zero values for some of the resources as inputs, and of course all resource entries, R^1, R^2, ..., will be zero as outputs. Further, among the material output (X) entries we will find reference to the different forms of economic "waste".

USE VALUE

What is use-value? Where does it come from, how does it change, how does it determine and how is it determined by its interactions? We have criticized orthodox Marxism's failure to focus on these questions, so what does our approach offer instead?

For a thing to have use-value means that it is desired to fill some need or purposes. This is simple enough, but are such needs and purposes unchanging or do they themselves constitute social relations with histories and interactions of their own?

In our view people have a variety of natural and species needs, including those for food, sexual gratification, security, knowledge, love, aesthetic development, self-esteem, sociability, and self-management of their activities. There are also a host of socially determined needs like those for employment in a firm, particular types of food, television, cars, and marriage. The extent to which we seek to meet various innate or derived needs, and the extent to which meeting all of them is simultaneously possible depends largely on the social contexts in which we function and the social opportunities we encounter.[5]

For example, in some social settings to get enough food to survive requires activities which preclude, or increase the difficulty of achieving dignity, love, aesthetic fulfillment, and self-management. This is the case with most means of achieving an adequate income under capitalism. Similarly, to attain security in a society which denies her skills and opportunities, a woman may develop personality traits aimed at capturing and pleasing a man, in which case the struggle to attain security requires dissimulation and passivity, and precludes self-respect and free and equal love relations. So in certain social settings meeting one need may very well preclude meeting others. To attain what we absolutely must have we may end up denying our potentials for reaching other ends as well.

Depending on one's past history and present social setting one has varying desires and means of fulfilling them. Whatever we pursue has use-value for us. But whether or not it is the best possible thing we could be pursuing, given full control over our setting and history, is a matter for analysis.

So use-value is neither an ahistorical given nor completely a function of our cumulative social relationships.[6] Rather, use-value derives from the interaction between our needs and potentials and the environments we encounter. It is variable. It develops over time, as do our personalities, skills, and consciousnesses. It changes as our human characteristics change, but it is not infinitely moldable.

The economy is one part of the social setting in which we function. Since use-value is partially governed by our innate needs, partially by the past history of interaction between those needs and our past environments, and partially from our present setting and the constraints it imposes, it is "endogenous" to economic conditions. That is, it is affected by the economy in which we work and from which we consume.[7]

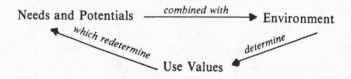

But not only are people not static creatures, we are not ignorant either. We change and we know we change. Our personalities, skills, and consciousnesses are changed by our daily activities and experiences. And although such "character development" is often out of our control, sometimes we do have some say, some influence over where we are going. Sometimes we seek to mold ourselves so that our futures might be as desirable as possible. We study and we train ourselves to develop certain abilities, to gain new insights, to be able to enjoy certain new pleasures. The choice to develop along one line rather than another, so that one thing, say a piano, or another, say a baseball glove, will have use-value for us, can be conscious. It is clearly influenced, among other things, by the future likelihoods of our being able to own and use a piano or a baseball glove. And in a capitalist society the likelihood of being able to use different goods depends on the future relative prices of those goods, or their expected exchange-values. This is a crucial point in the way the conformity between human center and institutional boundary comes about in capitalist systems. It comes as a disturbing realization that it is not just that we are "warped" and manipulated by "the system" but that in fact we warp ourselves!

People's needs (or what holds use-value for them) depend on their human characteristics at the time.[8] Based upon expectation of the relative prices of different goods in the future, it would be better to have certain needs or desires rather than others. It would be better to have developed needs for goods that will be relatively cheap and to have minimized needs for goods that will be relatively expensive. But since future needs depend on future human characteristics and future characteristics depend on previous consumption and work activities, including those we are about to choose in the present, our future needs are not completely beyond our control. In choosing which activities to engage in now, rational people will take this future "need developing effect" as well as the present "need fulfillment effect" into account. It is sensible to mold one's needs in so far as possible so as to conform with future availabilities, and it is in this sense that we conclude that use-value depends in part on expected exchange values. The line between use and exchange-value blurs as we incorporate the notion of praxis into the foundation of our economic theory, and perhaps not too surprisingly given our methodological disposition to emphasize relational thinking, we have argued that use-value is a human social relation in the strongest sense of the term.

In earlier discussions we stressed that societies reproduce their centrally defining contours at both the institutional and the ideological level. At that time we pointed out that the conformity between institutional boundary and human center was a necessary condition for even temporary societal stability. That is, for a society to persist, people's personalities must be largely in conformity with the roles they must occupy and the activities they must engage in. We must desire, expect, or at least accept the conditions we daily encounter. If this were not the case the disjunctures would lead either to terrible incapacities—inability to do what our roles require—or to disjunctures and struggles—struggle against doing what our roles require. In the specific arena of the economy, this translates into the assertion that what we pursue as use-values must be largely what the economy provides. There must be a general conformity between the kind of job roles and commodities provided by an economy and the economic desires of its inhabitants, or their perceived use-values. But whether this conformity comes about because the economy accommodates to the freely developing needs of the citizenry, or because the citizenry is forced to accommodate to the disfiguring requisites of the economy is a matter for close investigation. Moreover, the relation between our economic activity and our needs/ expectations can not be one thing, while that of cultural activity, family activity, or political activity and our needs/expectations is another contrary thing. Economic institutions and we as economic actors taken together are in relation to the rest of society, much as we as people have relations to economic institutions themselves. The argument for a "meshing" carries over just as forcefully. The economy therefore can never be understood in isolation, nor does it develop independently.

We have described a mechanism whereby people adjust their own needs as much as possible to expected job roles and commodity supplies, even though these might not be the most fulfilling ones possible. In effect, the reproductive requisites of any particular set of core characteristics in an economy might take on a "life of their own" independent of maximum human fulfillment, growth, and development.

COMMODITY CONSUMPTION AND MARKETS

Consumption is an economic activity. An individual or group "takes in" one set of items, acts upon and with them, and in the end gives off another set of items. Some of the inputs and outputs will be material—new cars, food, a prepared dinner, cars for junkyards, garbage—but some will be non-material—social relations, consciousness, skill levels, and degrees of fulfillment—all those things we earlier described and subsumed in our notation, a_h^t.

As a human act consumption is both network and process. Each act is connected to countless others—these are relationships between things but also between people. To abstract from the whole is to ignore important aspects of each act. Consumption is also process—in the first instance each act occurs as a flow through time. In the second, these flows are all one with a still "larger" flow which is the motion of the whole economy, A_h^t, from period to period. In a particular social setting consumers may or may not be aware of these complex features of their actions. This has considerable impact on the extent to which they can intelligently plan and benefit from them.

The market is one possible institution for coordinating economic activities of disparate groups of people. This coordination is accomplished by providing all individual units with the opportunity to offer the outputs of their activities in exchange for the outputs of other unit's activities, with a general assumption of non-coercion.[9]

Of course, markets can be combined with many different economic institutions to constitute, for example, capitalism, slavery, simple commodity production, or market socialism. But from the standpoint of the market these differences can be reduced to what things are permitted to be treated as commodities in market exchange and what things are not. In slavery human beings are treated as commodities, in capitalism labor power, but not the laborer him/or/herself is a commodity. In simple commodity production neither the laborer nor his or her power are alienable, whereas in market socialism management powers and privileges over group production activities are non-transferable. But once the set of commodities has been defined, that is, once the other economic institutions have settled what things can be alienated by their owners and what things cannot, all commodities are treated in a similar fashion by the market.

The common view of markets is that they are informational miracles and efficient mechanisms for coordinating separated economic activities.[10] That is, markets are like trucks. If you want to move goods, then trucks are efficient instruments. If you want to coordinate economic activity, markets are efficient mechanisms for doing this. We disagree completely.

We've already discussed the interrelation between exchange and use-values—how market relations can impose an acclimation between "people's wills" and constrained options for meeting their real needs and developing their capacities. But further, markets are a cybernetic disaster that delete all the information about different group's activities that would allow those groups to coordinate their activities in a way promoting social well-being. Additionally markets are inefficient at allocating resources: as "trucks" they have built in tendencies to travel routes and head for destinations we don't necessarily want to go, while they declare other desirable routes closed to traffic. We present these arguments in order.

MARKETS AS CYBERNETIC DISASTERS

Exchange between different economic units is an expression of the fact that people in those separate groups are actually engaged in social activity with one another. Although the two units involved in exchange are separated by distance and lack of information about the nature of each other's roles in their shared activity, neither of their processes makes sense, or could continue, without the other. The exchanged outputs of one group's activity would have no purpose were they not destined to be inputs of the other group's activity, just as the activity of the second group would be impossible without the inputs received from the first. We have no difficulty understanding that the workers at the beginning and end of an automobile assembly line are engaged in the social activity of making automobiles. And even though the workers in the blast furnace divisions are not connected by a physical assembly line to the workers in the rolling mills in a modern steel plant, we see their activities as integrated and part of the same process. But we frequently fail to understand that workers in a steel mill and workers on an auto assembly line are similarly involved in a shared activity. The reason for our blindness is that within individual units the activities of different individuals are consciously coordinated and planned to achieve a known goal.[11] However, in market economies the individual activities of different economic units are *not* consciously coordinated and planned by anyone. For those working on the auto assembly line do not appear to be engaged in a social activity with the steel workers, or bound by a specific set of production relations with those other people. Instead it appears that they are engaged in isolated productive activity and have relations only with other things—i.e. the sheet metal they utilize as inputs in their labor process and the automobiles they create as outputs.

In other words, in commodity producing societies people see individuals (or small isolated groups of people) consuming material inputs—relationships between people and things—or producing material outputs—relationships between people and things—or see things exchanging in markets for other things—relationships between things and things. Relations between people and other people in the economy either disappear from sight or are confined to recognition of relations between people in the same economic unit. By focusing on this surface appearance, we come to lose sight of the fact that in social economic activity people must also have relations with other people and that it is precisely these human relations that are disguised as relationships between commodities in exchange. Paul Sweezy describes this information-disguising characteristics of markets, originally identified by Marx as "commodity fetishism", as follows:

> The quantitative relation between things... is in reality only an outward form of the social relation between the commodity owners.... The exchange relation as such apart from any consideration of the quantities involved, is an expression of the fact that individual producers, each working in isolation, are in fact working for each other. Their labor, whatever they may think of the matter, has a social character which is impressed upon it by the fact of exchange.[12]

But the information-disguising character of markets goes further. For the auto-workers to really evaluate their work in human terms they would have to know the human/social as well as material factors that went into the items they need to work with, as well as the human/social outputs of their work—the uses to which their steel will be put, the societal contribution it will make, the needs met or aggravated, and the human and social characteristics produced. Suppose, for example, that autoworkers overcome the misinterpretation of economic reality called commodity fetishism and set out to discover the nature of their productive relations with steel workers or coal miners or any other group. Let's say the auto workers have complete information on the social relations of production within their unit and want to extend their understanding to their unit's relations with other group's economic activities.[13] The only information the market provides about the relations between auto workers, steel workers, coal miners, etc. is a price that accompanies the physical commodities that are exchanged. Even if these prices accurately represent the total human costs and benefits that have occurred in the various processes that have utilized this commodity as input or output—and we will shortly argue that this is not the case even when markets operate "ideally"—this information is totally insufficient to allow the auto workers to understand and evaluate their relations with the steel workers and miners. The price leaves us in ignorance concerning what went into a commodity's production, what needs were met or left unsatisfied, and what human characteristics were simultaneously produced. Prices someone will pay for goods we are producing don't let us know what concrete pleasures and character development they will promote. Market institutions hide all this information about the concrete relations that are necessary for morale and empathy, and they thereby preclude the development of solidarity based on each unit's concern with the well-being of all the others.

Markets make it almost impossible to think relationally and historically about one's involvements with other productive processes. Assuming that a group of workers, h, "sees" a_h^t with all its material and human inputs and outputs, what they need to expand their understanding from their own particular part of the whole is a vivid picture of $a_1^t, a_2^t, . a_h^t$, where t equals 0, 1, 2, ... T. The so called cybernetic miracle of markets is actually the surpression of all these information flows. Based on the prices of material inputs and outputs alone economic actors are totally unable to think in terms of network and process and therefore unsuited to judge whether a change in their own productive activity, shifting the relative amounts of material inputs and/or outputs, eases others' conditions or makes their situation more difficult. The very absence of information about the concrete effects of one's own activities on others leaves little choice but to consult one's own situation exclusively.

But the narrowing of the human dimension of consumption occurs not only in how we relate to each other and to each consumed item, but also in what is available. First, prices are skewed so they do not properly reflect "social as well as individual costs and benefits" (even in an ideally competitive market situation), and second, "what is offered on the market" is actually defined not by people's unfettered wills, but by the requisites of society's core characteristics. We consider these two points in turn.

MARKET BIAS AGAINST "PUBLIC GOODS"

In market transactions the balancing of costs and benefits goes on only between buyer and seller. If people beyond the buyer and seller are affected, if for example, there is more than one "consumer", then market exchange which *treats* commodities as if there were only one consumer, that is, as if the use of commodities were equally as "alienable" as their ownership, cannot be expected to generate an accurate evaluation of goods. The reason for this is quite simple: In a market system one economic agent pays for a commodity, and therefore will evaluate the worth of that commodity only in terms of its effect on itself, paying the price if its effect is deemed worth more than the loss of other commodities that the purchase out of a limited income implies. Therefore, the weighing and evaluating that takes place is only in terms of the effects on one agent. If the "consumption" of the commodity by one agent also produces effects on other individuals or firms, then these are ignored and there can be no claim to "efficiency" by the process involved. In other words, the market process misestimates the human worth of commodities whose "consumption" has use-value for more than one economic agent because it does not provide means for joint, or social expression of desires.[14]

This wouldn't be such a significant criticism if there were very few "public goods", and this is what the modern neoclassical approach to economics asserts.[15] Each good is a private good till proven otherwise. But our dialectical view, interpreting economies as networks of inter-connected processes, motivates the converse view—a good is a public good until proven otherwise. The vision of economies as millions of isolated Robinson Crusoes connected to one another only through the material goods they interchange is precisely the view we have criticized as commodity fetishism. Although in a market economy it is only material outputs that are exchanged, in fact what are *shared* are all the various economic activities that in combination produce the joint economic outcome, that is, the environment in which we all live and the changes in human characteristics and levels of need fulfillment that it allows. Moreover the processes that produce material outputs are the same ones that generate human outputs. Instead of seeing only the physical objects we should relate to them as proxies for the human activities that stand behind them. Viewed in this light, the public character of goods is more discernable. For once we recognize that a human being "is in the most literal sense of the word a *zoon politikon*, not only a social animal, but an animal that can develop into an individual only in society,"[16] that "people are invariably in a close relationship with one another because 'their needs... and the manner of satisfying them creates between them reciprocal links...' so much so that 'the history of an individual in particular cannot be separated from the history of preceding or contemporary individuals'."[17] It is clear that the human outputs embodied in others are of primary importance to ourselves as well. People are social; what occurs for each, affects all. As proxies for human outputs material commodities assume a public nature as well. Their costs and benefits are therefore incorrectly evaluated in even the most fair and competitive, single buyer, single seller market exchange. All goods are public or social; market transations either under or overestimate their worths precisely as they fail to take account of their impacts upon society as a whole.

Markets are therefore neither cybernetic miracles nor efficient "trucks", but by obviating the need for social planning of social activity they might be considered a "quick fix".

MARKET "CENSORING"

The commodities available for one to buy on a market are severely constrained. Barring "systemic" error, nothing is made available on the market whose consumption would produce needs or insights incommensurable with the reproduction of the class system. This is ensured by the dynamics of product definition and differentiation which are now in the hands of only the capitalist owners and which must occur in context of societal hegemony. A capitalist tells a worker what to produce, and then sells the product to other workers. The capitalist makes sure not to sell things whose consumption would obviously disrupt the system—this is simple self-preservation, and it transpires both consciously by clear choices, and perhaps even more often unconsciously via the fact of prior socialization of buyers, and via consumers' needs for non-disruptive pleasure from commodities in a capitalist setting. The whole process becomes simpler and more precise as monopolies develop vast advertising networks,[18] and as people's tastes become adapted by a history of past capitalistic production and consumption. Moreover, it is necessary, and the capitalist system operates in light of this fact, *that consumption not satiate desire.* To work and bring profit to the capitalist the worker must want income to spend in the market. This will be the case only so long as the worker has unmet needs which he/she believes he/she can meet in the market, but which in fact he/she cannot. There are two phenomena related to this analysis. One is constant product redefinition. One must own the new model because to not own it is to lack status or be backward. The second is built-in-obsolescence which forces one to buy the new because the old becomes worthless. In context of the profit and reproductive dynamics of capitalist class divisions, consumption becomes the main avenue to general fulfillment and yet it works only very partially and temporarily. Consumption is the only means available to many rational ends, it is the only game in town, and yet is a game we only rarely win. The pursuit of profit spreads the "cash nexus". Social relations mediate all innate needs via derived needs for commodities: toothpaste for sex, spiffy clothes for dignity, hotdogs for a happy family, cosmetics for security, or uniforms for work. And yet the consumption of these commodities only barely meets the driving needs, leaving the ritual open-ended, and the motive to work for wages perpetual. A remarkable situation: social relations simultaneously give people no option but to consume in pursuit of fulfillment and growth, and yet also insure that consumption never leads to very significant amounts of either. It is simultaneously rational and irrational to go to the store to buy things.

MARKETS AND THE CORE TOTALITY

As we described earlier it must at least be true that the social relations and ideologies associated with the various core characteristics are compatible. It cannot be, for example, that the role dictates of the economy require women to be above men while sexual core relations require the reverse. Nor could it be that sexual core dynamics require that women have no economic independence while class dynamics ensure that women have the same access to wealth as men. It couldn't be that race core relations segregate living environments and involve a consciousness that one group is inferior to another, while class relations treat the two groups equally and bring them together. For there to be a variety of fundamental divisions in the human community they must at least be so organized throughout the center and boundary that they do not continually clash with one another—otherwise one or the other of the conflicting modes would eventually have to alter. So extending our economic analysis into the realm of real history is not quite so difficult although there are many possible variations of analysis. Thus there are a variety of possible core characteristics in addition to class. And it is possible for each to be related to class dynamics and to one another in a variety of ways—primarily in a kind of compatible parallel but unentwined motion, or in an interlocking, co-reproducing motion.

Consider first the parallel case and the two core characteristics, race and class division. Two analyses are carried through. The first is of the economy beginning from the perspective of class; the second of black society as opposed to white, using the approach of racial categories. Each analysis is augmented by recognizing the impact of the other. So the economy is further analyzed in light of people of different races and of how their incomes, bargaining powers, and economic roles are brought into accord with racism, thereby allowing compatibility between race and class dynamics. Similarly ghetto relations are reexamined adding to a national consciousness a class awareness as well.

Likewise, if class and sex were the two characteristics and they were parallel, a similar dual investigation of the economy and the family would be indicated. One would do a class analysis of the economy and a sexual analysis of the family. The analysis of each would then be enlarged by recognizing that they exist in a single formation and therefore push and pull one another into mutual conformity.

However, what if the relation between sex and class were co-reproducing and entwined? Then it would make just as much sense to look at the economy with patriarchal categories, or the family with class concepts as does the converse. In studying the economy we would try to understand not just how women were relegated to positions below men and alloted income consistent with their position of dependence in the family, but also how the social organization of factories and the market involve familial patterns and how the distribution of income relates to sex divisions. And similarly we would seek to understand how family dynamics were class governed, rather than just class compatible or affected.

As an extension of our discussion of consumption and markets, let's discuss an actual society with class, race, authority, and sex core characteristics in mutual structural co-reproduction. Then social historical reproduction entails reproduction of a total nexus in both institutions and consciousness. Daily life is reinforced and defined by a *hegemony* that is not merely classist or economistic, but which is constituted by a totality of entwined mutually enforcing characteristics. Here it is still the case that the economic activity called consumption is constrained by the arena within which it transpires, as well as by the motivations brought to it—motivations which are themselves social outcomes of other alienated processes.

Commodities are sold in order to "fulfill" not only material desires but also needs for community, love, sex, power over one's own life, knowledge, dignity, and all the rest of what social/creative people desire. This is easy to verify even by simply watching what commercials appeal to. Of course at the same time commodities don't fully meet these aesthetic, emotional, social, and political needs nor do they enhance any of the associated human capabilities. Rather, individualized consumption—buying toothpaste to achieve sexual and love advantages, buying a car to cultivate self-respect, getting a motorcycle for freedom, buying clothes to conform and thereby attract friends—meets the ends people desire only in small part, though often to a greater degree than any other socially acceptable approach.

Individualized consumption reimposes exactly those features in our personalities and values, namely, racism, sexism, authoritarianism, and classism, which force us to seek pleasure through isolated consumption in the first place. Consumption activities give people as much pleasure as is to be had in the social settings they inhabit and yet simultaneously help to reinforce those settings in their most debilitating aspects. In addition to capitalist criteria controlling which products are sold in order to reproduce class relations, we have also the existence of racism, authoritarianism, sexism, and monopoly. There are different markets and products for blacks and women to buy from and also in which to sell their labor power. Goods and advertising cater to elitism. To make economic hierarchies consistent with attitudes of daily life this must be the case. Different groups of people are treated differently by advertising, product design, the fact that stores in different neighborhoods cater to different clientel, storekeepers, etc. The marketplace is one part of the total social arena. Its role dictates must fit into the whole web and they do. In market exchange we exchange commodities and ourselves as well. While we intelligently pursue the only obvious avenue to human growth, we simultaneously reproduce the chains of our bondage—in our environments and in ourselves.

Moreover, in advanced capitalism, there is also the social spending of the expanded state sector. This accounts for the so-called "public goods" such as defense and missiles, or security via SWAT teams, or enlightenment via tracked school systems. There is also a complex new set of processes involving the sale of social services and public goods all aimed specifically at maintaining societal stability—for example, the sale of psychological services and the provision of welfare services.[19] the whole framework is a historical development which prevails, most often, precisely because of its "reproductive utility".

Yet people are not infinitely maleable. At the same time that the market economy seeks to isolate us from one another and only impose upon us desires for what can be delivered, it is also increasingly compelled to address broader motives for buying. While telling us that clothes and cars are the only means to sexual satisfaction, advertising addresses the desire and thereby helps us recognize its need for fulfillment. While T.V. tells us that the means to family solidarity is through MacDonalds, it aggravates still further a need which will not be met within the confines of this system. And the same is true for other ads which promise more friends, more courage or knowledge, more dignity, freedom, or just plain fun. Showing people enjoying such benefits and calling attention to the absence in our lives, these commercials eventually have a subversive power. For while the consumption process tends to reduce everything to a cash nexus, it also aggravates precisely those needs which can't be so met. And it does this not by accident, but because the system's very reproduction requires that people be continually "in need and seeking" while never developing too many capabilities, insights, or expectations. While the consumption process tends to reproduce hierarchy by advancing different clothes, goods, selling places, styles and prices for society's varying groups—it also is forced to continually project images of idyllic social relations and community. As material needs for survival become increasingly met it becomes more and more necessary to admit the existence of other needs and therefore use-values. And because markets are never able to fully reach such needs—contradictions are created. (The only alternative, to "take away" from people some of the material well-being they have become used to, to motivate them as they were before, is an even more explosive approach. For once people become accustomed to certain levels of fulfillment they'll take very unkindly to anything less.)

On the one hand, as traditional Marxist analysis tells us, there is a consumption contradiction whenever the material commodities people are socially induced to desire become unreachable due to either high prices, low wages, unemployment, or crises. On the other hand, however, there is also a contradiction the orthodox Marxist analysis does not address, and it exists even when the system delivers to capacity, precisely because people's social/political needs come to the fore and are of course unmeetable in the marketplace. In the first case the society doesn't give us what it "promises" to deliver; in the second we're simply opting for a whole new menu. In the United States both these phenomena exist and help explain the recent liveliness of consumer organizing efforts, and also of worker unwillingness to work on Fridays and Mondays. Why bother when aroused needs can be better met by playing the guitar or baseball with a bunch of friends than by earning more in order to buy more, especially when the material needs can be met on three or four days income if the job is reasonably well paid, and not at all if it's poorly paid.

In a real sense the pursuit of pleasure under capitalism both is and is not reduced to an exchange relationship—and use-values both are and are not reduced to those things which the system is willing to deliver for its own reproduction. As consumers we produce in ourselves tendencies both *consistent and inconsistent* with the system's continual reproduction. This is the phenomenon of "post scarcity".[20] It is the phenomenon of the forces of production of all things including personalities and social relationships being able to deliver much more, while the society's social relations both deny that greater possibility and simultaneously call up our desires for it and our recognition of its potentiality. The "happy outcome" is a revolutionary conjuncture of unmet potentials to meet aroused desires.

> Each time that the Coca Cola Bottling Company informs us
> that their product is "The Real Thing©", implicit is the message
> that it isn't the real thing after all; and what is more, people do
> feel the need for the actual real thing."[21]

HUMAN LABOR

Marx himself considered the recognition of the difference between labor and labor-power as his singlemost important contribution to economic theory, since he believed it located the origin of capitalist profits in the production process and therefore provided an explanation for them even in the context of equal exchange. But while we reaffirm our critique of the labor-time fetishism that arose from emphasizing the supposed quantitative distinction between labor and labor-power, we applaud the pursuit of the qualitative difference between labor and labor power begun by Marx and taken up by contemporary radical economists such as Harry Braverman, Herb Gintis, and Paul Cardan (Cornelious Castoriadus).[22] We believe that the new theory we have outlined provides an excellent framework for expressing and extending the analysis of this qualitative distinction.

In capitalist economies the labor market is most generally a market for labor power, not for labor services. This means that the labor exchange, whereby the worker exchanges disposition over his or her laboring powers for a specified time period in return for a specified wage, is not symmetrical with other exchanges such as those for raw materials, capital goods, and final goods. In the latter there is a definite quid pro quo involved where each party gives up and receives a known quantity. But this is not the case when a capitalist hires a worker, for in that exchange the "outcome" cannot be known at the time of the exchange, but only after the production process is complete. The labor exchange leaves the worker with a specified wage and the capitalist with the right to try and extract whatever labor services he can during a specified time period. But whether or not the worker will give maximum, moderate, or minimal effort; "internalize" the capitalist production goals or need to be prodded every step of the way; produce 40 or 30 widgets per hour, depends on the internal character of the production activity itself.

By characterizing the capitalist labor market as a market for labor power we do no more than affirm one of the defining characteristics of capitalism, namely, that workers are divorced from the means of production until they agree to a wage contract that establishes that their relation to the mode of production is to be settled by the capitalist rather than themselves. Imagining that labor services (specified "quids") are bought and sold in the labor market neglects the fact that to sell a labor service one must have prior possession of the means of production needed for carrying on that service. Although there are always exchanges of this type in any real-world capitalist economy, they are actually the hallmark of simple commodity production economies, not capitalist economies. The difference between the two is precisely that in the latter the majority of producers have been separated from the means of production, thus creating the market for labor power.

As with all commodities, labor power has both use and exchange-value. Orthodox Marxism found the origins of capitalist profits to be the quantitative difference between the two. For orthodox Marxism the exchange value of labor power is the wage, which is supposedly equal to the average labor time needed to "produce" a worker for a day in a certain historical setting, whereas the use value of labor for the capitalist is the amount of labor time of average intensity that the employee embodies in the products made during a day's work. In all but subsistence economies the latter quantity is greater than the former, leaving the capitalist with surplus value, the origin of all profits.

Our theory leads to a different analysis of the distinction between the exchange-value and use-value of labor power. The exchange value of labor power is the wage it sells for, whatever this might be. In other words we make no presumption of a subsistence wage, and of course this exchange value of labor power is the same for both capitalist and worker. The use-value of labor power, on the other hand, is a great deal more complicated. The use value of an ordinary commodity is the value it has in its use for its user. But the first problem with labor power is who is the user? Capitalism and orthodox Marxism treat labor power as if it were an ordinary commodity that can be transferred from one owner to another. And the capitalist certainly has purchased the legal right to try and make use of the worker's labor power. But human labor power can never be completely separated, or alienated, from the laborer. In the first place, no matter how extensive the attempt to concentrate thinking and decision making aspects of human labor in the hands of management, the effort always remains incomplete. As Paul Cardan notes, it is ironic "that in real life, capitalism is obliged to base itself on people's capacity for self-organization, on the individual and collective creativity of the producers without which it could not survive for a day, while the whole 'official organization' of modern society both ignores and seeks to suppress these abilities to the utmost."[23] In other words, as much as the employer tries to make his employees' labor power completely subject to his will, the employees remain beings of praxis, and regardless of the level of suppression and frustration, their activity is always to some degree directed by their own purposes. So the employee is always a "user" of his or her labor power along with the employer under capitalism. Cardan drives the point home with the observation that it is fortunate that the efforts of economic theorists and capitalist managers combined are insufficient to reduce human labor to the mechanical responses of robots since such economies function only in science fiction, not in reality.

Furthermore just as the human "will" cannot be separated from the release of labor power, the effects of the "consumption" of labor power are even more obviously inseparable from the laborer her or himself. While orthodox Marxism focuses exclusively on the physical outputs of the production process and the labor time embodied in them as the "use-value" of labor power, our theory focuses on the human outputs of work activity, the transformation and/or reinforcement of the laborers' characteristics and the degree of need fulfillment, as consequences of fundamental importance to employees and employers alike. In other words, the modification or reproduction of personalities, skills, and consciousnesses is also part of the use-value of labor power to *both* of its users. We have already pointed out that the Labor Theory Of Value provides an acceptable explanation of relative prices in Simple Commodity production economies *only* if one abstracts the differential human outputs of production activities. In this kind of economy there is no schizophrenia of users since the employer employs only her or himself. We can see no reason she or he would not take the effects on her or his human characteristics into account when exchanging the physical products of productive activities with others. However, in our opinion, not only is the abstraction from human outputs unjustifiable in the determination of relative exchange values, but it is devestating to our ability to understand the qualitative reproduction of the conformity between the human center and the institutional boundary of economic systems. In capitalist economies, as there are two users of labor power, the human outputs embodied in the worker as her or his characteristics have use value to both.[24] Labor is a complex process not just a simple passing of time during which commodities come into existence in order to be sold. It involves a variety of complex outcomes for both the worker and capitalist. The worker is either being fulfilled and enriched or stultified. The capitalist is either having profitable conditions reproduced or not. It is not only the magnitude but also the *character and human aspect* of work that is determined by the clash between the profit/power interests of the boss and the human development interests of the worker. In even the simplest capitalist setting work both is and is not reduced to an exchange relationship. For the capitalist the desire is to produce surplus and a worker totally acclimated to the work he or she must do in the future and to the lack of control he or she will have over that work.

For the worker, on the other hand, the desire is to spend time as creatively and fulfillingly as possible or at least as painlessly as possible. Herein, in this conflict and in the social relations of capitalism which determine that workers must sell their energies though not their souls to the capitalists, lies the power of the Marxist differentiation between labor and labor power.

Before pursuing this point, which is critical to our theory of the firm, we should summarize the distinctive elements in our treatment of human labor. The important characteristic of human labor is that it is *qualitatively* different from all other inputs to production. It is not like a lump of coal or even a beast of burden. Labor is a human activity, the exercise of a human power, the effort of a being capable of conscious evaluation of his or her activities and their consequences. Inherent in the notion of humans as beings of praxis is the conclusion that the mechanical functions of labor can never be entirely separated from the mental, purposive elements, or that the use of labor power cannot be entirely alienated from the laborer. Furthermore, the nature of praxis tells us that we change ourselves at the same time that we transform the physical objects we work with, that human characteristics are outputs of production processes just as much as material products, and that in any state of dual ownership, these human outputs, as part of the use-value of labor power, must be analyzed with regard to all users. Orthodox Marxist economic theory lost track of these qualitative distinctions between human labor and all other inputs in its efforts to establish a quantitative distinction between the commodity labor power and all other commodities. It is our hope that our economic theory will re-incorporate the qualitative distinctions that are to be found in Marx's theory of alienation and were so much a part of the Marxist "project".

Finally, as distinctive as human labor is from all other inputs to production, we find it to be qualitatively indistinguishable from human consumption, human learning, and human play. That is, just as production and consumption processes in the economy are fundamentally similar, human labor is just one form of human activity, qualitatively similar to all other human activity and subject to the same means of analysis.

But perhaps most critically, our framework calls for recognition of differences not only in wages, but also in skills, consciousnesses, and social relations. In a society with core race, sex, and authority relations, in addition to core class relations, our framework would be suited to seeing each characteristic's defining impact upon work roles, inputs, and outputs. Insofar as the relations which had to be reproduced in the factory were patriarchal or racist as well as classist and authoritarian, our analysis would certainly retain its applicability. The fact that in this general discussion we have addressed the activity of labor abstractly in no way precludes adding such further dimensions in concrete analyses. Indeed, as we will certainly see in the next two chapters, our concepts and theoretical framework *propels* such additions.

THEORY OF THE CAPITALIST FIRM

Our overall theory conditions us to see the firm as one of the institutional arenas in capitalism where human activity goes on, where both material and human inputs are "consumed" and outputs "produced". Our theory of human labor under capitalism tells us there are two users of labor power in the capitalist firm and that the "consumption" of labor power has use-value for both employer and employee. The workers care about the human outputs of the production process because they have needs which are fulfilled or unsatisfied by their work activities and because of the modifications or reinforcements in their personalities, skills, and consciousness that take place through work. Capitalists care about the material output since their success in extracting more or less products through the consumption of labor power helps determine revenues. Of course both workers and capitalists are concerned with the exchange-value of labor power and have the same conflicting interests that any seller and buyer do.

At first it would appear that just as the workers have no reason to be concerned with the material outputs, employers have no reason to care about the human outputs, except insofar as the employees' evaluation of those might influence the struggle over wages. After all, the employer is not a slave owner and cannot sell human characteristics because he cannot sell the human being in whom they are embodied.[25] But this is not the case. Not only is the capitalist concerned with the quantity and quality of material outputs in the current time period, but he also cares about the material outputs he will be able to extract in future time periods. Not only is the capitalist concerned with the total wage bill he must pay his work force this pay period, but he cares about what the wage bill will be in future pay periods.[26] Since the future saleable outputs and wage bills will depend, in general, on the future human characteristics of the capitalist's employees, and since those characteristics depend, in part, on the human outputs generated by production in the present, the capitalist is as concerned with the human outputs of production as the worker. This is a crucial point in our theory of the capitalist firm and needs elaboration.[27]

On the morning of the work day the capitalist buys eight hours of "capacity to do work." During the day the capitalist has the problem of actually extracting that work, using that labor power to obtain material products. The ability of the capitalist to extract work depends on a host of individual and group characteristics of his employees. What are the employees' motivations? Do they accept the employer's values and attitudes toward the work process or do they view themselves as having opposing interests. Are they amenable to his "leadership" or stubborn and resistant? As a group do they have a great deal of solidarity and offer mutual support in opposition to the owner's efforts to define their individual work activities, or are they characterized by internal division and mutual suspicion? Can some workers be influenced to oppose the will of others? All of these characteristics affect the ability of the capitalist to "use" labor power as he would like. Similarly, although today's wage bill is settled and done before the workday begins, tomorrow's depends on whether or not the employees support one another's wage demands, whether they bargain individually or collectively, whether their union (if they have one) is strong and militant or divided and defeatist, and whether or not their productive skills and knowledge are spread among the work force or increasingly concentrated in a smaller group. In general any individual or group characteristic that tends to make the employees accept the capitalist's right to dominate the use of their labor power and any characteristics that diminish the employees' individual and collective abilities to oppose that use, enhances the capitalist's ability to extract labor from labor power. And any diminution of employee solidarity or "deskilling" of the employees' knowledge of production increases the capitalist's ability to lower the wage bill. The point is that these characteristics are not beyond the capitalist's influence.

The capitalist has a great deal of influence over the choice of technology and the internal supervisory and reward systems in his firm. It is tempting to say that these are the capitalist's choice variables, but this is not entirely the case. To the extent that the employees are the users of their labor power, there are limits on the employer's determination of these variables. But to the extent that the employer can choose among alternative technologies and internal reward systems it would now appear that in addition to choosing the criterion of efficiency (i.e. least cost per output) the capitalist will consider how any technology affects employee motivation, the information employees obtain, the extent of employee accountability, inter-employee relations, etc. In other words, once it is recognized that human outputs matter to the employer, the profitability of any technology is seen to depend not only on its efficiency but on at least three other criteria: 1-its effect on the capitalist's bargaining strength vis-a-vis his employees over the division of the net product of the production process, 2-how it affects the capitalist's ability to extract labor from labor power in the future, and 3-its effect on who will ultimately control the production process itself and receive the share of net product going to that "controller". For even though the efficiency criterion alone may be sufficient to maximize profits in the present, the other three criteria are important for maximizing profits over time.

This means that it is in the interests of capitalists to choose technologies and organize production in ways that aggravate antagonisms among their employees (within reasonable limits), that fragment knowledge of the production process, and that lead to an ever greater acceptance of authoritarian relations in which one expects and accepts production orders. Of course to the extent that the most efficient technology is not the one that best reproduces the capitalist's version of the integrity of the labor exchange, to the extent that the workers' most preferred assignment of job roles does not coincide with the assignment that minimizes the future bargaining strength of the employees over the wage bill or maximizes worker accountability under relations that give the worker no interest in the material output of his/her labors, to the extent that there is a conflict between technical efficiency and the most desireable job structure from the employees' point of view and any of the other three criteria, there will be a trade-off, and the employer will not choose the most efficient technology possible or the most pleasant internal job roles.

It is important to realize that we are not arguing that capitalists will choose a trade-off between profit maximization and promoting antagonisms or increasing their control over the work process. Rather all these criteria are important to maximizing profits. And in fact what maximizes profits will generally not be the most efficient technology and most desireable job structure, but those that achieve the highest trade-off between the profit maximizing criteria.[28]

Moreover this reasoning is not based on the assumption that labor markets are not competitive, that capitalists necessarily do other things besides maximize profits, or that there is a conspiracy among capitalists to mold the work force to reproduce capitalist relations of production and expand capitalist profits. We have argued that it is in the individual, competitive capitalist's interests, in terms of his long term profits and ability to survive in competition with other capitalists, to take these effects into consideration along with efficiency.[29]

To this point, the important conclusions of our theory of the firm are that under capitalism there are two users of human labor power, each with a different purpose, and there are two corresponding use-values of labor power. The workers attempt to organize their work activities so as to maximize the fulfillment of their needs in the present and the growth and development of their human characteristics in the future. The capitalist tries to organize the labor process to maximize the material outputs in the present and to mold the employees' individual and group characteristics in a way that maximizes the capitalist's domination over the structure of work and the future distribution of its outputs. The different use-values of labor power are the effects of its expenditure as seen from these two different goals.

Furthermore, we discovered that the dynamics of profit maximization even in a context of competitive markets should reinforce whatever antagonisms exist among workers and their general hierarchicalization—that is, most often the dynamics of racism, sexism, and authoritarianism. There need be no conspiracy of the capitalist class to reinforce these dynamics (even if class is the only *core* oppression) any more than there need be a conspiracy to organize the labor process in ways that mold workers' personalities, skills, and consciousness to accept the capitalist's domination of production. Individual capitalists will be driven precisely by the very forces of competition to do all these things precisely to maximize their long term profits.

Finally, we concluded that the neoclassical fantasy, from Adam Smith to Arrow and Debreu, that perfectly competitive capitalist institutions lead to the most efficient technologies and the most preferred job structures; that there is a one-to-one correspondence between efficient technology and profit maximization, between the most enjoyable job structures and cost minimization; that even though the owner has the formal authority to decide on product mixes and job role offerings, that by maximizing profits he makes exactly the choices that we as consumers and workers would make; and that the competitive capitalist firm achieves a state of consumer and producer sovereignty, is an unsupportable fiction, and nothing more.

But this is not the end of our story. For what if a society has not only class relations, but also race, sex, and authority relations at its core? And what if these are all entwined?

We will discuss this situation in some detail in the next two chapters. Here it is essential only to show that our economic theory is still powerful with these added dimensions operative. In essence the change is that in the factory both workers and management have more complex and varied material interests, needs, and consciousnesses, and that the role structures are more multiply defined, the market on which goods are sold, more complex, etc.

Now the totality that is manifest in the structure of the factory embodies not only class, but also race, authority, and sex—at the bottom of the hierarchies are the women, the order takers, and the third world people. Even more important, the social relations and consciousnesses of the factory and its very role definitions, are as much a product of race, sex, and authority dynamics as they are of class dynamics. In the plant we can see a kind of family or nest of families, with kinship relations—male patriarchs, female mothers, younger sisters and brothers.[30] We also find the ghetto/downtown interface in the division between, relations among, and views of all the various racial groups. Decision criteria are "enriched". Patriarchy, racism, classism, and authoritarianism in the very roles and mentalities of the factory and in its products as well, must all be reproduced. The kinship, racial, class, and elite divisions create ma:erial and psychological (conscious and unconscious) interests propelling these reproductive dynamics. The process we described earlier, that even profit seeking alone leads to aggravation of race, sex, and authority divisions, is now simply intensified and reversed as well. But about these matters we shall have more to say later.

QUALITATIVE REPRODUCTION: CONCLUSION

We have argued that use-value is endogenous to the functioning of economic systems because people orient their future needs toward goods and activities that will be relatively easy to obtain, and away from goods and activities that will be hard to obtain. That is, if there is a bias in the expected conditions of future supply of particular kinds of goods or roles, people can be expected to influence their own development in a similarly biased direction. We have also concluded that capitalists will use their power to try and define work roles that enhance their future ability to extract labor services from labor power, increase their future bargaining strengths over employees vis-a-vis the division of the net product, and maintain their control over the management of the production process, as these are important components of the maximization of long run profits. In particular, we have argued that there will be a tendency for firms to provide racist and sexist roles, roles requiring less and less knowledge, and authoritarian roles requiring that one give or accept orders. This last conclusion could be restated as the inherent tendency of capitalist firms to minimize the number of roles characterized by self-management. Finally we have argued that the informational, role, and allocative biases of markets, even when they are operating "as they should", promote the expression of individual needs and dampen the expression of social needs. In other words, market allocative institutions have an inherent tendency to provide a relative overabundance of private goods and public bads, and a relative scarcity of public goods. When we combine the first conclusion with the second we find that not only will there be an absence of "producer sovereignty" over work roles in any initial time period, but there will be a steady divergence away from producer sovereignty as employees "rationally" adjust their needs and preferences in order not to actively need or desire self-management, for example, but to accept authoritarian relations. When we combine the first conclusion with the third we find that not only will there not be "consumer sovereignty" in an initial time period but there will be cumulative divergence away from consumer sovereignty in future time periods which is increasingly disguised, as people "rationally" adjust their personal characteristics to diminish their needs for public goods, diminish their aversion for public bads, and increase their needs for private goods that the structural bias of market allocative institutions ensures will be in over-supply. What we have sought to explore in depth is the *mechanism* whereby people's perceived needs and desires come to correspond with the authoritarian characteristics of capitalist production institutions and the individualizing characteristics of capitalist market institutions, the mechanism of "rational" self-manipulation of personality structures, skill development, and consciousness that reproduces the core characteristics of capitalist economic institutions in the human center of capitalist citizens. In addition, we tried to show how the reproductive dynamic of profit maximization reinforces the structural characteristics of racism and sexism even when class is the only *active* core characteristic. We have also alluded to some of the ramifications when race, sex, and authority are also active, and have promised to discuss these matters more in the next two chapters. But in our desire to make the case for structural reproduction of capitalist social relations, we may have left the impression that there are no possibilities for qualitative interruptions. Therefore, we conclude by reiterating the existence and nature of the fundamental disjunctures in capitalist reproduction.

According to our view there is a divergence of criteria inside the capitalist firm. On the capitalist side is the criterion of long-run profit maximization (at least) which requires various human characteristics of employees, including an absence of needs for self-management and solidarity with fellow employees. On the workers' side is the criterion of human well-being or fulfillment through work activities with its requirement of worker self-management and cooperation. Furthermore there is a divergence of criteria implicit in the confrontation of humans as social beings with market institutions. Consumers have needs that must be fulfilled through social consumption, whereas the market provides means for expressing consumption needs only individualistically. People have human needs and potentials which, however stultified, are always present, while markets and factories are both organized to address only the reproduction of society's core totality irrespective of the oppressions thereby enforced. The divergence implies a continuous struggle between the core characteristics of capitalism's institutional boundary and the fulfillment of human potential. Furthermore, the question of momentum, i.e. which set of criteria is gaining and which set is losing ground, is crucial. If the criteria of profit maximization and market dominated allocation (and in many societies racism, sexism, and authoritarianism) are increasingly determinative of the actual conditions of availability—it will be increasingly rational for people to accelerate their adjustment toward those conditions. But if the momentum reverses, the disjuncture between societal role requirements and people's needs, expectations, and behavior will have a tendency to widen even further.

WAGES, PRICES, AND PROFIT
QUANTITATIVE REPRODUCTION UNDER CAPITALISM

Let us begin our analysis with the origins of a society's "social surplus" and of any individual capitalist's "private surplus" or profit. If the laboring activities of the workforce, using existing inputs and technologies, produces more commodities than are needed to replenish the stock of inputs and to feed, clothe, and house the population at some bio-historically determined "necessary" level, then the excess is the social surplus. It is output minus input replacement and necessary consumption where the exact definition of the latter is a considerable problem which we shall pass over for the moment. Clearly the actual surplus depends on the prevailing ownership and market exchange relations as well, since these relations can affect both the total output and the amount of necessary consumption. An individual capitalist will experience a profit if his position as a seller in the market of the commodities "he produces", a buyer in the markets for the factors he uses, an employer in the market for labor power, and a boss in the production process, are such that he exchanges less than 100% of his saleable output to obtain all his inputs including labor power. Though this may appear to be an unnecessarily complex statement about the origins of society's surplus and individual capitalist profits, it serves as an important reminder that both profits and the social surplus are determined by *both production and exchange relations*. Our task is to show how these relations are entwined, and how, even in this very abstract model, they also affect and are affected by relations in other spheres as well.

What our view of profits makes explicit is that every capitalist is in a *bargaining relationship* with other people. Every capitalist is in a bargaining relationship with the suppliers of his inputs, the workers he hires, and the buyers of his outputs. Similarly every worker is in a bargaining relationship with his/her employer-manager and with the seller of the commodities he/she buys. When we ask how a particular capitalist can increase his share of the social product, or expand his individual profits, or how a worker can increase her/his share of the social product or her/his real wage, we see that the answer must lie in the changing balance of people's bargaining relationships as these are determined by positions in production, positions in exchange, and also by broader socio-political relations. An individual capitalist can increase his individual profits by increasing the strength of his bargaining relationship with respect to his suppliers, employees, or buyers; and an individual worker can increase her/his share by strengthening her/his bargaining position with respect to her/his employer or the sellers of consumption goods.

The role of technology becomes more complicated when it is looked at in this light. Any new technology which results in the change of some production operation so that the same output is produced with fewer inputs, or more output results from the same inputs, will obviously increase the potential social product and most likely the actual social product and social surplus as well. But the effect of the change in technology on the relative shares of the aggregate product and surplus that different capitalists and workers will be able to claim is not so obvious.

Suppose the new technology were conceived by a single, fabulously wealthy person in the process of idle contemplation. If she were in no hurry, and if there were complete industrial secrecy and 100% effective patents, then perhaps the whole increase in the aggregate surplus could be appropriated by the inventor. But suppose that in order to be implemented, the new technology required five more workers when there was already full employment in unalienating, creative jobs. Then the inventor would be able to attract the workers only by offering them "a part of the take". Because of their strong bargaining position the workers would obtain much of the increased product.

Of course, neither of these examples has much to do with "real capitalism", but they do serve to clarify the effects of a change in technology on the relative shares of capitalists and workers. Again we find that although a more efficient technology will almost certainly generate a larger social surplus, the effect of the technology on individual's shares will depend on the bargaining relations between various human beings. What were these relations at the time the new technology was implemented and how were they altered by it? What was the social product and how did it change? What was socially necessary consumption and how was it altered? And finally, how do all these factors combine to determine the new output, the surplus, and its distribution? All these questions must be answered if we are to understand the effects of new production techniques.

Before leaving these scant beginnings of an approach we should review our analysis in light of the Marxist admonition to avoid fetishizing commodities. At this stage we are certainly not making the mistake of ignoring the social relationships lurking behind exchange. On the contrary, we have said that these govern people's bargaining powers which in turn govern exchange relations. However, we have wandered far from orthodox Marxism's formulations that only one property of a commodity enables us to see it as the bearer of social relations—its property as the product of labor—and that the value of a commodity represents abstract human labor and is determined by the expenditure of socially necessary labor hours. But our divergence is very much in tune with our earlier critique of the labor-time vulgarization of the original Marxist project. We have argued that the labor-time approach is expressive of equal exchange relations between producers who own their own means of production and perceive no difference in the use-value of the different kinds of labors they perform. That is, that the Labor Theory Of Value is the appropriate way of avoiding fetishism in simple commodity production economies uncomplicated by monopolistic markets or different human outputs from different work activites. The Labor Theory Of Value does not express unequal social relations between all capitalists and all workers accompanied by equal social relations among all capitalists and among all workers since labor-time exchange ratios in a competitive capitalist economy would mean unequal profit rates, and therefore presumably unequal social relations between capitalists in different sectors whenever the organic composition of capital was not uniform. But even the Sraffian theory of relative prices, while expressive of the orthodox Marxist assumptions of perfectly competitive capitalism leaves out too many social relations crucial to relative price and wage determinations to be of any great help in analyzing real-world capitalist economies. That is, not only are these value theories not helpful to understanding the ways in which unequal relations between capitalists and workers are reproduced when unaccompanied by a qualitative model such as the one we have outlined, but even these "properly corrected" quantitative value theories exclude too many important social relations borne by commodities. In our view the exchange relations between commodities express more than just the social relations between people as employers and employees; they embody the unequal relations between different capitalists as buyers and sellers of non-labor inputs and outputs and the unequal relations between different sectors of workers as sellers of labor power and buyers of wage goods.

Thus, the orthodox Marxist or Sraffian abstraction from bargaining power in its fullest sense affects not only the model's ability to illuminate movements of relative shares among different kinds of capitalists—between the "grande" and "petit" bourgeoisie, or between the manufacturing and agricultural sector—but also among different kinds of workers—between skilled and unskilled, organized and unorganized, male and female, white and non-white. The orthodox Marxist vulgarization of the general injunction against commodity fetishism to a rejection of any theorizing not in terms of labor-time as "unreflective of the social relations which determine exchange relations" is simply wrong.

We are now ready to specify our quantitative model. In order to compare different objects, all of which have use-value for someone, we need a unit of common account. But while we accept that "the exchange values of commodities must be capable of being expressed in something common to them all, of which they represent a greater or less quantity," we reject the logic of the orthodox Marxist assertion that obviously "the something common to all commodities must be the value creating substance, the labor contained within the article."[29] This approach is based upon an untenable abstraction and new type of fetishism that overlooks the fullness of the social relations that determine exchange relations. Our solution to the units problem is simply to assume that we are functioning in a monetary economy and that every commodity can be bought and sold for some quantity of money. In other words, what all commodities have in common qualitatively is that they are the bearers of all the social relations of an economy, while the "something common to them all, of which they represent a greater or less quantity" is the money they exchange for.

THE MATHEMATICAL FRAMEWORK

Let W equal wages paid to living labor; let M equal the amount paid for all material inputs to production; assume that all non-labor inputs are completely used up in the time period of the production process; and let R be the amount received for the product.

Obviously a necessary and sufficient condition for a particular production operation to yield a profit is that revenues exceed costs:

$$M+W<R$$

We can define the amount by which R exceeds $M+W$ to be S, the absolute value of the capitalist's surplus or profit.

Now, in light of our earlier discussion of how any individual capitalist obtains part of society's surplus, we define five more quantities and related ratios.

S_e is the capitalist's surplus due to his position as an employer, that is his bargaining power vis-a-vis laborers both in the market for labor power and in the production process itself.

S_b is the surplus accruing to the capitalist due to his bargaining position as a buyer of non-labor factors of production.

S_s is his surplus due to selling final goods.

S_t is his surplus due to knowledge of a particular technology.

S_n is his surplus due to ownership of some advantageous aspect of the natural environment.

$S_e + S_b + S_s + S_t + S_n = S$ is the capitalist's total surplus.

$S_e' = S_e/W$ is the capitalist's rate of exploitation as an employer.

$S_b' = S_b/M$ is the capitalist's rate of exploitation as a buyer of non-labor factors.

$S_s' = S_s/(M+W)$ is the capitalist's rate of exploitation as a seller of final goods.

$S_t' = S_t/(M+W)$ is the capitalist's rate of exploitation as a user of technology.

$S_n' = S_n/(M+W)$ is the capitalist's rate of exploitation as an owner of resources.

These concepts reflect our view that the surplus of an individual capitalist, S, can be derived from a variety of sources. If we strengthen a given capitalist's position as a buyer of material inputs, then we would expect M to fall and S to rise. This change in his bargaining strength as a buyer could come about as a result of a decrease in the number of other buyers competing against him for the inputs, an increase in the number of sellers of the inputs he uses, or the development of new products that serve as substitutes for the inputs even if he continues to use the old ones. These phenomena would be measured as a rise in S_b. If we strengthen a capitalist's position as a seller, R would rise and S would rise. This might result from a decrease in the number of other sellers, an increase in the number of buyers, or the reduction of availability of substitutes for the capitalist's outputs, and would be measured as a rise in S_s. An increase in S_e could come about from breaking up the union in his plant, an increase in the number of unemployed workers in the local labor market, an increase in racial or sexual antagonisms among his employees, the introduction of a new managerial technique allowing for greater supervision or the "deskilling" of a number of employees. S_t could rise if the capitalist developed or purchased the patent for a new production technique unknown or unusable by his competitors, and S_n would change if he gained control over any of the non-producible inputs to production such as a particular piece of land, a mineral deposit, or oil and natural gas deposits necessary for producing his goods.

Finally, we can define the rate of profit, r:

$$r = [R-(M+W)]/(M+W) = (S_e+S_b+S_s+S_t+S_n)/(M+W) = S/(M+W)$$

It is important, however, to realize that any capitalist's surplus as a result of being an employer, S_e, depends very much on precisely who is employed. Different types of workers have *different bargaining powers*. In general, unionized workers are in a better bargaining position than unorganized workers, men are in a better bargaining position than women, and dominant racial groups are in a better bargaining position than minorities. Therefore S_e is really a composite of other components which we can label S_r, S_w, S_u, respectively, thereby indicating the surplus appropriated from oppressed races, oppressed women, and unorganized workers. So the total surplus component, S_e, is really a sum of varying surpluses garnered from sectors of the workforce who have differing bargaining strengths.

Before discussing the theory's "value", there is one technical matter of some importance. That is, can a framework such as ours which includes not only differing bargaining strengths between capitalists and workers in general, but also among capitalists and among workers, yield a determinant set of relative wages, prices, and profit rates? Can we deduce a set of commodity prices which expresses all the social relations whose importance we have argued for and allows for the quantitative reproduction of the material flows necessary for the reproduction of the bargaining relations? If this were not possible, for all its heuristic value, the above discussion could not be legitimate as a theory of quantitative reproduction.

But since the derivation of an equilibrium, or reproduction wage-price vector for a "total social relations theory of value" is rather technical, and no further analysis rests on the techniques involved in the derivation, we relegate it to the appendix, "The Wage Price Vector".

THE THEORY'S VALUE

The principal advantage of our quantitative theory is that it incorporates unequal exchange, knowledge, and resource ownership relations, as well as unequal production and social relations. That is, it operates at a low level of abstraction that allows us to check critical questions about intra-capitalist and intra-worker distribution of society's material surplus, as well as inter-class distribution. Furthermore, since intra-class developments will always affect inter-class distribution, orthodox Marxism's abstractions are not even justified when addressing the limited questions it asks. For example, when women demand and win equal pay for equal time, what has actually occurred? In addition to women's share of society's surplus rising relative to men's, will a greater share go to workers as a whole, or is it simply that more hours of labor will be extracted for the same share of society's wealth?

If the latter is a possibility, is the solution a demand for equal pay for equal work and a growing family wage? And similarly what is the effect of black militancy for higher wages or better work conditions on capitalists and on other non-black workers? When the big unions win wage increases does it come from capitalists or is the bill passed along to unorganized workers in the form of higher prices? If the latter, shouldn't leftists urge that all wage demands be accompanied by price demands as well? What is the effect of technological changes upon income shares? What is the effect of consciousness changes?

Are shifts of income occurring between the agricultural and industrial sectors, between the natural resource extractive sectors and the manufacturing sectors, between the grande and petit bourgeoisie? If so how do these changes affect inter-class and intra-working class distribution? What strategies are indicated?

The second advantage of our theory is that it does not lead us onto any wild goose chases. The Labor Theory Of Value identifies the organic composition of capital as a critical variable in determining the rate of profit, if not for individual capitalists once prices-of-production have been amended to the labor-time theory, then for the capitalist class as a whole. Since most people's intuitions are that capitalist development has been accompanied by ever more capital intensive techniques, this leads us to the specter of the famous falling rate of profit. Of course, if such a phenomenon cannot be ascertained, one must decry the fact that national economic accounts are not kept in labor hours, making empirical calculations most difficult, or one must look for "counter-acting tendencies." This is the wild goose chase. There is no need to search for counter-acting tendencies because there is no falling rate of profit due to the introduction of capital intensive technology in and of itself. The average rate of profit will fall when the working class increases its bargaining strength vis-a-vis the capitalist class. And the profit rate could conceivably fall if the social surplus shrank due to natural resource depletion. But any other source of a falling rate of profit is an imaginary phenomemon—the result of a mis-specified theory. Our theory does not predict a historical trend that is not only completely undetected but contrary to our intuitions such as the flow of financial capital from capital intensive sectors to labor intensive sectors in order to equalize profit rates. This flow is only necessary to equalize profit rates if one begins with labor-time prices in the first place, that is, begins with the *wrong* theory of prices, prices that do not reflect the social relations of even competitive capitalism with homogenous labor—but we have discussed this before. In sum, our theory does not require that capital flow from steel production into goat herding.

The third major point about our model is its "non-economism" and "developmentalism". That is, the model recognizes that the economy exists only in society, not as an independent aspect, and the model achieves its full dimensions only via its concrete application. The model's texture develops as the model is employed.

The fact that S_e is a composite variable should make clear that the functioning of a capitalist economy is not carried out independently from the functioning of the rest of the society. Nor is it solely a matter of the economy fundamentally determining the rest of the society which then plays back on the economy because of time-lags and uneven development. In fact, the varying bargaining powers of different sectors of the work force as determined by their varying consciousnesses, skills, social relationships one to another and internally, arise partly from the dynamics of the economy itself insofar as it molds workers to fit varying patterns, distributes them in ways engendering different levels of organizational strength, etc. But differential bargaining strenghts also derive from such precapitalist historical factors as racism and sexism, which once capitalism appears continue to exist, both defining and being defined by the capitalist economy's particular contours. This last fact has particular importance as soon as we seek to concretize our economic model by recognizing the importance of socio-political, human factors to the definition of economic roles.

As to "developmentalism" we earlier discussed the application of the model to the problem of understanding an economy's development over time—we examine the sequence of complex matrices $A_h^1, A_h^2, \ldots$ In the very act of doing this our model develops as well, as we fill out the dimensions of its many variables. Further, if we are to move from description to explanation, we have to "merge" our qualitative and quantitative theories. Changes in the economy in our view come from such factors as investment in new technologies, alterations in management relations, changes in race and kinship patterns, etc.—all according to constraints imposed by society's core characteristics. Our economic model is adaptable enough to address and explicate these issues. Some of the required mathematical extensions are mentioned in the appendix, "The Wage-Price Vector".

To close this chapter we would like to present a couple of dialogues. The first explains our notion of unequal exchange and how bargaining power introduces a new wrinkle into our understanding of "income distribution". It is presented as a discussion between an orthodox Marxist, "OM", a neo-Ricardian, "NR", and "one of us," —a social relations Marxist, "SR". Non-economists may find some of the wrangling a bit obscure but it shouldn't confuse the main theme. To those familiar with the debates between Joan Robinson and the orthodox Marxists, it should be of some delight. The second dialogue, on the other hand, should be clear for all. It is between an orthodox Marxist, "OM", and a historical Marxist holding the views of this chapter. The discussion centers primarily around the issue of "economism".

VALUE THEORY'S VALUE

NR: Why do you persist in this word game—"value" and all the rest—why can't you just say what you have to say about exchange rates, profit, and distribution without all the labor-time metaphysics?

OM: "Metaphysics!" The concepts of "value", "use-value", "exchange value", and embodied "labor-time" are the tools by which I'm able to get beyond the commodity-blindness you suffer from. They are what keeps me from falling back to the superficial wage and price formulations you cling to. It's precisely these concepts which help me keep track of the underlying social relations, so I don't make the mistake you do of thinking that it's all just a fight over a big commodity pie!

NR: That's a lot of rhetorical nonsense. I understand as well as you that it's the existence of wage-labor separated from the means of production that makes exploitation possible; I get that from history and from studying the rich part of Marx's *Capital*. But yes, I do think you Marxists beat around the bush while Sraffa got right to the point on matters of exchange ratios and allocation. What does your Labor Theory of Value add anyway? Why not have a Donkey Theory of Value? Why not just calculate how much donkey energy is directly and indirectly embodied in everything—that would do just as well you know, and then...

OM: Oh shut up already! We don't use a donkey theory because we're not donkeys, you fool....

NR: Then you admit that it's all just a matter of accounting and that you choose labor over prices or real goods for a purely ideological impact!

OM: I admit no such thing! If you'd just let me finish instead of trying to pile up debating points, you'd find out what I think! Your Donkey Theory of Value, like a price theory or even a peanut theory for that matter, is, as you say, only an accounting framework. It's only a description; but the Marxian Labor Theory of Value is actually a real theory. It doesn't just describe, it explains; it locates the roots of exchange ratios in underlying social relations....

NR: There you go again with social relations as if you've got a monopoly on understanding them. Remember I know the differences between laborers and capitalists also...

OM: Yes, but your theory gives no place for that difference in the determination of exchange. Your approach is all technically centered except for the exogenous wage you just throw in....

NR: Now wait a minute. You're off attacking me on new grounds, and you haven't even begun to deal with any of my criticisms. I say we're the same except that you don't know how to say what you mean without a lot of political rhetoric. Sure, the Donkey Theory is just a description, but so is your Labor Theory until you can tell me what governs wages; and if you say that it's history and class struggle, well that's what I say also, so where's the big difference?

SR: I've been listening off to the side here. Perhaps if you'd let me interject, maybe I could help out a little....

OM: I doubt it...

SR: Nonetheless, I think that for your highly abstracted model of simple commodity production, The Labor Theory Of Value really is a theory and not just an accounting framework. And if the organic composition of capital were the same in all sectors and all the other mobility assumptions were justified in your model of capitalism, the Labor Theory Of Value would be a real theory there as well. But "NR" is right in pointing out that your solution to the transformation problem succeeds only in preserving the status of the Labor Theory Of Value as one possible accounting framework for the rarefied model of perfectly competitive capitalism you and "NR" share, and that under your own assumptions the Labor Theory Of Value cannot be justified as a theory of relative prices and the origin of individual capitalist's profits.

NR: That sounds like what I've been saying.

OM: It does, and it's as wrong as you are! The whole transformation problem shows how foolish such notions are. Certainly prices diverge from values, but they do so in a regular way, and the Labor Theory Of Value's power is thus preserved...

SR: Only as an accounting framework. "NR" has an explanation for relative prices under your assumptions of complete mobility of capitalists and workers but unequal bargaining strength between the capitalists and working class in general. It's a cost-plus mark-up theory of pricing that does not define living labor as the only exploitable input to production and therefore does not predict a constant flow of financial capital from capital intensive sectors like steel and oil production to labor intensive sectors like shoe manufacturing in order to arrive at equal rates of profit in all sectors. Therefore "NR's" approach is consistent with historical reality whereas an interpretation of your solution to the transformation problem as a real theory rather than an accounting framework is not.

NR: So you were with me all along!

SR: No, I wasn't. Your approach is every bit as backward as "OM" has said it is and then some. Your emphasis on "commodities producing other commodities" places technical relations rather than social relations at the center of your theory of price determination. And you abstract from all the unequal social relations in the economy other than that between labor and capital just as "OM" does.

NR: Sure, but that's only my present level of abstraction. Surely you'll grant me the right to make some simplifying assumptions before I try to deal with more complex situations?

SR: Yes, in general, if that's what you are doing, okay. But you treat labor as if it was just any old commodity—a shoe or a lump of iron. You fail to distinguish between labor and labor power, and, because of that, you lose track of the struggle over control of the labor process focusing instead solely on the wage struggle. And before you claim it's just your present level of abstraction, remember that you don't let the neo-classicals abstract from class struggle in treatments of wage determination, and admit that you shouldn't do it in reference to the problem of production relations either.

OM: So you're a Marxist after all.

SR: Yes, but not as you mean the word. For you don't really understand the labor/labor-power distinction either, especially its effects upon the structure of the capitalist firm and on your favorite "forces of production". This is because you abstract from the fact that workers produce themselves in production, except that you say it all the time to distinguish yourself from the Sraffians and to appear profound. But you really have very little to say about how the working class actually reproduces—you don't understand that use-value is as much a relation as is exchange value. You don't understand that there's no such thing as abstract labor, and you can't really explain why the economy reproduces racism and sexism and skill differentials rather than levelling all such differences. You don't...

OM: Wait a minute! I've got plenty to say on all those matters, and anyway what have you got that's so new and improved anyway?

SR: Fair enough question. But to really see what we have, to contrast all our differences, and to struggle out our disagreements further, we'll have to wait till next time we meet. We will need a chance to express our views more fully. Till then, think about this: The real reason you don't like the Sraffians is not just intellectual. It's because you think that they would settle for a reformed capitalism with stronger unions and social democrats in the government. Well, the real reason I don't like you is because you'd settle for a "revolution" that would give a new economic arrangement with redistribution and more enlightened folks in power, but with essentially the same social relations of production in each firm and the same lack of real self-management as persists now. What you lack is a totalist view that sees beyond a few essentially economist fetishized categories and thus, as we'll undoubtedly discuss more later, a true understanding of capitalism, socialism, or of revolution.

TOO MUCH "ECONOMICS"

OM: Let me get this straight: You actually claim that I'm too economistic? I, who critique neo-classical economism and who focus my attentions on history and class struggle, am in turn accused of economism as well?

HM: That's right. I don't deny your theory's power nor its vast margin of improvement over the neo-classical view. I simply claim that there's room for more improvement and that social practice has reached a point which makes clear the need for such advances.

OM: But that kind of statement is applicable to any theory. Why claim that the problem is specifically economism?

HM: Because from our perspective economism is in fact your problem. You look at the world as if all its most important features were economic—and moreover you also look at economics too quantitatively. Economism is overlooking the breadth and the mutuality of links between the economic aspect and the rest of society, and it's also misunderstanding the "economic" itself by insufficiently understanding its more social and psychological aspects.

OM: But how does this abstract formulation apply to me? I understand the relation between the economy, the culture, and the state. I know that class consciousness is an outgrowth of economic dynamics. I focus on these matters. My theory, Marxism, addresses matters of ideology, aesthetics, the state, history, and the economy. Sure there's room for improvement, but surely we should do the improving without throwing out what we've already got?

HM: It's true that you focus firstly, as you say, on history and class struggle, but you don't do it very well. You see, you actually work not with real concrete human history, but rather with the history and struggles that occur in your own "corrected model" of reality, and in doing so, however fine your motivation, you again diverge from Marx and also lose track of certain complexities which are crucial to social change. For example, in our society not everyone is white and male. Class is not alone nor even always the dominant determinant of consciousness....

OM: So what! Anyone in the least concerned with practice in the United States knows racism and sexism are important features and the working class is fragmented by their presence. Obviously they must be overcome as a prerequisite or at least in parallel with a socialist revolution.

HM: No, you're wrong. Not everyone concerned with revolutionary practice sees so clearly and unequivically as you. Feminists see sexual and not class demarcations as most critical. For them class is the "peripheral" feature: class divides women one from another rather than sex dividing the working class. And similarly some nationalists see racial demarcations centrally and class only tactically, as you see race. But you are right that simply recognizing the importance of race and sex to revolution is no longer a touchstone for judging revolutionary theories. All but the impossibly inflexible now pay at least lip service to the importance of class, race, and sex divisions. The issue now is "how is each viewed?" We say that you are economistic because you take class as a priori dominant in all societies. Of course you admit that momentarily a race or sex issue might be highly important, but it's always in context of effects on the eventually "more critical" class dynamics and class revolution. It's this understanding of race and sex as merely peripheral that leads to the opportunist and even paternalist ways that you treat feminist and nationalist movements. But at the theoretical level, what we deny is the a priori dominance of class that you insist on. People engage in many activities: production is only one, and the factory is only one "activity arena". In particular, because of its history and organization in the United States, class and also race, sex, and authority together constitute a totality of characteristics that dominate and determine social relations, consciousnesses, and human possibilities.

OM: Yes. I read your formulation and now I'm beginning to understand what you mean. But it seems to me a gigantic step backward. You're going from the essence of how our society works back to the appearance; from first and dominant causes back to a simple list of all the effects. Where we have a theory, you seem to merely have a snapshot—perhaps more detail around the edges, but complete fuzziness as to the key link we must grasp if we are to create revolution.

HM: Yes, I can see how to you it must look as you've described—how else could you interpret our view? We say you abstract too much; you must of course counter that we abstract too little. We say that you go right past the complex "key link" to focus on only one of its four primary aspects; and you say we stop short of naming that one aspect as dominant. The debate will not be resolved by such interchanges. Only a comparison of understandings of more familiar societal features, say consumption and production, is likely to more clearly distinguish the relative powers of our alternative approaches. Even more, the issue is finally whether or not racism and sexism and also authoritarianism, whatever their varying initial roots, now contribute to societal reproduction and even to the more specific reproduction of class relations. Must our oppressions be understood as a totality or can one be singled out for priority treatment? Must our demarcations of race, sex, class, and power social groupings be understood each as critically as every other or can class be given priority? These are the issues and, short of comparing strategies, a matter better left for awhile; it seems that the only thing to do now is to progress toward our varying pictures of some economic features themselves.

OM: That's alright with me, though I think my explanation of the origins of racism and sexism are probably more powerful than any others. I do recognize, however, that you're right when you say that the principal issue is not origins but rather how, after a long evolution, they now persist and interact in the modern United States context. But to get on.... From reading I know that your criticism of my qualitative analysis goes primarily to my definition of the concept "use-value". You say that I treat it too simplistically, but aren't you ignoring my rationale. In my economic analysis I aim to uncover the basic laws of capitalist motion. I know full well that "use-value" is variable, affected by advertizing, prices, and so on, but unless one is concerned with an evaluation of societal welfare, excess concern with this aspect of the economy is again just missing the forest for the trees—the essence for the appearance. It detracts from the effort to uncover those broad quantitative tendencies that can help explain capitalism's fundamental laws of motion.

HM: Okay, I'll accept your priority (and overlook my earlier critique of your "quantitative analysis"). We'll ignore questions of welfare to get at what you call "the laws of motion"—and yet I can't. For in my analysis part of what determines societal motion is the condition of its citizenry— how well-off or oppressed they are, and particularly how conscious they are of their condition and of alternatives. That is, I understand the economy to be a process involving the alteration of people as well as of things. As a result, use-value is a concept not only of great importance to welfare analysis but also to understanding societal motion. What you or I take to be desirable depends on our past and present, and it changes with changing conditions and also as we ourselves change due to accumulated experiences. This is a fact of immense importance, since societal reproduction depends upon our use-values, which correspond quite closely with what society allows us to achieve. Whether our understanding of these phenomena is seen as an enlargement or as an alteration of the classical view is of little importance as long as it is somehow incorporated. For only then is it possible to arrive at a full understanding of the internal dynamics of production and consumption: how do they affect participants, how are they structured, and how do they contribute to societal reproduction and to potentials for revolutionary change.

OM: Well, maybe some of what you're saying is true. I'm just not sure yet. But what I can't abide by at all is your sloppy way of flinging around words like "familial" or "ghetto" while talking about the factory. I can understand the factory quite well by analyzing in terms of class, of the appropriation of the surplus, and of the problems of dividing the working class along race and sex lines. I just don't see why I need some far more complex approach that will just make things more difficult and obscure.

HM: You just can't yet conceive of a non-economist approach to understanding society, but that is not hard to understand. We're all used to the economistic framework, we all see reality in terms of it, and alternatives are only very marginally developed. Still the need for something much broader is quite apparent. Race, sex, and authority relations are always at least core alongside class relations. Even the economy itself can not be fully understood if one starts with a class focus and no other. The workplace is structured partially in a familial way, partially in a racist or "ghetto" way, and partly in an authoritarian hierarchical way, as well as in a class way. These are very hard to specify because when we look at the factory we still see (especially if we are white, male socialists) only its class characteristics. Our assertion is that the rest of the characteristics also determine the factory's roles and that factories would be quite different places if our society had only parallel or only class core characteristics rather than a fourfold totality at its core. I suppose time will tell if this is correct. But it's important to realize the actual character of the assertion. We say any society has a center and boundary and core characteristics and that in ours these characteristics are mutually entwined into a structural totality. If so, this must be apparent at both the institutional and the human level. Therefore, we expect or intuit that both in people's consciousness and in our society's institutional role offerings, race, sex, class, and authority characteristics predominate, governing daily-life and imposing limits upon human fulfillment as a whole and not each separately or only in parallel. Certainly the best we can do in this first presentation of our new approach is to make the assertion and back it up with some arguments, as well as show its implications and judge how well they accord with our experiences. This latter step is most easily accomplished by considering the implications of this view for problems of revolutionary strategy, but that is something we won't get to for awhile yet.

OM: Well, I'm hardly convinced by all this loose talk, but I'll admit that much of what you say is provocative. Perhaps at a minimum some of my views need updating and reworking, but I just can't see the purpose in stepping outside of the orthodox framework—it's too powerful, too dominant, too effective, and simply too useful to brush it aside for such weak reformulations as you're offering.

HM: What you say is revealing. The orthodox framework is a paradigm. Everytime another criticism surfaces, from feminists, nationalists, anarchists, cultural activists, or ourselves, the immediate response is to simply plug the "hole". This is called putting aside or covering over the "anomolies". It can work for remarkable lengths of time, indeed precisely until the old view is replaced by a new and better one. And until that time the old view continues delimiting the kinds of questions people can ask, the thoughts they can have, even the things they—we—can see. Our orientation is simply inconsistent with the current dominant historical materialist interpretation of Marx. To maintain otherwise would be self-defeating opportunism. We see society as more complex, and thus feel the need for a broader set of concepts as well as a firmer basis in a more accurate understanding of human nature and human development. But without practical comparisons further discussions will likely avail us little. We've made what general theoretical points we now can in the material you've already read. We will only resolve our theoretical differences by contrasting our concrete analyses, our strategic orientations, and particularly our practical experiences; and for such comparisons we must regretably wait awhile.

FOOTNOTES
CHAPTER FOUR

1. See Lenin, *What Is To Be Done,* International Publishers, New York, N.Y., and Mao Tse Tung, *Selected Readings from the Works of Mao Tse Tung,* Peking Press.

2. X^1 or N^4 are simply symbols—they represent specific items. Perhaps X^1 is stereo records, and N^4 oil. Then if we say X^1 is ten we mean 10 records, etc. The purpose of such notation is to ease discussion by allowing shorthand and generalization simultaneously.

3. Obviously when we say that V^3 represents a specific value, or P^6 a specific personality trait, we're on fuzzier ground than with X's and R's. But even though there is a continuum of personality types, values, etc. so that our notation can only be approximate, it proves to be a useful abstraction.

4. Many intellectual advances have been "at root" inventions of new kinds of notation. The invention of the numeral "0" was responsible for all subsequent mathematical advance, at least as a necessary prerequisite. The laws of mechanical motion required the development of calculus which rested primarily on notational advances, and even Einstein's great contributions rested largely on his and others' development of tensor notations. Our simple matrix formalism is much more modest and nothing particularly new, but like all notations that are beneficial, if we let it, it can help us with logical manipulations, organizing our data, and giving it some clarity. It shouldn't be intimidating—think of it as you would a useful shelving arrangement to store your kitchen materials so that you might use them most easily and efficiently.

5. There is an implicit assumption here that in a "good and just" society people's needs and capacities would be internally consistent, mutually supporting, compatible, ecological. We will discuss this more in chapter seven when we consider socialist possibilities for the United States.

6. An analysis of use-value making either of these errors is very dangerous. Neo-classical welfare economics is guilty of treating use-value (or preferences) as a-historical givens, whereas orthodox Marxism tends to view use-values as almost infinitely moldable by societal economic requisites.

7. Obviously we do not confine ourselves to the economy as "sole affector of use-value" but see culture, familial relations, community life—the rest of society—as factors affecting use-value also. In fact use-values are one of the channels of interconnectedness between what we abstractly demarcate as "in the economy" and "outside the economy".

8. See Appendix two of chapter four starting on page 364 for a mathematical demonstration of the argument in this section.

9. Although there are important distinctions between barter-exchange and monetary exchange systems, they are not germane for our purposes here.

10. See any microeconomics text, for example, *Microeconomics*, Henderson and Quandt, McGraw Hill, New York, 1971.

11. Whether this planning is done by the workers themselves or a management chosen by the owners of the firm is of no relevance to the present argument.

12. Paul Sweezy quoted in Edwards, Reich, and Weiskopf, *The Capitalist System*, Prentice Hall, New York, Page 112.

13. We will presently argue that under capitalist relations of production the employer will limit and distort the information any particular group of employees receives, but this is irrelevent to our present concern with markets, and if it is easier, the reader should just imagine this discussion in context of a market socialist society.

Indeed, we will have cause to discuss markets again in chapter seven, there however for the purpose of demystifing the notion that markets can be valuable in a socialist framework.

14. In general, the recognition that markets can't adequately evaluate public goods and goods with effects on people other than the buyer and seller, is well known even to neo-classical economists. For example, see Richard Musgrave, *The Theory of Public Finance,* McGraw Hill, New York, 1959, Page 10-11. The problem is that neo-classical economists are unable to understand how consumption virtually always has effects on many agents and the public as a whole.

15. See Musgrave, op. cit.

16. Karl Marx, *A Contribution to the Critique of Political Economy,* translated by N. I. Stone, Chicago, 1904. Page 268.

17. Karl Marx quoted in Ollman, *Alienation: Marx's Conception of Man in Capitalist Society,* Cambridge University Press, London, 1976. Page 104.

18. See Stuart Ewen, *Captains of Consciousness,* McGraw Hill, New York, for a discussion of advertising and consumption in U.S. history.

19. This will be discussed in more detail in context of an analysis of a "new class", the coordinator class, in chapter five.

20. See Murray Bookchin, *Post Scarcity Anarchism,* Ramparts Books, San Francisco.

21. Ewen, op. cit. Page 189.

22. See Harry Braverman, *Labor and Monopoly Capital,* Monthly Review Press; Gintis, op. cit. and Paul Cardan, *Workers' Councils and the Economics of a Self-Managed Society,* Philidelphia Solidarity, Philidelphia, 1974.

24. In fact, if one felt the need to pinpoint a "primary" contradiction, or fundamental struggle in the capitalist economic arena itself, it would be the struggle between capitalist and worker over who is the dominant user of labor power.

25. In other words, because, under capitalism as opposed to slavery, the human output part of the use-value of labor power cannot be alienated, it appears that the capitalist would be unconcerned with this aspect.

26. By this we mean nothing more than that individual capitalists are concerned with profits in the long-run and not just current profits, since survival in the competition between capitalists depends on profits over the long haul, not momentary achievements.

27. Note that it is not necessary to see this concern as manifesting only around the reproduction of profitable relations. The criteria governing the trajectory of development of factory outcomes may also, in particular societies, include kinship, race, or other factors as well.

28. We repeat that profit maximization need not, however, be the only criterion governing factory outcomes, and we will discuss this issue further in coming chapters.

29. To argue that individual competitive employers cannot "afford" to pursue these strategies even if they would benefit the capitalist class as a whole is to misinterpret our argument. This objection assumes that the most efficient technology maximizes profits and that any deviation from this choice, for example, the calculated promotion of racial anatagonisms, must lower profits. But in fact, we have shown that the reverse is the case.

30. See Batya Weinbaum, *The Curious Courtship of Women's Liberation and Socialism,* South End Press, Boston, 1978, for a discussion about similar matters.

PART THREE

RACE - SEX - CLASS - AUTHORITY TOTALITY AND HEGEMONY IN THE UNITED STATES

The civilization and justice of bourgeois order comes out in its lurid light whenever the slaves and drudges of that order rise against their masters. Then this civilization and justice stand forth as undisguised savagery and lawless revenge... the infernal deeds of the soldiery reflect the innate spirit of that civilization of which they are the mercenary vindicators... The bourgeoisie of the whole world, which looks complacently upon the wholesale massacre after the battle, is convulsed by horror at the destruction of brick and mortar.

Karl Marx
The Civil War In France

CHAPTER FIVE
UNITED STATES
THE HUMAN CENTER

> In every cry of every Man,
> In every Infant's cry of fear,
> In every voice, in every ban,
> The mind-forged manacles I hear.
>   William Blake
>   "London"

Looking at the United States, different analysts see different phenomena. The orthodox Marxist sees one thing, the feminist another, the anarchist a third, and the nationalist still a fourth. Then there are the combination viewpoints: anarcho-communism, socialist feminism, nationalist socialism, and anarcho-feminism. How do we choose between their various descriptions and explanations? Or, how do we develop our own alternative?

None of the above listed orientations proposes an inconceivable picture. There could be a society in which class, race, sex *or* authority was alone actively core, or in which some combination of only two of these were actively felt in all daily-life interrelations. In such a society one of the above perspectives would prove very useful. The others, however, would all be off the mark. For example in a society where patriarchy and capitalist class relations were actively core but authority and race relations weren't active, socialist feminism would provide a powerful analysis, while the other approaches would all either miss the mark entirely, or address issues with only partial accuracy. In any society, determining the relevance of each of these various perspectives is a matter of concrete investigation. None is always accurate. Each often reveals much, but just as often conceals much as well.

In this and the next chapter we argue that the United States has four core characteristics. We discuss their impact in society's center and boundary, their mix, the associated concepts of totality and hegemony, and finally some of the implications of all these attributes for the dynamics of evolution and revolution in the United States. We discard old particularist (monist or dualist) orientations for a new totalist approach.

179

SUMMARY OVERVIEW

The United States is a complex, alienated, oppressive society. It reproduces rather efficiently and yet also embodies many potentially destabilizing contradictions. Pervading both the boundary and the center are a series of core characteristics which delimit and define the quality of daily life and the possibilities for constructive change. These we label racism, classism, sexism, and authoritarianism.

Life in the United States is alienated and oppressive not because advanced technology or human nature are innately evil, but because our institutions and consciousnesses have evolved historically, largely in "entwinement", each finally coming into accord with the requisites of reproducing society's core characteristics, and not with any more humane dictates. Our society is an alienated place to live because its main features are concerned not with human fulfillment but with the reproduction of the oppressive defining characteristics. We get law, schooling, technology, jobs, and even art, not to further human capabilities but rather to reproduce racism, sexism, hierarchy, and classism. In general, in our society, when people gain something worthwhile, it is either because they fought for it, or because it was in someone else's crassest interests for them to have it.

At times the police may actually help people, but it's just a by-product of their real purpose of protecting wealth and power; notice what happens when the interests of wealth and power clearly conflict with those of human development.[1] Even the medical system runs by rewarding wealth and power and reinforcing racial and sexual divisions; it serves health only as a means to these ends and not nearly as well nor as humanely as it might under a different social arrangement.[2] Non-elite schools are aimed at preparing people to endure boredom, to take orders, and to know precisely what they need to know to fit into awaiting social roles; they educate only as much as societal reproduction requires.[3] Similarly, by their organization, design, and technology our jobs tend to reproduce all those personality traits essential for the system's reproduction and to smother the rest. These phenomena are not often calculated and maliciously planned. Rather, they are usually an outcome of the way social changes in our system finally percolate into accord with our society's core characteristics.

Reproduction of society's oppressive aspects depends fundamentally upon a perpetual recreation of a general conformity between people and their environments and roles. But our society is not "one-dimensional". This conformity is never absolute, and it can completely break down for any number of reasons. As examples, socialization can lag behind the development of new role requirements; economic crises can undermine old beliefs; or social practice could generate beliefs which don't fit. When such "disruptions" occur, there is the possibility that people will discard their old perspectives and adopt new and more revolutionary ones. Through society's own tendencies, or through revolutionary activism, such ideas can spread until whole social groups develop revolutionary intentions. These groups or movements can then potentially overcome society's past core characteristics and generate in their place new relations better suited to human growth and well-being.

People who want to help this process occur have to understand the complex ways that our society reproduces and also have to see the contradictions in these reproductive processes, and how these contradictions create possibilities for revolutionary activism. Revolutionaries must understand how the various consciousnesses that allow society's continual reproduction are rooted in different social groups' needs and daily life practices, and how society's own motion and also the practice of revolutionaries can help to uproot these "conforming consciousnesses", develop revolutionary potentials in their places, and then also overcome society's more coercive and repressive impediments to revolution.

CORE CHARACTERISTICS IN THE UNITED STATES

The core characteristics in the United States are racism, authoritarianism, sexism, and classism.[4] Each pervades center and boundary. Each has a determining impact upon the life situation of a particular oppressed group and a defining effect upon everyone else as well. In this section we briefly describe each of these four characteristics as they appear in the United States giving some preliminary support to our contention that they are *all* core.

RACISM

In the United States, racism is a historical structural phenomenon.[5] It is rooted in age-old divisions, the dynamics of colonialism, slavery, and the murders and mutilations of countless Native Americans and blacks. It continues to thrive in legal and extra-legal forms which are new but still intensely oppressive. Racism is artfully rationalized genocide. It is the denial of various races' dignity, intelligence, and even of their very lives. It has taken its toll on Native Americans, blacks from Africa, Chinese, Mexicans, Puerto Ricans, Irish, Italians, Japanese, Arabs, Jews, and most recently the Vietnamese.

The structure of racism in our society, in center and boundary, has roots dating back to indentured servants, slavery, and the Civil War. But despite this heritage, no one is born racist. In an individual living in our times, racism usually develops as a response to current pressures to conform to racist role requirements. The need to see and think of others as racially inferior, the rationales "proving" such inferiority, and the associated behaviors of racists usually serve personal needs for security, self-justification, or community. Racism is born out of specific conditions, but once in existence it has a strong tendency to reproduce itself. The need for self-justification and for a positive self-image pushes racists to continually regenerate their racially stereotyped ideas, even against obvious counter-experiences.

Racism is a core characteristic of our society for third world people and for everyone else as well. It serves to divide people whose ultimate interests are really one and the same: the creation of a human community geared to human needs and ends.

Even for white people racism restricts potential solidarity, community, knowledge, objectivity, and frequently love, sex, and self-esteem. Racism requires the oppressor to maintain a distorted view of reality. It demands arrogance and blindness to evidence. It creates perpetual fear, and it requires inhumanity, just as it denies the skills and potential contributions of large numbers of oppressed peoples. Where there is now a constant tension between races, the threat (and practice) of violence, a lack of communication and of shared development, there could be solidarity. Of course, it cannot be denied that under the present organization of society, racism also delivers many advantages to the racist. It assures fewer competitors, cheap labor, people to look down upon, scapegoats, people for the dangerous and the menial jobs, maids, and dishwashers. Further, only a small portion of the products created by racially oppressed people accrue to them, the rest being unequally distributed among the rest of the population.

For third world people, racism in the United States is manifested in inferior health services; denial of dignity and identity; psychological oppression at the hands of any and all authorities; discrimination in hiring, advancement, and job definition; denial of a decent education and job training; and most blatantly direct physical and judicial persecution, including mass murder.[6]

Certainly no other feature of United States relations does so much to define the quality of life of a black living in Harlem, as does the fact of our society's pervasive racism. It largely determines culture, education, and economic position. It largely determines what a black person can come to think about him or herself and about the world outside. Certainly third world people are profoundly affected by class and sexual relations, but even more obviously they feel the effects of racism first and all the time.

SEXISM

Ways of human behavior that began for one reason often go on reproducing and hurting people for others. At some point early in human history differences between men and women led to unequal role definitions.

Men hunting and women farming—if indeed it even was the early norm—may have made some survival sense at the time, but because of the monopoly it gave men on certain skills and aggressive ways of thinking, it had very adverse effects upon the general relations between the sexes. Similarly, sexual divisions based on women's role in childbirth and nursing were at first probably rooted in developmental concerns— but then were over-extended to produce rigid "mother"/"father" (and still later "Wife"/"Husband") role definitions. Further, according to Marxists, with the genesis of private property there came also the practice of handing on wealth to fathers' sons, requiring restriction of women's sexual freedoms so that it would be clear whose sons were whose. Whatever the origins of these role divisions, their oppressive consequences have plagued the human race ever since. The important issue now is not so much how patriarchy was born; but rather why it persists, how it reproduces, and how it might in the future be overcome.[8]

In the United States sexism is a panoply of thoughts, actions, and institutional relations that mediate almost all modern man/woman interactions.[9] It includes the historically determined institutional inequalities of wealth, power, education, opportunity, and personality that exist between all men and women. It involves as direct victim half the society. There is no potential for genocide, that is for the elimination of women by the oppressors, but there is a constant direct person-to-person clash which is often violent.[10]

In the factories, courts, families, hospitals and sports arenas all institutionally defined roles relegate women to a "women's place", imposing demeaning requirements, and differential rewards. As women have come to define it, *Patriarchy* is a system under which virtually all power, wealth, knowledge, culture, skill, and dispensation of skill, law and dispensation of law, are in the hands of men. All rules, as we shall see in our upcoming discussion of society's boundary, require of both women and men sex-stereotyped behavior—"motherly", "fatherly", "brotherly", "sisterly" behavior.[11]

Patriarchy includes and revolves around the reality of women having to serve and please men; of women being defined and even defining themselves via their relationships to men. It mediates the way men and women relate in bed and on the street. It mediates the way men relate to men and the way women relate to women. It creates as expectations among all societal agents' that women have certain dispositions and men others—"motherly" and "fatherly"—with the latter always more important and dominant. It gives all people a variety of ideals to strive for (related to love, sex, and status) that are either more harmful than fulfilling, or else almost completely out of reach. In this society it is quite impossible to attain the media-defined "ideal" love relationship, family life, or sex life. People's attempts to do so (generally via commodities) are a self-defeating aggravation of the kinds of problems—insecurity, loneliness, sexual incapacity, family strife—they are seeking to escape in the first place.[12] This is just another of society's many vicious circles in which, once having accepted its goals we end up reinforcing the system against our own best interest.

Sexism in the U.S. gives men privileges that they defend through mythology and force. It denies women their own private self-identities as humans. It denies women the possibility of recognizing that they can themselves make initiatives and change the world. Women are forced instead to feel like their existences depend upon the nature of the men around them—because, indeed, institutionally this is the case—and most specifically upon the nature of the man who "owns" them. Women are forced to work in the worst paying jobs with the most demeaning role requirements; or to rely on a man's generosity. Women are forced to endure rape, to sell themselves for income, or to endure beatings as a price of maintaining a marriage. Women are maligned and mistreated by the culture, by their parents, by their husbands, by their children, by the institutions and roles around them, and by their own frequent "misconceptions" about themselves and their men. In this situation, love is sacrificed to a tenuous stability. Dignity is sacrificed for a security which is hardly ever achieved. Self-management virtually disappears as a womanly possibility.

A woman unused to it couldn't possibly endure the assault level that most women daily encounter. A woman who expected better treatment, who had experienced alternatives, who could see reality in terms of her own needs and potentials and act upon them, would unquestionably revolt against sexism. But a woman socialized all her life, accustomed to her situation, struggling to get as much as possible given its contours, in a sense believing in it and supporting it by her own personality, can certainly endure, at least temporarily, though only at immeasurable human cost.

We can reasonably redefine the abstract behavioral styles "masculine" and "feminine" as intersecting opposites that should be comingled to create a fulfilling whole. Masculine comprises confident, initiating, bold, active, etc. Feminine comprises humble, patient, understanding, flexible, sympathetic, sensitive, etc. Neither attribute set is worth much in isolation from the other. They are parts of a single whole and they degenerate when separated. But their unity is not the joining of a man with one set of attributes and a woman with the other. Neither party to such a couple is a whole person and the union is little improved. Rather both masculine and feminine attributes must appear in all individuals—each person must contain their unity.

Sexism exists in both oppressor and oppressed forms. It keeps both males and females from moving toward wholistic masculine/feminine character structures. But sexism affects each group differently. The man is free to meet many needs and he defends this advantage (however unself-consciously) even though the modes of defense and the actual quality of his position itself cut off various other fulfillment possibilities. The woman, on the other hand, is often unfree to meet even her most basic needs. Her character development is stunted and she is forced into a kind of "slave" role, slave to her man, slave to all men. She stays put because force keeps her there, because habit keeps her there, because mythology makes her believe it's right for her to be there, and because though awfully oppressed, she does get some needs met in her position. Thus she defends the security, income, and "companionship" her man provides even though the whole situation impedes many of her broader capabilities.

AUTHORITARIANISM

Authoritarian relations spring up whenever differences in skill, knowledge, wealth, or preparedness create differences in power, and when the latter then perpetuate and increase the former.[13] The United States has a history of unequal development among its peoples; we are separated one from another by race, sex, class, and countless other divisions of geography, upbringing, religion, and especially education. Hierarchical social relations and mentalities intrinsic to all these divisions have developed a kind of *force of their own* propelling them into all other aspects of daily life. Competition in the economy is a mark of capitalist class relations and it breeds hierarchy which then spreads to all other arenas. Divisions of race and sex also cause hierarchies which, once generated, lead to behavior patterns and beliefs which can become generalized beyond race and sex criteria into other sectors of society as well. No wonder almost all United States institutions are hierarchical. Almost every United States citizen has a tendency to order him or herself on a scale of relative value as compared to others, even others of the same race, class, and sex. The criteria for where one fits is always determined by those who can wield most power. Those who have most power invariably define themselves to be most worthy; those who must obey accept criteria of worth which deny their dignity.

The archetype authoritarian institution is the state. As the administrator of society, the state wields power over social life—in one instance perhaps dictatorially, in another perhaps by laws and "bourgeois democracy". The state takes different forms in different societies and epochs. Viewed historically and relationally it represents a complex institution serving reproductive ends, while also mediating societal conflicts. It is often, at least in part through the state that reforms "percolate" into shapes consistent with core characteristic requirements. It is also the state which carries the responsibility for law and order, when necessary, in the form of the violent defense of the status-quo. So long as society is oppressive and not self-managed the state is an alien institution above the will of the majority of citizens.[14]

Authoritarianism, order-giving and order-taking, blocks the potential for human community and for the fullest development of all people's capacities. It requires of the ones on top an arrogance and elitism, an insensitivity to the well-being and potentials of others, and a distance from others, which are together destructive of human warmth. It requires of those who take orders a sense of futility, of worthlessness, of obedience which stifle all attempts at personal creation. The way in which Americans take as gospel what the lawyer, doctor, teacher, newspaper writer, T.V. announcer, or other "authority" figures say is indicative of the degree to which we live in an authoritarian society. The hierarchical structure of our schools, factories, hospitals, even of our sports and drama, all attest to the pervasiveness of authoritarianism in our society. Save for a very few exceptions, people are outwardly controlled, inwardly docile. In the so-called land of individualism, there is little variety. At any one moment millions, even hundreds of millions watch the same T.V. programs and believe the same advertisements or lying news stories. Stanley Milgram's experiments with obedience show just how pervasive authoritarianism is in our society.[15] They show, how on the say so of a professor one person will in most cases literally shock another to death rather than disobey. They give clear evidence of the subtle and not so subtle reasons why we are able to say that authoritarianism is one of our society's core characteristics.

CLASSISM

There should be no need to argue here that class relations constitute one of our society's core characteristics. The problem with orthodox Marxism was not that it attributed importance to the concept class, but that it misunderstood the full ramifications of that importance and denied the centrality of other factors as well.

Class relations, like sexual, racial, and authority relations mediate all United States daily-life interactions. They help to determine income distribution, the social relations of production and consumption, and the character of culture, politics, sports, and health care. Depending upon our class position, we have different access to schools, housing, jobs, dignity, and even language. Our lives are thus differently structured depending upon whether we own capital, act as coordinators, or work to produce commodities in the traditional proletarian fashion. Whether we are black or white, woman or man, used to giving orders, receiving them, or both, our class position is also critical in the determination of our life possibilities. But to understand how class manifests itself, and for that matter how race, sex, and authority manifest themselves, it is necessary to go beyond these general introductory comments about "coreness" to a description of the place of each of the characteristics in society's center (in the remainder of this chapter) and boundary (in the next).

THE CORE CHARACTERISTICS IN SOCIETY'S CENTER

At the center of society are people with varying needs, desires, skills, and consciousnesses. To understand this immense whole is an impossible task. Still, we can develop insights into some general features of the center, and then, by piecing those insights together, we can get a rough overall view.

We look at society's citizens in terms of their "positions" with respect to sex, class, authority, and race: First, man or woman, what class, order giver, order taker or both, what race? This has an immense determining impact upon one's needs and personality. And second, for women, workers, order-takers, and non-whites, how do they react to their position—do they accept their oppression, or do they rebel?

Of course each individual in our society has her/his own particular immensely complex consciousness. But commonalities derived from shared positions in relation to society's core characteristics do appear over and over, and allow us to distinguish different sectors as being essentially homogeneous in certain needs, concerns, and desires.

At a very high level of abstraction we can thus distinguish between ideal oppressor, oppressed, and rebellious consciousness types for each of our society's characteristics. Real people don't have such stereotypical consciousnesses as these ideal types, and yet, at the same time, what consciousnesses we do have can often be understood as a personal adaptation of the ideal types in varying combinations and relative strengths.

To develop a general picture of U.S. consciousness types we choose to discuss representatively an ideal racist oppressor, oppressed order-taker, and woman's rebellious consciousness, remembering that these are only three of the nine general race, authority, and sexual consciousness "types". Then we discuss class consciousness separately as it isn't as easily explained via the "neat" dichotomous division between the oppressor and the oppressed. Throughout we do not assume that consciousness is simply a reflection of economic or any other "material" conditions and therefore to be ignored, but rather we see the centrality of human praxis and the power and equal causality of consciousness relations. Moreover, our approach allows, as orthodox Marxism does not, the understanding of racism, sexism, and authoritarianism—not just their labelling. And similarly, even our description of classism is enhanced because it is more complete and it deals with the human behind the "labels."[16]

THE RACIST OPPRESSOR CONSCIOUSNESS

Racists believe at least to some degree that the races were meant to be separate because of their differing characteristics and supposedly differing potentials. In the United States, racists invariably believe that blacks (and often Chicanos, Asians, Mexicans, etc.)[17] are mentally inferior and deserve what little they get, that blacks are lazy, that they are animals. Blacks supposedly don't need all the things whites need and they don't deserve what whites have. The "liberal" version of this consciousness: blacks seem a little slow; they have a different culture and seem happy enough; they certainly deserve an equal opportunity but not any extra advantages; if they can't do as well as whites in this society, well then that's their problem.

Racists are not innately malevolent. Their theories seem to explain reality; they correspond quite well to needs for rationalizations and scapegoats, and to the role expectations of society's institutions.

Racists daily "see" black ignorance, black poverty, black vandalism, black militance, and black violence. What are the obvious explanations? Either there is something wrong with the society or there is something wrong with black people. The first view about society is very distasteful for whites who must rationalize living in society, working in it, and succumbing daily to its requirements. The latter view about blacks (or other third world people) is much more "comforting". It has no disruptive implications and can even prove "useful" in allowing racist behavior.

When young, a racist might have been beaten up by a black person, or might have been told anti-Chicano jokes, or might have known only

Asian menial servants, or might have had to accommodate to parental racist views. Sometimes the surroundings literally force someone to be racist, as when neighborhood blacks are hostile, or when parents impose racist viewpoints. Other times it is more a matter of personal weakness, as when someone who knows better starts acting racist to be one of the gang.

Racists often maintain or extend their self-images via their views of black people: look at their poverty and see my wealth; look at their ignorance and see my learning; look at them down there and me up here. It's not injustice; it's because I'm better. I have more, and I deserve it. I earned it by working for it, and I have a right to defend it. If all this isn't said that often, it is at least felt. The racist conveniently overlooks the real roots of racial injustice, and in so doing creates a stable, defendable, personal niche.

The racist mentality is most often a part of a complex mechanism for maintaining self-esteem and for defending various short-term material interests. It is almost always rooted in needs for community and feelings of solidarity that identifying oneself as a superior group generates. It rationalizes advantages that would otherwise seem unwarranted and it justifies their defense. It deflects pressures to face the real enemy and thus also all the fears/dangers such an encounter would generate. It provides convenient scapegoats—again preserving the myth of the country's goodness which sustains working for it and submitting to its pains. Anyone with a weak self-image or societal position resting very much on beliefs in the country's goodness, can be well served by having an excuse for all problems—a way to avoid confronting difficult crises or painful truths, and most importantly, a way to avoid thinking about one's own shortcomings or the shortcomings of one's lifestyle or especially of one's environment, while also rationalizing the more extreme plight of other people. This is what we might call the scapegoat, guilt-complex, rationalization theory of racism. It is rooted in an understanding of people's needs for self-esteem, security, and a positive image of the country they work within.

The recent New York blackout and rioting/looting experience provides graphic illustration of some of our assertions. How was a white worker, suburbanite, or store owner to perceive the events? Either "they" ran wild, like "animals", trying to steal what "they" were "too lazy or dumb" to earn—or—the system has unjustly deprived a large group of people access to its products, including food, and given the opportunity, those people took back from the system what the system had in fact historically looted from them. In the absence of a vision of a better society and a movement to attain it, the second view is discomforting and guilt-producing. The first has more immediate "use-value". Remember that the Mayor called the looters "animals", that the press used "they" and other race-laden terminology, and that there were articles to be found not only asserting racist views but even advocating genocidal solutions to the "looting problem".

Many times racists adopt ideologies to rationalize actions they've taken for other reasons. A business manager hires blacks at low wages to seek profit and slowly becomes racist to rationalize his actions in a suitable self-serving way. Other times the "racist-creating" process is more complex: there are a variety of forces compelling most Americans to become racist including up-bringing, the need to conform so as to have friends, the pressure to succeed, the need for palatable explanations for inequalities, the effects of biased schooling, and the dynamics of U.S. courts, culture, and workplaces. Institutional and ideological racism both create and recreate each other over and over from generation to generation in the family, the workplace, and on the playground. Eventually everyone is in one way or another affected.

All the various racist attributes of U.S. institutions and people interact with one another across culture, production, and family lines. Together they form a kind of racist net which has tentacles reaching into every aspect of daily-life.[18]

The costs racists pay for privilege are quite severe. Racists are substantially cut off from a large part of the human race. As their position becomes more rooted in unmet needs and more threatened by reality, racists are most often forced to retreat ever further into self-deception. To persist in racist beliefs people must come to view the world irrationally. They must censor their view of their surroundings lest any new perceptions deny their beliefs. They must lie to avoid admitting they are lying. They must alienate themselves from themselves and others.

Racists rationalize their racial myth-making by accepting the abstract form of their "subjectifying behavior" as legitimate. They begin developing more and more myths in new areas cutting off more avenues of potential liberation. Self-deceptions around class, authority, and sex relations become entwined with self-deception around race issues. The myth-making tendencies tend to invade every area of life—convenience, not objectivity, becomes the criterion of "truth". The act of perverting reality's contours to suit one's own expectations or needs becomes a kind of habit. It serves immediate ends but only at immense costs in long-run ignorance and alienation.

A racist worker is constantly separated from and competing with black co-workers in order to advance and to maintain white friendships. He grows cut off from his surroundings as his activities become less and less related to real facts. His behavior is made hypocritical by the extents to which he is sometimes forced to relate to blacks on a more or less equal basis. Even when there is a modicum of solidarity during a strike in the

will not discuss its particular forms of consciousness.

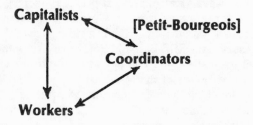

CAPITALIST OPPRESSOR CONSCIOUSNESS

The intelligent capitalist believes in the sanctity of profit and property. The capitalist organizes his (or in a few instances, her) life within the dictates of material self-interest, circumscribed by a belief that everyone else will do the same. He's sustained by the belief that the net result will be the best of all possible worlds. The capitalist says that people inevitably compete for individual self-advancement. The capitalist says that society should be organized so that competition will occur freely and things will be able to organize themselves optimally. This is certainly a convenient enough position for those who already own almost everything.[23]

The capitalist consciousness views everything in terms of narrow self-interest and accommodates all perceptions, desires, and philosophies to the same ends. In effect, capitalists see money as the source of all need fulfillments. Status is a function of wealth and power, and dignity comes with status. Knowledge can be bought. Love culminates in a contract and is won in a power contest on a "sex" market not insensitive to financial resources.

The United States capitalist leader sees the world as a huge marketplace where U.S. needs are the greatest, and our interests dominate. Profit is the key thing. Profit creates growth. But the capitalist's beliefs are not innate. They are caused by interaction with the U.S. boundary and especially by efforts to succeed in certain U.S. roles. The capitalists are indeed willing to speak for themselves:

> As the largest producer, the largest source of capital, and the largest contributor to the global mechanism, we must set the pace and assume the responsibility of the major stockholder in this corporation known as the world...nor is this for a given term of office. This is a permanent obligation.[24]

United States business leaders see the world in a subjectively circumscribed way. Areas of greatest personal interest, knowledge, and involvement are areas of greatest "personal concern". United Fruit leaders "cherish" South America; Firestone "covets" Liberia; the oil companies survey the Mid-East and Southeast Asia with intensity. If you were an oil magnate would you pay attention to the affairs of a sugar country, of Harlem, or of the Mid-East?

When something threatens their material interests, all of a corporate leaders' values come into play—but not until those interests are threatened. If there's a right wing coup in Liberia furthering Firestone's interests, Firestone's leaders won't perceive any threats to the personal liberties of the Liberians. But if the same coup threatens Firestone's interests, then they'll worry about the interests of the Liberian people as well. They associate human freedom with freedom of their interests. The humane aspects never come into play until the capitalist ones blaze the path. The capitalist consciousness acts first; and then, if conditions demand, human concerns can operate as well. The capitalist mentality orders incoming perceptions and determines priorities first according to corporate interests. The corporate tendency toward human freedom is invariably first a tendency toward freedom of trade, of capital penetration, or of plain exploitation and colonialism.

> Much more seriously than they themselves realize, property is the bourgeoisie's god, their only god. It long ago replaced in their hearts the heavenly god of the Christians. And, like the latter in the days of yore, the bourgeoisie is capable of suffering martyrdom and death for the sake of this god. The ruthless and desperate war they wage for the defense of property is not only a war of interests. It is a religious war in the full meaning of the word.[25]

Corporate leaders get their identities from their material wealth and from their capitalist beliefs. When you attack property or power you're attacking the corporate basis for life, the corporate rationale for existence, the corporate center for motivation, feeling, and self-esteem. You can expect a response.

Corporate leaders pursue noble or ignoble aims only after their attention has been drawn by threats to old investments or by possibilities of new ones. Under such conditions they are "forced by the total structure of society to operate without regard for the ultimate consequences for large numbers of people."[26] Corporate leaders necessarily internalize a wide variety of destructive, anti-social, oppressive ideologies; they undertake immoral actions with almost no noticeable reservation.

Capitalist rationales argue that by pursuing profit and power, the money holders actually do the most efficient possible job of filling people's needs.

The capitalist's definition of "crime" illustrates his mentality well. Deaths from malnutrition in the ghetto are perhaps lamentable but certainly not criminal. They don't threaten power, or profit; they augment it. Corporate theft, bribery, graft, and fraud, are not criminal. They are part of society's process of production and consumption; they don't threaten corporate power relations. Most corporate leaders would laugh at the suggestion that fifty thousand automobile accident deaths a year constitute mass murder; however, private theft is a heinous crime, looting is despicable, and strikes are un-American. The same leaders would listen carefully to the thesis that minority looting is a central problem in the United States today, or that international movements for nationalization are anti-life, anti-human, anti-property and thus deserving of intense, forceful opposition. When someone suggests to them that millions around the world die unnecessarily because of imperialism, they scoff; but for profit opportunities they always listen and act, no matter what the effects on anyone else. The corporate sense of justice is thoroughly alienated. Only when profit is unaffected or when its furtherance actually corresponds to what is just, is there any chance for humane decisions.

WORKER'S OPPRESSED CONSCIOUSNESS

Racism directly oppresses third world people in the United States. Sexism directly oppresses women and children. Classism directly oppresses the people who work, buy products, or suffer militarism at home or abroad. The classist economy and its various roles inculcate a whole variety of mythologies related to each of these many kinds of oppression. All these forms taken together collectively oppress and "infect" everyone.[27]

Work in the United States is alienated. The product escapes our control and the work's value almost escapes rational understanding. Work is not aimed at human welfare in either its character or product. The situation is artfully caught in Marx's observation that:

> First the fact that labor is external to the worker, i.e., it does not belong to his essential being; that in his work, therefore, he does not affirm himself, does not feel content but unhappy, does not develop freely his physical and mental energy but mortifies his body and ruins his mind. The worker therefore only feels himself outside his work, and in his work feels outside himself.

He is at home when he is not working, and when he is working
he is not at home. His labor is therefore not voluntary but
coerced; it is forced labor. It is therefore not the satisfaction of a
need; it is merely a means to satisfy needs external to it.[28]

Many workers "accept" their condition as inevitable. They accept
the ethic that says the only responsible and moral thing to do is to earn a
good living no matter how debilitating it might be. Once workers feel that
their situation is permanent—and to some extent they must because their
very survival depends upon their working and they certainly don't see
many alternatives offered elsewhere—they must also develop
rationalizations that allow some measure of personal dignity. If you must
show up for work every Monday through Friday or Saturday or else
suffer grave hunger, indignity with relatives, and ostracism, it becomes
essential to take work in stride, to acclimate, to not continually find fault
but rather to accept and "make the best of it." It even becomes necessary
to actively avoid literature and experiences that call your work-life into
question. For they can only bring pain and trouble, certainly no new life.
The weekend must not be enjoyed so much as to make returning to work
Monday impossible. Not only do the social relations of our work try to
reproduce docility within us, but in subtle self-defense we become
accomplices in our own stultification as well. Better to watch SWAT than
a documentary on Attica, better to read a "get rich through personality
improvement" book than Marx—the former activities don't disrupt the
"snugness" of our fit to what we must be doing; the latter generate
seemingly useless discomfort. The only other alternative which depends
on believing that one's plight is only temporary, is to literally work and
yet not work, participate and yet not participate. We go to work forty
hours and yet deny that those forty hours have any meaning or
importance at all. We simulate sleep on the job, using drugs and alcohol if
necessary. The whole process is made to seem outside the life that
matters. This approach is particularly likely where consciousness of the
unjustness of work is generally high, so rationalization is difficult; while
consciousness of alternatives is quite low, so political activity and
commitment is also difficult. Waking sleep seems to be a viable and
"popular" option.[29]

In any case effectively oppressed workers have ambivalent feelings
about the upper classes. They think authority is necessary. They don't
particularly like anything about their bosses but they respect their
existence. Most workers with homes of their own have a stake in
accepting that salaries and privileges are staggered according to one's
skills and sacrifices. They might want more, but they don't particularly
think much about changing the whole system, and when confronted with

the idea they think it is a daydream that couldn't possibly work. Moreover, the notion threatens their world view. Workers therefore frequently develop rationalizations that allow contentment with relative, regular advancements, and that give interests in defending those advancements and the honest hard-working means by which they were acquired. Workers believe that managers and doctors should get more, because upper class work requires more decision-making, engenders more tension and requires more education and skills. Workers have come to believe very strongly that material incentives are essential if anyone is to work hard to attain greater education and skills—and why should they not think this in a society where learning is painful and the employment of skills and knowledge always alienated?

To make it to the suburbs workers labor inordinate hours year after year, with little leisure, at dehumanizing jobs, and they feel entitled to what they finally get. Workers reach for self-esteem, dignity, and the power to help their children in the only ways our society allows; in the process they stunt their own lives.

Acquiesent oppressed workers believe in the system of hard work and reward that has given them their minimal but liveable incomes. They believe that its problems are simply facts of modern-day life. They fear attempts to equalize rewards because these threaten needed rationalizations, unjustly reward some folks to others' detriment, push workers too high, or eliminate necessary incentive mechanisms. But this isn't to say that such workers enjoy their jobs. Boredom is boring even if rationalized and irrelevance is irrelevant even if paid for. Being bossed around is no fun no matter how it is dressed up, but workers believe that there is no alternative.

Workers make this sacrifice within a framework determined by a belief in the power of profit and the sanctity of private property. In order to justify their "successful lives", acquiescent workers become more and more attached to defending those values. The oppressed worker who is totally "domesticated" by his/her plight (the one who will work harder than necessary) accepts the necessity of capitalism, profit, hierarchy, and property; accepts unequal wages; believes in his or her boss's dignity; and gains self-esteem through relative accomplishments, doggedness, and the ability to oppress others and feel superior to them. Such workers have only a classist vision of what an improved life would be like. They are made susceptible to all sorts of manipulation by a government and a productive apparatus especially designed to mislead them. They are used to buttress every imaginable kind of split among exactly those people whose interests are inextricably entwined. Workers have been pushed out of touch with their own solidarity among themselves and with others.

Moreover, they then must go to the Shoppers' Mall and buy their conditions of oppression as well.

CONSUMER OPPRESSED CONSCIOUSNESS

People are oppressed and become acquiescent in the market as well as in the workplace. Consumerism is a kind of pathology preying upon everyone living under capitalism, yet all buying is certainly not ill-conceived. Behind most purchases is reasonable need, such as when we buy a car for transport or to get companionship or sex. But there are still obvious problems. First, such purchases only partially meet our needs, and second, sometimes we become so consumerist that buying becomes a compulsive end in itself.

Consumerism is built into the nature of the capitalist class system. More and more goods must be sold, but no new social needs are to be aroused. If the cycle work-consume-work is to continue indefinitely, bought goods must aggravate needs, not really fill them. Commodities must be sold to answer our needs for self-esteem, dignity, success, love, companionship, and self-management (which they can never meet), as well as to meet material needs (which they can). The whole society is constructed so that so long as we take its reproduction for granted, there is no other course for us than to consume, for that is the only fulfillment game in town. Regretably most often we are eventually eaten up by our own undigested well-beings, and yet our behavior is all quite rational—short of offering major resistance to society's basic design.

People need commodities because commodities mediate interpersonal relations and because they are expected, though hardly ever optimally enjoyed. The car salesman needs a special suit. The nurse needs a uniform. And everyone needs to buy presents even when they serve no needs of either party save the official "holiday" expectation that they'll be given. But mostly people need to buy goods because goods determine status and because there are no other "conforming" means to gain respect, develop talents, or use leisure time. Commodities mediate everything. People have virtually no choice. We must buy, and we must rationalize our constant buying. We adopt as a part of our personalities a set of private acquisitive traits. In one part of our minds we come to believe in the divine powers of the bought article. This is fetishism. Our behavior is rational in that it allows us to survive and meets many of our most basic needs in the only ways that society respects. It is irrational in that it does little to further our whole development.

Consumerism isn't inherent in the human psyche. It arrives because of the setting we function within, and it stays as an oppressive character trait impeding our whole development, but it is rational and even self-serving in this society. Consumerism in the personality causes totally frivolous spending to an extent, to be sure, but its main effect is to prepare and make people desire to do the consuming that we must do anyway to survive and to gain some fleeting pleasures in an irrational setting, and to then rationalize that behavior—allowing us to continue with it over and over, and to live with ourselves as well. As it becomes rooted, consumerism makes us value all things as if they were commodities on markets: thus we view each other, knowledge, sex, love, and ourselves as "investment projects". And at the same time, it breeds individualism. The problem isn't that we stupidly get deceived by T.V. and buy nonsense. We have no choice but to buy nonsense, and the T.V. acclimates us to that necessity. Consumerist values foster the behavior, but also and more importantly they rationalize it, acclimate us to it, spread it throughout our non-material lives as well as our buying-selling lives, and keep us from seeing much beyond the most superficial understandings of the involved dynamics.

Consumers defend consumerism in much the same way as many other oppressed people defend their own particular alienations. One's dignity and self-esteem depend upon defending the values one submits one's existence to. What develops is "a mutilated frustrated existence: a human existence that is violently defending its own servitude,"[30] rationally, in the name of its own well-being.

> The second nature of man (consumerism) thus militates against any changes that would disrupt and perhaps even abolish this dependence of man on a market ever more densely filled with merchandise—abolish his existence as a consumer consuming himself in buying and selling. The needs generated by this system are eminantly stabilizing conservative needs: the counter-revolution anchored in the instinctual structure.[31]

Consider suburban especially "upper-middle-class" after dinner discussion: The recitals of recent purchases become a game wherein people compete to see who is smarter, has more dignity, more status, more intelligence. This is a self-defeating mentality at work—one that tries to meet needs it can't touch, prevents other needs from being expressed, and finally leads people to become alienated from themselves. We work as a means to consumerist ends; we don't realize that our work makes us incapable of fulfilling leisure activity, and furthermore that work should actually be an end in itself.

The market for labor and goods requires that each of us compete against the rest, ignoring our social cooperative side. The competitive ethic is the ideological rationalization for a form of behavior which is made inevitable by an economic system which pits each person against every other. Much like consumerism, competitive individualism makes sense within the system's constraints; but it also serves to produce and reproduce those constraints. It is a mind-set which feeds and is fed by our society's parallel racist, sexist, and authoritarian mentalities.

The Worker As Citizen

In the United States we swallow productive, competitive, consumerist myths as well as myths about our democracy and international generosity. We live in the belly of the imperial giant. If we are to be loyal Americans and get what our society's legitimate roles have to offer, we must reconcile ourselves to militarism, interventionism, and the threat of instant annihilation. We have to grow up in the United States. We need a consistent picture of the world we live in that helps us function and that allows us some self-respect. We must adopt anti-communist, almost jingoist awarenesses because only they can easily help us to live emotionally and financially stable lives. They help us to love our country and believe in it and thus rationalize slaving away within its confines. To slave for a war mongering country would not allow dignity; to slave for the best country in the world allows some. Pro-U.S. myths give us reasons for our pains and for our country's belligerence. Even the people who invent these lies eventually come to believe them.[32] They fit very well with what people need to hear so they are rarely questioned.

In U.S. decision making centers people act by corporate criteria and justify it to others and to themselves by anti-communist, American good-guy myths. It is preferable to be a bit subjective while remaining an upstanding citizen, than to be objective, hate one's country, hate one's own past beliefs and behaviors, and have essentially no where to go and nothing to do.

United States worker-consumers have complicated personalities that lead them to accept capitalism when it doesn't accept them. The framework goes relatively unbroken because it is enforced, because it meets many basic needs, and because, as Marcuse might well phrase it, it is eminently self-sustaining. The weaknesses are made to seem just, and the actually meager rewards beneficent.

U.S. capitalism's dynamic is technical advance and human stagnancy. Its result is continuous oppression accompanied by potentials for liberation. The injustice is made relatively tolerable by mythology, competition, and reaction to fear and previous experiences.

Life in the United States cultivates and rewards just about every way in which people could harm other people and themselves as well. The state only intervenes when social order is at stake. The result is that only insofar as society does not work, do we fully develop our humanness and rebel against our conditions.

ANTI-CLASSIST CONSCIOUSNESS

Anti-classists believe that every individual has the right to control her/his own work and the product of that work harmoniously with every other individual. They understand why people work for the system and defend it despite what it does to them. They understand worker loyalties to business, the myth's of the boss's dignity, and the dynamics of consumerism, and believe that all these can be overcome.

Working class rebellious consciousness is opposed to profit and private property. Its goal is to restore to work both dignity and craft, a usefulness to the collective welfare. This motivates a simultaneous opposition to the capitalist division of labor and thrust for workers' self-management and a redefinition of technology and the social relations of production. Consumption too is a sphere of activity which should be aimed to fulfill human needs and develop human capabilities. A rebellious worker has no patience for manipulative advertising and shoddy workmanship. The consumer is to exert collective pressure upon what is available for consumption. Competition is opposed to pursue solidarity—the rebellious worker with a clear anti-classist consciousness believes in a collective solution to the limits of capitalist economic relations—not in personal escape through a problematic individualist advance. The goal is economic relations which propel equity, restore human friendship, engender craft skills, and reproduce collective self-management—that is, "efficiency" in a human sense of the word. In chapter eight we will discuss revolutionary consciousnesses of a variety of types, focusing around race, sex, class, and authority taken separately and in combination.[33] Here it suffices to say that the two minimum foundation points for any working class socialist consciousness are: first, unshakeable opposition to the capitalist division of labor and profit motive, and second, unwavering insistence upon working class solidarity and collective self-management.

CONCLUSION

No individual is solely classist, class-oppressed, or anti-classist. In our society with its capitalistic orientation, each characteristic melts into all our consciousnesses to varying extents. Many corporate leaders motivated almost completely by capitalist ideologies also have anti-capitalist pro-ecology tendencies as well as oppressed consumer tendencies. Many consumers have an ambivalent understanding of their plight and empathize with Nadaristic attacks on big business and advertising. Most workers have a side which hates alienation, hates bosses, craves community, and avidly desires self-management. It's just that this side mostly emerges only off-the-job. Everyone has latent within her/him variations on oppressing, oppressed, and rebelling class traits. Most interestingly, anti-capitalists embody many capitalist oppressor-oppressed tendencies. Most of us are still competitive, status-oriented, insensitive to human dynamics, needs, and desires, consumerist, and often somewhat nationalistic. The corporate view of the world, and especially the corporate view of people as "investment projects" is quite widespread in the United States, even among capitalism's most ardent enemies.

THE IMPACT OF A NEW CLASS

So far the picture of class consciousness we've offered has been dichotomous, based on two classes, but the actual situation is more complex. In addition to the two polar elements we've discussed, the capitalists and the working class, there is also a "coordinate class" in the middle and the petit-bourgeoisis off to the side.[34]

With each group other than classes which we have discussed, men, women, blacks, whites, etc., the key aspect has been the position with respect to one or another of the set of four entwined oppressive features at society's core. With class this remains so. Capitalists, coordinators, workers, and the petit-bourgeoisie all fill different roles with respect to society's hierarchy of economic activities—i.e., with respect to making profits and to reproducing the conditions of making profits.

Historically, reproduction of the conditions for profit-making required the capitalists to often employ the power of the state (police, courts, troops) or private armies of Pinkertons—but as monopoly capitalism has advanced, the contours of control have matured in kind. There has been a steady effort to errode the intellectual and coordinative abilities of the workers over their own work—leaving them steadily less able to envision themselves as society's masters—and to then vest these skills in an intermediary layer of expert intellectual coordinators.[35] These new agents came to constitute a coordinate class of "workers above the workers", that is, of managers, teachers, social workers, health workers, psychologists, industrial engineers, technologists, advertisers, and a host of types of bureaucrats. These are enjoined simultaneously to "serve the people" and yet also to continually preserve the conditions which give rise to the need for such service in the first place. Thus they must act to insure a proper socialization of all sectors and must tend to people's needs and hurts, but always within the constraint of leaving society's basic relations intact. Teachers teach, but only as much as society says its various citizens should know; more for white men, less and different for blacks and women; more for the future capitalists and coordinators, less for the future working class.[36] Psychologists try to resolve people's tensions through accommodating them to the society, never vice versa.[37] The social worker seeks to alleviate pains and grievances but only within certain limits.[38] The coordinate class sells its labor to capitalists. It works and thus shares certain attributes with all other workers. But it also functions above other workers—seeing itself as superior to them and in a sense responsible for administering to their incapacities. The workers also interact with two classes: the capitalists and the coordinators; and indeed contacts with the coordinators are far more frequent than with the capitalists.[39]

The implications for consciousness are legion. To work effectively the coordinate class must be seen as legitimate and must therefore have considerable autonomy from the capitalists.[40] As a result there really is a tendency toward a "serve the people" mentality. But there is also a paternalism toward the working class. Thus we have a "middle element" who have certain antagonistic relations with both capitalists and workers and thus certain tendencies toward oppressing, oppressed, and rebellious relations toward each of these classes. The coordinators relate to the capitalists as intellectual workers. When quiescent, the coordinators accept the conditions of their work. They obey the will of their employers and pay proper respect.[41] But when rebellious they demand ever greater autonomy and take their "serve the people" rationales to their limits. This leads to an anti-corporate "populism" or even as far as a kind of technocratic socialist stance: socialist because of the anti-capitalist thrust and parallel extension of the desire for autonomy; technocratic because the coordinators often retain their own particular oppressing role toward workers—that is, their paternal relationship to them.[42] So there is a potential for a partially anti-working class "socialist" consciousness. On the other hand, if this coordinate class could overcome both its oppressed role/mentality with respect to the capitalists, and also its oppressor role/mentality with respect to the workers, a true full socialist consciousness could result.[43]

The worker's consciousness is similarly complicated by the presence of the coordinate class. For now workers can be anti-capitalist and yet oppressed because of their fealty to experts, and also anti-leftist because of their justified hostilities toward the worker-oppressing socialism of the coordinate class. To achieve a truly anti-capitalist class awareness, the workers must gain a full understanding of the trichotomous relation and a full faith in their own capabilities. They will attain this only through serious revolutionary study and struggle.

SUMMARY

Whatever their roots, the present critical features of racism, sexism, authoritarianism, and classism in the United States, are their pervasiveness, longevity, entwinement, and continued reproduction. People's consciousness in the U.S. is a complex amalgam of various oppressor, oppressed, and rebellious tendencies, all combining in varying strengths and textures in each individual and in each similarly situated social group. As racism, sexism, authoritarianism and classism penetrate all of society's institutions and role definitions, so too are they present in our very consciousnesses and personalities. Life options and needs are different depending upon whether one is white or black, male or female, owner, coordinator, or worker, an order-giver an order-taker, or both, and so too are the consciousnesses one holds and the ways they mesh one with each of the rest.

We have described such potential consciousnesses in a sequential, abstract fashion. In fact, there are no such sharp distinctions as those we've made. In the United States, no one is just an oppressor, just oppressed, or just rebellious—and neither is anyone only black, only male, only order-giver, or only worker. To the extent that society's core characteristics effectively dominate, people are primarily oppressor or oppressed in all four categories. The oppressor traits work partly to the advantage but partly also to the detriment of their holders—and similarly the oppressed traits hurt but also partly help their holders. With unchanging status-quo conditions, oppressor/oppressed consciousnesses serve their holders pursuit of very limited fulfillments; but with reference to absolute future possibilities, only rebellious ideologies make any sense. So in general, people are partially oppressor, partially oppressed, and partially rebellious around each of the four characteristics—with the balance of emphasis (and the exact texture of the three aspects) largely governed by the position each person holds with respect to each core characteristic.

For example, many women partially accept male definitions, partially think men are inferior, and partially hate all sexist roles and fight them. Similarly men partially look down upon women, partially fear them, and partially hate their sexist roles and those of women also. Likewise many blacks (and other third world people) carve out an oppressed existence accepting their supposed inferiority, while also harboring anti-white as well as anti-racist feelings. Whites on the other hand, partially find blacks inferior, partially fear their superiority, and partially hate racism in all its forms. In each person the specific traits take different form and also have varying strengths relative to one another. Yet, in the United States, despite all the individual variance social groups do tend to share the broadly identifiable consciousness types we have described.

It is also true that our society's core characteristics don't exist as independently as we have abstractly described them; each takes varying forms across different social groups. For example, sexism is different for women who are black than white, for working women than for coordinator women, etc., and also for married and unmarried women, for mothers and for daughters (for wives and for sisters). Sexism is molded by and molds the phenomena of class, race, and authority, and vice-versa. Each characteristic is but one manifestation of society's *core totality* of defining aspects. The feminist perspective of an independent sexual dialectic is wrong, just as the nationalist view of an independent racial dialectic, the anarchist view of an independent authority dialectic, and the orthodox Marxist view of an independent class dialectic are also wrong. In the United States there are no economic relations without race, sex, and authority characteristics, and similarly no racism without sex, class and authority characteristics, etc. People in this country do not live day-to-day lives in which main determinants of what makes up their values and roles exist in isolation from one another.

We have described a variety of consciousness types but to understand how they interact with one another and change over time, we must also discuss their presence in society's boundary. After developing a feeling for how the core characteristics define the roles of our society's institutions, we will be in a better position to understand the nature of the core totality that governs United States life, and especially the implications of the existence of this core totality for revolutionary potentials.

IS ALL THIS REALLY NECESSARY

In which a skeptic (S) with many orthodox Marxist ideas confronts an adherent of this chapter's totalist analysis (TA). The main question—"is all this really necessary?"—is pursued in a variety of guises. Some confusions are alleviated and some motivations analyzed, but the skeptic remains unconvinced awaiting further evidence and some practical verification.

S: I liked your preliminary description of the four core characteristics, but it all feels too undirected when what we really need is to focus on the key factor, class. Anyone can list descriptive attributes of some oppressions. That's not theory, its eclectic empiricism. Useful, perhaps, for some purposes, but it is not a theory tracing appearances to their roots—roots against which we can then focus our programs.

TA: But this is precisely what we are slowly developing an insight into, i.e., the central "root" of our society's "lifelines". It is true that race, class, sex, and authority are each core characteristics. But this is not at all empiricist. We have a theory of center and boundary, of human interaction, and of core characteristics and historical change, all of which inform our search for what we should "describe and evaluate" in our own society. But to know our society's core characteristics we have to "describe and evaluate" concrete examples. We have to empirically investigate if we are going to determine which factors are at our society's "roots".

S: Perhaps, but you stop at the description stage instead of pushing further to discover which one of the four aspects dominates.

TA: But we've really already been over the so-called problem of our not "finding the key link". You can question what we've pointed to and called the key link, but don't keep denying that the reason we focus on these characteristics is because we see them, in total, as the key factor, root, or core totality.

S: All right then, let's discuss the descriptions themselves. It seems to me that it is perfectly possible to discuss racism in the U.S. as being a result of economic forces—class forces—and so I don't see why you give it a separate position. And for sexism I have the same problem. You even include a little bit about sexism's possible genesis in a division of labor. So again, why not continue viewing it with class eyes? Then we'd have a much simpler, one-central-concept class analysis?

TA: But it's not a more useful analysis. As we've said before, when you try to understand race or sex relations as outgrowths of economic forces, as manifestations of economics—secondary, without a defining impact of their own—you miss much of what is most important about them. Class analysis of racism and sexism hardly ever even defines them, much less analyzes their manifestations in behavior, consciousness, culture, and roles—or how they reproduce themselves even when economic conditions temporarily favor alterations. Such analyses do not properly respect the contributions of women and third world people to social change, nor the deep roots of the oppressions these sectors endure. But this is ground we've already covered, and it will become even more obvious next chapter when we discuss institutional roles. Surely you must see that our view of consciousness formation and structural perpetuation is very different from a simple class interests analysis—we think the increased complexity is necessary to meet activists' needs.

   To the issue of the genesis of racism or sexism, we say what does it really matter?

S: What do you mean, what does it matter? That's ahistorical. Of course knowledge of the genesis is...

TA: Not very important. First we know that economic, kinship, community, and authority relations all exist "outside" concrete human history. That is, we know that they will be present in all human societies simply due to our knowledge of human nature. But the forms these relations will assume, their mix, and whether they are oppressive is all historically contingent. The origin debates focus on these matters. The most frequent question is when did the oppressive characteristics of each of these four types of relations become prevalent and why? But what would be more useful is to investigate how the earliest oppressive forms altered to become those we now endure. In this study we might learn something useful about the current mix and reproductive tendencies of these relations. But with respect to you question about the first oppressive forms, the chances of finding the origins of racism and sexism are slim. Our hypothetical stories about these origins, however, weren't class based at all. We hypothesized racism's birth in tribal warfare and sexism's in the transmutation of biological differences into socio-economic role differences—both across class lines. But assume we were wrong in these guesses. Assume racism as it now exists was born in the slave trade and that its origins were entirely governed by class relations, and assume similarly that sexism was born through class pressures requiring monogomy and governing the form of development of the modern family. In other words, assume that though the existence of community and kinship relations is independent of economic requisites, their first oppressive form was imposed economically. Even were this peculiar hypothesis true, it would only lend general intuitions about what we might expect to find thousands or even only hundreds of years later. It might engender a hunch about the present, but we'd have to check that hunch's validity. In our society, the only way to know about race and sex relations as they are now is to look at them, not at hypotheses about their origins. We have no historical theory so precise that if we knew our society's origins we could logically extrapolate its current condition and future history. The whole notion is absurd...

S: All right, your's is a consistent position, at least for race and sex, and all I question is its accuracy and power. But I'm not sure that you can get off so easy with authoritarianism. That seems different. It has no clear oppressing or oppressed sector nor any obvious focal arena in which it dominates. You've got to admit that its different from the other three?

TA: Yes, it is, precisely in the ways you say. But in the essentials, being a defining aspect, pervading center and boundary, and limiting human potentials, it is similar.

S: But it just seems like an aspect of the others. Why elevate it to a place of centrality in its own right?

TA: In a sense what you say is true. Racism, sexism, and classism all involve an authority relation as a part of their dynamics. In fact, many anarchists use this fact to argue just the reverse of what you're saying, namely, that we should view authority as the key link and the rest as particularist derivatives. But we think that you and they are both wrong. They simply focus on only one side of things; they miss the full complexity of class, race, and sex relations by examining them, if at all, only through an "authority focused" lens. You, on the other hand, by lumping authority relations as a part of the others, miss a core phenomenon which pervades all societal relations on its own account. In fact, its quite obvious that in the military, schools, and police, authority relations have a dominant impact. Even more importantly, this also holds in many bureaucracies and, as we'll discuss later, in certain socialist societies and socialist "visions" authority relations are at the core. Throughout the United States, authority role requirements and consciousnesses are pervasive and sometimes dominating in their effects—and this has tremendous implications for the strategy, issues, and organization of revolution, though we'll have to wait awhile to discuss these matters. And another thing, it's also possible to subsume the four given relations under each of the others besides authority—wrongly, but similarly to how the anarchists do for authority. For instance, community relations between separated sectors with inter and intra group dynamics obviously applies in part to male-female, order giver-order taker, and capitalist-worker divisions, as well as to racial, national, and religious ones. But to use it in this encompassing way all the time just wouldn't be as useful (perhaps straightforward is a better word) as our approach. The full extension of the concept would be encompassing, but most practitioners would not achieve as powerful a result taking only that one track approach to the whole. However, such an extension does become useful, once we have come at the whole from all four aspects, in understanding the mix of the four relations and in seeing how particular forms of activity seemingly unrelated to particular oppressions may in fact reproduce the contours of those oppressions. For example, the activity and consciousness associated with the notion of a vanguard party—we are the revolutionaries; they are the masses—can easily reproduce the underlying dynamics of oppressive community, authority, kinship, and class modes at the same time as it ostensibly confronts them.

S: You've got an argument, all right, but I'm not convinced—maybe, after we discuss institutions more and then strategic implications, there will be more clarity.

But, in this first presentation about four core characteristics, why did you spend so long discussing purely ideological relations? Why did you do the ideological presentation before the more basic institutional one? It seems backward...

TA: Why don't most other analyses spend equally long on discussions of consciousness? That's the real question to ask. We want to understand our society in order to change it. Isn't it obvious that one crucial piece of the whole picture we need to understand, is what do different people feel, think, and know? Actually our discussion was pitifully short. We only discussed a few representative examples in the most cursory way. We hardly even mentioned what needs were operative for the people in various sectors, and that's certainly an important part of what we need to know about our society's center. What are the active needs and how are our consciousnesses linked to them? The immediate task is to begin answering these questions and acting upon our answers.

And to your second point, we presented the discussion of consciousness before a discussion of institutions—the opposite order to what orthodox Marxists would usually do, if they discussed consciousness at all—precisely to make the point that the center is not "less basic" and just a reflection (however rarified) of the boundary. Rather, it has built in dyanamic trends itself and is in a co-causal relation with the boundary. Neither of the two is "prior" or "more basic", and the division between them is only an abstraction, useful for pragmatic purposes.

S: Yes, but then when you do it—when you discuss the examples of consciousness—you make it sound like the racist, and, I guess, the other oppressors by analogy, are innocent, or even sensible, and that the problem is in our heads. There is so little discussion of institutional racism that the whole presentation seems idealist.

TA: There's little said here about institutional racism because, for pragmatic purposes already discussed, we describe the center first, and will get to the boundary next. But your point about the racists has more to it. We don't say at all that racism is good or neutral, but you're right, we do argue that in certain contexts the adoption of racist views is an almost automatic, logical response to one's environment. It's strange, first you complain about our not having enough institutional stuff, then you're upset because we say that a sufficiently obscuring, hostile, coercive environment can inculcate racist views quite effectively. You can't have it both ways, or either way for that matter. As for the idea that something in our heads is a problem, we say definitely yes. Racism in its oppressor and oppressed forms does live in people's consciousnesses, and activists, indeed all people, should see dealing with racism as a priority at the consciousness as well as at the institutional level. And the same goes for sexism, classism, and authoritarianism. A focus at either the institutional level or the consciousness level without the other is self-defeating. And this isn't idealism. It's just recognizing that people's feelings and thoughts are themselves critical factors and not merely simple reflections of economic or other institutional impositions.

S: I don't want to get off this so fast. You make it seem that the oppressed person should fight with him or herself and not with the oppressor...

TA: Both, we should struggle with both. But in a real sense it is probable that the former struggle is the more important one. For when we oppressed overcome our own passive and otherwise self-constricting outmoded habits and consciousnesses, when we come to see the potentials for a new kind of social order and develop a desire and plan to achieve it, then the outcome of our struggle against the oppressors, however long, arduous, and costly it might be, is really a foregone conclusion.

But the two battles are nonetheless clearly entwined. As we struggle with the external institutional and human forces that oppress us, through the lessons of the activity we can also overcome the forces within ourselves. So if our tone suggests that we think the oppressed must wage an internal fight to improve their own consciousnesses, take responsibility and initiative, and learn skills, well that's because we believe that we do need to do these things.

S: Well the other really major problem I have with your presentation is that it is static. There are oppressor, oppressed, and revolutionary viewpoints and we each hold them all. But where do the latter come from and how does the change occur from the first two types to the third?

TA: It's true that we didn't have much to say about this, but we'll take up this matter more in the next and in our last chapter.

S: Well, on balance, it just seems to me that while what you've done is revealing, it is also too mechanical to be very useful for real analysis.

TA: It is certainly too brief and oversimplified, but the alternative is no presentation at all. We think that though it's still quite abstract, our "building block" analysis is useful for 1-the legitimacy it gives to the effort to continue the analysis more deeply, and, 2-because even at this early stage of development, the understanding we have of our society's four core characteristics and their center manifestations is actually going to help us make a number of important strategic assertions. For now, however, perhaps it is just better to get into the problems of society's institutional relations and its various tendencies toward evolutionary and revolutionary change.

FOOTNOTES: CHAPTER FIVE

1. In Studs Terkel's book, *Working,* (Pantheon Books, New York, N.Y.) there is a very revealing interview with a black policeman, Renault Robinson, giving evidence both about the police and the nature of racism in our country. But at the same time, it is indicative of the extent of further study required that there is so relatively little research and analytic material on the structure of police departments in the United States.

2. There are a number of studies of the U.S. medical establishment, for example, the "Health Pac" study, *The American Health Empire,* published by Vintage Books, New York, N.Y. and prepared by Barbara and John Ehrenreich.

3. For a powerful analysis of the U.S. school system, see *Schooling in Capitalist America,* by Sam Bowles and Herb Gintis, Basic Books, New York, 1976.

4. This is a minimal statement. We are as yet undecided on the centrality of age in the U.S. and other analysts may well determine other additions to our list.

5. There are a number of works on racism referenced in our bibliography but we would like to draw special attention to four here: *Wretched of the Earth,* Franz Fanon, Grove Press, New York, N.Y.; *Reluctant Reformers,* Robert Allen, Doubleday, New York, N.Y.; *The Colonizer and the Colonized,* Albert Memmi, Beacon Press, Boston, Mass.; *Racism and the Class Struggle,* James Boggs, Monthly Review Press, New York, N.Y.; and the pamphlet "Black Worker, White Worker", Noel Ignatin, distributed by the New England Free Press, Somerville, Mass.

6. For powerful personal descriptions of the nature and impact of racism, see: *The Autobiography of Malcolm X,* Malcolm X and Alex Haley, Grove Press, New York, N.Y. and *Soledad Brother,* George Jackson, Random House, New York, N.Y.

7. See *Toward an Anthropology of Women, Rayna Reiter,* Monthly Review Press, New York, New York, 1975.

8. See for example, *Women's Estate,* Juliet Mitchell, Vintage Books, New York, *The Second Sex,* Simone deBeauvoir, Bantam Books, New York, *Sisterhood Is Powerful,* Robin Morgan, ed. Random House, New York, and *The Dialectics of Sex,* Shulamith Firestone, William Morrow, New York.

9. For a complex discussion of the psychological side of patriarchy, see *Psychoanalysis and Feminism*, Juliet Mitchell, Vintage Books, New York, N.Y. 1976.

10. See the literature, for example, of the organization "Women Against Crimes Against Women".

11. For a fuller introduction to the use of kinship categories as well as a powerful critique of Marxism as patriarchal, see *The Curious Courtship of Women's Liberation and Socialism*, Batya Weinbaum, South End Press, Boston, 1978.

12. And this is precisely what is desired by the networks and the commodity dealers—it is what leads to continuous buying without "satiation" of needs.

13. For discussions in more detail see, *What Is Communist Anarchism*, Alexander Berkman, Dover Books, New York, N.Y. and *Anarchism*, Daniel Guerin, Monthly Review Press, New York, N.Y.

14. See *Anarchism*, Daniel Guerin, Monthly Review Press, 1970.

15. For a full discussion the reader should see Stanley Milgram, *Obediance to Authority*, New York, Tavistock, 1974.

16. The relative paucity of discussion of consciousness of classes or any other social groups in other "socialist analyses" is perhaps due to the fact that once one includes this sort of material the door is immediately open to hypothesizing the existence of important social groups other than traditional classes. Most orthodox Marxists simply label all such intellectual endeavors sociological or bourgeois and dismiss them as trying to hide class relations so as to mystify workers. Of course, in our view, it is the orthodox Marxists themselves who have forsaken objective analysis.

17. Most often we will oversimplify and refer only to blacks and racism against blacks. This is merely a convenience which does no harm at the high level of abstraction which we are following—however, for all deeper investigations it is very important to realize that while racism against blacks might well be most dominant of all racisms in the U.S., it is not the only prevalent form at all, and all must be studied on their own, to determine their own particular attributes, and so they might all be opposed by the most effective means.

18. A particularly relevant work on this point is the forthcoming book, *Science and Liberation*, a work of three members of the organization Science for the People, forthcoming from South End Press, Boston.

19. See Noel Ignatin, op. cit.

20. Stanley Milgram, op. cit.

21. It is impossible to overestimate the importance of this change in perspective. When a person changes from seeing an oppressive world as just, to finding it repulsive, the alteration is complete. It is as if one was blind to half of reality and then suddenly able to see all of it again. Such a change can obviously be a shock both to the person undergoing it, and also to those who know her.

22. Actually this was not really accurate. The relations were more complex, though we chose to ignore the extra complexities. Thus there are many races and ethnic groups, not just white people and non-white people; and rather than there being only men and women, there are people who are heterosexual and homosexual, married and single, daughters, mothers, brothers, fathers, husbands, wives, and grandparents. All of these categories represent increasing levels of complexity in the two-pole descriptions we oversimplistically gave.

23. For the archetype presentation see Milton Friedman, *Capitalism and Freedom,* University of Chicago, 1962.

24. Leo Welch quoted in *The Sick Society,* Michael Tanzer, Holt, Rhinehart, and Winston, New York, 1969. Page 78.

25. Bakunin, *The Knouto Germanic Empire,* quoted in Paul Berman, *Quotations from the Anarchists,* Praeger Publishers, New York.

26. Michael Tanzer, op. cit.

27. Perhaps the most complete introduction to capitalist political economy for those just beginning to investigate the area is *The Capitalist System,* edited by Edwards, Reich, and Weiskopf, Prentice Hall, New York, 1977.

28. Karl Marx, *The Early Writings,* tranlated T. Bottomore, London. 1963. Page 363.

29. We're describing a specific example of the general mechanism generating "conformity" between role dictates and human attitudes and actions. A view similar to ours is expressed in Maurice Brinton, *The Irrational In Politics,* Black Rose Books, Montreal, Canada, p. 43-44:

> It would be wrong to believe that working people fail to revolt because they lack information about the mechanisms of economic exploitation. In fact revolutionary propaganda which seeks to explain to the masses the social injustice and irrationality of the economic system falls on deaf ears. Those who get up at five in the morning to work in a factory, and have on top of it to spend two hours of every day on underground or suburban trains have to adapt to these conditions by eliminating from their mind anything that might put such conditions in question again. If they realized that they were wasting their lives in the service of an absurd system they would either go mad or commit suicide. To avoid achieving such anxiety-laden insight they justify their existence by rationalizing it. They repress anything that might disturb them and acquire a character structure adapted to the conditions under which they must live. Hence it follows that the idealistic tactic consisting of explaining to people that they are oppressed is useless, as people have had to suppress the perception of oppression in order to live with it. Revolutionary propagandists often claim they are trying to raise people's consciousness. Experience shows that their endeavors are seldom successful. Why? Because such endeavors come up against all the unconscious defense mechanisms and against all the various rationalizations that people have built up in order not to become aware of the exploitation and of the void in their lives.
>
> This somber image has far more truth to it than most revolutionaries can comfortably admit. But in the last analysis it is inadequate. It is inadequate because it implies totally maleable individuals, in whom total sexual repression has produced the prerequisites for total conditioning and therefore for total acceptance of the dominant ideology. The image is inadequate because it is undialectical. It does not encompass the possibility that attitudes might change....

30. Herbert Marcuse, An Essay On Liberation, Penguin, London. Page 23.

31. Ibid.

32. See Noam Chomsky, *For Reasons of State*, Pantheon, 1970.

33. It is worth noting here that we make no equation between what we have called rebellious consciousness and revolutionary consciousness. The one is certainly a step toward the other, but further steps are required as well.

34. Our approach is similar to that of Barbara and John Ehrenreich in their paper, "The Professional and Managerial Class", included in *Between Labor and Capital*, edited by Pat Walker, South End Press.

35. See Steve Marglin, "What Do Bosses Do", URPE, Vol. 6, No. 2, and Harry Braverman, *Labor and Monopoly Capital*, Monthly Review, New York, 1976.

36. See Sam Bowles and Herb Gintis, *Schooling in Capitalist America*, Basic Books, New York, 1976.

37. See the forthcoming book by Sandy Carter, *Understanding Mental Illness, A Marxist Approach*.

38. Ehrenreichs, op. cit.

39. For relevant discussions see Studs Terkel, *Working*, Avon, New York, 1972, and Sennet and Cobb, The Hidden Injuries of Class, Vintage, New York, 1972.

40. Ehrenreichs, op. cit.

41. Ibid.

42. Ibid. See also Anton Pannekoek, *Workers Councils*, Root and Branch, Detroit.

43. See Ehrenreich, op. cit. and also the writings of Antonio Gramsci as referenced in our bibliography.

CHAPTER SIX
UNITED STATES
THE INSTITUTIONAL BOUNDARY

I wander thro' each charter'd street,
Near where the charter'd Thames does flow,
And mark in every face I meet,
Marks of weakness, marks of woe.

William Blake
"London"

Having discussed our society's core characteristics as they appear at the center, we must now address the problems of society's boundary, of social change, and of lessons for revolutionaries. This admittedly cursory first attempt to apply our concepts is meant more to demonstrate their worth and to suggest various possibilities than to make any final statement about how our society operates. Full final statements will have to be made by movements which understand through their practice the details of our society's daily operations. Our purpose here is to provide methods that socialist movements might find useful, and partial analyses that can help such movements pursue their own studies and political activities.

CORE CHARACTERISTICS IN SOCIETY'S BOUNDARY

By the boundary we mean the institutional roles we are to fill if we are to be granted society's benefits. At least most of the time there is a general conformity between center and boundary. Each contributes to the evolutionary development of the other. The boundary roles require consciousnesses which become part of society's center. They meet or impede needs whose oppressions or fulfillment also becomes a feature of society's center. But the center also affects the boundary. As institutional roles vary they must still remain in accord with prevalent, self-reproducing consciousnesses.

To discuss the thousands of institutions and millions of roles that make up society's boundary is impossible. In this section we describe three example institutions and demonstrate some of the primary ways our society's four core characteristics are manifested in each. The example institutions are chosen for their relative simplicity. Our discussion of these is only a first unfinished step. Our extrapolation to more general statements about society's whole boundary is an argument in support of a hypothesis. More work is obviously required. Hopefully, we have given some useful road signs for these coming tasks.

SPORTS AND SPORTS TEAMS

How do race, sex, class, and authority aspects manifest themselves in the sports institutions of our society? Why, first of all, are football, baseball, and basketball our society's "big three status sports"? Why not swimming? tennis? or the biggest spectator sport of all, stock car racing? As they are currently played, these three sports cater to certain men's muscle formations and are therefore most easily kept "sacred to men". They are fiercely competitive, they are aggressive, and they emphasize size and strength attributes which are at least historically more prevalent among men.[1] Men dominate these "macho" sports, and, as a result, in our patriarchal society the sports themselves also become dominant.

Why do the rich play tennis and the poor run track or shoot baskets? Why do blacks dominate some sports and hardly make a presence in others? Why do workers bowl and bosses golf? Certainly in each case the accessibility of resources and their costs are a factor (this is itself core defined), but it is also a matter of general societal divisions manifested in the very definition of who will play which sports. Gym teachers and their students have prior expectations about what men and women, blacks and whites will be into—and these expectations are usually borne out because the sports themselves are structured along different cultural, race, sex, and class lines.

Each sport requires its own "mind set" as well as physical attributes and skills, and this often caters to the prior experiences of a particular group. Thus pro football requires one kind of mentality; sandlot softball for fun another, and gymnastics a third. Swimming has one culture; basketball another, and bowling is in another place entirely. The evolving definition of how our games are played (and viewed) largely conforms with the dictates of society's core characteristics. Sports and the rest of society must generally mesh; otherwise athletes wouldn't get along in daily life, sports fans would develop attitudes inconsistent with the rest of their life roles, and little leagues wouldn't produce "good citizens".

A society could have sports which promoted collective growth; emphasized excellence but not winning; promoted anti-violence; enhanced health and physical development; treated all people equally; and fostered collective self-reliance and sharing, rather than consumerism and competing—but, this could only occur if the rest of society had similar dynamics.

Why don't good basketball players get pleasure out of passing so as to enhance the play of less-skilled teammates? Why do volleyball players get more thrill out of a fairly good spike which scores a winning point than out of an excellent one which is returned, or an excellent set-up which is never converted? It is because certain behaviors are consistent with society's core role definitions and others aren't. Certain behaviors are expected and understood, while others are statistically strange and treated as abnormal. In our society nice folks do finish last and athletic roles are structured accordingly.

At all levels, athletics also involve economic considerations. At the professional extreme, who gets paid what? On average, the white male gets the most (especially as the owner), women the least, and when blacks do all right, it's racially alibied on grounds that "they are only good at that." The athletes are workers and commodities at once. They are bought and sold, traded and put on display. They have little freedom, and in all but the big leagues, little money also. The owners are capitalists; the managers are hired foremen. The profession is a business like any other. Pursue profit, compete, obey orders, reproduce divisions, don't rock the boat, and do what you're expected to—these are the watchwords.

At the amateur level, the situation is similar. Distribution of funding is skewed away from women. College sports are big business, and at the lower levels everything is aimed to conform to later "big-time" requirements. The little league is just that, a little big league with similarly constricting role definitions. Sure it's an attempt at a humane kind of fun—but the product, the elitism, competition, parental psychoses, wrecked pitching arms, frustrated "losers", triumphant "winners", and girls on the outside cheering all conform to big-time standards. They are only explicable via an analysis of the alienated role definitions built into the endeavors.

Each sport in our society is hierarchically structured: capitalist owners, coordinator bosses, experts/authorities, superstar elites, whites, men, blacks, women, some positions better than others.... On each team players have expectations to meet. Proper fealty must be shown the owners and coaches. "Cut your hair!" "Yes, boss." The superstars must get their say. Even in little leagues the better pitchers strut; they get the after game congratulations. They stand at the head of the line and begin to feel like they belong there. Certain jobs are for certain people. The thinking, play-calling quarterback and middle linebacker will be white; the bulky guard or fleet halfback may be black. Men will be macho (or at least nearly so) and generally sexist. This is expected. Other behavior is deemed strange. Friendships, being one of the boys, and image all depend upon meeting sexist role expectations. Toughness is mandatory or at least one must accept it in others. Though whites and blacks may get along, there are limits. There are expected mannerisms for each race. There are bounds on friendships. Blacks should/will dress and talk one way; whites another. Blacks get one kind of treatment from the press; whites another. The ghetto uptown division reappears, in disguise to be sure, but even in the locker room. Who will be manager and whose "brother" will sweep up after the game? Further, no one will express opinions counter to accepted core characteristic norms, or having done so, he or she will be canned, or if too good for that, ostracized. "Don't like steroids—don't come back." "Don't like capitalism—man, you're crazy." These pressures, and the general expectations all along the line, do their job. Athletes are "homogenized" to fill predefined slots. In this they are like us all, even if, like us, they too are well-motivated, function rationally, and often construct (as) humane (as possible) niches for themselves.

In college, on the way to the big-time, there is the meat line, profit-motivated, scholarship/jock course load, NCAA championship process, getting the vast majority of aspiring athletes no professional career and most often no education or degree either. Here too, there is the jock syndrome, the macho, and the roles which must be fulfilled if one is to succeed. Not to care about the opponent, not to care about oneself, care only about the coach, care only about winning, "cheer" the cheerleaders. Teams are half families with fathers, little boys, and sex objects doing the cheering. They are laced with race division and authoritarian "professionalism/superstarism". They are all aimed to make a buck. The women who do play, have to conform as well—they must almost become men—and to do so, in a society like ours is even a real, if severely constrained accomplishment.

And for the seven year olds it's all much the same. Play to win. Succeed or go home crying. The girls are immediately tracked into a very few allowable slots (swimming, gymnastics, maybe tennis, or cheering—all in "skimpy uniforms") or out entirely. The capitalist/coordinator offspring get the tennis lessons. The working class white men play the big sports, mimicing who they will, with whatever equipment they can muster. Blacks struggle to become great to make it out of one ghetto, and, unexpectedly into another.

And not surprisingly adult participation sports are mostly for those who have excess time and are almost all individualist/dualist: not volleyball, but tennis; not softball but biking or jogging. They require the greatest possible amounts of "up-to-date" equipment and the least human solidarity. For the rest of us, watch the tube—it fits our degree of exhaustion from work better anyway.

And for the "kids", there are skateboards, with hundreds of brand names, a consumer ethos not unlike that around car or stereo buying, and sexist fan magazines as well. Or even worse, there are plug-in T.V. wargames replete with battle sounds and images of destroyed "lifelike" targets. And yet, people persist because there is simply no other game in town—at least none that "fits". For the kids, where else could they develop some room of their own, some personal culture? What other little league is there? Where else is one to play? And isn't it the same for adults: Play the "accepted way", watch, or do nothing. There is no escaping the role requirements imposed by our society's core characteristics.

We face a boundary of institutions—role offerings and expectations—and to get along in society we must make do someplace within its options. In school or on the street, amatuer or professional—in order to belong and to succeed, an athlete must at least reasonably fulfill the expectations of some athletic arena. The person who does this is still a person, not a robot in a slot, not totally mutilated—but the effects are still real and oppressive. As with working in a factory, or being a parent, or even being a cop, while we come to fit, we also seek to retain integrity, and we often also harbor some notion of what's wrong and some rebellion.

Lombardi as patriarchal boss, the team leader as big brother, the black as jester, whites calling the tune, sexual joking, competition to win, for status, for salaries, and for the patriarch's respect, individualism, superstar elitism, women as supporters or in swim suits...it's only the surface of United States sports roles, but it should give evidence of some of the ways all four core characteristics make themselves centrally felt. From childhood through the pros, to understand sport in general, a particular game, a team, or a particular slot on a team, we say that you have to understand the ways race, sex, class, and authority expectations all define the associated roles. They are all core. They all mold expectations and define the bonds and contradictions between athletes. We can't do such a full analysis here, indeed, only the athletes and other participants themselves are in a position to discern how much and how subtly they are cast as fathers, brothers, lovers, and sons, mothers, wives, sisters, daughters, and girl-friends, honkies, niggers, order-takers, workers, and consumers, by the requisites of the athletic roles they seek to fill. But it should be clear that the game is not the same, depending upon whether one is a man or a woman, white or of color, coordinator or worker, or more or less skillful.

LAW AND A CERTAIN KIND OF ORDER

Perhaps most obviously, our police forces are authoritarian. The whole premise of "law and order" is unquestioning obedience. Internally the police are organized into a very extreme hierarchy. Externally their position is one of power over the people. Their very costumes are designed with the idea of furthering an order-giving, order-taking outlook. The motive of all this authoritarianism is not, however, efficiency in the service of "blind justice". Rather, the efficiency is of a type specifically conceived to serve a very skewed value system—a value system which self-managing people would quickly reject.

As the laws are class biased, so are the roles of the law enforcers. The main police priority is to protect private property. The great bulk of all crimes are crimes against property—theft. No one who robs a bank and gets caught does less than twenty years. Crimes against people are not so severely nor consistently punished. What would happen, for example, if there was a riot on Fifth Avenue in New York amidst the big stores, instead of up in Harlem amidst the black people?

Criminal activities that prey upon the poor—rackets, the numbers, drug pushing, and street mugging—are at best only weakly opposed, and are often even supported by the police themselves. Indeed, it was only when drug pushing found its way into wealthy suburban neighborhoods that the police began to seriously consider dealing with it. In the ghettos and downtown generally, the drug racket was not only too profitable to interfere with, but its effects, dulling out people who might otherwise have the energy and solidarity to complain about their situations, were also too welcome.[2]

There's a strike. The police don't carefully evaluate the merits of the workers' grievances. They follow their orders. They intervene to protect the owner's property and his "freedom" to pursue a profitable livelihood.

If cops were supposed to ask about every assignment "is this really serving justice the best way possible?," in time they would likely develop some rebellious notions.[3] Better that they just obey their "more intelligent", "better informed", superiors.

The police act according to racist role expectations as the courts deliver racist verdicts. A robbery occurs in a small college town—the police scan the local school's black student photos for likely suspects. This behavior is role-enforced. It is standard operating procedure. It occurs if there is the slightest evidence a black person might have been involved. A miscarriage arrest often results. The black victim is usually too poor to fight back properly. He or she will often wind up wrongly in jail. In many cities, the form this takes is a kind of random prosecution and even police sanctioned murder. Crimes are committed, "undesireable blacks" are rounded up, framed, and put away. It happens all the time. And even when the person caught is the perpetrator, where is the justice in first structuring society to trample the black underfoot, and then second, prosecuting her or him for lashing back, or out, or wherever?

Police are more afraid in black neighborhoods—with reason—but the result is a perpetual fostering of racist attitudes, and teenagers shot dead for petty thefts.

Sexism has its effects also. A call comes in about a loud ruckus in a private home. The police go investigate. It appears to be a fight between husband and wife. She asks for help. He asserts that it is just a family quarrel and tells the cops to leave. They go. Another wife beater is served by the sexist role expectations pervasive to police law enforcement.

A woman comes into the station to report a rape. The derogatory looks begin immediately, then the third-degree. It's assumed that the woman is promiscuous or otherwise at fault. She is guilty until proven innocent, and only at that point do the police start thinking about the rapist's possible guilt. And on the other side, there are the prostitutes, women denied skills and a means to income, who decide to sell themselves. They are victimized first by having to do it (though it's only a logical extension of what all women must do), then by their tricks, the Johns, and finally the police—who on the one hand employ their services, and on the other regularly bust them.

But the influence of class, race, and sex on the police is like that of authority. It molds not only the cops' relations with the public, us, but also the character of the job itself and of the roles cops must fulfill within the force.

Cops are in fact workers. In smaller towns it often appears to be a relatively high status service job with considerable security. In the cities also, some come to it with this expectation; however, for many others it is just the easiest route to power or even worse, a sanctioned way to be sadistic. In any case, the jobs are very much defined by class relations. Wages, work hours, supervision, and over-time requirements are all very much like they are in factories. Similarly, racism also exerts a defining influence. It governs the number of blacks hired, their slower and more limited advancement, their placement and assignments, their social treatment at the station-house, on the road and off-duty, and the general expectations they must fulfill and attitudes they encounter concerning culture, community involvement, interests, dress, and general life concerns. Similarly, women police have very constrained duties. Often they are glorified secretaries. Sometimes they'll investigate "female" crimes; often they'll be sexual decoys. Always they are "father-lover looked after" by their male comrades, and likewise expected to lend a "motherly" ear or warm body in times of need. Their pay, numbers, and advancement are also moderated by sexism.

Within the force, and between the police and the people, race, sex, class, and authority relations all help determine the role expectations people "must" fulfill. For the cops, the white boy is different from the girl, is different from the black boy, is different from the bourgeois child or gentlemen. Cops are father figures, bosses, white honkies, and Uncle Toms because their roles require it. Moreover the police force exists in context of the legal system and the distribution of wealth, power, knowledge, and lifestyles of the whole outer society. It must conform with these, and it does. Cops, and we when confronted by cops, are like everyone else in society—just people trying to get by in context of very constraining, often oppressing or oppression inducing roles. Some of us come to fit our "slots" all too well, often even going beyond what they demand of us. Others struggle to retain some self-respect and sense of human feeling and fight against their role requirements. But the deck is quite effectively stacked, and whatever the outcome for the single individual, the result for the force as a whole is predetermined—race, sex, class, and authority requirements dominate human concerns.

THE UNIVERSITY

Universities are corporate administered and controlled, and usually corporate owned. In fact, universities are most easily differentiated by purposes in serving corporate interests—delivering executives, professionals, scientists, technicians, high level workers, and low level workers, or new research, new sales methods, new product designs, new workplace technologies, new weapons systems, etc.—and structured in accord. More resources, better student teacher ratios, nicer everything go to Columbia; a lot less of the same for Boston University; and at the extreme classrooms in curtain partitioned gymnasiums for some two year colleges (the better to prepare students for the din of industrial work).

Within each college, there is a similar class-governed division of resources according to the job slots students will fill on the outside or to sources of research funds. Thus the department doing research that can be used for military purposes is likely to be well funded; the one proposing new means of teaching reading which promote the formerly illiterate person's sense of self-worth are less well funded. The department training future corporate leaders must have resources that accustom students to the autonomy they will have and the high culture they must exhibit. The vocational departments need not be so well-fixed. They need only prepare us to endure the boredom of capitalist work and no more.

Schools seek to educate up to societal requirements. Curricula must accord with the dictates of the job slots people are going to fill on the outside. A state university must not graduate people who expect more autonomy in their work than they are likely to have. The modern university is a people factory, a conduit between high school and adulthood, which insures that we fit wherever it is that we are "destined" to wind up. We arrive in one school or another because of who we are— what color, what sex, what class—what learned skills—and we go out the other side changed only as much as necessary. Since the slots we're aimed at are class-, race-, sex-, and authority-defined, it's no surprise that our education is also.[4]

The Univeristy's admission standards are race-, sex-, and class-biased as well. In the first place, all prior education has been doled out unequally to third world people, women, and workers; in the second, there are expectations about who can "cut it" and who can't, expectations which are largely valid because the language, culture, and style of university life all militate against women, third world people, and working class people.

The university is also like a factory in its employee hierarchy. Coordinate class people rise in academic departments; capitalists administer and own. Working class people, third world people, and women are sometimes low-level teachers but more often custodians and secretaries.

The social relations of university life are sexist, racist, classist, and academically authoritarian. Women's roles are highly circumscribed. Blacks and whites have different cultures, hang-outs, and styles. Curricula deny black and women's history. The working class exists for purposes of study only—by sociologists or even more frequently by managerial students. Authoritarian professionalism pervades the departments. The professor is a kind of patriarch and cop at once. Grades are like wages. Men define women and academic norms as well. The school functions "in loco parentis", and its faculty and administrative staff are accordingly structured to socialize, nurture, and discipline the student "children".

Collective work is minimal because it's perceived as "cheating." Theses on how to make a revolution are not on anyone's mind—the pedagogy and environment prevent the thought even arising. The Pentagon Papers, the closest thing to a written record we have of U.S. government policy making, goes unread in political science and government departments throughout the country. Dressing up and acting sexy is mandatory because how else do you get dates? The varsity blacks spend more time at sports then studying because how else are they to keep their scholarships? The custodians, cooks, secretaries, and other workers are denied equal access to knowledge. To expect and fit their condition they must be excluded from academic participation. Why should professors clean up after themselves sometimes, so that others might be free to study?

The grade, promotion, or financial grant is the external incentive monitoring all activity. Like in the factory, the activity at hand is not an end in itself.

The university's purpose, structure, pedagogy, and daily activities; the administrator's tasks and those of the faculty and other employees; the students, who they are, what they are doing, where they will go; the school's cultural life, its social life, its ethics; all these are determined simultaneously by class, race, sex, and authority requirements.

As but a first step to really understanding a university, all the sectors of people within it would have to look and see how the roles they fill are defined by all four core characteristics. To just do a class analysis and then tack on that blacks, Chicanos, and women get an even worse thrashing is insufficient. It's necessary to see how the university's roles embody sexual, racial, and authoritarian (as well as class) expectations. The former are not simply a peripheral product of the latter, nor are they felt that way. The black person experiences the university (whether as student, faculty person, or maintenance worker) differently than the white, and similarly the woman differently than the man, the worker differently than the coordinator differently than the capitalist, and finally the elite scholar differently than the average student. Even the white, male, ruling-class offspring, ruler-to-be, pre-law student experiences school differently because of its four core characteristics than he would just due to class factors, and never as simply an intellectual growing experience.

SUMMARY

The dynamics of being a part of a university, a police force, or an athletic team are alike in being largely determined by core characteristic requirements. The experiences are incomprehensible unless we realize that in the United States there are four such characteristics, and account for the effects of each. And this is just as true for all other U.S. institutions. Racism, sexism, classism, and authoritarianism are all institutionalized. Doing just a class analysis is enlightening but insufficient, and similarly for studying society from any other particularistic orientation.

Once we get out of old habits of thought this much is pretty obvious. It is why women and third world people generally feel slighted by orthodox Marxist analyses. It is why anarchists have little patience with Leninists and it is why Marxists themselves get so exasperated with feminists, nationalists, and anarchists alike.

Members of each persuasion focus on a single particular core characteristic and feel slighted or worse whenever someone comes along and contests that characteristic's centrality. Each activist thinks the others rather foolish, but, in fact, they all have a grasp on part of the truth. All four aspects are actively core in our society. It needn't have been so but it historically is. The pressing task is to do full analyses of our institutions and consciousnesses uncovering the impact of all four aspects. But going beyond the very general kind of treatment we've given here will require considerable work by all kinds of people. A necessary preliminary step, however, is to first get some understanding of the mix of our society's core characteristics. How do they interrelate, which are active, and how do they determine our society's core totality and reactionary hegemony?

THE MIX OF CORE CHARACTERISTICS

How do the four core characteristics of our society interact? There are two extreme possibilities with countless variations in between:

1. Each of the core characteristics operates essentially separately from the others, dominately in some societal arenas and only peripherally in others. The mesh of society's core characteristics is only an accommodation of each to the other three. Class might govern the economy, sex the family, race the geographic interface between blacks and whites and their cultures, and authority might govern the state apparatus. In the factories, for instance, the mix would simply be an accommodation wherein women, third world people, and order-takers would get the lowest *class-defined* positions. That is, class requisites would not contradict the role dictates of other core characteristics, but would encompass them, for example, putting women and blacks in the lowest *class-defined* factory roles. In the family, similarly, sex determined roles wouldn't contradict class, race, or authority relations, and similarly these aspects would not generally interfere with the reproduction of patriarchal relations. But family roles would remain only *sex defined*. Ghetto culture would be consistent with class requirements and would not place women above men, but race would remain the *sole defining* feature. In effect, the core characteristics would exist in a kind of parallel, mutual accommodation. At times there would be friction and one would interfere with another, but such disjunctures would be the exception and only temporary (though also very important for activists).

2. The core characteristics neither exist nor operate in isolation from one another. The manifestations of each reproduce and also help to determine the manifestations of the others. Rather than simple accommodation, there is "entwinement". All four core characteristics are always operative, each not only consistently with the other three, but also *reproducing* them. In different arenas different characteristics may play greater or lesser roles, but in all cases the whole situation is always defined by the entwined impact of all four. Different sectors of people may experience one core characteristic more intensely than the other three, but in all cases everyone's life experience is actually governed by the defining impact of all four aspects.

In our theoretical discussion we went to great pains to argue that history is very fluid so that if a certain situation usually predominates, others may come into prominance as well. The first task in understanding any society is to uncover the generally operative norms, and only then the common divergences including their frequency and importance.

To begin discovering whether the generally prevailing mix in the United States is parallel or entwined or something in between is actually not as difficult as it might at first appear. By answering three particular questions we can develop a fairly powerful argument for one option over the others. "Proof", however, is another story and will finally require much more research, argument, and practical evidence than we can muster here. In any case our three questions are:

1. Are each of the core characteristics more operational in one arena than in others?
2. If yes, are they only peripheral outside their key arena? That is, are they only of secondary importance, or do they have a defining impact? If the former then they likely only exist in parallel.
3. But if the latter, then is their presence in each arena independent or entwined? Do they move separately, pushing and pulling one another, or are they part of a whole? Do they help to reproduce one another's contours? If no, they move "merely" in parallel, but if yes, then we can reasonably assert that the society's core characteristics are entwined.

DEGREES OF IMPACT

Though it can be misleading, it is not unreasonable to tentatively identify each core characteristic with its own "key arena". Here the core characteristic has its roots. Here it is felt most strongly and clearly relative to the other three characteristics. Thus we identify class with the economy, race with the nation or ghetto, sex with the family, and authority with the state. Everyone makes this demarcation and it seems to help analysis considerably. For example, to understand class roles we look first to the factory, and for sex roles first to the family.

However, it is regretably also true that this route of analysis closes our eyes to the true pervasiveness of each characteristic. Indeed, it fosters the illusion that it is wise not only to analyze each separately from the rest, but also to seek to determine which of the four is most fundamental. Still we must admit that the commen sense division of characteristics according to arenas of greater or lesser consciously felt impact is basically accurate.

The roles of worker, coordinator, and owner are most obvious in the factory; mother, father, brother, sister, in the family; white and third world in communities; and ruler and ruled in the state. But do these roles really exist in their "pure" form, abstracted one from each other as we tend to describe them when looking at each arena in turn and separately? This is the "parallel hypothesis" that seems to flow directly from the logic of the points made thus far.

IS THERE A PERIPHERY?

However, this hypothesis is wrong. Although class, for example, is most clearly felt in the economy, the other core characteristics are not peripheral there. They also *define factory roles*; they do not merely appear in an accommodating manner. In the factory, men and women, blacks and whites, skilled and unskilled not only appear in different class-defined slots, but they also have different race-, sex-, and authority-defined expectations to meet. Though class is more apparently operative, the rest are not peripheral. They also define the character of factory life: how people relate to one another and to their jobs, what people do and expect others to do, what people think and how they feel.

In the family class, race, and authority help mold the quality and character of daily relations, not merely secondarily, but in the very definition of the roles people must fill. The family's income is class governed, but even more, as there are "father" and "mother" expectations in the factory, so there are classlike role expectations for fathers and mothers within each family. Production (and consumption) occurs in the family and different members play different roles in that activity. The father is owner-boss, the mother a worker, and the children even lower workers. Dispensation of wealth in the family is class as well as sex defined. The ghetto experience is not simply color versus white with accommodation for the other experiences. The ghetto family, for example, has a different experience, a different internal role structure, and different relations to the outside world for being black, or Chicano, or Asian, and similarly roles in the ghetto are sex, class, and authority defined as well as they are obviously race defined. In each societal arena, while the presence of one particular core characteristic might be most obvious, actually all four are present and defining. This was also the lesson of our analysis of economic roles in chapter four. The issue now becomes—how do these four characteristics interrelate?

PARALLEL OR CO-REPRODUCING?

Each of the four characteristics could be defining in all arenas and yet still only exist in parallel with the other three. In fact many socialist feminists claim this to be the case for patriarchal and class characteristics. Each defines, they accommodate to one another most often, but they are finally separate. We disagree.

We find that the norm for the core characteristic mix in our country is what we've called entwinement. By this we mean that each of the four:

1. exists only in relation to and in interaction with the other three, and
2. helps to reproduce the other three, so that
3. in fact we always feel the impact of all four as an entwined totality, however much (depending upon what sector and arena we are in) one or another part of the whole may have a greater importance to our own particular situation.

Class reproduces race, sex, and authority relations. In the factory these latter are not simply present, nor even only partially defining; but they are also reproduced. The dictates of pursuing profit help to enforce the perpetuation of racist, sexist, and authoritarian behavior. It is more profitable to take advantage of racism in hiring practices. Women can also be paid less, and moreover they can be given women's work at sharply more exploitative wages. To maintain profitable conditions it is also necessary to enforce a strict authoritarian hierarchy. Over time, these relations do not remain separately operative. As class dictates reproduce the others, so race, sex, and authority divisions help in the reproduction of class relations. Economic roles become simultaneously defined by the interacting impact of all four attributes acting as a whole.

The economy seen as purely class defined, *does not exist*. There is no factory without institutional and ideological sex, race, and authority relations. And, as we saw in chapter four, the same holds for the market and distribution arena. Class concepts alone are insufficient tools for economic analysis.

In the family, sex dynamics enforce the reproduction of class, race, and authority relations. The dynamics of early socialization, besides teaching sex-skewed personality, also inculcate authoritarian and passive habits. Racial attitudes are passed on both by mimicry of parents to gain favor, and by the very fact that families are like little competing nations with alliances that seldom cross race lines. Class expectations are taught through family concerns about income as well as by the fact that the family's material well-being is largely governed by the class (and race) affiliations of the parents.

Race and sex divisions provide a cheap work force and a reserve army of ready laborers. Fears of intermarriage and racial stereotypes generally enforce sexist beliefs and vice versa. Men "protect their women"; fear for their own masculinity; and guard their own children from the "others". Women feel a responsibility to hold families together in face of racial and class oppressions.

Authority in a sense links the three other characteristics. The abstract form of "one above another" pervades all four. Accepting its validity in any one form tends to enforce its legitimacy in the other three as well. Passive in the face of authority—then why not passive in the face of men, whites, or a boss? Comandeering with respect to those considered "less worthy"—then racist toward Chicanos, patriarchal toward women, and classist to workers.

The four core characteristics are ideologically and institutionally entwined.

First, all four are always defining—none is merely peripherally accommodating. How blacks feel racism depends upon their class. How women feel sexism depends on their race. How people exert authority depends upon their sex. What our lives are like is multiply determined. The slots we fill are multiply defined. At any point in time or while functioning in any particular institutional setting, one or another aspect may occupy our attentions more fully—a person may sometimes identify more as worker, or as woman, or black, or simply as "pushed around"— but actually our situation is always centrally defined by all four aspects.

Second, the four are institutionally linked. The role dictates associated with each actually reproduce those of the others. What the white worker must do to fulfill class requirements gives him interests in racism and sexism in his workplace and union, as well as in the society at large. "I've got a job, let the unemployed and welfare recipients get one too—and till then let them suffer. They're all black, so who cares?" "Keep the woman at the woman's work, so I'll keep my job for myself. When I get home from supporting the family, I need a ready meal, my kids need a dutiful mother." Similarly the family need for children to meet parental expectations inculcates passivity and reproduces not only parental sexual consciousness but also their race and class attitudes. The responsibility to keep the family together pushes hard on the worker to get ahead and especially not to rock the boat, not to be too militant for fear of losing work. The sports, police, university, and other institutional descriptions we've made all bear out our assertion: for all four characteristics and in all arenas, as a norm, the role dictates are mutually reinforcing.

And third, at least as the normal order, this mutual reinforcement prevails at the consciousness level as well. In our heads, the mystifications which justify oppressing or being oppressed are very similar from one characteristic to another. As the roles are entwined so are our associated ideas. If we see ourselves as superior or inferior in one mode, it enforces the likelihood and legitimacy of doing so in others as well. Even more, the consciousness we have in respect to each characteristic exists in context of those we hold with respect to the others. Black workers and bosses have different racial as well as class consciousnesses. Women coordinators or workers, of color or white, have different sexual self-conceptions. There is not, in our heads, a tinker-toy building block consciousness, but rather a whole very dynamic structure with the parts mutually interacting and most often co-reproducing due to their shared abstract form as well as in more concrete ways—for example, fear of racial intermarriage entwining with sexual notions.

Our argument concerning the mix of our society's core characteristics is as complete as we can now make it. Brief discussions of sports, the police, the universities, the workplace and family support our hypothesis. Much more evidence and argumentation is of course required but we nonetheless feel justified in drawing some tentative conclusions whose implications we can usefully investigate.

There is in our society, an identifiable set of dynamics we can label classism, just as there is also racism, sexism, and authoritarianism. The mistake is not to so identify these features nor to recognize that they affect different social groups differently, but it is rather to minimize their interrelations, assuming one or another form of simple dominance. We do not live in a society whose character is simply molded by a scarcity of material well-being, or love, or dignity, or equity, but rather by the scarcity of all of these interactively. We do not live in a society which is dominated by either class, race, sex, or authority requirements or even in which all are core and developing in parallel—but rather in a society which has at its core a totality of entwined relations which manifest themselves in the forms classism, racism, sexism, and authoritarianism in all institutions and in all people's lives. The laws of motion for such a society are more complex, it is true, than would be those for the societies imagined by an orthodox Marxist, nationalist, feminist, or anarchist— but that is a fact not to be wished or mystified away, and moreover it is of immense relevance to modern revolutionary strategy, a fact we will investigate in more detail soon.

THE ACTIVE TOTALITY AND HEGEMONY IN THE U.S.

This totality of core characteristics is not new to U.S. history. It has been at the center of U.S. development right from the beginning of our country. Now, however, there is a new phenomenon. All four aspects of the core totality are actively recognized (and not simply felt) by the oppressed. People's aroused needs—for material well-being, security, knowledge, self-management, and love—are perceived as knocking against the limits of these characteristics. Whenever people begin organizing to advance their lives, they tend to become sensitive to all the limits in their way. In a class issue movement blacks and women become sensitive to matters of racism and of sexism. In an anti-racist movement, there also develops a sensitivity to class and authority issues. Just as the oppressive contours of our society are linked, so too are the revolutionary orientations.

A white male worker striking around class issues might remain insensitive to the importance of racial and sexual injustices or even continue as a perpetrator of them, but black and women workers will not be so myopic. As they overcome oppressing class mystifications, they will also, sometimes even more easily, overcome old racial and sexual rationalizations. Each sector of society will minimally be aroused against its most direct oppressions. People who fit more than one oppressed category may first or primarily identify only one way—black women as women and not as black, or more likely, vice versa—or may identify both ways, or even may first identify around oppressions other than the one most central to their immediate situation. But what won't happen is for people to give on-going allegiance to a movement which continually denies a main part of their lives.

In times of quietude this has little relevance. But in times of social conflict, when old conforming ideologies are giving way, it is very important. It means that there will never be a single issue, particularistic class, race, sex, or authority movement which successfully unites people from all sectors of society. Even with such a narrow movement as a detonator, motion about all the core characteristics will inevitably develop. Whether any particularistic movement can hold a broad constituency will depend upon its ability to recognize the *centrality* of other struggles. Whether all four movements can work together, and whether they can each endure, has a tremendous amount to do with the fact that the United States core totality is entwined and actively recognized.

Women will not remain in a class-issue movement that is sexist, and they will see any movement that denies the centrality of sexual oppression as sexist. Black's will not relate to a racist women's movement, and they will see any movement that denies the centrality of racial oppression as racist. Anti-authoritarians will not be attracted to, nor long remain part of a hierarchical anti-racist organization. Workers will not trust a coordinator oriented women's movement. And so it goes. Each particularistic movement will have difficulty growing. Each will be internally fractured over how it ignores or even perpetuates "other oppressions".[5] Women identifying as women perceive viewing sexism-as-less-than-core to be sexist. Blacks identifying as blacks perceive viewing racism-as-less-than-core to be racist. Workers find coordinator movements to be anti-working class. Anti-authoritarians feel that hierarchically organized movements of any type deny the centrality of authority relations to the reproduction of oppressions in our society. And each group is right.

It is necessary to challenge all four core characteristics, not three peripherally to the other one, but all centrally. It is insufficient to say one cares about class and sex, but believe in a "class dialectic" or a "sex dialectic" alone. Developing a socialist strategy which can accomplish a totalist view, while simultaneously relating to the concrete divisions between sectors and also to the need people feel to develop separately in autonomous movements, is one of the main tasks we will address in the last chapter of this book. For now, however, we should continue with our theoretical evaluation of how the United States functions, reproduces, and creates conditions making revolution a real possibility.

We have added to the orthodox class perspective an awareness of the additional *defining* presence in the United States of racism, sexism, and authoritarianism. We've started the argument that these last three features along with classism constitute a kind of complex whole at the core of our society—that each of the four features are simultaneously separately active and yet that they also exist only interactively, each as a manifestation of all four entwined.

This is the notion of a *totality* at society's core which manifests itself both institutionally in social relations and also ideologically in people's consciousnesses, and which society's daily outcomes in workplaces, stores, homes, schools, hospitals, sports arenas, and music halls are all oriented to reproduce.

It is also the notion of *hegemony*—that is, that our society reproduces primarily via a historically generated and continually regenerated conformity between what its people seek, expect, or will at least settle for, and what society itself can and will deliver. Hegemony is what we name the imposition of an alienated set of needs, ideas, and capabilities into us all by way of our involvements in society's day-to-day life roles. We are molded and indeed mold ourselves to fit, during childhood, in the family, in school, and on the neighborhood street playing, and then later as adults in work, consumption, and family life. We do this in the context of social relations that have evolved precisely to insure reproduction of our docility, racism, sexism, and willingness to "sell ourselves" for a daily wage.

United States social relations of work, art, and family life, —and thus the life roles society puts foward for its people to fill; (worker, coordinator, or owner, advertising artist, child, wife, mother, husband, or father)—are all imbued simultaneously with racism, sexism, classism, and authoritarianism. As a result our consciousnesses are similarly alienated. We all have to varying degrees a reactionary constellation of mutually reinforcing views and habits which simultaneously 1-rationalize our day-to-day life activities, 2-reproduce their defining relations, 3-meet what needs we can in fact meet within the system's dictates, and 4-hide the truth that with the system's alteration life could be vastly improved. Hegemony is the totalist process that imposes and reimposes relative societal conformity via this constellation and it is not to be overcome, in our view, one pillar at a time. Instead, within each of us there is a tension, a kind of civil war between our total fluctuating reactionary perspective (varying from person to person but fairly defineable across certain large sectors), substantiating our current situation, justifying, and even propelling our oppressing others and being oppressed by them, and another set of objectively revolutionary views challenging the totality at society's core and seeking collective liberation for all people. For us, all in-between positions are unstable, for example a person "clear" on class but sexist. Hegemony is still operative, still present in the remaining reactionary views and constantly threatening to reinforce the entire prior reactionary stance and subserviance to the status-quo.

All of this implies the need for a totalist approach to social change. The fact that our society's core totality is active shows us that particularistic movements would be unable to consistently attract allegiance across sectoral lines. The movements would also internally fragment as their narrowness affronted the people most affected by other "less focused upon" oppressions. The lesson of hegemony is that particularistic movements, even if they somehow manage to subsist, have an additional tendency to regress even with respect to their key concern precisely because of the impact of the rest of hegemony.[6]

So from two directions, narrow one-focus movements are subject to forces of dissolution and reaction. To overcome these tendencies and retain a progressive aim is just about impossible. If all other hurdles are cleared, holding a single focus eventually requires a repressive stance with respect to "other" differently focused movements. This is invariably the end of any progressive possibilities (for the original one-focus movement).[7]

UNITED STATES "LAWS OF MOTION"

Theories of society are unlike theories from natural science. We can not know society the way a physicist knows a "projectile". We can not ascertain "initial conditions", calculate a path of motion or determine a final destination. We can't say with scientific precision, "If we interfere in this fashion the path and destination of our society will change by this exact amount."

The reason our knowledge of society and history must be approximate is that humans are unlike the physical systems other scientists analyze. People have consciousness and self-consciousness. Our past and potential futures can alter our present. The very knowledge of our situation in turn motivates us to alter our situation. People engage in activity with the very intention of changing the direction of motion of their "projectile". As we understand our situation, we seek to change it, and in so doing we change ourselves as well. And even beyond these ultimate problems of the "dialectic of consciousness", there is also the much simpler constraint that the study of human relations is only in its infancy. We are nowhere near the borders of what we can know (however the latter might be ultimately limited). We are at best like physicists of a hundred years ago, and learning from their experience, we would be quite wise to show a certain humility about our beliefs and predictions.

Still, we believe there are general tendencies built into any society's core, and we think it is reasonable for people to try to develop intellectual frameworks sufficient to discern and understand these, as well as the particular ways they manifest themselves and the specific counter factors that might operate in actual societies.

Orthodox Marxists certainly attempt this, even if only narrowly and incorrectly. As main historical dynamics they discern economic accumulation, the clash of forces and relations of production due to the development of the former, and the struggle of classes concerned to maintain or to overthrow economic relationships. They then show how these historical tendencies manifest themselves in context of other more societally bound factors. Here, for example, matters of race, sex, cultural heritage, or other relations may attain an important place.

But we have gone to considerable lengths to explain the weaknesses of this viewpoint. In short, it relegates human praxis to an inferior position, misunderstands subject/object relationships, is overly economistic in its understanding of economic and class relations, and overemphasizes the economy to the exclusion of other important societal arenas. Still, despite these broad criticisms, we do agree that material and broader economic phenomena are important, and that classes are critical actors in the historical development of modern societies.

Another attempt at discerning "laws of motion" is furnished by radical feminists who have asserted that history is a chronicle of the struggle between men and women over who will dominate social life. In this view history is dynamic because of the ever-changing interrelations between men and women. The motion has its roots in biological phenomena but manifests itself in a social struggle.

But this view is also inadequate. It ignores or at least insufficiently recognizes the importance of class (and other core) relations. It posits a biological basis of oppression which is a-historical and rooted in basic male drives for dominance which must finally be held down by woman-led institutions. We have a different view of human nature and of the way social interaction has historically led to a variety of core oppressions, but we do agree that sexual relations are among those central in history, and that sex-caste and familial differentiations among people are often key to people's life possibilities.

Similarly anarchists on the one hand, and nationalists on the other, propose that history has at root an authority or a racial dialectic. Progress occurs due to a power dynamic or a racial dynamic again dependent upon either innate human drives of an anti-social type or contingent institutional relations which totally dominate human potentials. Each viewpoint is myopic with respect to other important factors in history and unbalanced in overemphasizing *either* human nature or institutional compulsion. But, in each instance, although we disagree with the overall analysis, we do agree that the chosen aspect can be a critical factor in any particular society, and that the social groups focused upon are indeed often agents of historical advance.

We divorce ourselves from the particularistic orientations of the orthodox Marxists, radical feminists, anarchists, and nationalists and their one-sided analyses—either overly institutionally based or overly based in "human nature". On the other hand, we do retain recognition of the importance of class, sex, race, and authority relations to historical developments.

This is because we begin our analysis of history from an understanding of the central role of human activity and of the interrelationships between humans in society and the role arrangements they create and must fill. We start from an understanding of how humans organize together socially and develop institutions to fill their needs and develop their capabilities, and of how the interrelations between people and those institutions then lead to certain oppressive structures—racism, sexism, classism, and authoritarianism—which tend to reproduce within societies and even as societies undergo historical alterations. We argue that these structural aspects determine the character and quality of social life in the societies where they appear, and that they tend also to insure a reproduction of those aspects by forcing a "mesh" between people and society's roles—socializing people and also insuring that new roles fit recurring requirements of prior consciousness forms. We also argue, however, that major social transformations or revolutions are possible as a result of contradictions involving these same core characteristics.

The factor underlying historical development, in this view, is the continual interplay between human praxis and the societal arenas in which it must be carried out. People engage in the production and reproduction of all things relevant to human development—human capabilities and personalities included—and in so doing act as the "motor" of history. In concrete instances, this statement can be further refined. For example, in certain societies we might be able to say that certain social groups tend to produce and reproduce conditions of the accumulation of profit, or of the maintenance of patriarchal privilege, or of racial advantage, or political dominance. Then, the impact of existent forms of consciousness and of institutional role structures would propel these forms of activity and perhaps others as well. The problem of ascertaining "laws of societal motion" would reduce to the problem of how the existent core characteristics interact, how they reproduce, and also how they create conditions suitable for revolutionary alterations.

There are thus two very general laws of historical motion. On the one hand, there is a tendency in history for the *reproduction* of social arrangements via the reproduction of core charactertistics in both center and boundary. And on the other, simultaneously, there is also a tendency for *revolutionary alteration* in social arrangements propelled by the development of contradictions involving core characteristics and their manifestations in both center and boundary. The first tendency rests on the character of human praxis as a self-justifying process and on the requirement for conformity between center and boundary if people are to garner the benefits that the society's institutions allow. The second tendency rests on the fact that humans are not "infinitely moldable" so that the conformity between center and boundary in all societies to date has been oppressive and alienated; it has rested on the denial of some subset of human needs and capabilities to partially fulfill others. The mesh between center and boundary has therefore never been without rough edges. It's a round peg in a square hole—and the peg never entirely loses its resiliancy. At all times there is some resistance, some people are entirely in rebellion, and many more who accept their "slot" do so only with great tension, relenting in order to meet what needs they can, but aware of the cost and only partially convinced of its necessity and rationality.

In any particular society, bringing the "general tendencies" into relation with concrete conditions requires empirical analysis. By studying actual occurrences, one determines society's core characteristics, their interrelations, the ways they generate reproductive motion, the ways they generate potentials for revolutionary alterations, and who will be the agents of this revolutionary process.

With respect to the United States, we have offered only a very tentative begining on these tasks. We have hypothesized that there are four core characteristics entwined into a single totality pervading both our consciousness and the institutions we must daily relate to. The problem of the laws of motion of our society is therefore considerably reduced.

1. How do changes in what we think and in our institutional boundary tend to largely preserve race, sex, class, and authority relations? How is it that even when dissident sectors seek changes these generally percolate into accord with society's core reproductive dictates? In short, what are the dynamics of "reformist reforms" whether instituted from above or below, by technical or by intellectual proposals?[8]
2. What are the causes of and ways in which sectors develop oppositional consciousnesses? What are the attributes of the motion of society's core characteristics which promote this tendency? And finally, what will be the form of social struggle that will lead to revolutionary changes: who will be the agents, around what issues will they mobilize, how will they organize, and what will be their aims? In short, what are the dynamics of non-reformist reforms and of revolution?

In our two chapters on the United States we have presented many arguments relevant to these two analytic/programmatic points, and we will deal with them still more in the dialogue closing this chapter and in the next two chapters as well. But it would be ridiculous to assert that we have uncovered and described the "laws of motion" of our society. We have not even come close to such an achievement. Rather we have argued for an orientation for accomplishing a variation upon this end; an orientation which is quite new, and which we think is better suited to the task than those that have been used in the past. Perhaps the critical assertions of our presentation are 1-that there are no scientifically precise laws of motion of our society, and that the attempt to found such laws on over-simplistic assertions of the absolute (or last analysis) dominance of *either* "human nature" or "objective material conditions" are doomed to failure, and 2-that the only way to develop insights into the general tendencies of history and their operation in our society as well as into our society's own unique attributes is by large numbers of people organizing politically and combining their analysis with collective practical experience.

WEAKNESSES AND EXTENSIONS

For a change, this dialog is with someone sympathetic to the new veiwpoint, though concerned with some of its weaknesses and apparent implications. The sympatico is labelled "S" and the adherent of our totalist analysis, "TA".

S: I understand that you couldn't do more than a cursory analysis of the United States in the short space allotted, but nonetheless I was struck by how little use you made of the methodological approaches you developed earlier.

TA: You're right. For the most part we didn't really follow our own scenario of using a "relational" and "historical", as well as structural approach, except that, and this is critical, we got our central concepts— center, boundary, totality, hegemony, and our view of human interaction and history—by using those approaches.

S: But then what would a full analysis include? If you were to attempt one, how would you proceed?

TA: Well, I suppose it would make sense to start as was done here, only more extensively, so as to better develop the general analytic framework that would then guide the ensuing studies. The initial approach allows us to solidify our notion of the United States fourfold totality. Then we could begin anew studying racism, sexism, classism, and authoritarianism each relationally and historically...

S: Understanding society from the perspective of each?

TA: Yes. In a sense like Marx's project in *Capital* where he took the economic relation as the core totality, and through examining it in ever more concrete detail sought to understand the whole. We would first do that for each of the four characteristics. Indeed, that is the Marxist, anarchist, nationalist, and feminist project, or should be, in preparation for a final analysis from the angle or perspective of the whole core totality at once, again analyzed relationally and historically through center and boundary.

S: But you would have to make divisions—sections—which you would focus on a bit at a time to finally piece together into a whole view?

TA: In a sense, yes. We would have to keep starting from an abstracted aspect and work through it to a partial view of the whole. Thus we would come at society from the economy, but also from the polity, the culture, the family, as well as from a study of racism, sexism, classism, and authoritarianism. As we proceeded, we'd get an ever-fuller picture of what our society's roles, people, and contradictions are like.

S: It's clear why you opted to do so much less in your presentation here.

TA: But it isn't just a matter of space. We're not at all equipped to do a full study of United States conditions, nor even to take off from one particular orientation to a partial view of the whole. In fact, the only way such analyses can come about is through the accumulated social experiences and wisdom of countless people, all carefully analyzed and brought together through political activism and study. Only active political movements can arrive at as complex and alive a picture of society as we need—of its roles and people; its past, present, and possible futures; its network and process. Only a broad movement can gain a totalist view with concepts that place people first and that understand society from all relevant angles. Only by summing the lessons and analyses of women, workers, blacks, chicanos, children, and soldiers will we come to know how different sectors of people are affected differently by society's core totality, and how people's needs, powers, and personalities are both propelled and also severely constrained by life in the United States.

S: But if this totalist approach is as necessary and as powerful as you claim, why haven't others been employing it—why isn't it the dominant view?

TA: If only we could figure the exact answer to that question—but some partial answers do immediately present themselves. First, though all four characteristics are core, it's only fairly recently that they have all become simultaneously active (felt). Second, the class tradition is long, and in its orthodox form, sectarian. It is powerful and appealing for its logical consistency and seeming comprehensiveness. It prevents many people who have totalist intuitions from developing them. At one point class forces alone may have been actively felt as core oppressions and this would easily explain the early dominance of the class analysis viewpoint. Then its longevity itself would tend to preserve the class approach's dominant position. Also it is much easier and more spontaneous for people to key in upon the aspect of society's core characteristics which affects them most directly and clearly—and in the U.S. we historically get particularistic theories and movements focused upon each of the four aspects. Even more to the point, however, in recent times most socialistically oriented people have "voted totalist" by their very cynicism toward the other existent approaches. In the United States the great majority of people leaning leftward steer very clear of established left organizations. It seems reasonable to suggest that it's not that these people wouldn't join anything, but that the existing alternatives are lacking precisely in their doctrinaire narrowness and in their lack of a real explanation of the multiple problems we now confront, as well as in their lack of a vision of a new alternative way of living.

S: Well, maybe that's so. It's a comforting thought for you, I can see, but there are obviously many other possible explanations. Perhaps we'll soon see. But I'd like to get into discussing some of the implications of what you say for people who would like to try and make a socialist revolution in the United States. I keep trying to extrapolate the logic of your analysis into strategic notions and I'm not really so sure I'm succeeding.

I understand, for example, the Marxist Leninist logic of why they say the proletariat—or working class—makes the revolution. Historical materialism says revolution is propelled by contradictions in the core mode of production, and that classes are the group whose interests are defined by their relations to that mode of production, so that it is classes who become on the one hand revolutionary and on the other defenders of the status quo. The logic seems clear enough to me, and it's also easy to see the reasonableness of understanding other societal divisions and oppressions in terms of a class analysis. Thus, women and blacks are members of the working class and that is why they will finally become revolutionaries, though their distinct race/sex positions and experiences are also important to the unfolding process. Particularly, racism and sexism are critical to address and understand for the ways they impede working class solidarity and socialist consciousness. I also understand your criticisms of this view and feel a lot of solidarity with them, but I'm caught short at what the alternative strategic orientation is.

TA: You're raising specifically the problem of determining who are the most likely agents of revolution. In our view this translates into the question of which societal groups are capable of developing a revolutionary consciousness and practice, and moreover, by what paths might they most likely and most rapidly arrive at that consciousness and practice?

Since we no longer start from the premise that the economy is alone core, we now have the problem of seeing what other factors might be essential in determining people's activities and consciousness and interests. In fact, since we find a fourfold core totality and see revolution as a struggle against all its aspects and in favor of a whole new alternative, we see people who hold different positions relative to that totality to be the groups of key interest to us, the ones likely to either become revolutionary or reactionary.

S: I know that you trace consciousness to activity and argue both that activity isn't just economic, and also that even economic activity isn't simply class defined, and that much makes good sense to me. But when you get to the strategic level it seems to lead to such an eclectic view that I'm having problems with it.

TA: Well, I don't know what more to say, because we do argue from just the position you've described. People daily engage in a variety of activities each constrained in differing ways by society's core characteristics. Depending upon what people do and upon who they are—that is, upon what various castes, classes, and sexual groupings as well as finer sectors of each they belong to—they generally have quite different views of themselves and the world. There is a different likelihood they will achieve revolutionary consciousness at any particular time in history, and even more importantly, they start the march toward being revolutionary from different initial positions and must cover different ground.

People who hold different positions with respect to society's core totality face differing daily life situations. To the extent that they hold "conforming consciousnesses", it is in each case for differing reasons and with differing levels of obstinacy. In different groups, conforming consciousnesses reproduce by different processes.

S: So people in different places will react differently to revolutionary programs also—and then it makes sense that the programs should take that into account by clearly addressing the various starting places and differing needs of the groups.

TA: That's right. It's not that the historical materialist proletariat-bourgeoisie distinction is totally wrong, it's just much too narrow. The strategic logic of our analysis is that class is not a priori the only critical division between people. In the U.S., in fact, there are four critical demarcating factors. People from different sectors won't synthesize into a whole movement because eventually they all come to identify as proletarians, or for that matter, as women, or order-takers, or a minority, or some other oppressed thing, but because eventually many of them will identify as revolutionaries who oppose the totality of oppressing characteristics and who are for a well-envisioned socialist alternative.

S: So people will finally see that the things which kept them apart weren't really that important...

TA: No! That's a particularist understanding. Eventually everyone realizes that their commonness as workers or whatever else in this society outweighs their "false" differences. No, solidarity will come not because people decide that the things which kept them apart are no longer important, but because though different sectors are oppressed differently by society's core characteristics and even do oppress each other, they are able to eventually arrive at a shared opposition to all of them. It is the whole core totality which reproduces each sector's oppressions. Solidarity will not rest on believing everyone is somehow abstractly the same in this society, because the fact is that this is simply not the case. It will instead rest on us all having a shared desire to become equal members of a new socialist society.

S: All right, I guess I see that there really is a significant difference. In the old orthodox view it's necessary to overcome the material impediments to workers' solidarity and then to seize power. But in your view it's necessary to develop programs which address each of society's sectors where they actually are, and in terms of how society's core totality directly affects them, and then to bring all the sectors into a total movement precisely by making that movement relevant to what each most directly feels and to the whole complex of oppressions they endure. I know you want to wait until later to discuss matters of organization and how it's possible to simultaneously have all these different kinds of movements addressing particular oppressions and yet also be part of a whole, but just to ensure that I have a good feeling for the general strategic drift of your view, till we can get more detailed later, perhaps we can get into the matter of choosing the issues around which revolutionary activists might do their organizing.

Again, at least I understand the Marxist Leninist perspective, no matter how sympathetic I may be to your criticisms of it. Historical materialism tells us that the most important issues are those related to the contradiction between the forces and relations of production. It is dealing with these that the left can take advantage of the laws of history and capitalism. So the most obvious things to fight around are wages, work-day length, speed-up, and mandatory overtime. Then issues which promote class solidarity in the community are also important. Then, finally, matters of racism, sexism, and other oppressions may also be very important, but it will always be because of their impact on class solidarity.

TA: Yes, that's basically the logic but now, in fact, most of the Marxist Leninist groups are too much in touch with reality, with their own experiences, to follow the logic entirely. Thus they are forced by conditions to address whatever issues "the people" are most concerned with: be they racial, cultural, sexual, law and order, schooling, prices, wages, ecology, unemployment, rents, dignity, or even issues of control and authority. The problem is that the traditional Marxist Leninist left doesn't have any way to take the lead in anticipating and addressing all the most important issues, nor any way to do it most effectively in terms of the most effective criteria—continually developing the organizational strength, scale, and consciousness of the left. In fact, and this is reflected in their economic theory as well as in their practice, what happens is that most Marxist Leninist groups tend to see all struggles only in terms of their class dynamics, thus missing many of their most important features and often employing ill-chosen tactics, organizing styles, or programs.

S: If you're right about the core totality, then I guess what you say here about strategy follows as well. But I still don't see the positive side clearly. You just do what people are into doing, or does your theory tell you what issues are more important and why?

TA: The revolution is a continual enlargening and strengthening of the revolutionary left until it can gain hegemony over society's day-to-day life. This growth derives from continual struggles and programmatic and crisis activities which cause people to develop their consciousnesses and allegiances in revolutionary directions. The movement fights to gain a reform of wage rates or work conditions through a militant strike, or to establish some new institution or program like a food coop or health clinic, or to gain control over some institution like a school system or police force. The general purpose in each case is to 1 – uproot old "conforming" consciousnesses while also generating new revolutionary alternatives, 2 – strengthen the organizational and general material/positional power of the left, and 3 – construct new social relations that approximate the ways people will live under socialism so as to contribute to tasks "1" and "2" and so as to begin developing the foundation upon which a new society can be built. There is a procession of such struggles and victories each leaving the left better off than it was previously until final victory.

S: Sure, but what are the issues that such a progression would focus upon? Is it just a vague vision with no clear, specific areas of concern?

TA: Well, there is no precise revolutionary prescription, if that is what you're looking for, but there is more theoretical guidance than we've got so far. Society will be revolutionized not because it doesn't technically work, but because even when it is working perfectly it has an oppressive core that contradicts peoples' development.

The issues of revolutionary struggle are defined by the way society's core characteristics interfere with daily life, and particularly by the contradictions engendered between the core characteristics and people's desires for a better life, as well as by the more intermittent major disjunctures in daily life due to economic crises, socialization problems, political turmoil, wars, etc.

S: It's still a lot of vagueness. Can't you get more specific?

TA: In our view, revolutionary activists must be sensitive to the totality of issues significantly affecting daily-life and most particularly to the dynamics of race, sex, authority, and profit. We must understand how day-to-day conditions limit people's freedoms, impede their capacities for human development, and in more extreme, but quite prevalent, instances brutally hurt and kill them. And we must be able to identify how people perceive these oppressions and how leftist activities can help their awarenesses become more and more revolutionary. How do people perceive issues of crime and safety, of family living, of material well-being, and of dignity, and how might these issues come to have a revolutionary political impact?

For us, revolutionary consciousness is a threefold sensitivity to 1-how the institutional boundary and human center of present day society oppress people, 2-how an alternative socialist boundary and center could free and even enhance people's potentials, and 3-how a revolution carried out by society's many oppressed sectors is both necessary and possible.

S: And the issues, damn it, what are the issues?

TA: The issues are all those aspects of daily life whose character is such that related organizing can help develop revolutionary awarenesses of society's core aspects and socialist alternatives, and/or help strengthen the material position of the left.

In a factory or any other organizing place, activists would first notice the various constituencies of people present: members of different races, sexes, and age groups, doers of different jobs, etc. Then they would seek to undertand how the factory milieu manages to maintain relative stability, which rules and institutional relations and consciousness types contribute to the factory's relative stability, and why and how they persist.

Next activists would try to understand the specific ways in which the factory oppresses its workers, the community in its vicinity, and the consumers of its products. How do society's core characteristics manifest themselves in the factory with respect to the workers, the community, and the factory's products? What are the ways racism, sexism, authority, and classism limit the lives of the various workers and their contributions to society at large, and how can left activism bring these features to full and clear prominence? How can it bring each type of worker to greater, clearer insights, give evidence of and explain alternative possibilities, and also build the power and organizational means to fight?

S: But finally how are the issues you fight around different from those the Marxist Leninists address?

TA: We find and understand the issues differently, and we subsequently address them differently also. For us, the issues of concern are more comprehensive in both scope and depth. There are of course material issues of high rent, bad housing, low pay, private ownership in general, inflation, unemployment, the character of work if you do get it, police repression, the court and prison system, unequal wealth, and so on. But there are also and equally the more qualitative issues such as fear of crime, loneliness, lack of dignity, respect, and self-respect, lack of community, poor family relations, the generation gap, care of the elderly and room for them to express their wisdom, the quality of education and culture, and the constant issue of people's lack of power over the contours of their own lives. But we address each of these in terms of the core totality, all four aspects, and not class alone.

S: But now it sounds like a big shopping list. It's what I've been afraid of all along...

TA: But why afraid? It's a long list because society hurts us in a great many ways. The critical theoretical underpinning isn't useful because it tells us to ignore ways in which people are oppressed, but because it enables us to understand each of them and to address them in ways that effectively clarify root causes and also alternative possibilities. The left has to explain and also to continually learn how societal attributes oppress, how an alternative social arrangement could be better, and how revolution is possible by choosing foci that are in touch with people's most active concerns, and by discussing and acting upon them in ways suited to people's concrete conditions and consciousness. The left must explain why people hold views that are racist or are accepting of racism, sexist or accepting of sexism, etc., and show what real needs such views meet and what harm they nonetheless cause. It must understand why workers frequently feel that their plights are their own fault and learn address and finally uproot such views—not "propagandistically" but by showing the harm the views cause and also that they are wrong and unnecessary as rationalizations of capitalist day-to-day life, because such a life is not the only option. Resistance and revolution can create socialism. Rather than just attacking old views which give a semblance of meaning and dignity to day-to-day life as now experienced, the left must demonstrate the bad as well as the useful aspects these views have, and show how a new kind of meaning and dignity as well as potential for life improvement can be had from a new socialist perspective.

The left fights for ideological hegemony. That is, in its day-to-day functioning the left exposes the truth about the totality of United States oppressions in ways that penetrate people's prior rationalizations by providing new views and identities to take the place of old ones. Instead of "things may be bad but at least I get what I deserve," or "I'm better off than others, or I may get ahead, or my kid will get ahead, or at least it's the best country in the world," the left could generate a new understanding of why things are as they are while also giving people the insights necessary to their having the dignity and respect they will otherwise seek through rationalizations. To reach such a practice obviously requires a left which is not only sensitive to the real human contours of daily-life, but also by its organization and manner can communicate the possibility of something better. If a family is wracked by internal divisions and hostility and violence, is any member going to believe in a left that talks only about the workplace—is such a family member going to believe in the possibility of a "good society", or only in the credo of struggling for what little you can get in the world as it is?

Perhaps the most fundamental problem in developing a revolutionary movement in the United States is overcoming the cynical views that 1-no better society is humanly possible because people are just plain bad and one way or another there are going to be those on top and those on the bottom, and 2-even if a better society is possible, we'll never see it because you just can't fight city hall—the state and the rich are too powerful to be overcome. In dealing with each of these cynical perspectives the left will have to first address the totality of things about daily-life that make people feel that nothing better is possible, and will have to do this both theoretically and programatically. Second, through a steady development of solidarity, it must demonstrate the real power of the people.

S: But this whole discussion about consciousness seems to imply organizing only around ordinary day-to-day affairs. Do you just ignore the possibility of crises during which left activity would be even more critical?

TA: No, of course not. We understand that crises can provide a critical opportunity for organizers. For example, an economic downturn, the war in Indochina, Watergate, the C.I.A. exposures or other such events all allow for large scale left gains. But to be effective in context of such crises, leftists would have to understand that the important point is how the crisis induced motion can be translated into developments of new revolutionary consciousness or organizational strength. How do such events reinforce previous relations, or how do they disturb them making room for development of new outcomes? If the New Left, for example, had been better prepared to analyse various sectors' needs and beliefs and how the war affected them, and how various alternative left tactics would further affect them, many grievous mistakes might have been avoided.

The point here is not that existing Marxist Leninist movements don't try to function at least somewhat as we've been decribing, but rather that historical materialism—a particularistic, class dominated focus—is insufficient to the theoretical and analytic problems involved.

Even the most historical and relational historical materialist practitioner cannot overcome the handicap which is inherent to the initial set of concepts he or she brings to analyses. Beginning with only class focused, overly "materialistic" categories, even if she/he treats them flexibly—expanding them horizontally according to an uncovering of relational networks and vertically in tune with an awareness of historical process—they will not be sufficient to the task of strategically understanding matters of consciousness, race, sex, and authority. It is this "handicap", if you will, which has prevented even the most brilliant and useful of Marxist analyses from reaching a texture sufficiently rich to adequately help modern revolutionary activists.

Our concepts, on the contrary, avoid "class myopia", economism, and "objectivism" right from the outset, from their initial, most abstract postulation. Then as we develop them dialectically—extending them horizontally and vertically, as both network and process—they are brought into correspondence with activist's daily needs. To see this more fully we will have to discuss strategy showing these activist needs and precisely how a revolutionary councilist approach is well-suited to meeting them. But as a prior step it proves more useful to discuss the question of what kind of society we would like to create—what is our socialist vision?

FOOTNOTES: CHAPTER SIX

1. For a discussion of women and sports see *The Femininity Game,* Thomas Boslooper and Marcia Hayes, Stein and Day, New York, 1973.

   The "data" and assertions of this section are really quite commonplace; they hardly require evidence as they are so evident just from our daily experiences. What is new, however, is the way of choosing to organize and analyze this data and the basis this lays for further more detailed investigation. What is new is the way our discussion of sport becomes a part of our discussion of the whole society, informing it and being informed by it.

2. See "The Heroin Trail" by Henry Norr, New England Free Press, for detailed evidence and argumentation on these points.

3. See the interview with Renault Robinson in Studs Terkel, *Working,* Avon, New York, 1972.

4. See *Schooling in Capitalist America,* Sam Bowles and Herb Gintis, Basic Books, New York, 1976.

5. For a general discussion of this phenomenon see chapter one of *What Is To Be Undone,* Michael Albert, Porter Sargent Publishers, 1974. For a discussion of a particular movement that has relevance here, see *Detroit: I Do Mind Dying,* Dan Georgakas and Marvin Surkin, St. Martin's Press, 1975.

6. Ibid.

7. The point is that the oppressed of any particular sector will always become more rebellious in tune with the advance of active struggles. If a class oriented movement progresses, people who feel other oppressions intensely will certainly become aroused to these injustices and the possibilities of overcoming them. To limit their struggles would then require repressive coercion.

PART FOUR

GOAL AND STRATEGY
A REVOLUTIONARY COUNCILIST VIEW

...When the narrow bourgeois form has been peeled away, what is wealth, if not the universality of needs, capacities, enjoyments, productive powers, etc. of individuals, produced in universal exchange? What, if not the full development of human control over the forces of nature—those of our own nature as well as those of so-called "nature"? What, if not the absolute elaboration of our creative dispositions, without any preconditions other than antecedent historical evolution which makes the totality of this evolution—that is, the evolution of all human powers as such, unmeasured by any previously established yardstick—an end in itself? What is this, if not a situation where people do not reproduce themselves in any determined form, but produce their totality? Where they do not seek to remain something formed by the past, but are in the absolute movement of becoming?

Karl Marx
Grundrisse

CHAPTER SEVEN
POLITICAL ECONOMY

Two centuries ago a former European colony decided to catch up with Europe. It succeeded so well that the United States of America has become a monster.... For Europe, for ourselves and for humanity, comrades, we must turn over a new leaf, we must work out new concepts, and try to set afoot a new person.

Frantz Fanon
The Wretched of the Earth

Making a socialist revolution in the United States requires a clear vision of what the socialism we want will be like. How will it work, what will be its institutional and human relations, and how will its quality of life be superior to that we now endure?

United States citizens are not going to rally to rhetoric nor to an amorphous set of promises, nor to a blurry vision. They are not going to take great risk to achieve the kind of society they see in Russia, East Europe, or China, and this is to the good.

In order for people to care about socialism in this country, it will have to be evident that socialism means a new form of truly democratic society, a possible society which is so much more desirable than what we have now, that it is worth immense efforts to struggle in its behalf.

This is a minimum. Critiques of the present have their place, but without a positive formulation of the future there will be no powerful movement for socialism.

One would think that such a vision could evolve from the socialist heritage itself, but this is unfortunately not the case.[1] The visible practical heritage, and for that matter the prevalent intellectual heritage as well, do little to attract the allegiance of United States citizens.[2] A more subterranean heritage that might have exerted some attraction has been literally removed from view—the Paris Commune of 1871, the soviets and factory committees of the early years of the Russian Revolution, the Hungarian Revolutions of 1919 and 1956, The Italian factory councils of the early 1920's, and the Spanish revolution of 1936, as well as the intellectual heritage of the libertarian socialists are hardly matters of public

253

awareness.[3] A critical evaluation of the *whole* socialist heritage—both its theory and practice—would be very welcome. We are obviously unable to pursue such a task here. What we can do, however, is describe the critical flaws in the more orthodox socialist models and present the outlines of our own conception of what socialism can be like here in the United States.[4]

SOCIALISM'S DEFINING CONTOURS

Our concepts suggest a very direct way of determining what criteria we should use for judging a socialist societal model: describe as completely as possible the kind of human beings that we, as socialists, would like to become, and judge social institutions according to whether or not they embody the associated values as their core characteristics. For (assuming they are consistent with human nature) to the extent that the human characteristics we desire are the core characteristics of the economic and social institutions of a society, they will most likely come to predominate as human characteristics; while to the extent that they are not core characteristics of the society's institutional arrangement, they cannot persist as human characteristics.

What is it, then, that socialists want for human beings? First, all socialists envision adequate provision for all people's material survival and comfort, and most then assert that this will also ensure physical and mental security; bounteous fulfillment of all people's needs for sex, friendship, love, dignity; and the greatest development of all people's talents and creativity. But we don't believe that there is any absolute connection between "material survival and comfort" and the other qualitative, more social ends. While seeking the former, we see the need to simultaneously seek the latter as well.

We recognize that 1-people are always in process, creating and recreating themselves through their activities; 2-people are social beings, gaining fulfillment and reaching fullest potentials only in equal relations with one another; and 3-people require variety of environment and lifestyle, and experimentation in development.[5] This last is both for diversity to meet diverse human requirements, and also because planning decisions will only be as intelligent and as popular as possible, if as many alternative options as possible are experimented with.

We thus demand for ourselves and for all people, power over our lives, a condition of true community, and a condition of variety of life experiences. Thus *self-management, solidarity,* and *diversity of development* are beyond material sustenance, also fundamental socialist requirements for a true human society.

But how do these positive requirements mesh with our earlier theoretical assertion that all societies—presumably our socialist "vision" included—necessarily have economic, kinship, community, and decision-making core characteristic structures? The answer is straightforward. It remains true that people's needs and powers are socialized via the elaboration of social relationships of economic activity, sexual/socialization activity, decision-making, and internal as well as intra-group activity. However, these are no longer characterized by the division of society into opposed classes, sexual castes, racial castes, and authority hierarchies. Now, instead, the social relations demarcating each of these spheres of human activity function consistently with the requisites of human well-being and development, rather than being an obstruction to their accomplishment. Kinship relations still exist but oppress neither women nor men. They allow the translation of diverse human sexual potentials into a social mold, but they do so to the benefit and not at the expense of human potentials. Community relations still exist but they are no longer marked by competition, fear, or racism. Indeed, racial demarcations simply pass away—we no more classify people by the racial criteria now employed, then we would now think to use height or weight demarcations. Of course, decision-making must continue under socialism, but the translation of the human potential for creative, conscious activity is no longer marked by the monopolization of power among a few who hold positions at the top of various hierarchies. Instead, decision-making is marked by the equal involvement of all society's actors. Finally, there must still obviously be economic relations, but there need be no classes nor class struggle. Economic relations are equitable—people produce themselves and their environment collectively and without alienation or exploitation.

To the end of self-management, solidarity, and diversity of development, under a true socialism we must have institutions in all spheres with core characteristics such that the necessities of functioning within society demand initiative rather than passivity, sharing rather than competition, friendship rather than aloofness, love rather than callousness, and variety rather than uniformity. To attain self-management, we want institutions that allow people to initiate their own activities and to participate in all related decisions. To attain solidarity, we want institutions that guarantee equity of consideration and also of outcome, that provide full information concerning the effects of people's choices on the well-being of others, and that lead people to consciously apply the decision-making criterion of well-being for all. In a socialist society we must be free to experiment with the development of social and economic institutions that promise this kind of human development, and that moreover allow us to continually refine our insights about our own needs and capabilities, and thus to continually develop as people and as a society.

SOCIALIST ECONOMY

When studying various political economies we distinguish between "intra-unit" institutional forms, or economic institutions that directly mediate between people within relatively small economic processes, and "inter-unit" institutional forms, or economic institutions that provide for some kind of coordination between separated economic processes, thus allowing for an overall mesh, or plan. In the United States, for example, the intra-unit forms are primarily the hierarchically organized, racist, sexist workplace and nuclear family, while the inter-unit forms are primarily the monopoly market structure and a variety of state agencies. In this section we will discuss alternative economic forms of both the inter and the intra-unit kinds for a United States socialism.

We will also distinguish between the process of producing goods and the process of consuming them. But as we recognize that there is more to economic processes than merely a flow of material goods, we will stress that in each phase both "production" and "consumption" are going on.[6] For when a household consumes food, clothing, t.v.'s, books, and housing, it simultaneously produces human fulfillments (or oppressions), capacities (or limitations), consciousness (or unconsciousness), and altered social relationships. And similarly when an automobile factory produces cars as well as changed workers, an altered environment, and sometimes new social relations, it simultaneously consumes not only material inputs such as steel, rubber, and glass, but also human inputs such as worker's skills, consciousness, personalities, and social relations. In our view, as developed in the past sections on political economy and as exemplified in our discussion of the United States, it is essential to understand the "human side" of production and consumption as an integral factor of each process which makes each process an aspect of the other. This orientation must carry over into our discussion of socialist forms as well. Individual and group characteristics are both "inputs" and "outputs" of all economic processes, and the ultimate concern of socialists must be precisely with these human inputs and outputs of the economic processes. For not only does an economy provide the material objects we use to fulfill present needs and capacities, but its economic processes also generate us as we ourselves grow and develop or conversely have our future needs and capacities developed for us.

For purposes of understanding socialist possibilities it is important to remember that all human activities are social rather than private in their effects. Even when you, by yourself, decide to consume a particular "product", the decision has social effects. The people involved in the production of that item have a great interest in your decision and its rationale. It is different, for example, to produce what people can really use and thus want, than to produce waste, conspicuous luxury, or only partially rational commodities—that is, cars instead of means of public and safe transportation. Furthermore, when you consume something you change yourself and that can certainly have social ramifications for your whole community. On the other hand, what the entire economy does also has a large reciprocal effect upon the actual outcomes of any particular activity you may choose to engage in. Thus, your particular choices to develop certain skills or personality traits will have widely varying values for you as well as for society depending upon what other people are doing and upon what goods will be available on what basis in the future. In short, there is a quality of *universal interdependence* about an economy, where the merit of any one decision in terms of its social worth to individual units is only determinable in the context of society's whole economic plan.

However, any particular economic outcome inevitably has a greater effect on some units in the economy than on others. Moreover, there are always certain units which know much more directly the implications of any particular part of a whole plan. Workers in a given automobile factory both better understand the implications of choosing between assembly-line and work-team technologies for use in their factory and are more immediately affected by that choice than more distant units in the economy, even though many other units will also be affected, and the choice is a fully social one.

The task of creating a socialist economy is thus that of building inter and intra-unit forms, as well as of stipulating human decision-making criteria, that are able to focus on the human effects of economic processes, and that can recognize both the universal interdependence and the unequal effects of economic outcomes so that they can embody self-management, solidarity, and variety as their core characteristics. First, we will describe the intra-unit forms we believe appropriate to these tasks. Then we will present an inter-unit form that avoids the weaknesses of the two most commonly conceived socialist forms now in vogue: central planning and markets. Finally, we will conclude this section on socialist economy by addressing the issue of conflict resolution and why we believe it would be possible for an economy to work as we will describe.

INTRA-UNIT FORMS

We see the units of the new socialist economy as individual work places varying in size from a few workers to as many as several thousand according to the nature of the work process; and individual neighborhoods of several thousand people who would constitute a collective consumption unit. Each of these units would be organized as a *democratic council* that would be entirely reponsible for 1-the day-to-day management of the unit's activities, 2-initiating the unit's proposals concerning its inputs and outputs in society's economic plan, and 3-revising these proposals during the back-and-forth planning procedure we will describe below.

In contrast, in the United States (and existing socialist societies as well), most intra-unit forms are either individualist, as in consumption, or hierarchic, as in production. In the individualist format, we find literally no community, and variety and self-management only within the dictates of society's constraining core characteristics. In the hierarchic form there is passivity rather than initiative, a struggle to climb over one's "mates" rather than to work collectively with them, and a tendency to conform to achieve security rather than to experiment so as to grow.

A council form has very obvious advantages for local intra-unit organization. Councils are conducive to direct communication, long-term personal relationships, and conflict mediation involving all parties equally. Even in a hostile capitalist environment, small groups enjoying intimacy and long-standing familiarity are often able to generate considerable solidarity; the results should be that much better in a socialist environment where the councils' cooperative tendencies are aided from without and they are encouraged to establish various practices to foster initiative and solidarity.

Thus we expect that democratic councils would be the most likely form to adopt overall decision criteria emphasizing well-being of all the members of the council as well as of all members of society. The workplace councils would desire to meet responsibilities that the unit had agreed to during the development of society's economic plan, while also organizing work in ways most suitable to the development of the capabilities of the workers. To this end, until massive restructuring of the work situation was completed one necessary policy would be job rotation. Jobs with power over others, jobs that were particularly unpleasant, and jobs that were particularly rewarding would all have to change hands regularly. For example, until the hazardous job of working in the coke ovens in steel mills could be eliminated, the steel mill council would arrange rotation so that no one ended up doing this work continually while others worked in relative safety as crane operators or oversaw the completion of products as team captains in the rolling mill. Adequate training procedures would be needed to ensure that such rotation would work smoothly. Until health care could be radically transformed, doctors would spend much of their time teaching many of their skills to nurses and hospital aides who would be given time to acquire these skills through formal and informal training periods. Although surgery would never be carried out by anyone other than the most learned people available, the spreading of comprehensive medical knowledge and experience among all health workers would improve overall health care, and there is no reason save a temporary glut of patients, that doctors could not perform even the most menial hospital tasks on a rotating basis.[7]

In summary, short-run job rotation would be important both to ensure fairness, and to develop full solidarity and "totalist" rather than fragmented knowledge within the councils. Knowing you are going to rotate into the coke ovens can't help but strengthen your commitment to restructuring that aspect of the steel making process. To expect that coke oven laborers could develop true solidarity with other steel workers who didn't share this commitment would be unrealistic. Similarly, doctors washing out bed-pans is critical to the building of solidarity between hospital aides and doctors.

The more long-run restructuring of work is a question of the kinds of training that the council will decide to provide and the kind of technological improvements it will seek. We would expect the same criteria to be used by the worker's council in these decisions as in all others: will the changes minimize drudgery, enhance solidarity, and promote health, fulfillment, variety, and creativity? The worker as "product" would be considered. The determination of "use-values" in the factory context would be free and social.

The prevalent U.S. feeling that technology necessitates hierarchy and alienation stems from the fact that in the United States we experience technology governed not according to the above social criteria but to the requisites of increasing profits, disciplining workers, and preventing worker collectivity and solidarity. It's little wonder that those criteria have produced the debilitating and fragmenting assembly line with its extreme divisions of labor, for these certainly served the owner's desires for ever-growing personal power and profit.[8] In contrast, as we've already indicated, under socialism the steel mill council would put its greatest efforts into changing the coking process. And more generally, rather than aiming at profit and at control over workers, technology would aim for worker solidarity, pleasure, and growth. It would be designed to call forth artistry, to foster self-management and initiative, and to generate hospitable and healthy work settings. Computerization of the most dreary clerical tasks would be in the interests of workers rather than threatening their financial security. And the elimination of repetitive assembly line work would be high on any worker's list of requirements for new technology. In conclusion, we would expect workplace councils to adopt as a general principle that changes be instituted according to whether they improve the general conditions of work consistent with a detailed understanding of all the involved human factors. And thus we see an end to the inhuman criteria of organization that constitutes the alienation of present United States factory life.

Finally, as job structures and human skills are more and more transformed in the indicated directions, work will take on a new meaning. No longer controlled from without, instead of being a dreaded means to attain the end of leisure time consumption, itself molded to conform not to fulfill, work will become an *end in itself,* or as Karl Marx put it, "life's prime want."[9] The councils will eventually transform the workplace into an arena where people can effectively engage their creative powers. Jobs will come to be rotated not solely out of defensive concerns but also to allow people to experience many kinds of enjoyable work in their lifetime; to provide a more balanced and complete development of human capabilities; and to ensure that new ideas are constantly brought to every job, thus promoting continual variety, creativity, and development. The factory will be consciously seen as a place where workers produce not only socially valuable goods but also themselves— ever more fulfilled and capable human beings.

Under socialism as we envision it, neighborhood consumption units would also be organized as democratic councils, and their general decision criteria would also be the fostering of the well-being and development of all the members of their council as well as the well-being of all the members of society as a whole. Although we'll leave the description of how an individual consumption unit's inputs and outputs are arrived at to our discussion of socialism's inter-unit planning procedure, each neighborhood unit would eventually agree to a schedule of inputs and outputs for a given time-period that include not only material goods and services, but also the individual and group human characteristics that will enter into the neighborhood's activities, as well as the individual and group characteristics that are expected to emerge from those activities. Indeed, as we shall see, the process by which the neighborhood councils will justify their proposals and requests for material inputs will hinge almost entirely on the changes in human fulfillments and capabilities that will be thereby produced.

The neighborhood council would have to decide on how much to allocate to "collective" consumption (i.e. parks, roads, schools, etc.) and how much to "individual" consumption (i.e. radios, food, etc.) as well as how to distribute individual consumption among its members.

Beyond the satisfaction of all members' basic survival needs, recognizing that tendencies toward excessive individual consumption would be inherited from the capitalist past, neighborhood councils would likely establish principles giving priority to collective consumption activities over private ones: community music, T.V., and recreation rooms rather than "rec rooms" for individual nuclear families; and community busses and vans rather than private cars. Because basic material inequalities between individuals are indicative of unequal consideration and destructive of solidarity, neighborhood councils would likely also adopt a principle of overall material equality in the assignment of "individual" consumption goods. And even further, recognizing that materialistic consumerism will initially be a prevalent leftover from capitalism, councils might well adopt principles favoring individual requests aimed at developing talents and creative capacities over requests aimed at satisfying lingering needs for social prestige and power via status-laden escapest commodities. Yet simultaneously, the councils would have no interest whatsoever in imposing any standards of uniformity over individual consumption desiring rather to see the greatest possible variety and initiative.

The point is that the neighborhood councils would have to adopt these, or some such overall principles *prior* to the face-to-face discussion of actual individual and collective community proposals, to provide an institutional context for those discussions. They would be a safeguard against an alienated unconscious reemergence of old self-defeating habits. And there is certainly nothing undemocratic or mechanical about such a principled approach. It merely includes that we can recognize that in the early stages of socialism we will not yet be the people we want to be, so it would be wise for us to democratically adopt a set of guiding principles for subsequent debates, where otherwise some of our undesirable characteristics might run unchecked.

INTER-UNIT FORMS

As we mentioned earlier there is something about the personalized nature of a work-place or neighborhood council that increases our faith in its ability to help us develop socialist consciousness and behavior. However, a skepticism about developing feelings of solidarity and mutual concern between people who work and live far apart, who will never see each other or even know each other's names, is well placed. This skepticism is increased when we examine the two most common forms of inter-unit economic institutions that have been used to date, and realize that it is difficult to imagine how even the most "socialist" of work-place or neighborhood councils could retain its characteristics of self-management or solidarity for long if it were connected to other councils via either a market or a central planning inter-unit mechanism. After examining some of the failures inherent in each of these forms, we will proceed to outline an inter-unit form we believe consistent with socialist core characteristics.

Markets

Under both capitalism and market socialism markets are the dominant inter-unit allocative mechanism: different groups of people, functioning primarily as producers in the factories or consumers in the homes coordinate their effects by means of market-place exchanges. Materials goods and many services have prices which fluctuate in accord with supply and demand. Buyers and sellers go to the market and express their desires through "bids". Prices fluctuate so as to allow a mesh of supply and demand.

Traditionally cited difficulties with the market mechanism include people having unequal wealth to express their desires, monopoly and monopsony, and the uncertainty produced in a system of decentralized decision-making which does not coordinate decisions (allow "recontracting") before parties interact. Although there are good reasons to expect that the first two of these difficulties should be worse under capitalism than under market socialism, they would nonetheless remain a problem in the new form too; and there is no reason to expect that the last difficulty would be any less serious.[10]

However, there are other and fundamentally more devestating problems associated with the market inter-unit mechanism, especially when we view it from a socialist perspective. The market provides as information only the price and commodity character of goods and services; it requires as activity only individualized bartering and competition, it involves as motivations only the maximization of personal immediate consumption pleasure and profit (per worker). The market involves a continual possibility of competitive failure and thus creates basic insecurities, which themselves elicit defensive behaviors counter-productive to societal well-being. And finally, the market is inefficient in any situation where public goods are involved, which is to say, in precisely that situation which socialists understand to be universal to human interactions. We will briefly explain the significances of these various criticisms.

Markets are part and parcel of "commodity fetishism" wherein commodities seem to acquire human powers, while the real underlying social relations and human endeavors become lost to sight. When markets and prices form the medium through which people express their desires, those desires become abstracted from the concrete realities of what goes into creating an object of possible consumption, or of what will be gained from consumption of an object of possible production. Markets hide from consideration the actual concrete human costs and gains that accrue from economic activities. They instead emphasize a knowledge of an abstract price, in some way supposedly a measure of those same costs and gains. However, even if prices were such a measure—and they are not—human fulfillment demands something more than just an "abstract" knowledge. It requires empathy with others, and an understanding of the *concrete realities* of every aspect of the factors going into our life activities. To know how much of something we wish to consume, and indeed to fully appreciate its worth, we need to personally know what went into its production. To know how hard we want to work in turning out some particular final good, we need to know, not the abstract price someone will pay, but concretely what pleasures and gains the good will bring. Not only does morale and what we might call "in-tuneness" with the world depend upon this absence of fetishism, but so does the possibility for real human solidarity premissed upon each person's collective concern and empathy for every other person's well-being. Instead of providing the kind of information necessary for people to develop empathy and solidarity, markets hide that information and provide the reverse.

Even worse, markets simultaneously require competitive behavior and prohibit cooperation as irrational. For markets create a direct opposition of interests between those who produce a certain good and those who consume it. The interest of the producer is sale at the highest possible price. The interest of the consumer is purchase at the lowest possible price. Neither participant is concerned with the human situation of the other—to be so concerned would undermine the functioning of the market mechanism between them. The essence of every market exchange is an act whereby each party tries to take maximum advantage of the other. As an economic agency, markets establish the opposite of solidarity—they declare the war of each against all. In short, as Marx put it, with markets—

...every product is a bait with which to seduce away the other's very being, his money; every real and possible need is a weakness which will lead the fly to the gluepot....every need is an opportunity to approach one's neighbor under the guise of the utmost amiability and say to him: 'Dear friend, I give you what you need, but you know the conditio sine qua non [the condition that must necessarily be fulfilled]; you know the ink in which you have to sign yourself over to me; in providing for your pleasure, I fleece you.'[11]

Adam Smith was just as clear:

It is not from the benevolence of the butcher, the brewer, or the baker, that we expect our dinner, but from their regard for their own interest. We address ourselves, not to their humanity but to their self-love, and never talk to them of our own necessities but of their advantage.[12]

Although it might at first appear that maximizing immediate personal consumption satisfaction is maximizing human fulfillment, growth, and development, our previous analysis of where capacities and preferences come from—namely their partial production within the economic system itself—uncovers the shallowness of this proposition. As Herb Gintis has stated: "To justify a set of economic institutions on the basis of the manifest preferences of individuals who were formed through their preparation for a participation in these institutions involves making an arbitrary cut in a system of causal linkages."[13] Use-value is determined in part by the economy itself through a mechanism which skews it in an alienated way. And, similarly, there is no question at all that maximizing profit is not the same as consciously maximizing fulfillment, growth, and development in the workplace. So the decision-making criteria imposed by a market mechanism on both the consumer and the producer are alienated. They diverge from the decision-making criteria we want to anchor at the very core of a socialist society: that is, a concern with on-going human self-development.

Gar Alperovitz has pointed out that "as long as the social and economic security of any economic unit is not guaranteed, it is likely to function to protect (and out of insecurity, to extend) its own special status-quo interests—even when they run counter to the broader interests of society."[14] And this is precisely the situation a market system creates. Workers in a plant generating pollution but thereby making money have an interest in hiding the weakness. Workers in a plant creating useless or even dangerous products have an interest in advertising to generate market demand, even while knowing that consumers are being duped. Consumers will pay for goods whose production causes intense pain to workers, and thereby to the whole community. And workers in an auto factory would under a market system be tempted to oppose desireable changes in the nation's overall transportation system, since the market system would not ensure their continuing employment, secure income, or dignity in their work. To put it most generally, markets systematically establish false contradictions between individual and societal well-being.

Finally, we return to the question of whether the prices that markets generate as signals for economic decision makers are in fact a "precise measure of the human costs and gains." Despite all their weaknesses, market prices retain an appeal because of this supposed characteristic. Unfortunately, however, the prices generated by "free markets" can lay claim to this characteristic only in situations where the involved commodities are limited in their effects to one and only one individual or firm who we can therefore unequivocally identify as their "consumer". The explanation for this is straightforward. When a person buys from a market it is an isolated, individualist act. The person evaluates whether or not to buy something only in terms of how its purchase would affect him or her and no one else. The person pays the price if the effects are deemed worthy of the outlay from a limited budget. The judgements that occur in market transactions therefore only involve the effects upon two agents, the immediate buyer and seller. If the consumption of a bought article by its purchaser in fact has effects on other people these will not have been taken into account in the decision to buy nor in the pricing, and the overall process can make no claim to "efficiency".

This is not a proposition discovered by radical economists who oppose the market system, but a fact long recognized and admitted by the staunchest defenders of the market system. How can this be? The defenders of markets refer to these problems as "externalities" and "public goods" (or "bads"), and have created a whole subdivision of the neoclassical economic discipline, Public Finance, to deal with them. But the crucial point is that the defenders of market systems view these problems as aberrations, exceptions, and infrequent occurrences requiring admittedly "social" or "political" mechanisms for their resolution. Socialists, on the other hand, have an entirely different view of the interconnectedness of the world we live in. Not only is the present capitalist world tremendously more interconnected than neoclassical economists admit, but the socialist world we want to create is infinitely more interconnected still! Not only do we recognize that we are inevitably social beings, but we want to develop our social potentials and become even more social. The inter-unit mechanism of markets is a structure that leads to generally inefficient allocations in an interconnected human world, but more importantly, it is an institutional boundary that prevents people from exercising their social aspects and developing their social potentials. Even under socialism, if one insists on maintaining markets, the necessity for an eventual mesh between consciousness and institutional relations will enforce a modified continuation of capitalist characteristics. Far from being an appropriate institution for socialism—one that embodies solidarity as one of its core aspects—markets are exactly what leftists have always suspected, an appropriate institutional boundary form for capitalism embodying individualism of the worst type, competition, and greed. As Marx put it, those who want markets under socialism "want competition without the pernicious effects of competition. They all want the impossible, namely the conditions of bourgeois existence without the necessary consequences of those conditions."[15]

Central Planning

The most predominant alternative to the market inter-unit form is central planning, wherein some politically determined central group generates society's plan in accord with a calculation aimed at maximizing a social welfare function, or, as Engels describes the process, "the useful effects of the various articles of consumption, compared with each other and with the quantity of labor required for their production, will in the last analysis determine the plan."[16]

Beyond the obvious problems that central planning has no real method for discovering society's welfare function, and that the planners' estimates would invariably be biased by their personal needs and much more critically by the reproductive needs of "their" organization of society, the fundamental difficulty is that, even if the planners were all-wise and altruistic, there would still be no self-management.

The easiest way to understand central planning is to abstract from all the technical problems that have been the exclusive concern of most authors. Stripped down to its essentials, the central planning agency is assumed to know what the social welfare function is, the technical capabilities of all the economy's productive units, and the availability of all resources. It then proceeds to formulate the economy's programming problem—maximize the social welfare function subject to all the constraints imposed by the technologies, capacities, and resources available—and then solve it on some giant computer. The result is a listing of what all the material inputs and outputs should be for each economic enterprise in order to maximize "social welfare". The central planning board communicates these values to each unit with the instruction to perform the indicated economic activity.[17]

This doesn't sound much like the iterative procedure known as "material balances," nor like the down-up, down-up idea often referred to as the planning procedure in socialist countries. But the key to interpreting these "more elaborate" procedures is to understand that, all too often, their exclusive motivation is that the central planning agency does not in fact have all the technical information we assumed it did, and so some way must therefore be found to generate that information. In central planning the iterations are not proposals from units that are then coordinated by a planning agency and sent back for revision, but rather, 1-production targets posed by the central planning board and responses from the units concerning what inputs would be necessary in order for the unit to meet the output targets, or 2-input proposals from the center and responses from the units concerning what output they could achieve with those inputs. These are practical procedures by which the central planning agency overcomes the technical difficulty that it does not know the technological capabilities of the production units. During the back-and-forth procedures of central planning the individual units are not participating in the social generation of an economic plan, but are instead only supplying data to the central planning board so that it can unilaterally calculate an "efficient" plan and inform the units of the part they are to play. The only "management" left to the individual economic units is to manage to fulfill the centrally planned targets.[18]

Although it would be possible to elect the central planning board to accord with the fullest of known democratic principles, to conclude that this would resolve the problem is to miss the point. Self-management does not mean electing some person or agency to make our decisions for us. The inter-unit mechanism of central planning is an institutional boundary that delimits workplace and neighborhood self-management. It doesn't provide local councils with information concerning all the human gains and losses associated with the inputs each council receives from the others, nor with the human consequences of the outputs each provides to all the rest. And it does not provide a vehicle through which councils can propose and collectively decide upon activities based upon knowledge of their full consequences. Instead central planning embodies as a core characteristic an *authoritarian command relationship,* which, if it persists, can only eventually erode any self-management characteristics that might be initially present within the economic councils or any broader political sphere. For it very quickly becomes evident to any central planning authority that it is easier to give instructions to a *manager* and hold him responsible for carrying them out then to try and deal with workers' committees. And once this is done, the manager must obviously be granted powers over the work process. Similarly the workers accustom themselves to a condition of "following orders" and in time accept it as inevitable, seeking desirable alterations in matters of income, work pace, etc. but not control. Authoritarianism becomes a part of the core of any centrally planned socialist society, and as such it pervades all arenas of life—or contradictions ensue. The social relations of work itself under central planning allocative forms are essentially as they are under capitalist market forms.[19]

At this point some clarifications are in order. We consider central planning to be the procedure whose essence we outlined above, and we insist that any communication between the central planning board and the individual economic units that serves merely to provide data to the center does not alter that essence. Nor do we consider this interpretation a straw-person. Other than markets, only central planning as we have described it has ever been rigorously presented as a feasible inter-unit mechanism for a socialist economy. Furthermore, this interpretation of central planning captures the essence of much of the planning that has taken place in countries trying to build socialism.

However, we do not mean to imply that there have never been any experiments departing at all from this essence, nor that all forms of socialist planning need be so detrimental.[20] As we hope to show, there is a type of socialist planning other than the centrist variety. But while we do not see any inevitable dilemma between individuality and collectivity, or between self-management and solidarity, our optimism does not stem from the belief most common to socialists aware of the intrinsic weaknesses of both market and central planning, namely that some combination of the two forms can achieve a "shrewd trade-off" that will negate the ill-effects that each form would incur if it were used alone. The limited use of markets can provide a decentralizing counter-force to the centralizing of central planning. And the limited use of planning can provide a collectivizing counter-force to the individualism and competitiveness of markets. But the combined use of both forms in whatever balance can in no way overcome the fact that each embodies core characteristics we have discovered to be antithetical to the development of socialist human beings. Their combined use is at best still a trade off between two evils. Looking at work incentives under the two systems provides a practical summary of the problems.

When actual work processes cause more pain than pleasure there must be some "external incentives" providing motivation to do them. In market socialism one works for the wage negotiated in the labor market plus one's share in the profits of the enterprise. Beyond this there is the possibility of motivation from comaraderie with one's fellow work-council members, but, significantly, not from any broader societal solidarity. Over time, as workers discover that their seeming internal self-management is actually severely circumscribed by the dictates of market profit dynamics, even the motivation from limited internal self-management will diminish and the external material incentives will reign supreme. Indeed, the council members will "save valuable time" by electing an "expert manager" to make the essentially technical maximum-profit-per-person decisions for them.

In central planning the ultimate incentive to work will also come to be material reward. There is no illusion about structuring the work situation together with one's fellow workers, and only a feeling of societal responsibility can compliment material incentives. The degree to which a centrally planned economy can rely on the "moral incentive" of social responsibility will depend on the degree to which workers feel that the central planners' decisions are made in accord with their well-being rather than with the reproductive needs of the planners themselves. Yet even in a situation where there is tremendous trust in the leadership's motives, there is a limit to the motivation of general societal responsibility in the absence of meaningful participatory involvement in grass-roots decision making. In the context of on-going central planning without participation the diminishing motivational power of "moral incentives" eventually leaves the planners with no other resort than to increase reliance on material incentives or on political coercion.[21]

Participatory Planning

Each council in our envisioned socialist society has a variety of possible ways that it can organize its economic activities. Each way requires and yields different social and material products, and thus has different effects upon the council itself and also upon the broader society. The inter-unit problem is to find a mechanism which allows councils to settle upon those particular activities which are as socially fulfilling as possible, in such a way that all council's decisions fit together into a feasible plan. What are needed as inputs by any one council must either exist already or be created as outputs by other councils.

For socialist allocation we then propose a social, iterative procedure in which fetishism is excluded, activities are proposed according to criteria of well-being, and are decided via direct participatory collective self-management.

In this system each work-place council would propose the amount and style of labor that it would do, and each consumer council what it would like to "take-in". The criteria that councils would use would be the worth to others of generated outputs, the difficulties for others implied by required inputs, and the effects upon the council's own members' capacities, personalities, and social relations.

In making an initial proposal each council would have to estimate from past experience the kinds of efforts required of others to supply a given list of proposed inputs, and the uses to which others would put a given list of proposed outputs. Then, learning the results of all units' first proposals, each council would get much new information to work with: 1-For each material good or service there would be information about whether it was left in excess demand or supply by the sum total of all first proposals. 2-The descriptions of the human inputs and outputs of the different neighborhood councils would provide new information about the human value of the different goods that the work-place councils provide. 3-The descriptions of the human inputs and outputs of the different kinds of work-place councils would provide new information about the full human gains and costs associated with making different goods. 4-A comparison of the proposals of different neighborhood councils would show what were the average and total proposed intakes for various goods. And 5-a comparison of work-place proposals would show each work-place council how it compared with similar councils in the same industry in both choice of technology and degree of effort.

Thus, let's say for example, that you were working in a council producing tools for neighborhoods and other work-places. The procedure we described would provide you with exactly the kind of information you would need to formulate a second proposal. That is, 1-What must other workers do to produce the inputs you use and how would that activity affect them? 2-How much would your effort aid the other work-place and neighborhood councils? Unlike with either the market or central planning inter-unit mechanism, our participatory procedure provides both the necessary information and the institutional opportunity for councils to make non-fetishized decisions and engage in meaningful self-management.

However there is no reason to suppose that the initial proposals will provide an immediate mesh or economic plan. Consumers might well have asked for more than workers offered to produce, and some work-places wouldn't be planning to produce enough of the inputs other work-places would need. If the sum total of tools offered was less than the sum total of requests, then as a tool-maker you would know that it would be socially beneficial if your council could increase its output. Of course you would check to see how your proposed efforts and the inputs you thought you needed compared with the average in your industry. If you were in a neighborhood council requesting tools, on the other hand, you would know that there were more difficulties than you had assumed, and you would check other neighborhood council's requests to see how you might operate with fewer or different tools. In the second go-round the workers, seeing excess demand for tools, and learning the reasons for it, either would be impressed and increase their proposed tool production, or would feel that the needs were not so significant compared to the increased problems the additional production would generate. Consumers of tools would make a similar assessment and either cut back on their requests or not.

Before dealing with the question of whether or not all these local proposals and revisions could eventually converge to a feasible annual plan, we will discuss how such a procedure could deal with three often raised difficulties: 1-unforeseen changes, 2-long-run decisions about "new technologies", and, 3-very large choices that radically transform production processes and affect great numbers of councils.

Federations of councils would be necessary. Every "industry" would have regional councils with representatives from all the work-place councils, and national councils made up of representatives from all the regions. Neighborhood councils would federate similarly. Representatives would in all cases be rotated and strictly recallable.

Now consider a consumer unit that has agreed to a year long food consumption plan on the basis of expected eating habits and estimated agricultural output; but that the unit's desires change due to changes in tastes, to an unexpected growth in numbers, or to some sickness that alters the mix of foods needed. The change would be communicated to either the regional or national agricultural council (depending upon the size of the change) along with an explanation. Often the totality of such local changes would cancel each other and only distribution—not production—would have to be changed. When such changes did not cancel out, the industry councils would have to consult the different local agricultural councils, who would in turn evaluate the possibilities of meeting such demand changes, in exactly the same way they formulated their plan proposal in the first place. When alterations were possible they would be made and when they were not, or when the workers simply didn't consider the change justified, this would be communicated to the consumers who would have the opportunity to react again. In essence, such difficulties would be handled by conceiving the planning procedure as a potentially continuous process, although between planning periods regional or national councils would be mediating among the few councils which had to bend their activities in accordance with changing circumstances. One practical way to meet many contingencies without such emergency adjustments would be to build a comfortable "slack" or planned excess supply into the yearly plans.

Long-range decisions introduce two different kinds of problems. Workers carrying out their daily activities in their work places cannot know all the consequences of changing the organization of production even though they will often conceive of the changes originally. Only people spending a considerable part of their work-time analyzing production operations will be in a position to formulate the full consequences. Second, certain changes require commitments of inputs and work activities in many different time-periods. We'll take transportation planning as an example of both.

Each community has a variety of industries making or repairing cars, busses, roads, trains, airplanes, airports, subways and operating these services. Each of these industries would have their own regional and national councils, which could in turn send representatives to make up regional and national transportation councils. Similarly the consumer federations could have subcommittees concerned with transportation problems. Consideration of changes in society's transportation plans would go on at all levels.

Each of the work-place councils would have some sort of "research and development" department through which all workers would rotate. The research and development department of a factory making automobiles and vans, though it might investigate more radical long-run changes to recommend to regional and national councils, would probably focus on changes in the work process as it affects the human development of its council members, and on "product innovations" in cars and vans as they affect consumers' well-being.

The regional transportation councils would establish R&D operations (workplaces), staffed by rotating and recallable delegates from local councils, to investigate the implications of major changes in the region's transportation system. These units would report findings to the regional transportation council and the regional neighborhood federation committee on transportation. Now suppose the regional transportation council and its member councils had agreed on the substitution of mini-bus neighborhood service for taxis—or the development of a new air transport facility—and had worked out an operational plan for the implementation of this change over a number of planning periods. Their proposal would include all the relevant data concerning what would likely be undertaken by all the different units in all the years involved and the human gains expected as a result. The proposal would then be considered by all the economic councils just as in the procedure for establishing the yearly economic plan. If it were accepted after back-and-forth revision and agreement on inputs and outputs, it would be implemented immediately and commitments for all the economic units involved would be considered to have been made some number of years into the future. Thus, in general, for each annual plan some features will have already been decided in the past as parts of longer-term projects that were previously agreed upon and already under way.

In analogous fashion a national transportation council would establish R&D operations to investigate more radical changes such as the replacement of cars by new kinds of subways in major cities and high speed train service for cross-country travel.

The important points to remember in all these instances, are: 1-The R&D operations are for the sole purpose of conceiving and formulating the exact implications of changes that would have been otherwise only vague ideas to work-place council members and consequently impossible to vote on. 2-Workers in the regional and national R&D operations would be sent on a rotating basis by the member councils. 3-The iterative procedure for their adoption by work and neighborhood councils is exactly the same as described before. And, 4-the fact that certain decisions can only be sensibly made in the context of a number of years simply implies that shorter planning periods will generally contain prior commitments they must work within.

Since not all changes can be undertaken at once, how will choices be made between transforming the transportation system, decentralizing cities, eliminating underground coal mining or strip mining, or converting from assembly lines to work-teams?

The same back-and-forth process will determine where the proposals are in conflict and where they are not, they will be revised, and finally some order in which to undertake them will be voted on. This "long-run" plan will imply definite commitments of resources and human activity in the first few subsequent years, and vaguer expectations for more distant years, so it is this procedure that would reassign workers to different units. But the criteria used in long-term planning—the greatest human fulfillment, growth, and development for all the nation's citizens—and the democratic, social, iterative procedure for its adoption would be the same.

The general character of our inter-unit economic institutions should now be clear. It is a procedure in which units coordinate their activities by essentially governing themselves, consuming according to need and in light of the social relations of production, and producing according to capability and in light of the social worth of related consumption. It is a means of social planning without fetishism, centralization, or competition but rather with a dynamic that reinforces empathy between democratic councils. It is a system wherein decisions are made in light of their direct human implications—both in immediate fulfillments and in the development of peoples' capacities and tastes over time. What to build, what technologies to create, how to structure factories, dwellings, and even whole cities, how to conduct day-to-day economic activities— all are determined in accord with the dictates of people's desires and skills. The economic plan is socially decided yet its aspects are at every step proposed and elaborated directly by people most intimately involved. We believe the participatory iterative model is the only inter-unit economic form that can embody both self-management and social solidarity as core aspects, reinforce both in the intra-unit council forms described earlier and simultaneously develop both in all people who engage in economic activities.

In the *Grundrisse* Karl Marx spelled out his view of the alienation of modern capitalist political economy most clearly:

> The social character of activity, and the social form of the product, as well as the participation of the individual in production, appear here as alien material things in opposition to the individual; not in their behavior to each other, but in their subordination to relations which exist independently of them and arise out of the collisions of indifferent individuals. The universal exchange of activities and products, which has become a condition of life for each individual, and the bond between individuals appears to them as something alien and independent, like a thing.[22]

We have argued that under central planning and market socialism the essential problem Marx describes—*the divorce of social outcomes from the wills of those most affected*—still prevails; on the one hand due to the adverse effects of market exchange relations, and on the other due to those of hierarchical centralized decision making, even though in both instances there is state ownership of the means of production. And we have further presented an alternative economic form in which "the universal exchange of activities and products" is still at the core of social life, but in which it finally occurs according to people's desires, at their behests, and to their advantages. What is now essential is to argue the feasibility of this model as a real world goal.

SOCIAL FEASIBILITY

Is the model socially feasible? Can people function in such a system even after it has been well-established, or won't they take advantage of each other, some being gluttonous and others lazy? During a transition period when people still have considerable leftover capitalist characteristics won't there be racism, sexism, and tendencies to greediness and power which would undermine the operation of the intra- and inter-unit forms we have described? Or, put another way, haven't we confused socialism with some more distant "utopia" and proposed institutional forms that are perhaps appropriate for the latter, but unrealistic for what is essentially a long period of transition?

In this section we will try to answer these questions while simultaneously giving an ever-more-concrete picture of our vision of what socialist economic life would be like. The answer comes in three parts:

1-People's daily-life characteristics are developed in particular socio-economic settings. If we succeed in constructing settings that foster solidarity and concern for others while discouraging greed, people will come to develop these aspects as well.

2-To the extent that capitalist characteristics survive into socialism, we will have to establish means for resolving conflicts within both the economic councils and the planning procedure.

3-However, if the means established for resolving "transitional" conflicts are destructive of the very core characteristics we seek to develop, either reinforcing old capitalist characteristics, or creating new undesirable ones, then it won't help to continually speak of a distinction between socialism and a future utopia, because there won't be any utopia and socialism will become a transition to something else.

CONFUSING SOCIALISM WITH THE UTOPIAN GOAL?

It is important to clarify the last point further before attempting to discuss the first two. Capitalism and socialism are fundamentally different social systems with fundamentally different core characteristics; some sort of revolutionary transformation must occur in passing from one system to the other. However, there should be no such distinction between the core characteristics of socialism and those of a future utopia or "true communism", and we do not expect that a revolution will be necessary in passing between these two societies. The only difference between a future utopia and a more immediate socialism is not the achievement of material plenty, but the degree to which solidarity, self-management, and human variety have come to pervade all aspects of society. If the distinction between the socialism we desire immediately and our longer-run expectations serves to remind us that there will be a period after the overthrow of capitalism when old human and institutional characteristics will "hang on", then the distinction can serve some useful purpose. But if the distinction is used to justify the continued existence of social institutions that are inimicable to the development of self-management, solidarity, and variety, or if the failure to achieve "material plenty" is used as an excuse to establish new institutions destructive of the core characteristics we desire to create, the distinction becomes counter-productive and the activities most likely reactionary.[23]

So if we have proposed institutional economic forms that are appropriate to an ideal society of the future, that's fine since it means we have largely succeeded in embodying the very core characteristics we most desire to pursue. However, our economic institutions must additionally include mechanisms for resolving transitional conflicts stemming from the "residual" characteristics inherited from capitalism. Within the councils the ultimate means for resolving such conflicts (as well as all others having to do even with differences about socialist policies) will be majority vote. In the inter-unit mechanism too, a voting procedure will settle issues that have led to an impasse in the planning iterations, but which councils vote will depend on just what kind of problem has arisen.

It will be important to distinguish between different types of disagreement. It is possible that continued discussion within a council or continued iterations in the planning procedure are failing to resolve problems simply because someone (or some group) is being lazy or greedy. Or the conflict could be between one policy which clearly embodies socialist values and another which does not. Or there could be an honest disagreement over which of two policies is more in conformity with socialist criteria or a disagreement could result simply from ignorance or disagreement about a proposal's long-range consequences. And finally, there could be disagreement about priorities or even developing standards or values. An example of this last that might come up very frequently would be disagreement over whether to stress immediate fulfillments or future development in cultural matters, design, etc. Although the procedure for resolving disagreements in all cases will ultimately be a democratic vote, determining the source of a conflict will be very important in deciding how to handle it.

For instance, imagine a neighborhood council that has agreed on the operating principles discussed earlier favoring equal treatment and collective consumption. If an individual insisted on continuing to unreasonably request significantly more than the average for the council, or refused to give his or her consent to a near unanimous choice of increasing the proportion of collective consumption in some particular way, this would be a disagreement of one of the first two types. The councils could overrule the individual and seek to change his/her understanding of the issues. On the other hand, suppose that two-thirds of a factory council that assembles T.V.s votes to replace the assembly line with work-teams but the other third insists work-teams would be too slow and that it would be better to keep the line with increased job rotation. If the factory were large enough, work-teams could assemble most of the T.V.s but the workers particularly convinced that increased rotation would better solve the human development problems could be allowed to test their beliefs on one remaining assembly line.

Now, on the inter-unit level, suppose that a lack of proposed steel output stands in the way of a feasible plan and that one steel mill continues to propose working only a twenty hour week. Unless the local, was proposing that all steel workers work a twenty hour week, they would be voted down at the national steel council for violating the principle of equality of consideration. If the local in question were seriously arguing that steel workers should all work less than the national average because their jobs were less satisfying and more hazardous, and if the national council agreed, then a twenty hour week would be proposed to all the other industrial councils. (However, if the need for high steel output under difficult working conditions stemmed from a major social decision to decentralize urban centers before transforming the steel-making process, then we would expect most steel council representatives to vote against the local's twenty hour week proposal.)

If the national steel council did propose a reduced steel workers' week, the federation of all worker's councils would pass on it. If this group couldn't reach a concensus, the ultimate decision would have to be made by a societal wide vote. But since it is difficult to imagine that an entire industry would contain a tremendously higher proportion of workers who were "lazy" or less-socially conscious than all the other industries, the failure to reach concensus would be considered a signal of failure on someone's part to understand the human implications of a decision. Therefore, in voting down such a proposal from the national steel council we would expect the other national councils to also vote 1-to reinvestigate their decisions requiring high steel inputs, 2-to hasten the investment necessary to transform the steel making process, and 3-to institute a large program of temporary job rotation between the steel industry and all other industries (steel workers and others trade jobs intermittantly).

An example in the inter-unit planning procedure where conflict resolution could allow a dissenting minority to experiment would be if there was significant disagreement over what kind of major transformation was best for improving ecological balance. If the majority felt that decentralizing the cities as quickly as possible was the answer, while a minority felt that it was better to transform large scale production operations such as steel and building materials into smaller operations able to produce more diversified products even if that slowed down the construction of decentralized living centers, the majority vote could establish the first policy for the country while allowing several regions to proceed with the second approach.

Finally, we would envision one particular institutional variation for resolving conflict involving racism and sexism. The kind of majoritarian movement for socialism necessary to overthrow capitalism in the United States could only develop with a general recognition that racism and sexism are oppressive core characteristics of the U.S. system. And therefore, we would expect during the beginning period of building socialism a committment to overcoming racist and sexist consciousness and establishing institutions necessary to the accomplishment of those tasks. Not only do we envision regional and national federations of minority groups and of women, but we believe there would be women's and minority caucuses within all the different economic councils in workplaces and neighborhoods. And we would suggest that the resolution of any conflicts that were judged to be ones involving racism or sexism be delegated to review and "leadership" by those caucuses.

For instance, should the black caucus in a Birmingham steel mill feel that a workers' council majority decision about the rotation and training program for hod-carriers and bricklayers was racist they would ask the worker's council to grant them the "autonomous" right to review the decision and veto it. Under normal circumstances we would expect the council would be happy to have this internal check preventing decisions that would hinder the development of solidarity. However, should it not agree that racial issues were involved, and thus decide to refuse the caucus review privileges, the caucus would take its case to the black caucus of the regional steel council. If that regional black caucus agreed that it was a racial issue, they would ask the regional steel councils to over-rule the local mill. If they refused, the regional caucus would have the right to appeal to the national level. And any national minority caucus or women's caucus that was in fundamental disagreement with its national industry or consumers' council would have the right of appeal to the political arena we will discuss below.

All of these kinds of democratic "forcing mechanisms" would be used when necessary to make the intra-unit and inter-unit planning procedures finally converge to a feasible economic plan. But is the system toward which it moves really compatible with human nature? Aren't there instincts for aggression and domination inherent in all human beings that would inevitably disrupt the operation of the kind of economy we have pictured?

As we have emphasized, we believe that people "make" themselves insofar as their social activities affect their consciousnesses, skills, fulfillments, and personality and thus their desires and behaviors. But this self-creation occurs not in isolation, according solely to one's own personal dictates, but rather in specific socio-economic settings according, at least thus far in history, very much to dictates outside one's own control and frequently aimed at things other than one's own best interest. We believe that people need and have capacities to attain not only material survival, comfort, and sex, but human solidarity and friendship, love, creative aesthetic fulfillment, and self-management. But we also know that historically the economic and social roles available to people have been directed away from the simultaneous fulfillment of all these ends, most often only toward assuring material survival and comfort for the few to the detriment of attaining the other ends. History has incorporated a host of detrimental dynamics in the institutions of society and personalities of its people but these are not endemic or permanent. Thus the kinds of individualistic, competitive, and materialistic personality-types one finds in capitalist societies are on the one hand irrational, because they foster the reproduction of capitalism's oppressions, and yet on the other hand quite rational, for so long as capitalism exists more humane personality traits are often even more self-defeating.

We have thus far defined a set of socialist economic institutions very different from those that now prevail under capitalism, or for that matter, under market or centrally planned socialism. Are they practicable? Let us ask how workers would have to act, and whether or not we believe people could be expected to do so—remembering in each instance that we are now talking about people living in a very different kind of environment, after a considerable period of development of that environment where many "old personality types" are no longer necessary.

Socialist production must create the goods necessary to meet all people's needs. It must produce food and clothing, build cities and transportation systems, create parks, hospitals, and dwellings. But at the same time it must also create a climate of cooperation and growth suitable to participatory decision making and worker fulfillment. Liberated production must allow workers to comply with Marx's admonition: "Produce with consciousness, as human beings, not as atoms without consciousness of your species, and you will have elevated yourself above all...artificial conflicts."[24]

Through the iterative mechanisms we've described, councils will have to formulate their proposals for activities and their opinions about other council's activities both in tune with their own immediate situations and an honest assessment of the conditions of other councils. Worker activity will have to foster societal growth at the same time that it furthers worker fulfillment, and each consumer's tastes will have to reflect a sensitivity to workers' conditions as well as to the consumer's own needs. In sum, individuals and groups of workers will have to be motivated by very different values and understandings than those which prevail now. Is this humanly feasible?

We believe that the kinds of shiftless, lazy, greedy, racist, sexist, and competitive consciousnesses that exist in present day societal forms are intrinsic to those forms but not to us as people. We believe that the mesh between personalities and roles under capitalism leads to oppressive traits, but that in a socialist society, where survival is assured, institutions are remolded, and role dictates altered, people could be sociable and empathetic and both human nature and society's institutions would make other types of behavior as irrational as humane behavior is in the present system where it is all too true that nice folks finish last.

We believe that under socialism workers will do their tasks because they understand their importance and the ways they interrelate with other tasks, because they determine their tasks themselves, and because of the direct rewards of socially valuable, self-managed, collectively-shared creative labor. To the extent some jobs are painful, they'll be rotated, and their importance along with the fairness of their assignment will be continually reevaluated. In most jobs workers will be able to have "artisan" values and, quite contrary to the present situation, to take pride in their efforts. When all the socially useless labor in the United States is eliminated—war production, insurance company work, lawyers to protect private property, advertising, etc.—the free time so generated, rather than going solely into leisure, will go into allowing useful work efforts to be done more carefully and artistically. Work places and processes will be designed with human scale and need in mind.[25]

Consider yourself as a worker in the type of socialist society we are attempting to describe. Do you skimp or do you try to honestly assess your capabilities and society's needs? Remember that everyone has an interest, and has come to understand that they have an interest, in the overall well-being of the community. Remember that the character of work life has changed entirely, and that others understand where it is still painful, and try to moderate their requests accordingly. We believe that workers will come to approach their tasks with the desire to produce so that they and everyone else benefits to the greatest possible collective extent. We think the type of collective behavior we've described would come naturally in the new social context because it would be in the interest of each worker seeking community and self-management, just as competition, authoritarianism, laziness and racism are "rationally" defensive responses of people seeking to survive and to rationalize work-life under present day capitalism.

But what about when you-the-worker go home and become the consumer in your local consumption council. Why won't you continue to ask for the most you can conceive of?

Again, consider yourself as a member of a council which collectively determines a set of consumption activities and thus of desired inputs from many different workplace councils. You are working in knowledge of the social relations that lurk behind the production of goods you might want, in knowledge of what your unit consumed last year and of what other units did too, in knowledge of what investment was and thus of changes in productive capability, and in awareness of the importance for the whole community of proper functioning within the inter and intra-unit forms. Won't all the pressures of the system, as well as your own desires for community work against excessive requests and won't you come to assess possibilities socialistically?

In a socialist society people will come to understand that their well-being is not a function of the number of goods they have. For, contrary to the situation under capitalism, there is no possibility that the goods necessary to survival can be here today and gone tomorrow. Nor do commodities impart status or power in a socialist society; they do not have to take the place of unachievable goals of community or love. By pursuing consumption that was not necessary but that caused producers considerable difficulty, a person would be sacrificing friendship, sympathy and community for some useless hoarding. In general, the difference is between trying to squeeze what you can out of a system hostile to your needs versus trying to further a favorable system of which you are, and feel, an integral part.

Incentives

Just as we summarized the essence of market socialism and centrally planned socialism by analyzing their implicit incentive mechanisms, we can summarize the essence of our economy by discussing incentives in participatory socialism. We recognized that as long as the transformation of work places has not been completed, we could not rely on the intrinsic quality of the work experience to provide the only motivation. However, it should now be clear that both the internal structures of the economic councils, as well as our iterative planning procedure provide much stronger impulses to the transformation of daily work-life than exist under either market socialism or centrally planned socialism.

But as great a difference as this may be, there still must be a rather lengthy period before the transformation of work is complete. During that period the incentives in our socialist economy are an integral part of the intra and inter-unit planning procedures. As immediately unpleasant as any task you have may be, you know that it was a fair assignment and that others are willing and going to do it too. Within your work place there are all the social pressures we have discussed to bring you to offer a personal labor plan that is in your own, your fellow workers', and your society's best interest, backed by the final sanction of a majority vote of the workers' council. In the neighborhood councils there are all the social pressures we have discussed to bring you to request a personal consumption bundle that is in your own, your neighbors', and your society's best interest, again backed by the right of the neighborhood council to give you a bundle of their choice should you prove intransigent. Similarly, the inter-unit iterative process provides all the social pressures and ultimate sanctions we have discussed to prevent both work councils and neighborhood consumption councils from attempting to "live off of" the rest of the economy.

As we have explained, the advantage of organizing the economy in this way is that every individual is involved to the greatest possible degree in the construction of the social plan and her or his own part in it. And every conceivable effort is made to bring the individual to arrive at his or her own proposal in a voluntary manner because it is in his or her best interest as a social human being. The system's chief advantage is therefore that the answer to the question, how do you get people to do what they have decided, themselves, to do, is rather obvious. You don't have to. Even to the extent that the methods of conflict resolution involve "forcing mechanisms", they too are democratic, emphasize equity of consideration, and allow for frequent experimentation with minority proposals.

So the problem of incentives during the transition period reduces to what happens if someone didn't really agree with the work plan that was proposed for him or her by some forcing mechanism. And what if he or she does not respond to the social pressure of the other workers in the workplace? As might have been appreciated by the separation of the workplace councils and the neighborhood councils, and therefore the separate treatment of the "work-effort" aspect of a person's life from the "consumption-effort" aspect, as long as the transformation of work and consumption are not in fact complete, participatory socialism is constructed to insure that "material incentives" are only a last resort. In participatory socialism "material incentive" is considered a euphemism, at best, for bribery and, at worst, for black-mail by threatening a person's basic security needs. They certainly are not an economic institution that will lead us toward "communism". But, nonetheless, should all efforts by a person's fellow workers fail, and they felt it was necessary, the workers' council could appeal to an individual's consumption unit to take sanctions against lack of effort in fulfilling one's plan. In nicer terms, it might be necessary in certain unusual circumstances for a worker to "receive a certificate from society"—signed by his work council—"that he has furnished such and such an amount of labor...and with this certificate he draws from the social stock of means of consumption."[26]

POLITICS AND THE STATE

Many modern capitalist systems have political forms that we call representative or parliamentary democracy. However, the fact that all economic decisions in these bourgeois democracies are made dictatorially by the owners and managers of corporations, and that these corporations are in control of the means of reproducing the society's material survival, renders the area of "democratic" decision making in the political sphere much less meaningful. Moreover, the particular representational forms usually further limit participatory democracy. However, a rejection of capitalism does *not* entail a rejection of democratic forms in the political sphere, or even of some representational forms under appropriate circumstances. Only after the economy has been democratized in a way such as we have described can democratic forms in the political sphere come to fulfill their promise. So the job of creating political institutions for socialism is to *retain* all the truly democratic aspects of bourgeois democracy, while replacing the unnecessary representational aspects by participatory democratic forms.

Just as there is a network of work place councils, their regional federations, and their national industrial councils, and a network of neighborhood "consumption" councils, their regional federations, and the national consumer's council, there would be "governmental" councils in localities, regions, and finally a national governmental council. However, the delegates elected to these governmental councils, who would of course be recallable at any time by their constituency, would view their function not so much as making decisions on political matters, but as formulating important proposals in such a way as to maximize understanding and to bring out the potentially controversial aspects so that a referendum could be held on all important political questions. We certainly have the technology necessary to conduct referenda easily: a voting device could be attached to the phone in each home which would send a message to a central computer in the area recording the vote. There are only two possible reasons for not using this (or some similar procedure) on all important political matters. Either a democratic decision is not desired, or it is believed the electorate cannot be sufficiently informed on a particular issue to understand what is in their interest.

In order to insure that the latter reason would not be applicable, a principle function of the government councils would be 1-to see that prior to all referenda the issues were debated on T.V., in the newspapers, and in all communities, and 2-to guarentee and extend civil liberties beyond our present conceptions. Freedom for corporations to own the press, and freedom of individuals to speak on street corners (sometimes) but not on T.V. and radio are a far cry from full civil liberties. The government councils would see to it that every community had several newspapers and T.V. stations, as well as a number of radio stations, and that all interested groups could develop their programs and have them put in print and on the air. The right of dissenting groups to use all forms of communication media would be especially safeguarded and any group that could gather the signatures of even a small percentage of the population of an area could insist on having a referendum on a proposal of their formulation.

The principle areas of decision formulation for the government councils would be foreign policy, education, criminal justice, and important economic decisions that were received on appeal from the economic councils. We will conclude this section with a brief description of how these areas would be treated.

It is very possible that the economic councils may conclude after using their iterative process that, particularly concerning some of the major long-term transformations or other major economic decisions we have discussed above, it would be helpful to have the government councils initiate a full public debate of the issues and conduct a referendum about the general direction that people prefer. However, during our discussion of the transition period we indicated that there was another kind of referral possible. A women's or minority caucus might appeal the decision of an economic council. In this case the government council would ensure a full public debate of the issue and would formulate a referendum not on the immediate proposal that caused the appeal but simply on whether or not the issue of sexism or racism was relevant to the case. We find it hard to imagine that a population capable of establishing the kind of solidarity necessary to overthrow capitalism in the United States could fail to vote that an issue concerned either racism or sexism when a succession of minority or women's councils had said that it did and considered it important enough to pursue. But if such was the case, even after the fullest presentation of the appealing council's position, we see no alternative but to accept the role of the referendum.

Concerning the state role of keeping the peace and punishing criminals, we must first ask who would disrupt the peace or commit crimes in our socialist society? With a just distribution of wealth, dignity for all, and a role in decision making for every individual, there would be no reason for theft or other such crimes. When people are the society they no longer need to rebel, certainly not in a "criminal fashion". But when people do commit crimes against one another during the transition period, the goal will be to restore them to society by respecting their needs and capacities rather than punishing them and isolating them from the community. Courts will be run not by "professionals" but by real juries of peers within the community who will guarantee immediate trials that use understandable procedures which simultaneously protect the rights of all parties.

Socialization and education are also considered by many essentially state activities. Socialization in general is just the process of "molding" new citizens to the requisites of the societal forms they must function within. When the society is alienated and oppressive, socialization is a process of repressing a person's truest abilities and desires while building up instead layer upon layer of alienated personality. In capitalism, for example, life in the family is a process of acquiring the habits and values of one's parents so as to be able to please them and live with them successfully. And schooling teaches authoritarian and competitive values and behavior patterns preparing young people for the roles of oppressor or, more often, oppressed. In the new society we envision socialization as an entirely different affair. For the key quality of socialist society will be that people have to be in touch with one another, able to formulate plans and understand the implications of social decisions, able to function collectively, and also able to recognize and further all the various kinds of human capacities that they and their neighbors possess. Socialization therefore will not mold people to fit a constraining environment, but be a process whereby people become better in touch with themselves and therefore better able to mold their environment rather than having their environment mold them.

We believe that socialist education will be simply every individual's and group's continual consciousness-forming process. People with advanced insights will be interested in spreading them for the furtherance of the whole community. Under capitalism people try to monopolize knowledge and insights because wealth and power accrue to those who do so; in our socialist society there are no hierarchies and thus there is nothing to be gained from such monopolization. On the contrary, eveybody stands to gain the most by the widest possible dissemination of all new insights. Education resources will be readily available everywhere, in specific schools, but also in the community and work places. There will be no mammoth, impersonal, "educational" institutions devoted more to testing and differentiating among students than to helping them learn. Each person will be teacher in some contexts, student in others, and always both learning and helping others to learn. Many curricula will still have "expert" teachers and special places for learning, but no mystiques. People will learn what they choose, when they choose, deciding among options by the same socialistic criteria used in all decision-making: an assessment of the capacities and needs of both the individual and community.

Having eliminated all expansionist behavior within our socialist economy and polity, and having established self-management, solidarity, and variety as the core characteristics of our new society, there would be no reason for the kind of imperialist foreign policy the United States presently pursues. And at the same time we would enjoy a supreme advantage compared to all past attempts at socialist construction—we would not have to concern our foreign policy principally with defending ourselves against the threat of being destroyed by a hostile and overpowering U.S. capitalism. The national governmental council would be responsible for the conduct of foreign policy and we would expect that important issues would be submitted to referenda as described above, and that the society's solidarity would manifest itself by the development of programs of truly beneficial economic aid to countries struggling to overcome a lack of modern technology.

There is no reason to expect that the citizens capable of constructing the kind of socialism we have described would tolerate any attempts to interfere in their internal affairs by any other country. And the best guarantee against such a possibility would be precisely the internal organization and consciousness we have described as our socialist vision. Only a fool would contemplate occupying such a society!

In conclusion, there are two criteria that political and state institutions must satisfy under socialism. They must be capable of resolving the conflicts that arise in the transition period, and they must truly be such that they "wither away". In a system where there would be no lasting divisions between social classes or interest groups so that all political debate would be due to differing beliefs and ideas and *not* to clashing interests or criteria, we believe that the democratic councils and referenda, as well as the program of civil liberties we have outlined, meet both these requirements.

CULTURE AND EVERYDAY LIFE

In this section we would like to round-out our description by very briefly extending the discussion to matters of culture and everyday life.

Culture will be more participatory and collective than now and yet standards and tastes will remain personal. Sports, for example, will be aesthetic and also productive in the sense of creating physical well-being and community. Everyone will seek their own limits rather than to exceed other people's achievements, and participants will get fulfillments and pleasures from other's accomplishments as well as from their own. No one will remember Willie Mays' batting average or Hank Aaron's home run count because these individual statistics will probably not even be kept. But personal memories and films will preserve Willie's dash to the center field wall and stab of Vic Wertz's line drive as well as the flick of Hank Aaron's wrists as unforgetable moments of human beauty and accomplishment. Architecture will be devoted to enhancing sensual enjoyment, human cooperation, and aesthetic pleasure. To accomplish such ends architects will have to be very much in touch with the people who will live and work in the structures they are designing and will naturally incorporate these people into design development, both teaching and learning from them in the process. Although no one will spend his or her entire life as an artist, and everyone will spend some time creating art, there will be people who have a special talent and interest in art. They will be equally incapable of focusing exclusively on an introverted progression of artistic endeavors meaningless to all but a few hundred people, and of foregoing all attempts to expand the ways art interrelates with the human psyche through freeing our unconscious fantasies and desires. Abstract art without any program for making it relevant to other people will be viewed as uninteresting, just as "proletarian art", in its usual interpretation, will be seen as a self-imposed stagnation.

But exactly what should be the mix between concern for immediate fulfillment and for on-going development will likely continually be a matter for hot "debate" and much experimentation. Viewing the building of a house relationally and historically, in terms of both immediate fulfillment and on-going development, there is much room for debate about whether a design sacrifices either aim to the other. And this is a kind of evaluative problem that will arise over and over in all aspects of democratic participatory socialist planning. It in fact gives evidence that there is real self-management, and its prevalence is one powerful factor in favor of including variety (and thus experimentation) as a socialist core characteristic.

We cannot really say what particular things socialist people will value most, but our belief is that people will appreciate and do many more types of things than they do now, and that people will be in much deeper touch with themselves, their environment, and their neighbors. How many people will live in families and how many in communes? How much monogamy and how much polygamy (for both sexes)? How much homosexuality and how much heterosexuality? Unclear. But that men and women and children will all be equal partners in social communities without sexism and ageism is quite clear. People will not engage in sex to dominate others or to prove themselves, or to gain security or to deceive, but to give and receive sensual and emotional pleasures and satisfactions.

We will not learn in order to get good grades or higher salaries, but to understand our world for the pure joy of understanding it. People will not make friends to get ahead but to make friends. And no one will love in order to survive or be supported, but to love and be loved.

Participatory socialism will not be a society free of troubles, debates, differences, and struggles. But the nature of all such dynamics will be vastly altered from what we know now. Contests will be to move all parties forward, rather than, as now, to determine which shall advance at which other's expense.

We have discussed capitalism and socialism. There remains the matter of going from the former to the latter. The programs of revolutionary struggle must be appropriate to the socialist goal people wish to attain as well as to the concrete conditions (and thus possibilities) they immediately encounter. In the next chapter we shall try to draw from our theoretical study a variety of lessons for the actual problems of developing a revolutionary process in the United States. Now, however, we have a discussion to relate.

A ROUND TABLE DEBATE

The following is a fictitious but realistic debate between 1-an adherent of centrally planned socialism ("CPS"), 2-an adherent of market socialism ("MS"), and 3-an adherent of democratic participatory socialism ("DPS"):

CPS: "MS", I just can't understand your blindness. You say you are a socialist but you persist with the markets and their competitive dynamics and mentality. You have no bourgeoisie and a good distribution of wealth; why can't you just go on to recognize the need for planning to insure production for use rather than for exchange?

MS: Sure, and trade in our efficiency for your deficits, our workers' management for your bureaucratic authoritarianism, our balanced development guided by consumer and worker desires for your heavy industry and excessive military focus—no thanks! We use markets because they are the best way to ensure an efficient mesh between all the separate units of our economy. They ensure us efficiency while also allowing our workers' councils and our consumers to exert real power over their pressing local concerns. You do alright with social services but little else—you've basically got a big, well-oiled, super authoritarian welfare state.

CPS: You can't be serious. Authoritarian welfare state hell! Not only do we succeed in such matters as health, transportation, and housing, as you admit, but our growth rate is immense; we've overcome the kind of petty competitive individualist mentality that's still at the core of your society, and with our down/up down/up planning procedures we're well on our way to developing the kind of initiative at the base necessary to Communism. You're wallowing in competition, and we're promoting social values. You've still got an economy geared to profit and we're oriented around social use-value. You've got a market governing allocation and we've got the proletariat in power through its Party's control of the central plan. Authoritarian? What's authoritarian about the people efficiently and socially administering their own economy? And what's all this garbage about the virtues of the market—you'd think the only thing wrong with capitalism was private ownership. What about the unequal development between sectors, the individualism, the profit motive...

MS: Shove it! "Down/up down/up" my ass! Down goes the order, up comes whether it can or can't be technically achieved; down goes a revised order, up comes "Yes Sir." And is it even the workers and planners who dialogue? No! It's little bureaucrats and big ones and no workers anywhere. And do the planners calculate allocations based upon the consumers' and the workers' real concerns, or on their own bureaucratic needs and the needs of their overlord, the Party? More of the latter, I bet. Capitalism has a host of rotten institutions but markets aren't one of them. Sure monopoly and uneven development aren't good, and sure we have to struggle against certain competitive and destabilizing tendencies—but those are minor problems which can be dealt with. In any case they are outweighed by the market's worth in generating efficient allocations that are desired by workers and consumers.

DPS: I've been listening here—do you think I could inject a few points of my own?

MS: Why not? We're not getting very far as is.

DPS: Maybe because you're each so unwilling to admit the weaknesses of your approaches. For instance, you "M", seem completely unwilling to admit the full complexity and depth of the negative side of markets that "CP" points out, while you "CP" don't seem willing to admit the authoritarian and bureaucratic tendencies of central planning.

MS: Oh, I'm willing to admit to problems all right. I just think we can handle them and that the strengths of our system offset them anyway.

CPS: Certainly we're not talking about some utopian arrangement. Obviously there are problems, even with central planning, but they are all of a peripheral impact when compared to the important advances the system represents.

DPS: But neither of you really understand the full magnitude of the weaknesses. For example, you "M" fail to see that even if you had perfect markets, the information they deliver and the motives and roles they generate in the name of efficiency all promote capitalistic values and horribly biased economic outcomes that lead away from real social use-value and toward the individualistic ends of capitalism. Even your well-focused desires for worker and consumer power become nothing more than wishful thinking or self-deceiving rhetoric in face of the constraints of markets—your workers understand this and so they use their vaunted powers to hire expert managers to make all their decisions for them; why not, since the decisions are forced by market dynamics into a mechanical profit-loss mold anyway? And similarly, and for similar reasons, your consumers have no choice but to function just like people do in shops in the United States. And then there's the pollution and the advertising, and lack of social goods, and the unemployment problems and all the other capitalistic problems with consciousness and culture as well!

And for you, "CPS", you don't even understand what use-value means despite your willingness to scrub democratic participation to achieve it. Why are the internal social relations of your factories the same as those of the factories in Detroit? Your planning doesn't sufficiently take into account the workers' need to develop skills, nor the consumers' potential for making social judgements. And even worse, you minimize central planning tendencies towards hierarchy and power differentials, which lead to privileges, competition to climb the hierarchy, increasing material incentives, and general authoritarianism and repression. Your myopic insistence that all that counts is whether the Party is in control of the state and planning apparatus is poor disguise for the fact that workers are no more powerful under your economic system than they were under capitalism. In short, neither you nor "MS" advocate an allocation system consistent with the fullest development of your citizens through their economic activities. Moreover, neither of you understand the profound links between your economic arrangements and the other aspects of your society—values, consciousness, culture, schooling, family life, and so on...

CPS: That's a lot of young utopian garbage! You've got to choose either our planning or "MS'S" markets and then deal with the debits. All you do is criticize, criticize, with your head stuck in the clouds, and without any feeling for just how hard it is to make an economy work at all. The "democratic participation" we scrub is your bourgeois democracy, worth nothing in the first place. Our factories look the way they have to look given the advanced nature of our technology. In time, as we get more and more efficient, people will work fewer and fewer hours, and that's what really counts: freeing people from the realm of necessity so they can get on with true freedom in their leisure. We have incentives and the rest because at this stage we need them, there is no other way to produce for a country as complex as ours, short of the kind of market approach that the capitalists and our friend "MS" here advocate. And as for your claim that it doesn't matter what Party controls the economy, that is just testimony to the backwardness of your political development. What could matter more! It's the fact that our workers produce not for the capitalist, but for the people through the agency of the Party, that makes life qualitatively different in our country, and that is the only thing that could have such a profound effect.

MS: I must admit that I finally agree with you. Our critic here seems a mite out-of-touch with the dynamics of advanced economies, unless, maybe "DPS" thinks the right approach is to try and combine our allocation techniques, using markets to offset the authoritarian tendencies of planning and planning to counter the individualizing, competitive tendencies of markets?

CPS: But a little market, is too much market, so...

DPS: But no, that's not what I mean to propose at all. I believe you don't have to choose between two methods inconsistent with socialist values in hopes of some future improvement which they preclude anyway; and you don't have to take them both in some supposedly clever mix either. We can develop an allocative mechanism consistent with the fullest participation of both consumers and producers in the decisions affecting them through the institutions of democratic councils and iterative planning where the councils retain the power of initiative in proposals as well as in the ultimate resolution of conflicts. And only through that form can we build a system which promotes solidarity rather than competition; equality instead of differentials; efficiency toward human ends rather than toward the goals of profit or power; participation in place of expertise or bureaucracy; work that is fulfilling rather than a means to alienated consumption; life that is fulfilling now rather than a means to Communism—a stage always in the future....

CPS: I just don't accept all this—our planning system achieves all those ends without risking the chaos that some harebrained scheme you'd suggest would likely generate. And anyhow...

DPS: Anyhow nothing! Your planning doesn't meet any of these ends and the reason you don't see that is because your thought has become so narrow that you don't even know what the "ends" really are all about. You can't accept what I'm saying, nor even fully hear it, because to do so would undermine your privileged position and even more, the beliefs around which you've built and rationalized your whole life. You'll sit there and tell me that working in a factory with a boss and no workers' management under the behest of a so-called proletarian state is superior to doing the same thing for a capitalist until you are blue in the face—and I'll reply, for just as long, that in all essentials it is the same; the social relations of work are every bit as detrimental to human fulfillment and development in your world as in the capitalist one...

MS: And you won't accept markets and workers' councils?

DPS: No! Markets don't solve the problem. They sacrifice the social aspect of "CPS'S" planning procedures with little gain in participation and perhaps even a further sacrifice in human solidarity and the pursuit of social well-being. No, what I have in mind is councils all right, but in a setting where they have real power to determine the plan—where they receive the information they need about social relations and human potentials, and where they can exercise and implement their judgements about their own economic roles, in conjunction with those of everyone else. I want to see work become an end in itself, as well as a means...

(The discussion continues with "DPS" spelling out in detail the envisioned new socialist inter and intra unit forms and general societal characteristics, much as in this past chapter, and then the "debate" continues.)

CPS: Good God! Maybe in a hundred years, but not now. People just aren't like that. Someone's got to take leadership...

DPS: And no doubt you'll volunteer for the job. No thanks, I'll struggle for the participatory approach—sure it'll be hard at first with all the old consciousness still prevalent, but flowing from a mass revolutionary process it can work, and it will work, and if it sounds utopian to you, so much the better as that means that at least what we've got in mind for a goal really is consistent with our vision of socialist people.

MS: Come on! You must have gone on drugs! I don't care how long we wait, that model is never going to work. The information problems alone are much too great to cope with, and anyhow who in hell would want to go to all your meetings. What a bore. Better to have some efficient way to handle all those decisions automatically so people have time to enjoy themselves.

DPS: What hypocrisy! The market method of solving the information problem is to suppress the most important information! I think it is possible to take account of the human side of economic relations. And moreover it's the only way to produce for use and promote solidarity. The model needs to be developed much more; it especially needs to be elaborated by people from all parts of society, each lending their lessons gained from concrete experience as well as their own evaluations, values, and visions. But surely, despite its incompleteness, the model we propose obviously offers far more in the way of what we as socialists want, than does either a traditional market or central socialist approach.

And we have yet to even discuss aspects outside the economy. All societies, including participatory socialism, have economic but also kinship, authority, and community relations. We've discussed primarily the economic and authority relations because for the most part they are the sole focus of your attentions. But a full elaboration of our model would have to include detailed reference to community and kinship relations as well. As to the latter, it will be necessary to elaborate socialist institutions which promote initiative, freedom, and equality between the sexes. Kinship relations do not disappear with the development of socialism, but we can consciously restructure them to new ends. And the same is true of community relations. The solution is not to try to eliminate all communities save the whole, all divergent cultures, heritages, and norms, but instead to insure that all inter community dynamics are marked by sharing and compassion, solidarity rather than hostility, while intra-community relations are marked by the general socialist values we've discussed with reference to other aspects of socialist activity. The actual concrete elaboration of such kinship and community relations as of economic and authority relations, is a problem for collective political practice, though the development of flexible general visions is a helpful first step.

FOOTNOTES: CHAPTER SEVEN

1. As it has been historically implemented, socialism certainly provides many lessons both in "what is" and also in "what is not" to be done. But there is certainly no easy way to extrapolate from existing socialist models to a vision of socialism as it can be in the United States. Even more, the creation of socialism in the United States is going to require a break with many of the guiding principles of the socialist heritage. This we will show in the chapter to come.
2. This is not merely a matter of anti-communist propaganda. To a great extent the U.S. public has a critical sense and *accurately* perceives that the socialist heritage in practice has been fraught with anti-democratic and conformist tendencies antithetical to what they feel is socially desirable. Anti-communism, read anti-totalitarianism, is nothing to be defensive about.
3. This is a matter of conscious media denial, both east and west. See, for example, Noam Chomsky, "Objectivity and Liberal Scholarship", *American Power and the New Mandarins,* Pelican Edition, New York, 1969, and Cornelious Castoriadus, "The Hungarian Source", Telos, No. 29, Fall 1976, Dept. of Sociology, Washington Univ. St. Louis, Miss.
4. To the libertarian socialists and Marx, the communist anarchists, the council communists, and the revolutionary people of the Russian soviets, Spain, and Hungary we owe a debt for: 1-our allegiance to councils as a socialist form, 2-our inclusion of a psychological aspect in our analysis, 3-our emphasis upon self-management as a crucial socialist goal, 4-our recognition is only one arena in

which people produce themselves and their environments, and 5-our recognition that human history is social and that humans are beings of praxis.

What we put forward in this chapter is not a finished plan. It is our view. It is an application of the ideas developed in earlier parts of the book, hopefully a contribution to the development of a workable socialist vision and practice—an end finally attainable only by a socialist movement.

For more on council organization see our bibliographic references to Anton Pannekoek, Antonio Gramsci, and Cornelious Castoriadus. On the psychological aspect, see references to Wilhelm Reich, Phil Brown, and Michael Cattier. With respect to points 3,4, and 5 our references to Marx are most informative.

5. See *The Closing Circle*, Barry Commoner, Bantam Books, New York, N.Y. for a beautifully argued treatment of the interrelations between ecological stability and the need for variety.

6. One can certainly find in Marx passages consistent with our desire to eliminate this false distinction, but more prevalently one finds passages which uphold the distinction and order production ahead of consumption in importance. For example:

> Production predominates not only over itself, in the antithetical definition of production, but over the other moments (ie. distribution, exchange, and consumption) as well. The process always returns to production to begin anew. That exchange and consumption cannot be predominant is self-evident. Likewise distribution as distribution of products; while distribution of the agents of production is itself a moment of production. A definite production thus determines a definite consumption, distribution, and exchange, as well as definite relations between these different moments.

The *Grundrisse*, Pelican Edition, London, England, Page 99.

7. For a powerful and very readable discussion of some facets of socialist medicine, see *Away With All Pests*, Joshua Horn, Monthly Review Press, New York, N.Y.

8. See Steve Marglin's article "What Do Bosses Do" in the radical political economist's journal, RRPE, Vol. 6, No. 2, and *Schooling In Capitalist America*, Sam Bowles and Herb Gintis, Basic Books, New York, N.Y. as well as *Labor and Monopoly Capital*, Harry Braverman, Monthly Review Press, New York, N.Y.

Job enrichment and related schemes introduced by capitalists do not refute our analysis but merely reflect the view of some capitalists that maximizing drudgery does not always maximize profits. Historically there often have been differences of opinion among capitalists on how best to generate profits and preserve power. But as the goal remains profit and power, the work process remains alienated and fundamentally different from self-managed socialist work aimed at human goals.

9. Karl Marx quoted in *The Social and Political Thought of Karl Marx*, Sholomo Avinari, Cambridge University Press, London, England. See also the forthcoming work by Bertell Ollman, *Social Revolution and Sexual Revolution, Essays on Marx and Reich*, South End Press, Boston, Mass.

10. We do not analyse these weaknesses as we feel that there are other matters of more fundamental concern. However, interested readers might examine the wealth of literature that exists on the "Yugoslav" model some of whose titles appear in our own bibliography.

11. Karl Marx, *Economic and Philosophic Manuscripts of 1844,* International Publishers, New York, N.Y. Page 148.

12. Adam Smith, *The Wealth of Nations,* Modern Library, New York, N.Y. 1965, Page 14.

13. Herb Gintis, "Alienation and Power: Toward A Radical Welfare Economics", unpublished Ph.D. dissertation, Harvard University, 1969, Page 118.

14. Gar Alperovitz, "Socialism as a Pluralist Commonwealth," in *The Capitalist System,* edited by Edwards, Reich, and Weisskopf, Prentice Hall, Page 527.

15. Karl Marx in a letter to P.V. Annekov dated Dec. 28, 1846, *Collected Writings,* International Publishers, New York, N.Y.

16. Frederick Engels, *Anti-Duhring,* International Publishers, New York, N.Y., Page 338.

17. Recently a host of mathematically oriented neoclassical economists have developed different iterative planning procedures for arriving at a central plan. Arrow and Hurwicz, "Decentralization and Computation in Resource Allocation", in *Essays In Econometrics,* edited by Pfouts. Malinvoud, "Decentralized Procedures for Planning", in *Activity Analysis in the Theory of Growth and Planning,* edited by Malinvoud and Bacharach. Heal, "Planning Without Prices", Ph.D thesis, Cambridge University, are representative examples. Montias, "Planning With Material Balances in Soviet-Type Economies", American Economic Review—1959, is the most accessible brief description of the general practical procedures. But in each of these articles the mechanisms discussed are purely means of bringing information to the central planners, just as we pointed out in the text.

18. This is true of all the supposed decentralized procedures in the literature as with those cited above. However, there is one other possibility as an inter-unit mechanism, namely not having one. We refer to this organization of the economy as "decomposition." Nor is it as ridiculous from the perspective of developing socialist characteristics in people as it might at first seem. The early anarchist vision was essentially decompositionist, as seem to be the visions of such authors as Gar Alperovitz. It seems to us that many of the forces pushing for socialism in China are ones coming not from what the Chinese themselves seem to consider their most advanced sector—the highly centralized heavy industry sector—but from participatory consciousness arising from the rural communes where solidarity and self-management are nurtured in relatively self-sufficient communes (that is, they have very limited planning or market relationships with other units in the economy).

19. The following quotation is from the conclusion of a cross-cultural study of political behavior covering five countries. It is from *Participation and Democratic Theory,* Carole Pateman, Cambridge University Press, London, England, Page 47.

If in most social relations the individual finds himself subservient to some authority figure, it is likely that he will expect such an authority relationship in the political sphere. On the other hand, if outside the political sphere he has opportunities to participate in a wide range of social decisions, he will probably expect to be able to participate in political decisions as well. Furthermore, participation in non-political decision making may give one the skills needed to engage in political participation.

20. Certain aspects of Chinese, Cuban, and Vietnamese planning appear to come closer to the model we will present below than to central planning. We will not however attempt to evaluate third world socialist models in this book.

21. A number of studies of socialist planning in Cuba and China make arguments and give evidence relevant to this point. For study in the area, readers might like to refer to the Union of Radical Political Economy's annotated bibliographies. The most recent covers a host of areas, including socialist history and planning. *Reading Lists in Radical Political Economy,* URPE, 41 Union Sq. West. Room 901, New York, New York.

22. Karl Marx, *The Grundrisse,* Vintage, New York, 1973.

23. Batya Weinbaum's forthcoming book *The Curious Courtship of Women's Liberation and Socialism,* South End Press, has a very effective discussion of this "stage phenomenon"—The problem will be resolved in the next stage; but when the next stage comes, of course it is no longer even considered a problem—centering on the issue of patriarchy but generalizable to other matters as well.

24. Karl Marx quoted in Fleischer, op. cit. Page 11.

25. See Schumacher, *Small Is Beautiful,* Harper and Row, New York, 1976.

26. Karl Marx, *Critique of the Gotha Program,* International Publishers, New York, Page 8.

CHAPTER EIGHT
THE ART OF
SOCIALIST REVOLUTION

It is necessary with bold spirit and in good conscience, to save civilization.... We must halt the dissolution which corrodes and corrupts the roots of human society. The bare and barren tree can be made green again. Are we not ready?

Antonio Gramsci
L'Ordine Nuovo

The purpose of this chapter is to investigate the general strategic implications of our theoretical ideas. Our effort is in the tradition of libertarian socialism milestoned by people such as Luxemburg, Gramsci, Pannekoek, Korsch, and Whilhelm Reich.[1] We will criticize modern Marxist Leninist views, and also simultaneously seek to refurbish some of their antecedents and competitors and to "bend" them to our own circumstances.

THE GENERAL ISSUES

Consider yourself a revolutionary activist. You are concerned to work collectively in a factory, a community, or another of society's many institutional arenas of struggle. You and your comrades have in common a general analysis of capitalism and a shared socialist vision. What are the various short and long-run problems you encounter in your work? What are your solutions? There are three principle kinds of problems faced.

First, there is a whole set of problems that all United States activists inevitably encounter concerning matters of racism, sexism, classism, authoritarianism, and their mutual interrelations. For in almost all struggle arenas there are people of different races, of both sexes, of different classes, and of different positions in power hierarchies. In addressing matters of racism, should revolutionaries ever take positions that tend to polarize white and black people temporarily against one another, or should leftists always avoid such issues, seeking only to bring whites and blacks together—and likewise for men and women, as well as for people of different classes, or of different levels of authority? Furthermore, are men and women, whites, blacks, Chicanos, Mexicans, Asians, Puerto Ricans, all to be in the same organizations—are they fighting the same struggle or different ones? How are organizing focuses to be chosen?

What is the relation among the various sectors? How do they come together and yet simultaneously retain their autonomy, or is this even a relevant goal? The issues can be most easily understood in terms of *totality* and *hegemony:* which are the societal features that are central to social reproduction and motion and to the character of daily life; and which are only peripheral or subordinate? Is sex, race, class, or authority dominant and what are their interrelations? Depending upon one's answers to these questions there is a different choice of programmatic focus and organizational forms.

The second set of revolutionary problems concerns matters of *leadership and internal structure.* People develop revolutionary consciousness and commitment to varying degrees. How should the left deal with the differences which inevitably accompany such "unequal development"? Should those moving first develop their own separate organizations? Should those who are more "advanced" and committed always persist in having separate organizations? How would they then relate to everyone else—what of the tensions inherent in the role of organizer? What forms should organizations have? How is leadership to be exercised? Who makes decisions and according to what criteria? If there is more than one organization in the revolutionary process how do they interrelate? In short, as a factory or neighborhood activist, are you to be a member of an organization? What kind of organization? Are you to recruit others? What are to be the criteria of membership and participation? What are the decision mechanisms?

Finally, the last major division of problems involves matters of revolutionary process: that is, of the *general issues, style, and tactics of revolutionary activity.* In the community or institution where you do your organizing how will you choose what issues to focus upon? What are the criteria of daily judgment? Are there to be study groups or would these tend to be isolating? What is to be the tone and content of leaflets? What is the role of creating a movement culture and of "serving people's needs"? How will you decide on a balance between local issues and regional or national ones? How do you struggle for reforms and yet not become reformist? How will spirit be maintained, and in fact what constitutes a "revolutionary spirit"? How do you relate to matters of culture and of repression? When do you work "quietly" building a small local base, and when do you seek a larger constituency, address city-wide or national issues, generate publicity, and use the media? How do you allocate energies between alternative programs? Where is money to come from and how is it to be allocated? How will meetings be run—how often will you have them? How will you criticize your comrades and accept their criticisms? The list is long and while no perspective can give fixed answers, a perspective suitable to our present conditions could and would have to provide tools sufficient for answering such process questions over and over in varying settings and for varying periods of revolutionary development.

Yet before addressing these major strategic issues there is the prior matter of the title of this chapter. Why did we choose "The Art of Socialist Revolution" when for most leftists the word "science" is much more popular?

REVOLUTION: ART OR SCIENCE

Einstein said that "As far as the laws of mathematics refer to reality, they are not certain; and as far as they are certain, they do not refer to reality."[2] All the more so for the laws of revolution. As Lenin put it: "An icon is something you pray to, something you cross yourself before, something you bow down to; but an icon has no effect on practical life and practical politics."[3] "Theory, my friend, is grey, but green is the eternal tree of life."[4]

The world we confront is a whole one. There are no separate units; no fundamental building blocks. There is only a complex totality. There is only interpenetration and process: a vast mosaic in which no single thread is the axis around which all others ebb and flow. The universe is not a collection of fundamental parts as Newton thought, but rather it is a dynamic web of interrelated entwined events. To say one aspect is more important than some other is only possible in context of some human purpose. That is, a part can be more fundamental, not as a building block, but only to some particular end.

Thus physicists understand the world with one set of purposes and ends in mind and revolutionaries with another. Our thoughts, be we physicists or revolutionaries, are always a map and not the real terrain itself. They are abstracted. And they are abstracted not only from what is truly peripheral to our immediate concerns (the particle physicist ignores the biology of snails and so does the revolutionist) but also from matters that are important to us but whose importance we have yet to perceive. As physicists have taught, Euclidian geometry is not inherent in nature but it is imposed upon it by the mind. There is a similar phenomenon in revolutionary theorizing as well.

The revolutionary theorist has a set of concepts and sees reality through them. Sometimes and to some ends they act like microscopes highlighting what is most crucial. But at other times and to other ends they act like blinders hiding what is most crucial. "History is not a mathematical calculation; it does not have a metric decimal system...."[5] Revolution is an art because living reality is always richer than any theory, even one functioning as a powerful guide to action. The alternative to the "scientific approach" to revolution is much more flexible, while it sacrifices none of the care and discipline of the former. "A better approach would be to identify certain broad tendencies operating in a given society, a knowledge of which might facilitate political intervention in a particular direction and lay the basis for strategy and tactics."[6]

What is required is a "philosophy of the act, not of the pure act, but rather of the real impure act, in the most profane and worldly sense of the word."[7] While guided by theory, revolution always also enriches theory and moves in a realm somewhat beyond theory: the living realm of real interactions. Theory should identify tendencies. It should highlight major features from a variety of angles. And it should thereby provide a guide to political intervention. But it is practice that is essential. And revolutionary practice is an art because it is a matter of experience, of sensitivity, of "touch", of practical translation and transcendence of theory as well as it is a matter of theory itself. The most crucial first step is not to learn "The Theory", but to learn to think and act in the context of a knowledge of the fuzzy map which is the most any theory can be.

Certainly it is difficult to become a revolutionist, to learn and spread the "art of revolution", and to believe in victory while also admitting that society is a tapestry without one strand which dominates all others—yet this is the task. For history can be very laggard and it is we who must give history a push toward socialism. And it is precisely our understanding of totality and of hegemony—two abstractions suitable to our strategic ends, not excluding too much, and yet simultaneously not cluttering our field of vision with the unimportant—that can situate us in the societal tapestry and provide insights that can guide our assault upon that same tapestry. The "normal" which is imposed by hegemony is immensely powerful. To make our way through it we must not make the mistake of thinking that theory gives forth answers—it does not. It provides either a powerful or a misleading guide for the practice which can alone generate answers. In the rest of this chapter we shall see how our theory contrasts with others in the practical orientation it suggests. The "art of revolution" itself, however, while well within the grasp of all of us, is finally a matter of experience and not of booklearning, however important the latter might also be.

TOTALITY: FOCUS, CONSCIOUSNESS, AND ORGANIZATION

For any society to persist with relative stability, it must enforce a general conformity between the roles its people necessarily fill and the consciousness they daily manifest. The process creating this conformity, as well as the conformity itself, in the factory, community, state, school, culture and ballpark is called hegemony. The core characteristics of society's roles and "meshing" consciousnesses constitute what we call society's core totality of defining aspects.

Revolution is a struggle waged at both an ideological and an institutional level.[8] It requires institutional power, but also popular allegiance and the suppression of society's "deadening normality", which is just its hegemonic influence upon people's self-conceptions and desires. Hegemony is a world view or series of world views internalized as a part of mass consciousness, reproduced in the factories, markets, and bedrooms of society, and inducing the oppressed to accept and even enforce their own plight. A revolution to successfully alter society's daily contours requires a break in hegemony, and this means that it requires a counter-hegemony. In opposition to a consciousness which mystifies and legitimates oppression, there needs to be a consciousness which reveals oppression and clarifies the potentials for revolution. The ideological aspect of our anti-hegemonic struggle is to destroy consciousness which reproduces societal normality and to instead build new awarenesses suitable to overcoming the grasp of normality and to struggling for socialism. It involves addressing the core totality as it manifests itself in people's personalities. Thus determining what centrally defines and reproduces daily life is critical to revolutionary struggle. What is the consciousness that reproduces oppression and what is the alternative revolutionary consciousness?

Juliet Mitchell has written, "The process of translating the hidden individual fears of women into a shared awareness of the meaning of them as problems, the release of anger, anxiety, the struggle of proclaiming the painful and transforming it into the political—this process is consciousness raising."[9]

In our terminology this is the process of translating daily awareness from hegemony to counter-hegemony: ie., from a fragmented view to a whole one; from self-deprecation to liberation; from acceptance or support of oppression to rebellion. This is a practical counter-hegemony—but of what is it constituted? To what precisely is a woman's consciousness to be raised? What is a full revolutionary awareness?

Lenin has argued the activist must know the workers' lives minutely so as to address them in ways overcoming the hold of normality and generating revolution.[10] But what are the parameters of normality—what is it in the workers' lives that we are seeking to understand and address? Sartre has remarked that the modern capitalist system provides needs which it can meet so that revolution must instead be about what it tells us we don't want, and therefore about overcoming alienation and hegemony.[11] But what are the contours of this alienation which must be overcome? What is the totality which limits our development and against which we can organize revolutionary struggle?

Gramsci wrote for a journal in Italy about which it was said: "The workers loved L'Ordine Nuovo... because in it, they found something of themselves, the best part of themselves; because in it they sensed their own inner striving: how can we be free? How can we become ourselves?"[12] This is a journal identifying what is possible and bursting the myths which normality uses to deny such possibilities. But what is possible in the present and what are today's critical myths?

Sheila Rowbotham in a plea for modern concrete revolutionary strategy has asked, "How can we mobilize the resistance of many different sectors of society? How can we bring together in our practice the separations in ourselves which paralyze us? How can we connect to our everyday living the abstract commitment to make a society without exploitation and oppression? What is the relation between the objective changes in capitalism and our new perceptions of social revolution? What are the ways in which we can organize together without sacrificing our autonomy?"[13]

In our terms these questions can be reduced to "what is it that is crucial to societal reproduction?" What must be confronted in each person's daily life if we are to overcome the reactionary hegemony now prevalent in the United States? This is certainly a theoretical matter and yet it is also empirical. The answers for the present are not timeless; the answers for our society are not generalizable to all others. In a powerful book about Antonio Gramsci's politics, Carl Boggs Jr. has propounded an abstract conception of the dynamics of societal totality:

> The various aspects of ideological hegemony—whatever their different histories and peculiar dynamics, whatever their relationship (past or present) to given structures, whatever their origins in a particular kind of oppression—constitute at the same time the totality of bourgeois hegemony in contemporary capitalist society. Each dominant system of beliefs has its specific quality, yet all are intertwined to such an extent that this totality is bound to permeate most concrete institutions, situations, events, personalities, and even the oppositional movements themselves. With the increasing complexity of civil society and its interpenetrations with the state, the attempt to abstract and isolate particular elements from the larger whole— what Gramsci called the "ensemble of relations"—becomes

more and more hopeless. The subversive attack against one area of hegemony must therefore, at some point, move to the level of totality that incorporates a broader struggle against all the dominant ideologies that support oppressive structures. All areas of hegemony function together, with varying impact and emphasis from one context to another, to produce and reify a generalized alienation that results in passivity, a sense of powerlessness, subcultural fragmentation, separation of the personal and the political, etc. Sense of community in any truly public or liberating form is consistently denied by the reproduction of bourgeois hegemony in people's everyday lives, from the family to the workplace and the neighborhoods. Since, as Gramsci emphasized, the oppressed must demystify the ideological armor of the status-quo and create their own integrated culture prior to and within the process of achieving economic and political control, it follows that destroying this hegemonic totality must be central to the calculations of any revolutionary movement.[14]

But this is still abstract and allows for a host of consistent, yet different, approaches. For all these commentators have yet to specify what is the active totality here and now in the United States. Is it society's capitalistic class relations? Is it racism? Is it sexism? Is it authoritarianism? Or is it some combination of two or more of these taken in parallel or in some form of interpenetration?

There are a host of revolutionary strategic orientations—Marxist Leninist, Nationalist, Feminist, Marxist Syndicalist, Anarchist, Socialist Feminist, Anarcho-Communist, etc.—each of which apriori designates a different active core totality and then also develops differing perspectives on what should be the primary focus of revolutionary struggle, on what is revolutionary consciousness, and on what organizational relations are needed to "mobilize the resistance of many different sectors of society."[15]

The following three charts give an outline understanding of sexism, racism, and authoritarianism, as each is treated by the different revolutionary perspectives. On all three charts, roman numeral I indicates the orthodox Marxist Leninist view. Roman numeral II designates those theories which hold one of the other three characteristics to be of unique central importance—much as the orthodox Marxists view class. Under roman numeral III are the more modern Marxist Leninist approaches that account for other characteristics than class, but assign them a clearly subordinate role. And finally, roman numeral IV indicates those views that treat one of the three characteristics as co-equal in importance to class.

SEX AND REVOLUTION

	Socialist Feminist	Marxist Leninist Womens' Liberation	Feminist Separatist	Marxist Leninist "Unite and fight"
Totality	Parallel sex-class dialectics are each critical to reproduction. Race and authority dynamics derivative.	Economic dialectic with class central but also a sexual dialectic causing divisions in the working class and requiring tactical responses.	Sexual dialectic; sexism central; sex an issue only to attain sexual solidarity.	Economic dialectic. Class central to reproduction; sexism a mere impediment to class solidarity.
Struggle Focus	There is a dual family and factory focus with issues of sex and class each deemed strategically central. All other focuses are tactical to further sex and class solidarity.	Focus on workplace and family, on issues generating class and sex solidarity. Class central to socialism, and sex to women's liberation.	Focus on the family and on all issues allowing the development of women's consciousness and solidarity.	Focus on the workplace and on all issues allowing the development of class consciousness and solidarity.
Revolutionary Consciousness	Revolutionary consciousness is an awareness of both the sex and class dialectic; of how they interact, of how they propel societal reproduction, and of how a two-focused movement can overcome the dual sexist-classist hegemony to finally create socialism.	Proletarian class consciousness for the masses; Marxism Leninism for the leadership. But now the sexually oppressed also have an anti-sexist consciousness and progressive men support them because of the strategic importance of solidarity to the class struggle.	A detailed understanding of the sexual dialectic and the oppression of women and of the solution via equality for women, or, in some versions, the subjugation or elimination of men.	'Proletarian consciousness for the masses; Marxism Leninism for the leadership. Anti-sexism required tactically as a means to class solidarity, is not itself a part of revolutionary consciousness.
Organization	The movement against the capitalist totality includes sexism. There are also autonomous women's organizations providing leadership in the sexual struggle, but taking equal part in other struggles as well.	There are two parallel organizational frameworks. One, mixed, focuses on class and the transition to socialism; the other, exclusively women, focuses solely upon the struggle for women's liberation.	Whatever the specific organizational forms chosen, they are to allow membership exclusively to women.	One big movement with no special demarcations along sexual lines.

RACE AND REVOLUTION

	Socialist Nationalist	Marxist Leninist Black Nation Thesis	Nationalist Separatist	Marxist Leninist "Unite and fight"
Totality	Economic dialectic. Class central to reproduction. Racism a mere impediment to class solidarity.	Race dialectic. Racism central to reproduction. Class an issue only to attain racial solidarity.	Parallel race-class dialectics are each critical to reproduction. Sex and authority dynamics are derivative.	Economic dialectic with class central but there is also a racial dialectic causing divisions in the working class and requiring tactical responses
Struggle Focus	Focus on the workplace and on all issues allowing the development of class consciousness and solidarity.	Focus on the ghetto, on issues allowing the development of race consciousness and solidarity.	Focus on the workplace and ghetto, on issues generating class and race solidarity. Class is central to socialism and the liberation of national minorities.	There is a dual ghetto and factory focus with issues of race and class each strategically central. All other focuses are tactical to further race and class solidarity.
Revolutionary Consciousness	Proletarian consciousness for the masses; Marxism Leninism for the leadership. Anti-racism required tactically to attain class solidarity, is not itself a part of revolutionary consciousness.	A detailed understanding of the race dialectic and the oppression of third world people and of the solution via national secession or, in some extreme versions, the subjugation or elimination of whites.	Proletarian class consciousness for the masses and Marxism Leninism for the leadership. But now the racially oppressed also have an anti-racist consciousness and progressive whites support them because of the strategic importance of solidarity to the class struggle.	Revolutionary consciousness is an awareness of both the race and class dialectic; of how they interact, of how they propel societal reproduction, and of how a two-focused movement can overcome the dual racist classist hegemony to finally create socialism.
Organization	One big movement with no special demarcations along racial lines.	Whatever the specific organizational forms chosen, they are exclusively for non-whites.	There are two parallel organizational frameworks. One, mixed, focuses upon class and the transition to socialism; the other, exclusive of whites, focuses solely upon the liberation struggle of non-whites.	The movement against the capitalist totality includes racism; there are also autonomous non-white movements providing leadership in the racial struggle, but also taking equal part in other struggles.

AUTHORITY AND REVOLUTION

	Totality	Struggle Focus	Revolutionary Consciousness	Organization
Communist Anarchism	Class and power are both core and move in parallel. Race and sex divisions are der-ivative.	Focus on any arena where class or authority issues may be confront-ed. Race and sex tactic-ally addressed.	An awareness of both the class and power dialectics, of how they interact, propel societal reproduction, and of how a two-focused movement can build socialism.	Participatory councils in both factories and all other arenas where class or power relations are manifested, but not along race or sex lines.
Marxist Syndicalism	Economic dialectic. Class is central but there is also an auth-ority dialectic which can cause class divi-sions and corrupt revolutionary organ-izations.	Focus on the workplace and issues generating class consciousness and solidarity, but there is also an emphasis on solidarity and guarding against authoritarianism.	A Marxist understanding of class coupled with an awareness of the impact of power relations. Class is central but there is rec-ognition that authority can impede class solidarity and also impede the develop-ment of working class self-management.	No hierarchy or central organ-izitional forms. Instead the focus is most often on spon-taneous or perhaps pregener-ated workplace councils.
Individualist Anarchism	Power dialectic. Po-wer hierarchies cen-tral to reproduction. Other divisions all manifestations of the power principle.	Focus on power rela-tions between individ-uals or groups. Other issues addressed when in power relations are in-volved.	A belief in the integrity of the individual and in the need for self-management. A recognition of the roots of all oppressions in hierarchy and of their solution via anarchism without government.	Personal autonomy via spon-taneous federations of locally constituted, completely demo-cratic organizations. No hier-archy in any form.
Marxist Leninist Dem. Cent.	Economic dialectic. Class central to re-production. Author-ity good or bad de-pending on its "class content."	Focus on the workplace and on all issues allow-ing the development of class consciousness and class solidarity.	Proletarian consciousness for the masses; Marxism Leninism for the leadership. Anti-authoritarianism is an individualist aberration counter-productive to revolu-tionary possibilities.	To attain a single will and im-mense flexibility, revolution-ary organization must have a strict hierarchy and centraliz-ation of power and experience,

SEXISM AND REVOLUTION

What differentiates the various strategic approaches are their views of the capitalist totality. Their different focuses, views of revolutionary consciousness, of tactics, and of revolutionary organization all follow logically.

Let us first consider chart one. Juliet Mitchell has stated that "to this point the liberation of woman remains a normative ideal, an adjunct to socialist theory, not structurally integrated into it,"[16] and thus she has made clear the feminist and socialist-feminist concern over orthodox Marxism's economistic understanding of the dynamics of sexism. "The position of women then, in the work of Marx and Engels, remains disassociated from, or subsidiary to, a discussion of the family, which is in its turn subordinated as merely a precondition of private property. Their solutions retain this overly economistic stress, or enter the realm of dislocated speculation."[17] This general critique is responsible for all three major alternatives to the orthodox orientation on the matter of sexism.

The first response to the "unite and fight" orthodox approach is separatism. In this view the dialectic moving history is sexual.[18] The totality determining social reproduction and change has completely altered—from class it has become sex. Organizations may take a variety of forms but membership is necessarily exclusively female. Men, male definitions of life, and male power are now considered the principle problem. Men have innate or at least very deeply rooted propensities to competition and authoritarianism. Only women can generate a new style of life. "Patriarchy then is the sexual politics whereby men establish their power and maintain their control. All societies and all social groups within these are sexist—not in the sense that one could maintain all societies are racist, but in the far more fundamental sense that their entire organization, at every level is predicated on the domination of one sex by the other."[19] The revolutionary focus is on the family and all other arenas and issues via which patriarchy is felt and recreated. The separatist perspective sees revolutionary consciousness as most often an awareness not only of the existence of patriarchy but also of its absolute dominance in societal determination and of 1-the need for women to organize separately to overthrow patriarchy, 2-the general superiority of "female" and the natural negativity of "male".

Even if it is possible to grant a considerable amount of accuracy to the separatist's perceptions, the weakness of their perspective is obvious: Sexism is not the sole pillar upon which modern oppression rests. The notion that women alone, organized solely around an opposition to men, could overthrow modern society is horribly flawed— if it were even desireable in the first place. Mitchell has a short passage criticizing the myopia of black nationalism which is equally applicable to feminist separatism: "The totalist position is a precondition for this realization (blacks can't go it alone), but it must diversify its awareness or get stuck in the mud of black chauvinism, which is a racial and cultural equivalent of working class economism, seeing no further than one's own badly out-of-joint nose."[20]

The second non-orthodox view merely appends to Marxism Leninism recognition of the special oppression felt by women, and of a strategic need for women to organize together to address this shared "problem". However this is all the autonomous women's groups are to do—struggle for women's liberation in parallel with the broader and more basic class movement for socialism. So there are two parallel struggles, one addressing the woman's question and rather subordinate; the other addressing the laws of capitalist motion and clearly prior. Autonomous organization is respected but clearly confined in its focus and responsibilities.[21] In actual fact, according to separatists and socialist feminists, this approach rapidly degenerates to "sexism on the periphery" handled solely opportunistically and economistically. Particularly if progress is made organizing around class issues, the sexual focus fades; and at all times it is subordinate to the class focus and to the leadership of the class organizations. In essence this approach represents a kind of plugging of the dam, or perhaps even more aptly, a hiding of the "anomoly" in the favored paradigm.[22] It represents a plus for reality but only a very small and generally temporary one.

The third response to the Marxist Leninist approach is socialist feminism, and it is much closer to our own perspective. In this view society's determinant core includes both patriarchy and class division. The revolutionary focus is therefore dual. Revolutionary consciousness includes an opposition to both sexism and classism in all their forms, each in both the community and the factory.

But now, as compared to the separatist approach, the differences between men and women are understood historically, not as givens but as contingencies. Women are not overglorified. It's recognized that "the indignity of femininity has been internalized for millenia,"[23] so that women manifest many imposed traits which contrary to being superior, are in fact self-detrimental. In general the act and condition of oppression not only disfigures the oppressor, it also maims the oppressed. The spontaneous culture of women oppressed by patriarchy is not an automatically revolutionary culture—far from it, it is automatically quite suspect as are all other creations of the oppressive hegemony.

While men are not viewed by socialist feminism as innately the enemy, their oppressor traits still remain very much a part of the problem. "For while we realize that the liberation of women will ultimately mean the liberation of men from the destructive role as oppressor, we have no illusion that men will welcome this liberation without a struggle..."[24] And while no doubt being disfigured and denied by sexism, men have also been the principal oppressors and developed a psychological and material attachment to their advantages.

In terms of organization there is again a subtle but critical improvement over the previously discussed positions. There are no longer two parallel struggles nor merely one simple big one of either a class or sexual definition. Instead there is now a whole struggle with a variety of component aspects precisely reflecting the fact that the totality to be overcome is itself a mosaic. With respect to organization, as Mitchell says, it's clear "that it's women as a group who are oppressed, and that, though all oppressed groups should work to a point of solidarity with each other, their own understanding of their situation comes from their own analysis."[25] And to develop such an analysis certainly requires "a room of one's own."[26]

Organizationally there must be autonomy within collectivity. Whatever the chosen structure of the movement's organizations, some must be mixed and others exclusively composed of women. But the latter, far from dealing only with matters of sexism would be struggling for a total revolution. They would function collectively with all other branches in developing *general program and practice*, but they would also *take the lead* in the struggle around sexism and in general be woman rather than man defined. Because women begin from a different position in society and a different consciousness than men, and develop themselves along different paths; and because they and only they can fully understand and develop counter-programs to their own oppressions, there is need for autonomous women's organizations even within a broader totalist movement. Autonomy in self-definition and in leadership of anti-sexist struggles; collectivity in dealing with the totality of oppressions, and solidarity with the whole movement—these are the organizational principles of socialist feminism.

The difference between the socialist feminist approach and our own becomes clear as we move on to discuss race and authority. For on these matters the socialist feminists are theoretically much like the orthodox Marxist Leninists. That is, they assert that the totality does not include racism or authoritarianism as core, but rather in its motion creates each as peripheral. The socialist feminist approach encompasses two of the crucial four pillars in their central focus. This is certainly an improvement over Marxism Leninism but it nonetheless still needs further enlargement. Moreover, most socialist feminist groups understand patriarchy and classism as interrelated only in a kind of parallel but relatively unentwined, if sometimes conflicting, motion. This sometimes

causes lapses to the "two parallel movement" or to the "men are the
ultimate enemy" positions. The alternative perception which was
developed in chapters three to six sees that there is an entwined totality,
which, however, manifests itself in four different identifiable oppressive
modes, and which must therefore be fought simultaneously as a totality
and also in recognition of its varying effects upon varying groups of
people, who must themselves each exercise leadership with respect to
their own particular predicaments. To understand further, it would be
best to move on to the question of racism and the correct revolutionary
orientation toward its elimination.

RACISM AND REVOLUTION

With racism as with sexism there are four prevalent understandings
of what constitutes the capitalist totality and thus of the proper
revolutionary focus, consciousness, and organizational forms.[27]

The general initial concern with the classical "unite and fight", one
big movement approach is that however much tactical importance it may
sometimes grant racism, it only understands it economistically, only in
terms of impeding or of generating class solidarity. It overlooks the
depths of racism's roots and thus mistakes the methods by which they
best can be eliminated. In a powerful pamphlet, "Black Worker, White
Worker," Noel Ignatin has written:

> A common approach to the problem posed above is that of the
> white radical who goes into a shop which has a typical pattern
> of discrimination against Black workers, instead of directly
> taking up that issue, and attempting to build a struggle for
> equality, he looks for some other issue like speed-up, which
> affects all workers to one degree or another. He aims to develop
> a struggle around this issue, to involved all the workers in the
> struggle. He hopes that in the course of the struggle the white
> workers, through contact with Blacks, will lose their attitudes
> of racial superiority. This is the approach to the problem of
> unifying the working class which prevails within the radical
> movement today.
> I don't think it works. History shows it doesn't work. The result
> of this false unity always leaves the Black worker still on the
> bottom. It always seems to be the demand for racial equality,
> the last one on the list, that is sacrificed in order to reach a
> settlement and celebrate the great victory of the struggle.[28]

The point is clear: To have a united revolutionary movement
capable of confronting capitalist hegemony and of overcoming it, racism
must be confronted head on. As Ignatin formulates it, "it is Black and

white together on the picket lines, and after the strike is over the white workers return to the skilled trades, the machining departments and the cleaner assembly areas, and the Black workers return to the labor gang and the open hearth..."[29] Ignatin finally quotes Tom Watson, a Georgia agrarian protest leader from about eighty years ago, and his words have deep meaning in terms of our own understanding of the interpretation of hegemony:

> You might beseech a southern white tenant to listen to you upon questions of finance, taxation, and transportation; you might demonstrate with mathematical precision that herein lay his way out of poverty into comfort; you might have him 'almost persuaded' to the truth, but if the merchant who furnished him his farm supplies (at tremendous usury) or the town politician (who never spoke to him except at election time) came along and cried, 'Negro rule,' the entire fabric of reason and common sense which you had patiently constructed would fall, and the poor tenant would joyously hug the chain of an actual wretchedness rather than do any experimenting on a question of mere sentiment...the argument against an independent movement in the South may be boiled down to one word—nigger.[30]

The separatist response to "unite and fight" is to call Marxism Leninism a white man's ideology, and then adopt in its place a more psychological and race centered perspective.[31] The focus becomes the ghetto. The issue orientation switches to matters of national well-being and separation. Revolutionary consciousness is essentially cultural. But the problems are all too obvious: racism is simply not the whole of the totality responsible for reproducing society's defining contours. A single minded racial focus is strategically unsuited to overcoming present day hegemony whether in its racial or in any of its other oppressive manifestations. Overlooking class, sex, and authority issues, nationalist movements in the U.S. are only interest-group oriented. They can neither garner sufficient numbers of people to their cause nor themselves successfully break with capitalist normality. Over time they either reproduce that normality internally and become coopted, or they move beyond their narrow definition to embrace a more totalist perspective.[32]

More in line with Marxism Leninism, and in fact an outgrowth of it, is a second response to the simple "unite and fight" approach which can lay claim to considerably more sophistication. This perspective accepts the classical view concerning the central economic dialectic governing capitalism's motion. Class struggle is still seen as the single key to socialist revolution. But the new view also grafts on an analysis of what is called the "national question", which is the fact of colonial oppression of subjugated nations and of the progressive character of national liberation struggles. So this view sees two parallel struggles, each progressive, the racial struggle if properly engaged aiding the more critical class struggle. The colonially subjugated peoples are responsible for their own liberation and organize autonomously to achieve it—though of course also with the aid of the most progressive of the colonizing people as well. Thus, in the United States in this view there is the socialist struggle and a variety of parallel national liberation struggles, each with autonomy, each dealing within that autonomy solely with matters of their own national liberation. The problems are again fairly clear: minorities in the United States don't constitute nations. The exception to this is the case of Native Americans who in fact are a nation waging a national liberation struggle. The southern belt is not the black people's homeland. The notion of secession as a strategy of liberation is totally false as well as impossible. In practice the nation approach leaves black and other Third World people pretty much where "unite and fight" left them, except now alone. Their struggle is still not a true part of the socialist revolution, and their role is peripheral, or, if central, it is so on class rather than race grounds. In practice there is more opportunism than solidarity—a totalist orientation is precluded and thus there is only an incomplete understanding of both class and race issues.[33]

In the final socialist nationalist view, which comes still closer to our own perspective, there is recognition that both racism and classism are central to societal reproduction.

It is understood that "white workers who can accept racial cooperation on the shop floor often then remain hostile to similar co-operation in matters of housing, schooling, health care, and a whole range of social issues."[34]

> On the one hand displays of democratic cooperation and frat-ernal relations with Black workers, and, on the other hand, examples of backwardness and selfishness which are unbecoming the members of a social class which hopes to reconstruct society in its image. What is taking place is a "civil war" in the mind of the white worker. In the community, on the job, in every sphere of life, he is being faced with a choice between two ways of looking at the world, two ways of leading his life. One way represents solidarity with the Black worker and the progressive forces of society. The other way represents alliance with the forces of exploitation and repression.[35]

Racism exists and has a set of powerful roots in all aspects of daily life, both institutional and ideological. It isn't important simply because it divides the working class—but rather because it is itself a part of a hegemony capable of reproducing both race and class "normality" against any partial movement of insubstantial theory or program. The classic "unite and fight" thesis is scrapped in recognition that neither racism nor classism will be overcome if the former is only understood peripherally to the latter. For then no programs confronting white racism will be adopted and in the end the dynamics of hegemony functioning through racism will undo any advances achieved in temporary workplace "alliances" made around obviously shared material interests. Similarly the separatist view is discarded in recognition that race isn't everything even if it is a part of the totality which is "everything". And finally the national liberation alongside socialist struggle approach is also scrubbed as an essentially opportunist attempt to fix up an insufficient viewpoint in light of the obvious practical importance of national movements.

The separatist tendency to overglorify the colonized's history and culture is gone. Now there is respect for the oppressed's achievements right alongside an understanding that racism is so crippling to spirit and capability that much study and preparation is necessary if those who have been racially oppressed are going to generate insights, culture, and practice suitable to their own liberation and to the socialist revolution. Organization partially requires autonomy as the racially oppressed are the only ones capable of generating an uncompromised full program to combat the racist manifestations of society and can do this only in isolation from whites; but it also involves mixed struggles and institutions as in many arenas the manifestations of totality affect people of different races similarly. Thus there is a need for a complex organizational form stressing autonomy at the same time as collectivity.

The differences between such a socialist nationalism and our own councilist perspective derives from their only very narrow and peripheral understandings of sexism and authoritarianism. For on these matters they don't see, as we do, the links between all the core characteristics and so they often generate movements which are at best insufficiently anti-sexist or anti-authoritarian. Further there is the additional problem that the socialist nationalists don't always recognize the interpenetration of racism and classism, each reinforcing/reproducing the other, and thus the tendency to fall back toward the "parallel movement, two struggle" approach or the "whitey is the enemy" approach. This is the question of the "mix" of the core characteristics, once their presence and form is recognized.

AUTHORITARIANISM AND REVOLUTION

Consider now the third chart, "authority and revolution". Here again we've suggested four viewpoints: First the classical Marxist Leninist, which, far from finding authority in any way bad, instead views it as a tactical-organizational necessity; and then the three counter views—the anarchist, Marxist syndicalist, and nearer to our own view, the communist anarchist and council communist views.

The Marxist Leninist view is clear enough: The main problem of revolutionary organization is efficiency and self-defense. To achieve these ends it is necessary to be able to function with a singleness of will—it is necessary to have punch as well as fine analysis. These are acquired by way of a hierarchical party organization which respects the greater experience and scientific capabilities of those at the center and simultaneously makes the greatest possible use of them. Class is the central analytic and programmatic category. There is nothing to fear from efficiency and discipline if they are carried forward in the interests of the proletariat. What's wrong with authority is that up till now it has always been the authority of the ruling clases against the interests of those who toil. With the Leninist party this is to be changed about—the proletariat exercises full power through the party vehicle.[36]

The anarchist response is immediate: Authoritarianism and the dynamics of state power are the feature that gives modern society both its oppressiveness and its relative stability. Hegemony is the imposition of follower/leader mentalities and hierarchic organizational relations. No Leninist party can overcome the forces reproducing present oppressions by "mimicking" those same forces. The best such an approach might achieve is a *change of bosses*. The dialectic at history's center is one of power and if people are to be free the only route is through an anarchism which eliminates centrally imposed authority—the main focus must be the struggle for each individual's free control over their own lives, in all of society's institutions.[37] The Leninist party is no vehicle for such an end. Rather it merely changes the shape of authoritarian "normality" replacing one justifying catechism for another.

Historically the problem with this extreme individualist anarchist approach is "similar" to the problem with nationalist or feminist separatism. While recognizing one aspect of totality, authoritarianism, which Leninism largely ignores, it often denies the equally absolute centrality of class, race, and sex, and thus itself also generates only a very incomplete assault on capitalist hegemony.[38]

In contrast the Marxist syndicalist approach retains the classic view of class as central while now adding a parallel concern for the ills of bureaucracy and hierarchy. The focus is on factory organizing but with a disavowal of the Leninist party form and an emphasis instead upon local councils. In essence this view sees the socialist struggle as very much class governed with however, a parallel authority dynamic which must be tactically addressed, especially so as to avoid a corrupting of the movement's goals.[39]

The transition to anarchist communism is simply a broadening of totality to include both class and authority, and thus of the struggle to all arenas where either are manifested. The hallmark of this approach is its simultaneous critique of democratic centralism and of economism. The weakness is the exclusion of sex and race relations from the understanding of totality.[40] The communist anarchists were not as theoretically prolific as their near neighbors in ideology, the council communists, and indeed, we find ourselves very much in tune with many of the latter group's viewpoints.

"If the revolution comes by decree from above and the worker simply changes his boss... the factory will remain alien and work a slavery..." says Gramsci.[41] And Anton Pannekoek echoes: "The road towards liberty will remain closed till the day the working class realizes the importance of independent action and of worker's control."[42] And we add that in the modern world of the United States, with its own particular history and present conditions, racism and sexism are similarly central. Organization must be anti-authoritarian and anti-capitalist so as not to replicate society's hierarchical and class relations thereby reimposing the old society's hegemonic normality. But organization must also be anti-racist and anti-sexist. It must provide the means for a total struggle against the four, entwined co-causal aspects with leadership coming from different sectors in different situations. It's sort of like fighting a societal octopus. You cut off one arm and it will grow back, supported by the others which still remain. To kill the creature you must get all the arms and the head lying beyond as well.

As Sartre says of revolutionary organization: "How could it be sufficiently receptive to react, not by saying 'Let us see what we can get out of this?' or 'Let us try to attract that movement to ourselves so that it does not escape from us,' but by saying, 'Here is reality and we must serve it by trying to give it theoretical and practical generality so that it may grow and be further advanced.'"[43] The Leninist party is always dominated by those groups who are already in the strongest position under capitalism—the sons of the white ruling, petit bourgeois, and coordinate classes. It reproduces hierarchy instead of countering it. It blinds its adherents to at least one aspect of totality, authoritarianism. It doesn't allow for autonomy within collectivity, except when it says, "okay, you can go off and autonomously deal with this sharply circumscribed set of issues, assuming of course that you do nothing to disturb the larger strategy we're formulating for the revolutionary struggle as a whole."[44]

TOTALITY AND REVOLUTION

As Sheila Rowbotham urges, "There are no short cuts. The making of a revolutionary socialist organization which is capable of taking the offensive without being either absorbed or smashed, which can at once safeguard the interests of groups within it and not simply reproduce the structures of authority and domination which belong to capitalism, is a gigantic task."[45] Our discussion should make clear that this task's successful accomplishment in the United States has as a prerequisite an understanding of our society's core totality. Accordingly, what is needed is 1-autonomy within collectivity, 2-non-authoritarian organizational forms, 3-a wholistic revolutionary consciousness, and 4-a total revolutionary focus aiming at all aspects of capitalist hegemony. Autonomy is necessary because the oppressions various groups feel are real. And yet an overall collectivity and a totalist approach is necessary to overcome every arm of society's hegemony. In this dual orientation there lies an immense energy and moral force. Thus we can now include on the next page, a final, fifth approach for each of the charts we've examined.

In the modern U.S. women, third world people, workers, and those under the boot of authority all say:

> We will not be part of a revolutionary struggle which relegates our particular condition to the level of "problem", while addressing other conditions as theoretically and strategically prior. We are not going to be in a movement which disrespects our heritage of cultural and material struggle, which ignores our lifestyle, and denigrates the importance of our achievements as well as our right and capacity to lead.

This sentiment reflects the fact that U.S. society has a fourfold core totality. The immediate task is to translate ourselves from conflicting interest groups who compete, to a revolutionary bloc creating a counter-hegemony. This can't be done by emphasizing any one aspect of society's core oppressions over all the rest—movements based on such biased perceptions will be neither large nor secure. More than anything else they represent "interest group" approaches to affecting reality.[46] They are fragmenting and competitive and have no potential to envision and enact a truly revolutionary future. In contrast, what is now necessary is to go beyond all narrow world views and finally develop a new totalist approach. We must respect all major struggles and yet simultaneously merge them in one united framework. This new framework must allow us

Revolutionary Councilist

TOTALITY AND REVOLUTION

Totality	Struggle Focus	Revolutionary Consciousness	Organization
The totality core to society's reproduction has four entwined co-causal pillars: sex, race, class, and authority. The four move as a whole and are thus together responsible for reproduction as well as for the contradictions which make revolution possible. The four oppressive manifestations affect differing setors of society's citizens differently. Still they reproduce interactively and must be overcome that way as well.	The focus is now multi-manifestations of totality are addressed. The split between foci is now only tactical, deriving from the fact that different groups are affected by the totality differently. Class, race, sex, and authority foci are all addressed, however as but one part of the whole which is to be overcome.	An awareness of the full totality, of how it reproduces, and of the socialist alternative. It is an awareness of how society's institutions and consciousnesses mold our daily lives, limiting them, and yet simultaneously create opportunities for revolutionary program. It's an awareness of what socialism in the U.S. would look like and of how it would be a living solution to present limitations. It is finally also an awareness of how a revolutionary movement united via a shared consciousness of totality and by an organizational form promoting solidarity while simultaneously respecting the different conditions and needs of men, women, white, and non-white peoples, could fight and achieve revolutionary change. It embodies at its core not only concern with class, but also with race, sex, and authority.	There is one big movement for socialism, but this movement recognizes the varying principal manifestations of totality, and has autonomous branches which take leadership around each, while also functioning equally in the whole. There are workers', women's and third world people's organizations. Further, in recognition that authoritarianism is core, it is realized that organizational forms must promote equity, self-management, and flexibility as well as autonomy and efficiency. There is a movement of various branches united by a shared analysis, program, and goal developed continuously and collectively, and also by an organizational federation stressing autonomy and solidarity.

to attain autonomy within collectivity at both the theoretic and the strategic levels.

The discussion and charts of this section should have given useful clarification to our own theoretic view as well as demonstrating where it leads. We see all the various prior strategic conceptions as lacking precisely in that they key in on only a part of the totality as if it alone were singularly dominant. This has been crippling to focus, program, and organization, but perhaps more to the ability of activists to even situate themselves in society and relate to one another. By using faulty concepts activists have worked with a map of their world which was in fact only very partially suited to the ends being sought. The need for a more complex map is not engendered by a penchant for detail or by a false or exaggerated sense of what's important. Rather it is an accurate response to the complex world we live in. Our view is not a simple amalgamation of those which have gone before, but instead a completely altered perspective which approaches society at both its institutional and also at its ideological levels, and which understands it in the fullness of its reproductive and revolutionary tendencies. To go further in our strategic presentation it is necessary to take up the next pressing set of issues on the left today: that is, what is to be the exact mix of organizational forms (party, council, union—spontaneous and planned) that the left will employ?

ORGANIZATION AND REVOLUTION

The chart on the next two pages depicts four major approaches to the organizational problem of "unequal development"—the fact that not all people develop revolutionary consciousness and commitment at the same rate and depth.

"EXTREME" MARXIST LENINIST ORGANIZATION

In the extreme Marxist Leninist analysis the solution to this uneven flow of revolutionary development, as well as to the inherent difficulties of taking power from a highly organized military state, lies in the vanguard party. It is to be organized hierarchically: those with greatest experience and knowledge must be at the top. The overall logic of the approach is clear enough.

On the path to revolution no matter how many people become generally active only a small percentage will have both the opportunity and disposition to become professional revolutionaries; that is, cadres who concern themselves almost always with politics and especially with

ORGANIZATIONAL FORMS AND FUNCTIONS

	Party Role	Party Structure	Council Role	Revolutionary Process
M.L. Jacobin	The Party is an organization of professional revolutionaries. It must 1) engender support from the masses, 2) provide leadership, focus and tactics for popular struggles, and 3) seize power.	The Party must be structured according to democratic centralist principles precisely to take maximum advantage of the skills and insights of those cadre who have the most experience and scientific preparation.	In this extreme Jacobin model the councils have no role at all. It is the party which is the means and end of revolution.	The Party is built carefully and over a relatively long period. During popular struggles it intercedes gaining legitimacy useful to its leadership tasks in the revolutionary moment itself. Finally crisis brings the conjunctural struggle for power which the Party, through its discipline and scientific preparation, wins, thus becoming the mechanism of the dictatorship of the proletariat.
Spontanest	There is no role for an organized revolutionary party. Such forms, created under capitalist hegemony, necessarily replicate capitalist social relations and thus serve to perpetuate rather than overcome them.		The councils are the means and the end of revolution. They must generate mass confidence and the skills necessary to administer the new society. They must seize control of society's economy and replace the state with the decentralized infrastructure of a new self-managing society; the free federation of people's councils in all workplaces.	The revolution comes as a result of a crisis. It is organic, not organized in advance. Councils erupt spontaneously and achieve consciousness in the actual moment of revolutionary struggle. Organizations that seek to prefigure or influence this process from outside the people's own spontaneous vehicles are inevitably doomed to failure; or even worse, they cripple the movement itself, either causing it to fall short of the mark, or destroying its organic forms and replacing them instead with authoritarian forms from the past.

ORGANIZATIONAL FORMS AND FUNCTIONS

	Party Role	Party Structure	Council Role	Revolutionary Process
Bolshevik	The Party is an organization of professional revolutionaries. It must to 1) engender support, 2) provide leadership, 3) infiltrate and help build councils, and 4) use the councils to seize power.	The Party must be structured according to democratic centralist principles precisely to take maximum advantage of the skills and insights of those cadre who have the most experience and scientific preparation.	The councils are the vehicle whereby the Party exerts the proletariat's power during the revolutionary moment. They are to coalesce the workers, generate spirit, communicate the Party's plans, and take the factories from the capitalists. But they are only a temporary necessity of struggle which arise as needed and pass away when no longer required.	The Party is built carefully and over a long period. It works to attain the workers' faith. It helps to construct their councils and its cadres play central roles in their development. Crisis brings the conjunctural struggle for power. Having attained a position at the head of the proletariat and hegemony over the councils, the party is in an ideal position to orchestrate the final uprising and proletarian victory. It then becomes the vehicle of the proletariat's power via the dictatorship of the party itself.
Councilist	The Party is an organization of revolution. It coordinates their efforts to: 1) develop and popularize analyses and culture, 2) build the councils, 3) combine theory with council experience, and 4) participate in the revolutionary process furthering the dominant role of the councils.	The party must be structured democratically such as to protect the greatest possible generalization of skills and such as to ensure a proper development of initiative and sensitivity to authoritarianism at all levels.	The councils are the means and ends of revolutionary struggle. They are a conscious product of the merging of theory with the concrete experiences and feelings of the people. They are an arena where revolutionary skills are forged, the insights necessary to self-management honed, and strategy formulated, and by which people overcome hegemony and develop socialist institutions.	The revolution is built by the people. Crisis provides opportunities but that is all. The revolution develops as a struggle for institutional and ideological hegemony at all levels of daily life. The party is a kind of detonating agency. It serves as a means through which those who become revolutionary first coordinate their efforts to "bring others along", and to also further develop themselves. But it is the councils which serve as the real vehicles of people's power. They wage the struggle and attain the critical position in the new society.

the strategy, tactics, and personal implementation of revolutionary struggle. Through their commitment, experience, and example, this group will take the lead and thus come to constitute the membership of the vanguard Leninist party.

And yet even in this special group without development of a "unity of purpose" and of a "singleness of will", individual efforts will clash and come to chaos. Marxism Leninism argues that there is need for strict coordination and discipline to attain the kind of collective force that can guide the whole proletariat and overcome the bourgeoisie's repression. And this unity is to be acquired essentially by delegating the rule of the party to a small central committee composed of the most disciplined, scientific, and in all other ways advanced cadre: a group which over time can develop the cohesion to really lead the party in all its struggles. Dialectically relating to the masses the party can act as the leading force of the revolution. Continually criticized by the whole party, the central committee can develop programs suited to revolutionary struggle in times of worsening crisis. Finally, upon achieving power the party can become a vehicle of proletarian authority. It can become the ruling party, whose central committee is the medium of the "dictatorship of the proletariat". The democratic centralist party is thus consistent with the Marxist Leninist view of capitalist society and of socialist revolution. The main concern must be steeling it to its revolutionary tasks: 1-taking power; and 2-employing power effectively in the proletariat's interests— and also ensuring that it can achieve these by developing for it a position of hegemonic leadership of the revolutionary movement of the proletariat.

SPONTANEIST "ORGANIZATION"

The general spontaneist critique of the democratic centralist view is straightforward: Seizing power in a statist form with a hierarchical party constructed during the reign of the capitalists is a complete dead-end.[47] It can only reproduce the contours of the old society. Indeed any organization formed under the domain of on-going capitalist hegemony will reflect that hegemony and serve in one way or another to continually reinforce it—albeit perhaps in new forms. To fit into an authoritarian party is to give up one's concern with fighting authoritarianism and promoting initiative. It leads internally to sectarianism and externally to an inability to relate adequately to the workers' concerns to control their own lives. Hierarchical parties are doomed not only to replicate the social relations of capitalist hegemony, but also to be divorced from the real life of the masses, and horribly inflexible. Far from bending with changing conditions they have a tendency to become captive to yesterday's formulas or "lines", thus missing immediate opportunities.[48] As Sartre puts it in a modern discussion: "If the cultural apparatus of the C.P.'s is practically null, the reason is not that they lack good intellectuals, but that the mode of existence of their parties paralyzes their collective effort of thought. Action and thought are not separable from organization. One thinks as one is structured. One acts as one is organized. This is why the theory of the C.P.'s has come to be progressively ossified."[49]

In the spontaneist view the solution lies in recognition of the power of revolutionary struggles to create their own organizational forms. Thus, as the capitalist crisis develops workers engage in struggle. Their consciousness develops in proportion and they come together in spontaneous councils in their work places. These, then, are the vehicles, the *means and ends* of the socialist revolution. They are formed not during the period of capitalist hegemony, but rather precisely when that hegemony is breaking down, in the moment of struggle and crisis. There is no Jacobin vision of seizing power at the center as the key step—rather a worker's self-management orientation prevails. The councils must take over the economy and the society as a whole. Decentralism rather than the reverse is to be the natural order of things. The contrast with Leninism is most stark: spontaneity instead of careful drawn-out preparation; councils instead of the party; the masses and more experienced revolutionaries as one, rather than the former following the latter; and finally direct self-management rather than a dictatorship through the party vehicle. In its most extreme versions the spontaneist school literally disavows the notion of "being revolutionary" before the actual revolutionary moment. For it is felt that while capitalism prevails relatively undisturbed all attempts at organized opposition are doomed to succumb to hegemony—there is nothing to do but school oneself, perhaps better the world a bit through some temporary local reform struggles, and wait for the revolutionary conjuncture when the working class will emerge and one's role in the struggle can become graphically clear.[50]

LENINIST-BOLSHEVIST ORGANIZATION

For our purposes it's useful to understand Bolshevism as a kind of intelligent Leninist rejoinder to the spontaneists. It is admitted that professional revolutionaries isolated from the people would become either "ultra-leftist" through impatience and frustration, or bourgeois through cooptation. However, it is also argued that total immersion in the affairs of the local factory units breeds economism—a loss of touch with the broader political struggle. Even in a moment of crisis the councils can slip into reformism. Moreover, while the councils do arise and are important, they are uncoordinated. They are unschooled and indeed more than any other institutions of revolution spontaneously reflect many residues of capitalist belief and behavior. They provide muscle but no real punch unless guided by those who are prepared to understand the ebb and flow of revolutionary struggle—the necessary slogans, tactics, and programmatic formulations. Finally, there is really no such thing as spontaneity in the sense of something pure and positive. There is only preparation and no preparation; the utilization of experience and instead the utilization of inexperience and confusion. The purpose of the party is to "fuse" the masses into a coherent revolutionary force. It must provide leadership and ideology. It must give direction and discipline without which the councils of the moment will fall helplessly prey to reaction. The councils (or soviets) are critical but are essentially *tools of revolution*. They must be built and consciously structured as a means of exerting the power of the proletariat. They must coalesce the proletariat not as a disjoint, decentralized force, but rather under the disciplined central leadership of the party. The soviets are essential for bringing the masses together, for creating unity in the struggle, for disseminating the party's programs and tactics, for awakening the interests of the masses, for fostering their morale and strength.[51] But they are not the actual means of seizing state power. They are not the means or end of revolution but rather only one tool that it employs. The party is still the solution to uneven development: not by making believe that it doesn't exist, but by taking advantage of those who move most rapidly and develop most revolutionary experience and wisdom. They are to be the central element. Revolutionary consciousness is maintained in a bourgeois world not via the masses in process, but through the patient, disciplined, study and practice of the party. Revolutionary consciousness is not arrived at spontaneously, nor is anything else of real lasting value. Rather it is a product of immense effort, as is the revolution itself. The result, a party steeled in practice, disciplined, prepared, and wise—able to lead the proletariat, to guide the temporary councils, and to finally, artfully and effectively administer the new socialist society.[52]

REVOLUTIONARY COUNCILIST ORGANIZATION

The revolutionary councilist tradition to which we attach ourselves tries to learn from and then move beyond all sides in the debate. Surely an absence of organization is a dead-end. Surely spontaneity can only by luck even approximate intelligently planned practice.

But must the approach to revolutionary organization be deadening? Must it suffer from all the weaknesses the spontaneists enumerate and more besides? In Sartre's words "Is it not possible to conceive of a type of political organization where people are not barred and stifled?"[53]

The Leninists are right that there is unequal development of revolutionary opportunities and that those arising first must be seized upon lest they're forever lost. But eventually revolutionary consciousness must become mass—for if it remains solely the possession of those who moved earliest the hierarchical social relations of capitalist society will inevitably be reproduced with the professional revolutionaries at the center and everyone else taking orders. Spontaneity is insufficient but so too is an elite theory and organizational form. For it inevitably distances the organs of revolution from the people themselves, from their needs and their capabilities. The end-point will then not be self-management but either a failure of "morale" or a new form of tutelege.

Leadership and theoretical direction must be ultimately merged with the self-activity of the masses. And this is necessary both to avoid a new hierarchy and to insure that leadership and theory are actually rooted in the masses real needs and potentials. There is unequal development but in the end the masses must make the revolution through their *own institutional forms*; in no other way is their any chance for true socialist democracy.[54] But the Leninist critique that councils operating by themselves tend to become reformist and economist is certainly well-taken.[55] Hegemony is a powerful force; normality is pervasive and is not to be effectively countered by appeals to spontaneity. While the daily life of the people opens possibilities of revolutionary development, it does not insure such development nor reward its occurence.[56] The people's own local institutions, to even come into existence as tools of revolution seeking ideological and institutional hegemony, must be carefully constructed.[57] This is accomplished by revolutionaries aware of precisely what they are doing. It is aided by the coordination of these first-moving revolutionaries through a democratic party of their own construction. This party is not a repository of some full revolutionary science or of determinant lines, but rather "only" of a world view which can unite the revolutionary movement and give it intellectual tools requisite to its strategic tasks.

But if such a party comes into existence first and helps construct the councils, why should it ever bow to their will? Why will it not end like the Bolshevik organization, ruling and indeed even dismantling the councils after they've aided in the seizure of power? This is the central question of the councilist approach.

The party is not viewed as the future holder of power and is not constructed for such a purpose. *The party is a tool* enabling those who become revolutionaries in the earliest stages to exert their potentials in the most effective possible fashion. It gives them collective strength and hones their theories and strategies through collective criticism and development. But the emphasis is on pursuit of the self-organization and expression of the people themselves in the factories, communities, and all other arenas of revolutionary struggle.

> Self-determination of the purposes and methods of struggle; self-management of strikes and/or production through permanent debate in open assemblies; the setting up of strike committees, at the shop and factory level, whose elected members are answerable to the general assembly of workers and may be recalled at any time—all are liberating experiences that reveal to the working class its capacity for self-rule and for mastering and modifying the work process, and that prepare it to refuse domination by management and by the state as well as by party and union bureaucracies.[58]

In the councilist approach the premium is on self-management and on the preparation of the workers for their role in the new participatory socialist society. The institutions of revolution become those of the new type of socialist society. They are prefigurative.

To become a revolutionary in the United States requires that one break with normality, step outside hegemony, and yet retain touch with the life of the people. Unequal development refers to the fact that the conditions which cause people to take such a route before the existence of a prodding revolutionary movement, indeed as the first members of such a movement-to-be, are not generalizable. Whether the few learn first from literature or personal experiences; whether they move to activism out of necessity or solidarity, because of their dispositions or relative freedom or for opposite reasons, their position is initially both tenuous and very difficult. To retain morale while motion is slight, to best use one's energies in building the left, these first revolutionaries must be entwined one to each other. They must have *organizational bonds* which allow each *to be part of a larger whole*, and which further allow the development of a coherent program including literary aids, support systems, and strategic aims. This is the party in the earliest stages of revolution. It is a vehicle of *solidarity* designed to bring disparate energies to a suitable focus.

> The motivation lying at the root of this "organizational voluntarism" is a refusal to wait "as if for the Messiah," for councils to form themselves: the duty of the revolutionary is to fight for their formation, in line with the current movement of

history. The only criterion of revolutionary authenticity for an autonomous group will be the degree of congruence between its critical theory and its practice.[59]

The problem is how to have such an organization without creating a schism between the earliest revolutionaries and the people who are to become the whole movement. How shall there be a vanguard without a rearguard, leadership but no followers? The councilists "demand that the organization intervene as an organization while still retaining the objective not of seizing and exercising power, but of struggling to further the seizure and exercise of power by the whole working class."[60] The party is not seen as the "conscience" of the revolution, nor as its "general staff," nor finally even as its "representative". Instead the party is aimed to simply contribute to the development and self-management of the councils through the "development and diffusion of revolutionary theory and day-to-day participation in the class struggle."[61]

There are three key features that councilists require of a revolutionary party: 1-internal democracy, 2-a self-definition as a tool of the revolution rather than as its chief means and ends, and 3-a self-clarity concerning the membership who are not "professional revolutionaries" divorced from the community, but instead, in Gramsci's phrase, "organic intellectuals" merged with the community. And we add a fourth, which is just the provision that there be caucuses of all types allowed within the party, and especially that there be caucuses paralleling the existence of autonomous council movements, as with say women and blacks.

The party must be democratic so it will not replicate and thus reproduce capitalist relations of hegemony. It must be democratic to insure the fullest development of all its members and of their collective revolutionary consciousness and culture. It must be democratic to insure that the movement will be sensitive to matters of authority within and without. It must be democratic to give living evidence that the new type of socialist interpersonal and institutional relations are actually possible and desirable. And it must accomplish all these ends precisely because otherwise its "counter-hegemony" would be incomplete and unable to persist. In general we agree with Andre Gorz who argues that "decisions based on considerations that cannot be conveyed to and understood by all those who are concerned, cannot be politically 'correct', however 'right' and 'justified' they may be in the eyes of the specialists. There can be only one correct line: the line of revolutionary mass democracy, that is, a line that leads people to organize their own liberation and to rule themselves collectively."[62] While it is the councils which will best implement Gorz's injunction, the party which helps generate those councils and which by its example has much to say about their structure, must of course also comply. The party is built slowly and with care as an agency of revolution which will promote council self-activity and which will lend it a variety of political insights. As such, the life of the party must effectively support the first revolutionaries in their daily tasks, while making them apparent to all who are touched by the party. The party "must not be a mere organization specializing in politics and political leadership, but also a place where people come together to experience a different life, to work out practically and theoretically the politics of life."[63] The party is the "detonator" of the revolutionary councils and they are the means and end of a truly liberating socialist revolution—as such the party must be suited to the conditions of the present as well as to the requirements of the desired future.

As the Lotte Continua people assert with relevance for both the party and the broader council movement: "Our struggle must make it quite clear to all that our life, which the capitalists make us curse, can be beautiful; that the program of proletarian struggle is not a "better life" but a totally different one; that the organization of the proletariat is not simply a part of their lives as they are—something whereby certain benefits can be attained—but that it is the only way to overcome the material and moral misery of everyday life, its loneliness, unhappiness, hopelessness."[64]

But still the party is initially a creation of a small group of "early revolutionaries," or in Gorz's words, an "external vanguard." The initial focus of this organization of militants is to offer each a "center" they can relate to and around which they can generate and collectively carry out revolutionary activities. It must provide leaflets, knowledge, communication, a linking of sectional struggles so that they can become the basis for a whole program—in short, all the resources of daily organizing as well as the strength that can come from collective membership in a viable organization. And yet the party must also not degenerate to sectism nor to an inflated self-conception. The task of this party is "not to direct and control from above, but to stimulate and deliver the capacity for initiative, improvisation and self-organization of the masses themselves."[65] The party is no longer designed to determine the course of struggle nor to affix its own conceptions on what can only then appear to be the "primitive" efforts of the people at large.[66] Rather, the party functions "as an active element within the masses which, like a ferment, stimulates action wherever this is possible, helping the masses to create their own organs of struggle and collective leadership, and to achieve the political vision implied by the carrying of their own experience to its logical conclusion."[67] The party helps to construct a revolutionary counter-hegemony without itself succumbing to society's "cooptive forces". Rather than replicating capitalist social relations either internally or in its relation to the rest of the left, the party fore-shadows socialist relations. The party is a solidifying agency in the sense of bringing disparate struggles into touch with one another. The party thus instills by its broad involvements a broad perspective. It counters tendencies to localism. But most of all, as the home of the earliest revolutionaries, the organic intellectuals, the party fosters their programmatic activities and particularly the development of the main means and ends of socialist revolutionary struggle, the revolutionary councils. There will be more concrete programmatic examples in the next section.

Those who move earliest to revolution have an awesome responsibility: To develop revolutionary theory and practice, to propel struggles and particularly development of the people's own councils, and yet to be of and with the people rather than somehow above them. Historically the first revolutionaries are well-informed at the start and early on achieve significant levels of historical and theoretical background. This is to the good as it potentially "insures" the relevance of their efforts, but it is bad in that it also contains seeds of elitism via the gap it digs between those in the party and everyone else. Thus arises Gramsci's prescription for organic revolutionaries. Those achieving revolutionary conscious-ness first must "inject" such awarenesses into the daily life of the people and also inject the feelings of the people's daily lives into revolutionary consciousness. In the early stages the party is indeed the tool by which revolutionaries can hold onto and further their understandings of the world and of how to change it. But avoiding compromise the party must also avoid isolation; avoiding incorporation it must also avoid sectarianism. The party's organic intellectuals must embed themselves in the daily life of the people, there to explain that life, to propel it to its logical revolutionary conclusions, and to foster the indigenous councils in their struggle for a revolutionary counter-hegemony. The merging of the first revolutionaries and the people, the internalizing of the vanguard, the continual unity of the movement in theory and practice and the perpetual growth of each—these are the hallmarks of the councilist approach and the opposite of the Leninist vanguard prescription. As the councils "melt into" the new socialist society, so in our view the initial party form "melts into" the motion of the masses and their indigenous struggles.

As Gramsci urges, under capitalist hegemony "the popular element feels but does not always know or understand; the intellectual element knows but does not always understand and in particular does not always feel."[68] Revolutionaries cannot afford to make the error of thinking that knowledge isolated from feeling and passion is true knowledge, that there can be effective intelligence in isolation from the life of the people.

Similarly, passion and feeling unguided by theory cannot be confused with intelligent program. There must be praxis—a merging of the theoretical, emotional, and experiential awareness, and this requires a party which is democratic and oriented around the complete immersion of its cadre into the life of the people—and even more, around furthering the people's self-activity so that ultimately the democratic council form can become central. The organic intellectuals take the experiences of daily life and 1-explain them so as to overcome hegemony and free the people's revolutionary potentials, 2-promote the people's revolutionary self-activity, and 3-promote development of the people's own revolutionary councils.

Now consider the councils themselves: The people's own partic-ipatory organizations which struggle to attain ideological and insti-tutional dominance in all of society's arenas of struggle. They are not bourgeois organizations which only reproduce society's defining contours—serving the left only as means to reach the people but not as means to popular power. No, the councils are the institutions of *revolutionary counter-hegemony.* They are the vehicle through which we the people prepare ourselves mentally and socially to administer our own lives and to overcome all obstacles to such self-management. They are the vehicle through which we spread our understanding of the world as against the now dominant bourgeois, racist, sexist, authoritarian understanding. They are the vehicle through which we struggle for progressively more and more power over the day-to-day lives of the factories, schools, hospitals, culture, and communities; through which we demand and attain progressively more power over assembly lines, wages, architecture, city planning, day care, the government's budget, taxes: in short, our day-to-day lives. The councils are the answer to Gramsci's question: "How to weld the present to the future, satisfying the urgent necessities of the one and working effectively to create and anticipate the other?"[69]

The factory councils are the means through which workers can learn to control their own environments taking into central account not profit, but their own social and creative needs as well as those of the people who will consume the fruits of their efforts. The neighborhood councils are the means through which consumers can break commodity fetishism and false individualism; rediscover their collective capabilities and their social needs, and then begin to act upon these in their own interests and in solidarity with the conditions and desires of those who labor in the factories. The women's councils are the means through which women can exercise autonomous power over the definition of their own liberation without in any way limiting themselves to only that involvement, but instead, functioning as one powerful arm of the whole totalized council movement. Similarly the national councils will propel those most oppressed by racism to the position of leadership in the struggle against racism, again including concern with all other issues of revolution as well. The councils will be bound institutionally in a federation and ideologically by their shared consciousness of the totality of capitalist oppression and socialist liberation. The councils respect autonomy and yet overcome the tendency toward narrow, interest-group politics.

The councils are the organizations which wage the war for material power which itself makes possible and is in turn fostered by the development of a revolutionary counter-hegemony. The two moments of revolutionary struggle, the material and the ideological, which are separated in the Leninist model of taking power and only then building the socialist person, are now combined in the simultaneous two-level councilist approach. The councils distinguish themselves from all other institutions as being best suited to this two-fold encounter. For example, in the workplace the contrast between the councils and the unions is stark.

"The companies and the union had developed a division of labor. The companies looked after the machines and the union looked after the workers."[70] There will be no such happy relationship between the companies and councils: rather there will be a continuous struggle for who will define daily life, its institutional, interpersonal, cultural, and ideological relations—a struggle which will run from the factory right into the community where the neighborhood councils will wage the battle.

"What the companies desire—and receive—from the union is predictability in labor relations." "...G.M.'s position has always been, 'give the union the money, the least possible, but give them what it takes,' says a former negotiator. 'But don't let them take the business away from us.'"[71] And yet taking the business away, taking the communities and schools, the hospitals and the parks, taking our lives away is exactly what the councils will do.

The unions are designed for the purpose of making collective bargaining agreements, not revolutions.[72] And indeed this has been the union's legitimate role—defending the interests of workers *within* the contours of the system. But the councils will not have to respect these contours. The union is a competitive institution seeking gains within a status-quo. While serving workers, it also reflects and even perpetuates capitalist hegemony by its bureaucracy (and often its racism and sexism), by defining work as a commodity, by separating workers and consumers, by its economism (and frequent willingness to enforce labor calm), as well as by many of its specific tactics.[73] While the average union is subordinate to dominant ideology and an institution of defense and enlargement, the council is counter-hegemonic and an institution of struggle and power. As important as the former might be, and as progressive a role as it has at times played, the latter is the primary *means and end* of revolutionary socialism.

As revolutionaries we can foresee a variety of ways in which a revolutionary process could fall to bitter defeat: 1-a new assembly could merely reform capitalism while "buying off" an ill-conceived movement in the process; 2-toothless councils might be crushed by a resurgent capitalist state; 3-the disarray of an organizationless movement could fail to sustain itself; 4-a partial movement for only material power could internally dissolve suffering the uncountered power of hegemony; or 5-the accession to power of a revolutionary authoritarian party could lead to merely a new reactionary hegemony. As a counter to all of these prospects we have proposed as organizational forms for the United States a democratic party of organic revolutionaries, and even more centrally, a federation of people's democratic councils organized to promote struggle within collectivity, to foreshadow and prepare for the socialist future, and to win it by a struggle for counter-hegemony at the ideological and material relations levels. In the traditional Leninist model the Party is the means of revolution via the conjunctural Jacobin struggle for central power, and also the end of revolution as the infrastructure of the dictatorship of the proletariat. In the councilist view the party is a "detonating", organizing, and ideological agency—the councils are the means of revolution via the two-level struggle for counter-hegemony, and also the end of revolution as the infrastructure of the new participatory socialist society. The distinction we have drawn between the economistic view of society and our totalist view has a parallel in the organizational sphere: the elite party versus the democratic party; the soviet as tool versus the participatory council as means and end; and a one party structure versus autonomy within collectivity. This is the crux of the organizational differences between Leninism and revolutionary councilism.

REVOLUTIONARY PROCESS

Socialist revolution is not spontaneous, automatic, or mechanical. Conscious preparation is essential. Revolutionary praxis requires theoretical guidance but also demands an accuracy which can only come from experience. Revolution means defeating capitalist ideological and institutional hegemony. It is thus a two-level struggle. Further it must be fought on all "fronts" where society reproduces: that is, against the full totality, including race, sex, class, and authority manifestations.

A party of revolutionaries begins developing a revolutionary perspective—an ideological counter-hegemony—and then through practice furthers that perspective merging it into the common sense of the masses and the feelings of the masses into it. Active programs arise from the people's own most pressing concerns—they allow continual elaboration and enlargement of the two-level struggle for hegemony. Revolutionary councils are brought into being, consolidate, and grow. Leadership comes to reside in them. The councils forge the attitudes, insights and skills necessary to socialism at the same time that they struggle for the power to implement it. The war is total; the means are varied. The new society is first prefigured; then constructed. By the final stage when the councils grow more numerous and rapidly larger, they are institutionally and humanly prepared. The revolutionary process is not found wanting.

What are the requisites and what are the characteristic features of daily revolutionary practice?

First we know that theory is the guide. It provides the general perspective, the lens to tell us what is most critical, and then the tools for concrete analysis of those most critical features. Our vision of socialism is the goal toward which we aim. Our general strategy—address the totality, build a participatory party and federation of councils, foster autonomy within collectivity, wage the two level struggle—provides the framework within which we daily orient ourselves. Tactics are last and most flexible in their definition, but also always our most pressing concern. "What do we do next, and how do we do it?" is our constant question.

You are a revolutionary. You join your city's chapter of the new revolutionary councilist party. What role will you now play? You have gone to a number of meetings, familiarized yourself with the chapter's present activities, and of course share their general ideological perspective. At present the group is at work in three factories, a community college, a university, two hospitals, a local community newspaper, and seven local neighborhoods. After evaluating your own skills and disposition you decide that on the list of high priority places to go, you would feel most comfortable at a job in an auto plant and living in a home in the nearby community. This then, after some general discussion, is where you finally go.

The party chapter in this city has existed for only a short time and as a "center" it has so far only been helping activists by providing leaflets, a little research, and a means of collective discussion and advice. Now, however, people feel that chapter membership is up enough—to about 50—to begin some broader chapter projects. Funding, however, is still only through tithes on member's salaries.

In the first place it is readily agreed that an immediately critical task is research. The revolutionaries must know their community and its institutions fully if they are to help engender, elaborate, and clarify its revolutionary struggles. So a group is collectively determined and delegated to begin a research and information coordinating committee. All the chapter's members have to keep journals outlining the issues, key information, etc. of their own areas of contact and the committee people accumulate these and also add in more general research on the social relations of the community's institutions and on the "make-up" of its citizenry. This knowledge serves as a perpetual fund in further tactical analyses. It is continually augmented. The goal is to have clarity about where people are at, about how that state of "normality" is perpetuated, about how institutions function and entwine, and about how these relations are reproduced, with emphasis on finding and understanding active contradictions.

Let's say the city is Detroit. Some of the initial data is very revealing. Many people seem genuinely afraid for their safety and thus concerned with public security. Study shows that the number of homicides and thefts is astronomical.[74] But it also shows that the police operate primarily in the ghetto and that some special branches have ghetto "kill ratios" rivaling those which Vietnam commando units used to attain.[75]

Work, particularly in the auto plants, is obviously terribly unfulfilling. There is a general "low-level kind of unconscious awareness" that it is not good work, that it is much more oppressive than necessary, redundant, of low quality, and underpaid; and so, on the assembly line the predominant mode is to simulate sleep as closely as the need to be continuously moving—and seeking to avoid accidents—allows. Life is to be lived away from the plants. But it seems from contacts that in off-time everybody is so tired and habitually "dulled" that they can't really get all that much out of their hard-sought leisure anyway. Moreover, there seems to be a constraint on just how much pleasure weekends can be organized to bring—for if they're too good going back to work becomes unbearable. So it is hard to be happy, and even if one can achieve it, maybe it's not so wise. There doesn't seem to be too much community. People certainly aren't proud of themselves, but rather seem almost embarrassed over their conditions. There seems to be a lot of loneliness and families seem one after another fraught with tensions. Fights about drugs, sex, and particularly schools, abound. Throughout the city racial and sexual tensions are intense. The blacks call automation "niggermation." They have the worst jobs, with other Third World minorities close behind.[76] The "hillbillies" from Appalachia are also near the bottom. There are a host of cultures but none have real means to flourish or even hardly survive. There is little sense of personal or group integrity. Rapes are frequent and women are beaten in a lot of families. There are many single and working women and their jobs are invariably demeaning and low-paying. Competition is intense cutting severely into the potentials for warm friendships of any kind. Even the athletic leagues lack camaraderie. This rough picture is continually filled in with ever more detail and scope. The character of work and of grievances in job after job, the health care and welfare and transportation conditions; the sectors of people and their views and values and all their particular oppressions—all are elaborated in continuously increasing detail, especially as the party grows, becomes involved in the people's struggles, and then finally even more as the councils form and take initiative.

Now there's a party debate about another step forward. Members are immersed in the community, making friends, discussing issues, and beginning to organize. A few have become involved in local shop struggles and indigenous tenants' groups. Some of those who are doing community work think that their efforts would be enhanced if the chapter had more city-wide visibility and reputation. They want some broad projects that will garner publicity. As possibilities they propose: a campaign around repression and fear focusing initially on unseating a particularly hated "hanging judge" and then moving on to issues of police brutality and perhaps community patrols;[77] or a consumer campaign around rent control and utility rates, and then also eventually around high prices in general using boycotts and eventually perhaps even community mass expropriations;[78] or finally a general campaign around education focusing on the public schools first, but then also on the possibilities of adult education, of schools within the plants, and so on. Another group working in a Ford plant argues that such broad programs would sacrifice the intense local efforts building a base requires, and only for the glory of a little publicity.[79] They argue instead for the slow, patient generation of a newspaper which everyone in and close to the party could share in producing and which could tie different struggles together, develop counter-hegemonic politics, and be an aid in local organizing as well.[80] The debate rages for a time. Finally the vast majority admits that eventually city-wide campaigns of precisely the types proposed could indeed propel local organizing and base building efforts, but that to embark on them too soon would be a big mistake, in a sense creating a major building without having first begun a foundation. The newspaper is adopted as a tool to reach people and spread new ideas and information, to build up a communications network, and also to develop members' skills and push research even further. It addresses the totality of daily-life so as to elaborate how oppressions exist, affect us, and persist.[81] There is a mix of articles focusing on local and national concerns, but in every instance the effort is to non-rhetorically link a personal perception to a general analysis, to perceive problems as well as the means of their future resolution. Sections on sex-life, problems of the family and community, racism, sports, culture, and the quality of work, and on how socialism would improve each are immediately popular. It is funded by the party tithe, by a purchase fee, and by the members' first efforts to gather contributions for the party, a practice which now becomes continuously pursued.[82]

Shortly party members become close to or involved with a large number of workers and community people, particularly women and black people. The paper touches all aspects of daily life and is avidly read. More and more people wish to contribute but not all are prepared. Also party people have been studying all the research committee's work (and have rotated through its membership) and have been elaborating their theory and strategy ever more fully in regular collective sessions, in their organizing work, and in their leaflet and newspaper writing. The "gap" between people in the party (now about 100) and those who are their friends and fellow workers and neighbors seems to be growing. It is proposed that there should be study groups and even a kind of decentralized "movement school" to spread the ever enlarging talents and knowledge. Some are worried that this will take away from further organizing work so the movement's development will stagnate as it becomes overly academic.[83] A compromise is outlined. Each week everyone associated with the chapter's projects is urged to meet in a small group to discuss a particular practical problem of their own prior choosing after having read some essay or other literature relevant to its solution, again of their own choosing. But also everyone is urged each week to simultaneously be reading a more theoretical work and to discuss it with one another informally whenever time permits. The newspaper summarizes the results of such discussions in a special column. This approach seems best suited to the party's intellectual needs, to the members' time and resources, and also to the needs, time, and resources of the people close to the party and involved in active struggles.[84]

With the party becoming ever stronger, more and more actual struggles are engaged. The general criterion followed is that any reforms themselves somehow improve the movement's position at one or both of the two levels of struggle. The process must enhance the general balance of forces between the activists (later the councils) and the authorities, between the counter-hegemony and the hegemony itself.[85]

The first struggles are characteristic: Two party members work in banks as tellers. They discuss with other workers what is most painful about their activities, and focus attention on those aspects which are simultaneously "felt as oppressive" and also critical to the reproduction of the "local hegemony". They choose to organize primarily around the overly fragmented character of the work and the rampant sexism. In time the workers develop a series of powerful reform demands for a general rotation of all teller and other clerical tasks, the elimination of barricades between tellers, and the elimination of all sexist employment and job role practices.[86] There is an on-going effort to develop a fighting spirit, to discuss the totality of councilist views, to discuss socialism, and to begin developing a councilist methodology and structure.[87] Morale comes directly from the immediate worth of meeting the demands, but also more and more from the perception that this activity is part of a much broader and deeper process.[88]

The party as a whole contributes advice, literature, and other aids as requested.[89] Many members become involved in neighborhood tenants' movements. They seek to organize and enrich these beyond their spontaneous limits. They try to organize tenants and general neighborhood councils and to generalize their concerns beyond rent—to collective shopping, sharing of chores and resources, social and intellectual clubs, reallocation of rooms to accord better with renter's needs, etc.[90] As the community councils develop legitimacy and size they elaborate ever more comprehensive programs: peoples' courts and patrols to deal with juvenile delinquency and mugging, neighborhood planning to overcome redlining and to develop racially balanced communities, community consumer boycotts, etc. In the automobile plants black party workers especially have striking successes.[91] They agitate around the already live issues of racial and general class abuse, form councils, and generalize the political discussion. With white workers they form general worker councils and they also organize caucuses in these workplace councils. The primary work demands are for freedom to determine breaks and work methodology separately from management intervention, to have control over the quality of the final product, for wage stability, price rollbacks, and an end to compulsory overtime. There is a tremendous effort to understand and address the workers' feelings of a lack of respect, power, and dignity on the job. The women's and black caucuses of the work councils (in the plant the latter would often be a majority) ensure that demands always put the fighting of racism and sexism organically out front in job allocation, job definition, and wage struggles.[92] The black and women's caucuses in the party begin general city-wide programs (eg. around police brutality, sex life of youth, and day-care) hold community meetings, and generally begin building black and women's council movements. This work progresses quite rapidly and focuses on both sex and race programs as well as on the more general problems of class and authority oppression and their socialist correction.[93]

All these programs are chosen, to repeat, for their value in the two-level struggle; for the ways they strengthen or enlarge the party or the councils; for the ways they enhance revolutionary consciousness; and for the ways they alter institutional relations to the movement's advantage. Their success means the continual enlargement and "solidification" of the councilist movement, ideologically and organizationally.

At this point repression starts to be a serious concern. When you address life at the plants you confront the power of the state and likewise when you seriously address racism and sexism in the community. These matters are discussed via the study groups like all others. Adventurism is carefully avoided. The problem of infiltration is understood and guarded against as well as possible.[94] Premature strikes that get cadres fired, "showyness" that brings down the cops—these errors are to be avoided.[95] Legal preparedness is high. All developing councils are brought into a network: 1-to generalize their lessons and enhance the totalist development of each, and also 2-to act in support of each other giving positive aid both in reform struggles and in warding off repression.[96]

Solidarity, however, is based on more than "you scratch my back, I'll scratch yours." The entire process has been geared to overcome particularistic approaches. All sectors are developing a totalist politics and practice even while often focusing more on one aspect than on others. The resulting solidarity is positive as well as defensive, empathetic as well as pragmatic.

Now the councils proliferate and federate. They exist in communities, among all types of workers and sectors of the population, in schools and for elderly people. They formulate localized and federated two-level struggle programs. They prepare to exercise self-managing power under socialism by gaining the knowledge, skills, and attitudes they will need. They function at every level, addressing racism, sexism, authoritarianism, and classism in institutions and personalities, in the economy and in the culture. There is no longer any contradiction between the "local" and the "city-wide". Each reinforces the other and indeed now there are regional and national programs as well, all determined by the involved councils and federations of councils. The role of the party diminishes as its cadres work full time in the people's own institutions "pushing" totalist councilist analyses and adapting them through new lessons as well. As hegemony is steadily overcome via two-level struggle of all kinds—strikes, rent withholdings, occupations, consumer actions, all without and also often with militant self-defense—the conditions of socialist self-management are simultaneously elaborated. The transition from contestation for power to the general construction of the new society is finally achieved.[97]

Of course this is a highly abstract and streamlined scenario, not meant by any means to be more than an indication óf general possibilities. The key point, however, is to note that for councilists the main problems and approaches are very different than, say, for Leninists; precisely because the theory and thus the world-view guiding councilist program is very different from that guiding Leninist program, even when both movements claim membership in the "real" Marxian heritage.

THE ROOTS AND ROLE OF IDEOLOGY

Marxism says ideologies reflect the interests of social classes but we've now argued that there are a variety of other social groups whose positions in society are such as to naturally give their members similar social ideologies—either oppressing, oppressed, or revolutionary.

In Chapter Five we show how women, men, third world people, white people, order givers, order takers, bourgeoisie, coordinators, and workers all naturally evolve toward a variety of different understandings of their particular positions and roles in society precisely due to society's differing impositions upon each of these groups. In this chapter we discussed a variety of revolutionary orientations and now it is rather easy to see that they represent the efforts of particular groups or pairs of groups to understand and affect the world in their own interests. Each of these revolutionary ideologies pierces at least a part of the mystifying veil behind which hides the truth about our society. Thus, feminism is an outgrowth of women's positions and insights into their world. It sees behind sexist stereotypes and sexist oppressing and oppressed rationales to a more accurate awareness of women's positions and interests. And similarly nationalist orientations develop powerful understandings of racism and of the interests of third world groups. And though less obviously, one could make an argument that U.S. Marxism Leninism often represents an elaboration of the coordinate class's interests (as perceived under capitalism) into a revolutionary perspective. Thus, the coordinators become the new administrators of their goal society, free of capitalist control but still above and "serving" the workers. On the other hand, council communism more clearly elaborates the workers own interests though again as they are narrowly defined in tune with the workers' own specific orientations and position in society.

It is also easy to see how and why these various ideologies are adopted by various groups as they correspond well to a translation of at least some of each group's specific experiences into a program also for that group's specific "isolated" advance. However, our analysis has shown that what matters is not a particularistic perspective but a total one, and thus not an ideology serving the partial interests of only one group (developed only from that group's perspective), but rather an ideology serving all the progressive interests of all the groups simultaneously (and developed as well via a meshing of the insights garnered from all their perspectives). As we hope we've clarified, this has a host of implications for revolutionary theory, goals, and practical activity. Perhaps most indicatively, where under Leninism a party was needed essentially to "impose" a particularistic ideology on a host of elements, under revolutionary councilism a party is needed precisely to help a host of elements to come together, to themselves elaborate a shared totalist ideology, and to then further their specific and also their shared revolutionary struggles so as to create a truly participatory socialist society. The purpose of our discussion has been to elaborate some of the new ideas needed for such tasks. Hopefully the organizational forms suited to further elaborating such notions and more importantly to putting them into practice will soon come into being. For only then will people in the United States stand a chance of building a future worthy of our capabilities and free from our past inadequacies.

NO PLACE FOR CYNICISM

Our last dialogue is between a revolutionary councilist (RC) and a "cynical" ex-revolutionary Marxist (CE). The focus is on whether we really are proposing something different, and on whether there are any grounds for optimism. The discussion is especially timely in light of recent developments among ex-revolutionaries in the French "intellegentsia".

CE: Why do you still call yourself a socialist? Socialism has offered little more than capitalism. At least under capitalism there is room for self-criticism. In Russia there is none.

RC: But we don't call ourselves socialist out of allegiance to Russia. In our eyes Russia doesn't deserve the name socialism at all. Socialism must mean the social self-management of all institutions and of human development by the people themselves. Anything less, is insufficient. We should coin a new concept for the Russian arrangement. But, at the same time, we should not be deluded into calling it capitalism, nor should we be deceived by the appearance—through western eyes—that Russia is even politically much worse than the United States. Though there is nominal freedom of speech and information in the United States, there is also the most sophisticated control of public discourse in the world. The barrage of media information is thoroughly monitored and even administered by state and corporate institutions. The forms of control of public discourse and the method of dealing with dissent are more varied and sophisticated and generally less extreme in the U.S. than in Russia, but no less effective. What is accomplished in one by blatant state control of social roles is accomplished in the other by more subtle socio-psycho-economic pressures and privileges.

CE: Come on, there's obviously a difference between Pravda and the New York Times...

RC: Yes, and also no. One is state controlled; the other is institutionally/ideologically molded and state/corporate monitored. One doesn't report about the Czech invasion, the other lies about Vietnam. They both report most of the sports and the pronouncements of national leaders.

CE: If you just said the Russians have a little better distribution of wealth (though less of it), I could go along, but to extoll their political system too...

RC: But I've said nothing about its being good. It's a horrendous dictatorship that has nothing at all in common with what people need and desire.

CE: But then why do you persist in taking the name socialist?

RC: Perhaps it's correct to avoid the word "communist" and let its public definition as "the Russian system" stand, though of course this wasn't its historical meaning. But the bad connotations of the word "socialism" are far fewer and unjustified. They must be overcome head-on, otherwise there will be no end to people's negative illusions about human possibilities.

CE: But then, on top of this, why do you persist in trying to elaborate an ideology? I can see calling yourself a socialist, maybe, but why a Marxist, even with a new formulation? Certainly history has demonstrated that all such ideological creations only serve as manipulative tools, as vehicles for concretizing social life in "scientifically consecrated," but still oppressive forms.

RC: Historically, what you say is largely true, but history needn't be a perpetual revolving door. If by ideology you mean a set of inherited formulas lorded as the acme of all human potential, then of course we agree. There is no place in our movement for that. But that's not what we're trying to help create. We see revolutionary councilism as a flexible mass of insights about the world, developed collectively, and continually altered via expansion and in accord with changing situations. It is not to be a province of the few; its tools are not obscure, they do not mystify. The very concepts at the root of the theory are variables. They themselves unfold with unfolding human relations. The guiding methodology addresses issues of network and process and forces a historical approach while also being sensitive to issues of continuity without being unintelligable to all but a few philosopher kings. Of course there's always danger of intellectual conservatism, but at least we've stacked our methods against this tendency, and we also envision and outline a non-elitist social practice which puts a premium on changing the theory, rather than on its continual verification and preservation.

Faced with the difficult problems of ideologies, you (on the other hand) merely throw up your hands and disavow all ideology. We each must have concepts, methodological tools, and ideas that we use each day as our world view or ideology; you included. The issue is whether one will hold a sectarian, dormant one, or a live, growing one. Your act of abnegation really amounts only to disallowing a consciously and collectively shared ideology. You preclude self-awareness of our consciousness, a sharing of it, and its collective social elaboration. In opposition to sectarianism you cut off the possibility of the very means to fight it. Your view is self-defeating and merely frantic.

CE: But at least I don't claim to deliver a "new politics of revolution" that's really just the same old prescription in a new bottle. You still have a party and cadres, you still have a favored body of knowledge—you don't call it a science anymore. The party and cadres will inevitably see themselves, armed with their greater insights, as superior. They will ban freedom of press and speech in pursuit of their own scientifically correct party press and speech. Why not opt instead for complete autonomy of activity in equal small groups?

RC: You go from one extreme to the other with no critical analysis of alternative possibilities. Your's has become a politics of hysteria. Of course it's necessary to avoid centralism, elitism, and authoritarianism, but one must also recognize the tasks at hand: the need for coordination, and the necessity to break repressive hegemony with a collective, revolutionary alternative. Our party is a detonator, not a central leadership. The cadre's consciousness is only partial—it moves toward sufficiency only in the councils, at the concrete level, and with everyone else's. Separated from the people, what the theorists know is worth little; it is certainly not superior to a concrete knowledge of daily life relations. The body of revolutionary thought is collectively elaborated and shared and its content is worlds away from what has previously rightfully repulsed you and also given largely undesirable results. With our premium on the advance of consciousness rather than on its deification, we have reason to pursue a free press allowing all voices a turn and even subsidizing those in dissent. You're right that there is such a thing as justified concern, but there is also excess blind concern that all too often becomes paralysis. The latter serves no valuable ends, no matter how you dress it up in rationalizing philosophies.

CE: Again you attack me for what I can't deliver, but don't promise either. So what? Look, there's another less abstract way to get at some of this. You're from the United States, and it's not surprising that you have less sensitivity to Stalinism than some of us here on the continent, and also that you get over emotional about your own country's ills...

RC: Now patriarchal wisdom to go with your cynicism. Sure, our experience with Stalinism is less, but you needn't endure cancer to understand its devastating effects. Indeed, sometimes distance, as you suggest about your vision of the U.S., allows more clarity. But we are not like those who explain Russian repression, low standards of living, and foreign manipulations or invasions as "accidents". Enough bad apples, we label the tree sick; enough sick trees, we check the ground they grow from. Stalinism is rotten in all its forms, whether they are temporarily "liberalizing" for tactical advantage, or showing true colors all out.

But perhaps on your second point you are right. Perhaps we should grant that there is a certain emotionalism in our hatred for what our country has become. A country which underdevelops a vast part of the world, which in the name of morality supports torturous butchers in Chile, Brazil, South Africa, Iran, and dozens of other countries. A country which uses the most advanced science people have created to control thought, to peddle unhealthy hamburgers, to maintain inhuman housing conditions in its own ghettos, to invent weapons and tortures or to "prettify" ugliness—the list is endless, and the cause for emotion infinite. Just to function rationally each day it is necessary to dull oneself to the full impact of the system which simultaneously creates international horrors and beggars on 42nd street, assembly lines and 5 & 10's selling cosmetics with subliminal advertising. But such acclimation should never go so far as to deny the magnitude of the crimes the United States commits each day, and what it is capable of on the merest provocation. No one should forget Vietnam, its barbarity or who won.

CE: But caught up in all these admitted faults, you miss the accomplishments. Where once unemployment was a threat to existence, now there is government support. Where once daily-life was threadbare, incomes have doubled across the board, or even more. Lynching is gone. There is a pluralism, ...

RC: But we have never claimed that the system is stagnant, only that there is an oppressive core which reproduces largely invariant. Sure there is evolutionary advance, due, however, almost entirely to the struggles of those who are most oppressed. But there are three points to be made about such progress: 1-It is often conceived on the backs of people in other parts of the world or minorities in the United States. 2-When it is at all progressive, a-this is due to pressures from the oppressed—for example for education, unions, unemployment insurance, better medical care—and b-it is finally molded to fit the contours of our society's core characteristics, that is, it never reaches its real potentials. And, 3-all such changes occur along a bounded trajectory. There are limits to what can be achieved, not so much in quantity of output, but in the quality of human relations and daily-life. We literally rip-off and rape the world, and you are correct, the system is not so totally disfunctional that there is nothing at all to show for this grand theft. It's just that there is little, most of it oppressive, all of it limited, and all save that bit reflecting the demands of the oppressed, dripping with international blood as well as the memory of Native American genocide, slavery, child labor, and all the rest, including the underdevelopment of much of the world.

CE: But the Russian state has also been militarist and even more repressive within its own borders. Big structures are all terrible. General Motors and the Communist Party as well. And now your network of councils too...

RC: And next the human race. If everything is crap, you have no responsibility and you can live your cynical dreams in peace. How much have you already debased your humanity to concoct rationalizations for your political cynicism? It's true that artificially big systems are unecological, alienating, and authoritarian. But the network of councils we propose is a means for people to self-consciously administer their own development, their own social advance. It won't be trouble free, but it is by no stretch of the imagination just a new kind of General Motors or Communist Bureaucracy. It's not worth arguing this again point by point; we've already made our case. Anyway it's something else that causes you to grasp at your cynical criticism.

CE: How do you escape manipulation? I'm just not convinced there won't be new leaders setting up new oppressive regimes.

RC: You worry about the manipulation that springs from centralist voluntarism, the notion that a few must lead. With no real confidence, you suggest the alternative of spontaneism—a revolution (or perhaps just reform) which unfolds without any organizational planning and coordination, even without any shared intellectual tools and conscious world views. On the other hand, we take a road which sees people as both created by and also creating history, a road which recognizes the strength of hegemony and poses a counter perspective, and which sees the need for organization but preserves autonomy and self-management. You abrogate all responsibility, and your centralist adversary claims it all, but we offer an approach that entails collective responsibility. I think you could see and appreciate the difference if you weren't so blinded by hopeless despair of ever really winning.

CE: Perhaps that is the real root of our differences. It seems that all the logical arguments you muster, and I held to a version of them myself not so long ago, no longer compare in impact upon me to the weight of revolutions gone awry, of the Gulag, of China recognizing Chile's junta and fabricating transparently preposterous public campaigns against defeated leaders, of Vietnamese and Cambodian revolutionaries spilling one another's blood. It seems so ridiculous to me now to put one's faith in a grand revolution aimed at total change, where these only seem to bring us full circle. It seems more sensible to take hope that there can be some gradual amelioration—maybe even by people like Carter.

RC: In the name of reasoned wisdom you invoke Carter as a hopeful sign. But he is no better nor worse than his predecessors, only packaged differently. Instead of free-enterprise and anti-communism, it's fundamentalist values and human rights—but the truth is still support for Pinochet and the Shah of Iran, destabilizing progressive regimes like Manley in Jamaica, total opposition to serious movements for national liberation, and the same fundamental racism, classism, sexism, and authoritarianism at home. Instead of taking the depressed outlook which reduces you to seeking hope in a criminal like Carter, why not see Hungary in 1956 and France in 1968 as signs of the coming self-managing revolution? Why not see the victory of the Vietnamese people as a sign both of the strength of a committed people and also of the weakness of the United States? Why not focus on the accomplishments of the new left movements of the sixties—helping to end the war, placing racism, sexism, and socialist revolution on the agenda of discussion, and temporarily threatening the most sophisticated reactionary hegemony in history—and the promise that their return in new forms augers even more? What's needed now is neither blind cynicism, nor ridiculous prophesies of inevitable revolution. What's needed is to get down to the hard work at hand—in all its forms. We'll win when the time is right and our efforts are complete, and this will come all the sooner insofar as we develop a capacity to understand our own potentials.

FOOTNOTES: CHAPTER EIGHT

1. For a general history of the revolutionary council communist heritage see Richard Gombin, *The Origins of Modern Leftism,* Penguin Books, London, England.

2. Albert Einstein quoted in Michael Harrington, *The Twilight of Capitalism,* Touchstone Books, Page 18.

3. Lenin in Tony Cliff, *Lenin Vol. 1,* Pluto Press, London, England. Page 255.

4. Ibid.

5. Antonio Gramsci, *History, Philosophy, and Culture in the Young Gramsci,* edited by Pedro Cavalcante and Paul Piccone, Telos Press, St. Louis. Page 150.

6. Carl Boggs, *Gramsci's Marxism,* Pluto Press, London, England. Page 27-28.

7. Gramsci quoted in Boggs, op. cit. Page 131.

8. For Gramsci the battle at the institutional level was called the "war of conjuncture", while that at the ideological level was called the "war of position". For him, however, these notifications seemed to emerge strategically never to be very clearly incorporated into theory. For us they derive very naturally from our guiding theoretical perspective. See Boggs, op. cit. Page 52-53. Another revolutionary who keys us to the ideological level is Amilcar Cabral. See *Return to the Source* and *Revolution in Guinea,* Monthly Review Press, New York.

9. Juliet Mitchell, *Women's Estate,* Vintage Books, New York. Page 61.

10. See Cliff, op. cit. Page 56-57.

11. Jean Paul Sartre, *Between Existentialism and Marxism,* Morrow Paperback Editions, New York. Page 125.

12. Gramsci quoted in Williams, op. cit. Page 95.

13. Sheila Rowbotham, *Woman's Consciousness, Man's World,* Penguin Books, London, England. Page XV.

14. Boggs, op. cit. Page 122-123.

15. Rowbotham, op. cit.

16. Mitchell, op. cit. Page 81.

17. Ibid. Page 80-81.

18. See Shulamith Firestone, *The Sexual Dialectic,* Jonathon Cape, London.

19. Mitchell, op. cit. Page 65.

20. Ibid. Page 23-24.

21. In a sense the woman's organization has still not escaped sexism—for it is still defined with reference to men and to women's relations to him—it is not "woman centered", and it is certainly not equally respected in all matters.

22. The reference here is to Thomas S. Kuhn's formalism, also mentioned in our introduction. He might argue that the Leninist strategic orientation is insufficient and thus suffering a variety of weaknesses, which are all becoming steadily more visible. One approach is to graft on new insights to "plug-up" such weaknesses. Another is to recognize the basic inadequacies and correct them in a whole new approach.

23. Rowbotham, op. cit. Page XI.

24. Ware quoted in Mitchell, op. cit. Page 51.

25. Mitchell, op. cit. Page 58.

26. Virginia Wolff, *A Room of One's Own,* Harcourt Brace and World, 1929.

27. These approaches, as with and perhaps even more so than in the sexism cases, are idealized—most groups have more complex "amalgam positions".

28. Noel Ignatin, "Black Worker, White Worker," New England Free Press, Somerville, Mass. Page 6.

29. Ibid. Page 6.

30. Quoted in Ignatin, op. cit. Page 7. Watson's later degeneration to racism does not take away from this early insight—indeed perhaps it provides evidence for the phenomena itself.

31. See Socialist Review, No. 37, Jan.-Feb. 1978 for a discussion of these issues between Harold Baran and Robert Allen. See also Robert Allen, *Reluctant Reformers,* Anchor Books, 1975, and James and Grace Lee Boggs, *Revolution and Evolution in the Twentieth Century,* MR Press, 1974.

32. Ibid.

33. Ibid.

34. Dan Georgakas and Marvin Surkin, *Detroit: I Do Mind Dying,* St. Martin's Press, New York. Page 7.

35. Ignatin, op. cit. Page 11.

36. See Georg Lukacs, *Lenin: A Study on the Unity of His Thought,* MIT Press, Cambridge, Mass. or Cliff, op. cit. or Lenin's own writings for favorable presentations. See Albert, *What Is To Be Undone,* Porter Sargent Publisher, Boston, Mass. for a summary review and highly critical appraisal.

37. See Alexander Berkman, *What Is Communist Anarchism?,* Dover Publications, New York, or Daniel Guerin, *Anarchism,* Monthly Review Press, New York.

38. Albert, op. cit.

39. See Rudolf Rocker, *Anarcho-Syndicalism,* London, England.

40. Albert, op. cit. contains a critique of Anarchism along just these lines.

41. Gramsci in Williams, op. cit. Page 149.

42. Anton Pannekoek, *Worker's Councils,* Detroit, Root and Branch.

43. Sartre, op. cit. Page 127.

44. See Anne Bobroff's "The Bolsheviks and Working Women, 1905-1920", in Radical America, Vol. 10, No. 3, Cambridge, Mass.

45. Rowbotham, op. cit. Page 126.

46. The multitude of ways that "interest group" politics appears in the United States is bewildering, but gives considerable evidence of many of our major theses. There are, for example, union politics of varying kinds, minority politics, women's politics, gay politics, lesbian politics, ruling class politics of varying kinds, etc. etc. Moreover, in any given struggle there are those who approach the problems at hand with a "self-first" orientation, and those who take a wholistic view in terms of a totalist revolutionary process. James and Grace Lee Boggs and Freddy and Lyman Paine have concerned themselves extensively with some of the problems arising from "interest group orientations" in their book, *Conversations in Maine,* South End Press, Boston, Mass.

47. For an argument in this direction see the latest edition of *Strike!* by Jeremy Brecher, South End Press Boston, Mass.
48. Cliff, op. cit. Page 93.
49. Sartre, op. cit. Page 131-132.
50. This position is like the most mechanist Marxist approach, except with an immense faith in the will and capabilities of the workers. See Brecher, op. cit. as a modern adherent.
51. For a fuller discussion see, *Lenin,* Tony Cliff, Pluto Press, London.
52. See Lukacs, op. cit., Cliff, op. cit. or Lenin, especially *What Is To Be Done,* International Publishers, New York.
53. Sartre, op. cit. Page 120.
54. See Andre Gorz, *Socialism and Revolution,* Anchor Books, New York, Page 101.
55. Herbert Marcuse, *Counter Revolution and Revolt,* Beacon Press, Boston, Mass. Page 44-46, reiterates and respects the Leninist critique: ie. that without revolutionary consciousness the councils can be reformist, workers' control can be reformist, and spontaneity can easily be "spontaneous capitalism".
56. Gorz, op. cit. Page 37, discusses the French events of May 1968 arguing precisely that their spontaneity gave them both the strength of originality, surprise, breadth, and depth, while also hurting them via the lack of coordination and political clarity.
57. In Paolo Spriano's analysis of the Italian factory occupations, *The Occupation of the Factories,* Pluto Press, London, Page 8, he argues that only those councils which had been developed and rooted in struggles preceding the actual spontaneous upsurge were capable of sustaining themselves against counter activities and the forces of capitalist hegemony.
58. Gorz, op. cit. Page 33-34.
59. Richard Gombin, op. cit. Page 110.
60. Ibid.
61. Ibid.
62. Gorz, op. cit. Page 68.
63. Ibid. Page 64.
64. Quoted in Gorz, op. cit. Page 64.
65. Gorz, op. cit. Page 176.
66. Ibid. Page 176.
67. Ibid.
68. Gramsci quoted in Boggs, op. cit. Page 79.
69. Gramsci quoted in Williams, op. cit. Page 104.
70. Georgakas and Surkin, op. cit. Page 33.
Consider also the Philadelphia Solidarity Group's formulation that:

> It seems quite obvious to us that the socialist organization must be managed by its members. Unless it can insure that they work together in a spirit of free association and that their activity is genuinely collective it will be useless. It will appear to people as no different from any other organization or institution of capitalism, with its rigid division into order givers and order takers.... During strikes, repre-

sentatives of the various political groups gain control of the committees. Demands entirely unrelated to the dispute then make their
appearance. The outcome is inevitable. A lack of interest, a diminution
of activity, sometimes even a vote to return to work. The feeling of
identification disappears and is replaced by a feeling of being used.
When the direct management of an organization by its members is
replaced by alien control from above, vitality is lost, the will to struggle
lessens.... The revolutionary organization must see its job as serving
the working class, not leading it, helping coordinate its struggles, not
imposing methods of struggle upon it, learning from the struggles that
are taking place, not ramming its learning down the throats of others.
It must realize that correct as its ideas may be, they are dependent upon
workers agreeing with them.

Philidelphia Solidarity, op. cit. Page 9, 10, 12.

71. Ibid. Page 32.
72. For a discussion of unions see Stanley Aronowitz, *False Promises, op. cit.*
73. For example, even the "dues check off", which makes excellent sense from
the perspective of defending workers' interests, has its drawbacks from the
perspective of increasing worker militancy and ensuring a tendency toward self-
management—for it separates union leadership from rank and file witholding
pressures.

Consider the words of Gary Bryner, President of the main Lordstown Local
of the UAW, speaking to the U.S. Senate Subcommittee on Employment,
Manpower, and Poverty, July 25, 1972, Sen. Edward Kennedy presiding:

There are symptoms of the alienated worker in our plant....Absentee
rate, as you said, has gone continually higher. Turnover rate is enor-
mous. The use of turning to alcohol and drugs is becoming a bigger and
bigger problem. So has apathy... (The worker) has become alienated to
the point where he casts off the leadership of his union, his
government. He is disassociated with the whole establishment. This is
going to lead to chaos...
We (the union) have got to take the quality of life issue, we have got to
meet it head on, and we have got to reach out to the people of this
country who are the mainstream of the economy, who do take the tax
burden. And if we alienate them to government, to the union
leadership, where in hell are they going to go? They are going to go with
a radical group. They are going to throw off every part of the
establishment and go somewhere else.

Quoted in Ken Weller, "The Lordstown Struggle", Solidarity Pamphlet no. 45,
Page 5. And Bryner's position, while liberal for the union in its insight, is
representative in terms of its horror over the possibility of radical inroads. The
history of unionism in the United States is marked by concerns to function within
the system. It is marked simultaneously by the blood and strain and solidarity of
countless activists, and the all-too-frequent sell outs of their leaders. Unions are
critically important for the improvements of life standards they bring and

particularly for the job security they can secure. But they are certainly not revolutionary organizations in form, purpose, or intent. In some cases it is even arguable that they have ceased to be "working class" organizations. In the first place, as our social relations theory shows, the gains they accrue for members might come not from capitalists to workers but from unorganized workers to organized workers—and this is perceived by both groups. And in the second place, it is often the case that union leadership isn't working class in its background or outlook at all, but rather more often of the coordinator class. For more on such matters see Stanley Aronowitz, *False Promises*, McGraw Hill, N.Y.

74. Georgakas and Surkin, op. cit. Page 4, recounts that in 1973, as an example, the number of Detroit homicides was triple the death toll on all sides in Northern Ireland.

75. Ibid.

76. Ibid. Page 35.

77. The judge focus approach was used by a community group organizing in Dorchester in Boston, Mass. a few years back. The judge's name was Jerome Troy and the response was immense and successful. Examples of campaigns around police brutality and community control are prevalent, although few if any have yet achieved significant institutional victories.

78. Rent control campaigns and utility rate struggles are also prevalent; in France there have even been a number of disorganized chaotic attempts at community appropriation of consumer goods from major chain stores. In Italy butchers have actually been kidnapped, not to be returned until prices were lowered.

79. This debate on orientation is perpetual on the left and one particularly revealing account of its specific dynamics in a particular context is put forward by Georgakas and Surkin, op. cit.

80. See Williams, op. cit. for an account of how journals in Italy served such purposes, or Cliff, op. cit. for Russia, or finally Georgakas and Surkin, op. cit. for Detroit.

81. Selections of Gramsci's writings from "L'Ordine Nuovo" in Williams, op.cit. and in Cavalcante and Piccone, op. cit. give one a good feeling for this.

82. In Detroit the alternative procedure was to simply take over the Wayne State University paper thereby avoiding funding difficulties. Cliff, op. cit. also documents the immense importance of the revolutionary papers in Russia for the purpose of building up networks of entwined active cadre.

83. One mechanism for this to occur is that people who study a lot begin 1-to lose touch with the realities of concrete circumstances, 2-to look down upon people who are less well informed, and 3-to become accustomed and enamored of the conditions of quiet study rather than those of active difficult organizing work.

84. Clearly with this discussion as with all those of this section, we are cutting corners, abstracting, over-simplifying, etc. The actual multiplicity of factors going into all these tactical decisions would be difficult to relate after the fact, and are obviously quite beyond any effort at precise prior prediction. Thus the schematic, though hopefully revealing approach of this chapter.

85. See Gorz, op. cit. Page 168, or consider Kenneth Cockrel expressing his viewpoint very succinctly at the 1970 Detroit anti-repression conference:

We don't engage in bullshit arguments about "that's reformist" or "that's not reformist". That which is reformist is that which is counter-revolutionary. What is not reformist or counter-revolutionary is any action that conduces to the creation of a larger propensity on the part of most people to view revolution as the only course of conduct available to end oppression. That's what we relate to—that's what we understand and see very clearly as being real.

Georgakas and Surkin, op. cit. Page 222.

86. See Jean Tepperman, *Not Servants, Not Machines,* Beacon Press, Boston, Mass. for a host of job discussions with office workers showing their conditions of work, greivances, consciousness, etc.

87. Here we have the debate about revolutionaries being "out front" about what they believe in. Obviously it's a tactical question and the approach chosen should vary in varying settings. In general, however, the councilist position is that the burden of proof is very much on the activist who wants to delay letting people know about his or her beliefs. This is because positive work relations demand honesty and also because unless one is addressing clearly how socialism represents an alternative to current oppressions, one is likely not really effectively waging the two-level struggle for hegemony. At the same time the use of rhetoric or catch words which alienate people from hearing the actual content of what one wishes to say, is obviously counter-productive.

88. By this we mean that though any reform struggle has a particularist or "interest group" aspect, each also has a relation to the whole revolutionary process and to broader collective interests. Clearly perceiving this fact and being as much or more motivated by the collective impact of a struggle as by its "personal returns" is essential to moving from reformism to revolution.

89. The extent of this depends upon how acclimated people are to receiving such aid. It is given when desired and when it can have a positive effect, not merely to be able to produce an impressive list of recipients, nor certainly to try to recruit new members irrespective of the effects on on-going struggles.

90. For example, elderly people could all move into first floor flats, people who require quiet all into one sector, and noisy people into another, etc.

91. Georgakas and Surkin, op. cit.

92. This acts to counter the otherwise prevalent one-pillar approaches. Ignatin, op. cit.

93. This is in tune with our understanding of the totalist role of autonomous organizations.

94. It is impossible to completely prevent police infiltration but the more totalist a movement is, the more its members have to live like socialists, overcome sexism and racism, as well as classism and authoritarianism, and participate at ideological as well as daily work levels, the more difficulty agents will have in retaining their cover. The best guard against agents doing much havoc is to have a level of awareness high enough to be unflappable by agent provocator tricks, and a system of decentralism effective enough so no one agent could know anything too damning about too many people.

95. As Georgakas and Surkin describe the Black revolutionaries in the Detroit

Union Movements, they felt that legal decimation was an essentially internally rooted phenomenon. They felt that with proper precautions against infiltration, proper care in all activities and planning, and effective legal support groups and community support, they could largely avoid the ills so many other groups suffered at the hands of the police. Their practice seems to have largely borne out this contention (despite its other problems), thus giving even greater hope of effective policies along these lines in the future.

> Cockrel said that all revolutionary organizations which find themselves in numerous conspiracy trials should look to their own structures, because this should not be happening at all, and never on a wholesale basis if the organization were properly set up. He noted how grand juries and police had failed to jail people like Mike Hamlin, Chuck Wooten, John Williams, Luke Tripp, Ron March, and Fred Holsey. The attempt to dislodge Watson from the South End and the attempt to disbar Cockrel himself had also failed, as had attempts to expel high school supporters of the League. All this and more had been accomplished because local people had been engaged in a local mass struggle. They had not been obliged to call on national celebrities to defend them. Their tactic of defense had not been to complain or moralize but to take the offensive in court and out of court.

Georgakas and Surkin, op. cit. Page 220. The League experience that Georgakas and Surkin recount is one of the most important modern organizing attempts in the United States, in a single locale, around community and factory issues. It functioned at two levels, used a kind of council approach, and was certainly strong on matters of race and class—but it suffered greatly for its nationalist tendencies, for its sexism and authoritarianism. Both its achievements and failings offer much information for activists to learn from.

96. Certainly the greatest defense against repression is an offensive capability which the state does not want to risk prodding. Consider, for example, the case of the Italian mass council occupations in 1920. Spriano, op. cit. Page 56; recounts an interchange between Agnelli of Fiat and Gioletti the Premier, which is particularly relevant in this context:

> Gioletti: Only time can solve the problems. Otherwise there is no policy but force.
> Agnelli: Precisely...
> Gioletti: Maybe. But let us understand each other. I will not allow the security guards to stay in the streets, defenseless if the Red Guards open fire from above (from within the factories). To drive the workers out of the factories we need artillary...
> Agnelli: I agree...
> Gioletti: We are in a position to supply it immediately. At Turin, there is the 7th Regiment of Mountain Artillary. I will give the orders at once. At dawn tomorrow, Fiat will be bombarded and liberated from the occupiers.
> Agnelli: No! No!...

Gioletti: Then, what?

Agnelli: No reply.

97. If it seems to some that we are proposing an essentially non-violent dynamic, that is regretably not the case. For there is considerable violence likely during the whole preparatory series of struggles leading up to the actual final seizure of power. But the seizure itself and the following period of construction will likely be relatively peaceful. Revolution will actively involve in at least a non-opposed role the bulk of society's military forces. The actual final uprising and seizure of all of society's major institutions and communities will itself be fairly unopposed, just as it was in Russia, Spain, Hungary, and Czechoslavakia before outside interventions. If anything this tendency will be more pronounced in the United States because of its greater levels of literacy and political development and because its movements will be councilist in form and in ideology.

Violence is a last resort. The only thing that has worse effects on the internal development of the left is defeat. Thus even defensive violence is to be employed only as absolutely required and with great self-awareness of its potentially deleterious effects. As Che Guevara has said, it is true that in revolution one either wins of dies, and that this necessitates revolutionary violence, the responsibility for which rests ultimately with the state. But it is also true, again as Che said, that revolutionaries must be moved by feelings of love and not hate. In a time of great struggle, Rosa Luxemburg clearly expressed the same sentiment:

> Rivers of blood have flowed in torrents during the four years of imperialist genocide. Now every drop of the precious fluid must be preserved reverently and in crystal vessels. Ruthless revolutionary energy and tender humanity—this alone is the true essence of socialism. One world must now be destroyed, but each tear that might have been avoided is an indictment; and a man who hurrying on to important deeds inadvertently tramples underfoot even a poor worm, is guilty of a crime.

APPENDIX TO CHAPTER ONE
SOLUTION TO THE TRANSFORMATION PROBLEM

In this appendix we wish to show how "prices of production" can be derived from labor-time "values". We have seen that when the organic composition of value varies from sector to sector, labor value prices do not allow for equal rates of profit in all sectors. To equalize profit rates, the output of sectors of high organic composition must sell above their "values" and the output of sectors of low organic composition below their "values". Here we show how the exact degree of variation can always be calculated.

While most orthodox Marxist solutions to the transformation problem are calculated in a three sector model (see Paul Sweezy, *Theories of Capitalist Development*, p. 109-130) we lose nothing significant by here using the two sector model we developed in the text of chapter one. Thus, we continue to divide the economy into one sector producing the means of production and another producing consumption goods. Finally, we should mention that we are deferring all questions of the explanation for how this transformation of "values" into "prices of production" actually occurs to the appendix to chapter two. In that appendix, "The Problem with the Transformation Problem", we analyze the various possible explanations and to what extent they are satisfying.

Let us assume that the price of a unit of machines, or constant capital, is x times its labor time value, the price of a unit of consumption goods (either wage or luxury goods) is y times its labor time value, and r is the rate of profit in both sectors. Then the simple reproduction scheme that appeared on page 28 in terms of labor time prices:

$$C^1+V^1+S^1=C^1+C^2$$
$$C^2+V^2+S^2=V^1+S^1+V^2+S^2$$

should be rewritten as:

$$xC^1+yV^1+r(xC^1+yV^1)=x(C^1+C^2)$$
$$xC^2+yV^2+r(xC^2+yV^2)=y(V^1+S^1+V^{2.1}S^2)$$

expressing the fact that the cost of all inputs (now in terms of price of production prices), plus the profit gained on these costs, must equal the revenue received (again in terms of price of production prices) in both sectors.

In these equations all of the labor time values are "known", that is C^1, V^1, S^1, C^2, V^2, and S^2 can all be determined in advance, and the unknowns that we must solve for are x, y, and r. But that is three unknowns with only two equations—an underdetermined problem. But since we are not interested in a unique solution for x, y, and r, but only in a solution that gives us relative prices and the rate of profit, we are able to add a third equation to get a "determinant" solution. Of course the easiest equation to add would be x=1 or y=1. This was essentially the procedure used by Borkiewicz in 1907 when he corrected Marx's mathematical error and "solved" the transformation problem. Or it might be nice to have a set of prices that allowed total price (the value of all outputs in terms of their prices of production prices) to equal total value (the value of all outputs in terms of the total amount of embodied labor time). This could be accomplished by adding as the third equation:

$$x(C^1+C^2)+y(V^1+V^2+S^1+S^2)=C^1+C^2+V^1+V^2+S^1+S^2$$

Or alternatively, one might want to have relative prices such that total surplus value equals total profit:

$$S^1+S^2=r(xC^1+yV^1)+r(xC^2+yV^2)$$

But whichever of these or many other possible equations one chooses to add to the two original equations, the three together allow for a determination of the three unknowns x, y, and r, and it is then possible to calculate the price of production prices from the labor time values by multiplying the labor values of the commodity by either x or y depending upon which sector it was produced in. If we had chosen x=1 as our third equation, then y would be greater than one if the organic composition of sector two were higher than that in sector one and y would be less than one if the organic composition of sector two were less than that in sector one.

Specifically, substituting x=1 into both equations, using the first equation to solve for (1+r):

$$(1+r)=(C^1+C^2)/C^1+yV^1)$$

and substituting this expression for (1+r) into the second equation one obtains:

$$[(C^1+C^2)/(C^1+yV^1)](C^2+yV^2)=y(V^1+S^1+V^2+S^2)$$

which can be reduced to the quadratic in y:

$$(V^1V^1+S^1V^1+V^1V^2+S^2V^1)y^2+(S^1C^1+V^1C^1+S^2C^1-C^2V^2)y-(C^1C^2+C^2C^2)=0$$

And finally this equation can always be solved for y using the quadratic formula. x and r could be easily found once y is known. There is, for those interested, the additional arcane problem associated with the fact that the quadratic will have two roots for y. Presumably, one can show that for reasonable' ranges of the labor values the two roots will in fact reduce to one positive and one irrelevant negative root thus determining one set of prices and profit rate.

APPENDIX TO CHAPTER TWO
THE PROBLEM WITH THE TRANSFORMATION
PROBLEM

In chapter one we saw that if we are willing to abstract from the human outputs of different kinds of work, the Labor Theory Of Value provides a powerful explanation for relative exchange rates in perfectly competitive capitalism with equal organic compositions of capital in all lines of production, just as it did in the case of Simple Commodity Production economies. But we also saw that neither Marx nor any of his orthodox followers argued that there was reason to expect equal organic composition of capital in different lines of production. The issue was of no importance in the case of simple commodity production because there was no point in keeping track of the proportion of present to past labor. The producers were conceived as doing both kinds themselves and supposedly would not care about whether more present or past labor was embodied in their products. (We see no reason to accept this assumption which amounts to a zero rate of time discount for simple commodity producers who are presumably still mortals, but this is not crucial to our present argument and we therefore let it pass.) So whether it be at a later stage of competitive capitalism or on the morning after the transition from a simple commodity production society, there is no reason to expect equal organic compositions in different sectors. But with unequal organic compositions, Marx recognized that labor time prices would not prevail if there were to be equal rates of profit in different lines of production. He thus determined the formula for what "prices of production" would have to prevail if profit rates were to be equal. Orthodox Marxists have subsequently corrected Marx's mathematical mistake and we can choose among any number of transformation schemes. However, deriving a formula for the relation between values and prices of production is not the same as presenting a theory explaining how those prices would come about. We have already pointed out that the formula $S^1/S^2 = (1-q_1)/(1-q_2)$, which tells us what the relative rates of exploitation would have to be in two sectors if there were to be equal profit rates despite unequal organic compositions, is accurate but insufficient since there is no reason why the rates of exploitation would come to this ratio. So we are in search of an explanation of how and why the price of production prices come about.

If there were no mobility of capital between sectors, if the bargaining strength between employers and employees were unequal, and if there were no other unequal social relations that an individual employer could exploit, then labor time prices would result. But in this case the fact that certain capitalists are in industries with lower organic compositions than others confers upon them an advantage vis-a-vis other capitalists whose technology forces them to lay out more constant capital to exploit the same amount of living labor. In other words, if there were no capital mobility but only labor mobility, unequal social relations between employers and employees in general necessarily implies unequal social relations between different capitalists stuck in sectors with different organic compositions as seen by the different rates of profit they would enjoy.

But if equal social relations between different capitalists is assumed due to complete mobility of capitalists between sectors, then even though the technologies in different sectors are such as to yield different organic compositions, no capitalist will be willing, or can be forced, to sink his financial capital into any sector with a high organic composition as long as labor time prices prevail since this would imply a lower rate of profit. There are only two possibilities at this point: 1-we can accept the original explanation for why there is a tendency for labor time prices to come about in competitive capitalism and search for a further argument for how and why labor time prices will subsequently be transformed into price of production prices. In this case we stick to the essence of the Labor Theory Of Value as applied to competitive capitalism and we explain the subsequent equalization of profit rates by flows of financial capital from sectors of high to sectors of low organic composition, thereby, through the pressure of supply and demand, creating price of production prices. Although various critics of the Labor Theory Of Value such as Pareto and Boehm-Bawerk have interpreted this flow of financial capital to mean that the organic compositions become generally equalized, and attacked Marx for employing this argument, we agree with Ronald Meek's conclusion that there is no evidence that Marx intended this, and there are numerous passages to indicate that Marx meant only that the flow of financial capital would change the relative supplies of output in different sectors. In the passage below this seems clearly to be the explanation Marx had in mind:

> Now if the commodities are sold at their values, then, as we have shown, very different rates of profit arise in the various spheres of production, depending on the different organic composition of the masses of capital invested in them. But capital withdraws from a sphere with a low rate of profit and invades others, which yield a higher profit. Through this incessant outflow and influx, or, briefly, through its distribution among the various

spheres, which depends on how the rate of profit falls here and rises there, it creates such a ratio of supply to demand that the average profit in the various spheres of production becomes the same, and values are, therefore, converted into prices of production. (Marx, *Capital, Vol. III,* p. 195-196)

Or, 2, we can argue that the equality between individual capitalists manifests itself by a mark-up of price above costs of production—whether they be labor or non-labor costs—that is equal for all capitalists regardless of what sector they are in and the organic composition of that sector. In this case our explanation does not require the "incessant" flow of financial capital from sectors of high to sectors of low organic composition. Although it is somewhat less obvious, this would appear to be what Marx was referring to in the following passage:

> As soon as capitalist production reaches a certain level of development, the equalization of the different rates of profit in individual spheres to a general rate of profit no longer proceeds solely through the play of attraction and repulsion, by which market prices attract or repel capital. After average prices, and their corresponding market prices, become stable for a time it reaches the *consciousness* of the individual capitalists that this equalization balances *definite differences,* so that they include these in their mutual calculations. The differences exist in the minds of the capitalists and are taken into account as grounds for compensating. (italics in original—Marx, *Capital, Vol. III,* page, 209).

The problem with the first explanation is that it predicts an event that has never been observed in capitalism: an "incessant" tendency for financial capital to flow from industries with high organic compositions to industries of low organic compositions. That is, capital would constantly flow from industries like oil and steel to industries like shoe manufacture and goat-herding in order to "transform" labor time prices into prices of production. Not only has no one ever dreamed of documenting that such a phenomenon has taken place, but most people's impression would be that, if anything, the very opposite seems to have occurred.

The problem with the second possibility is that it explains price of production prices in a way that denies the prior existence of labor time prices. It offers a *direct* explanation of the price of production outcome rather than an explanation of how labor time prices are constantly transformed into prices of production in capitalist economies. It argues against any supposed tendency for labor time prices to develop in capitalist economies and contradicts the essence of the Labor Theory Of

Value that only living labor is exploitable. In effect it asserts precisely the opposite: that in a competitive capitalist economy the equal social relations between freely mobile employers makes all inputs to production equally exploitable by individual capitalists as evidenced by their ability to set a mark-up on all forms of costs that is of equal magnitude regardless of whether they are labor costs or non-labor costs. In other words there is no problem with the second explanation itself, except that it is the neo-Ricardian theory of relative prices for competitive capitalism as developed by Piero Sraffa rather than the orthodox Marxist explanation of prices of production as derived from and based upon the underlying reality expressed by the Labor Theory Of Value.

In sum, the first explanation, which presumes the Labor Theory Of Value as the appropriate means of expressing the social relations of competitive capitalism must be rejected because it predicts an event contrary to all experience. But by accepting the second explanation we conclude: 1-There is no transformation of values into price of production prices, there is only a transformation in the minds of people starting with the wrong theory in need of arriving at the right conclusion. 2-All inputs are equally exploitable by individual capitalists in the form of cost-plus mark-ups on all inputs to production. And, 3-the extent of the mark-up is determined by the extent of the inequality in social relations and the consequent bargaining strengths between the capitalist and working classes as wholes, not by the difference between the labor time embodied in the commodity labor power and the number of hours in the working day.

So the Labor Theory Of Value is not even the appropriate value theory for orthodox Marxist's rarified model of competitive capitalism that excludes racism, sexism, monopoly, unionization, different bargaining strengths for different categories of worker, and the reality of human inputs and outputs of all economic activities. It is the appropriate theory of value for a rarified model of simple commodity producers. And it is also the appropriate theory for a super-abstracted capitalism characterized by equal organic compositions of capital. But as soon as we admit the reality, right from the first morning of capitalist production, of unequal organic compositions of capital, we must also admit that the Labor Theory Of Value does not provide an accurate theory of the social relations between participants, even when we retain all the other super abstractions in full. Instead the neo-Ricardian derivation of the price of production outcome, not from labor values but directly from the assumptions of equal relations among capitalists and unequal bargaining strength between capitalists and workers is the appropriate theory of value for the orthodox Marxists' model of capitalism. But while Piero

Sraffa solved the problem posed by orthodox Marxists, all our previous objections to orthodox Marxist value theory are applicable to Sraffa's neo-Ricardian value theory as well. It abstracts from too many important social relations in capitalism. It abstracts from the human outputs of economic activities thereby forfeiting any ability to analyze the crucial effects of human characteristics generated by the functioning of the economy on the bargaining power of workers and capitalists. And it offers no theory of qualitative "system" reproduction. We only mention these objections here since the argument is identical to the one we developed against orthodox Marxist economic theory in the body of chapter two.

APPENDIX TO CHAPTER FOUR
THE WAGE-PRICE VECTOR

Let R stand for raw materials used in production; K for machines used in production; H for workers' sole consumption good, huts, and P for capitalists' sole consumption good, palaces. Also let L represent labor hours. We will develop a wage-price vector for this simple economy in a way easily extendible to more complex conditions.

Assume that each of the four physical commodities is produced by one production operation under one technology acording to the following schemes:

$R_R + K_R + L_R$ yields one unit of R
$R_K + K_K + L_K$ yields one unit of K
$R_H + K_H + L_H$ yields one unit of H
$R_P + K_P + L_P$ yields one unit of P

where each of the inputs with a subscript stands for the physical amount of that factor required by the specific technology for that sector to produce one physical unit of its output. (Here it is clear that the wage price vector is concerned directly only with marketed outputs.)The R_i's and K_i's are completely used up and disappear in the process of making one unit of output. This is a complete summary of the technical conditions of production.

Now the social relations theory of value would expect that there would be different rates of profit in different production operations and different production sectors. These different profit rates are reflective of differences in bargaining strengths between capitalists that need not be non-equilibrium, or ephemeral phenomena. While capitalists would always want to move from low to high profit sectors, the high profit sectors are only high profit for firms capable of attaining bargaining strengths in production and exchange equivalent to the firms already producing. That is, attaining a sectoral profit rate is a much more complex and difficult matter than simply moving in some financial capital. But even if these "barriers to successful entry" didn't exist, there is no apriori reason to believe that the profit equalizing forces of financial capital flows operate fast enough to overcome the profit-disequalizing forces of developing unequal bargaining strengths between capitalists. As a matter of fact, there is no reason to believe the competitive forces are even "catching up"! Therefore we define: r_R, r_K, r_H, and r_P, to be the rates of profit on the means of production (excluding labor) for the respective sectors; and P_R, P_K, P_H, and P_P, to be the prices of the respective commodities. Now assume that there are n different types of labor l_i, i runs from 1 to n; where for each type there is a different hourly wage due to different bargaining strength, and where the n bargaining strengths also vary from sector to sector, so that, for example, type j has one wage in sector R and another in sector K etc. Write W_R, W_K, W_H, W_P, as the wage vectors in each sector; and write L_R, L_K, L_H, L_P, as the labor vector going into production of one unit of each output, using labor types i, j, etc., such that $W_R L_R$, for example, is the "dot product" of the two vectors, or the total wage bill spent in producing one unit of raw materials. Then we can write the following four equations:

$$(1+r_R)(P_R R_R + P_K K_R) + W_R L_R = P_R$$
$$(1+r_K)(P_R R_K + P_K K_K) + W_K L_K = P_K$$
$$(1+r_H)(P_R R_H + P_K K_H) + W_H L_H = P_H$$
$$(1+r_P)(P_R R_P + P_K K_P) + W_P L_P = P_P$$

which show that in each sector when you add the amount you must pay for that amount of each factor necessary to produce one unit of output, plus the profit you realize on your means of production (excluding labor), you must get exactly the price of one unit of output. (We assume labor is paid after production takes place out of revenue from sales. The only necessary financial outlay is for non-labor inputs.)

Now, if for simplicity's sake we temporarily abstract from the multiplicity of labor types and wage levels to say that there is only one wage equal to W, and only one kind of labor so that each L with a subscript represents hours to produce a unit referred to by the subscript, we get a new set of equations:

$$(1+r_R)(P_R R_R + P_K K_R) + W L_R = P_R$$
$$(1+r_K)(P_R R_K + P_K K_K) + W L_K = P_K$$
$$(1+r_H)(P_R R_H + P_K K_H) + W L_H = P_H$$
$$(1+r_P)(P_R R_P + P_K K_P) + W L_P = P_P$$

This leaves us four independent equations in nine unknowns: the four prices, the four rates of profit, and the wage rate. But things aren't so hopeless as they might appear. First, we can eliminate one equation by simply letting $P_R=1$. Now we have eight variables, and the value of anything is the number of "numeraire" units of R it will exchange for. One unit of R is our measure of value.

Furthermore, just as our knowledge of the actual production technologies used allowed us to write down the production schemas, our knowledge of the actual bargaining strengths of capitalists in different sectors allows us to write down the proportions that the profit rates in the different sectors bear to each other.

$$r_R = N_R r$$
$$r_K = N_K r$$
$$r_H = N_H r$$
$$r_P = N_P r$$

where the N_j's are (for now assumed to be) known constants determined by the bargaining relationships of the different sectors with respect to each other, and each N_j represents the percentage that r_j is of the average rate of profit of the whole economy, r.

Making these substitutions we have the following four equations:

1. $(1+r)(R_R N_R + P_K K_R N_R) + W L_R = 1$
2. $(1+r)(R_K N_K + P_K K_K N_K) + W L_K = P_K$
3. $(1+r)(R_H N_H + P_K K_H N_H) + W L_H = P_H$
4. $(1+r)(R_P N_P + P_K K_P N_P) + W L_P = P_P$

in five unknowns: P_K, P_H, P_P, W, and r. Solving the first equation for P_K in terms of W and r gives:

5. $P_K = (1 - R_R N_R[1+r] - W L_R) / K_R N_R (1+r)$

Substituting 5) into 3) and 4) we can derive expressions for P_H and P_P in terms of W and r also. But before doing that it is revealing to substitute for P_K from equation 5) into equation 2) to solve for W in terms of r:

6. $W = \dfrac{(1 - R_R N_R[1+r])(1 - K_K N_K[1+r]) - R_K N_K K_R N_R[1+r]^2}{L_K K_R N_R (1+r) + L_R (1 - K_K N_K[1+r])}$

Rearranging terms we get:

7. $W = \dfrac{1 - (R_R N_R + K_K N_K)(1+r) + (R_R N_R K_K N_K - R_K N_K K_R N_R)(1+r)^2}{L_R + (1+r)(L_K K_R N_R - L_R K_K N_K)}$

Examining this equation is worthwhile. First, only when this equation represents a straight line in the W,r plane is the value of K independent of the average rate of profit—a result which can be ascertained by substituting 7) into 1) and solving for P_K in terms of r. But this could only be true if the expressions multiplying $(1+r)^2$ in the numerator and $(1+r)$ in the denominator of equation 7) are both zero. That is, if:

$$R_R N_R K_K N_K - R_K N_K K_R N_R = 0$$
$$L_K K_R N_R - L_R K_K N_K = 0$$

With $N_R = aN_K$ this reduces to:

$$\frac{R_R}{K_R} = \frac{R_K}{K_K} \quad \text{and} \quad \frac{aK_R}{L_R} = \frac{K_K}{L_K}$$

which with a=1 is a *slightly more stringent* version of the equal organic composition abstraction of orthodox Marxist theory, and with $a \neq 1$ is a *more general condition* yielding the same "price of capital is independent of the rate of profit" result. Obviously, however, in our model there is every reason to suspect that the first null conditions will not hold.

The most important characteristic of equation 7) is that it expresses the wage rate not only as a function of the profit rate and technological conditions, but also as a function of the social relations among capitalists and it permits a determination of the effects of a change in *any* of these conditions on the wage rate as well. We finish our present analysis of the wage price vector by expressing the bargaining strength between capitalists and workers as a whole, $W = lr$, which when substituted back into 7) allows a determination of r in terms of known constants. Once r is determined, W can be found by using equation 7) and then P_P, P_H, and P_K can be determined from equations 5), 4), and 3) respectively. It is also worth noting that by setting r=0 we can derive an expression for the net product per worker of our economy, or, more precisely, per work hour of labor; expressed in physical units of R:

$$NP = \frac{1 - (R_R N_R + K_K N_K) + (R_R N_R K_K N_K - R_K N_K K_R N_R)}{L_R + (L_K K_R N_R - L_R K_K N_K)}$$

This net product, NP, represents the quantity that employers and employees are fighting over. When wages per labor hour rise, profits decline, and vice versa.

Our presentation of a social relations wage price model is now complete. The essential tasks, however, remain. First there remains the task of analyzing the manner in which the alteration of various parameters affects the whole system's structure. Further, we have to drop the abstraction of one type of labor and of one wage rate and resolve the system to the more complex form. We also have to clearly express the relationship between the N_j's and l on the one hand, and the actual bargaining ratios on the other, especially in the more complex model where the problems of different powers for workers of different races, sexes, industrial sectors, levels of unionization, etc. will all come to the fore.

Further, there is the problem of growth over time. We still need to develop an expanded reproduction dynamic model where in each sector some of the surplus is reinvested in various manners and with varying structural effects. Thus, over time, the actual social relations of the model, which underlie its exchange relations, are themselves variable— the bargaining parameters are not constants, but change with changes in concentration, product character, work roles, labor organization and consciousness, social relations in the workplace, social relations and consciousnesses of sectors of the workforce in and out of the workplace, and so on. But in all such work it also becomes necessary to incorporate the qualitative theoretical results of our earlier discussions. It is these which provide insight into why investments will be made and by what criteria, who gets hired and fired for what jobs, product definition, wage scale determination, workplace design, etc. In other words, a powerful dynamic quantitative model could only develop in parallel with a qualitative analysis of the development of an economy over time. Mathematically, we might surmise that the easiest way to deal with these problems will be via a matrix notation which incorporates the use of operators on economic processes, but this is only conjecture and the problems remain to be tackled.

Perhaps the most crucial distinction between this quantitative reproduction scheme and Sraffa's is not that we include social relations in our determination of an equilibrium wage-price vector, but in the difference of our interpretations of the origins of the different bargaining parameters themselves. Sraffa gives one the impression that l is settled outside the economic sphere, as the outcome of the struggle between capital and labor in the political arena. In opposition, the orthodox Marxists, at the opposite extreme, look entirely to the workplace for the roots of exploitation. But we begin our discussion of economic theory with a qualitative theory designed to indicate how not only l, but N_R, N_K, N_H, and N_P, are all affected by processes of production and exchange, as well as by processes in other arenas "outside" the economy as well. That is, before undertaking the task of finding the wage-price vector for any combination of technological and social relational conditions, we attempted to trace the effects on bargaining strengths of the operation of the economy itself. To leave the impression that these bargaining relations are not themselves a concern of economic analysis, or that they are only governed by economic relations, are two mistakes we hope we have successfully avoided.

APPENDIX TO CHAPTER FOUR
USE-VALUE: A FUNCTION OF EXCHANGE-VALUE

In this appendix we offer a formal model expressing the facts that the use-value or utility that one obtains from a consumption/work bundle depends on the particular characteristics one has at the time, and that these characteristics are, in part, the products of previous choices of consumption-work bundles. We then demonstrate that for a rational individual who evaluates the need-development effects as well as the need fulfillment effects of different choices of economic activities, the use-value of commodities becomes dependent upon their exchange-values.

THE MODEL OF PEOPLE AS BEINGS OF PRAXIS

1. Let $P_p(t)=(P_1(t), P_2(t), ...P_p(t))$ be a vector of individual personality characteristics at time t.
2. Let $T_z(t)=(T_1(t), T_2(t), ... T_z(t))$ be a vector of individual talents of skills at time t that are of any relevance to either consumption enjoyment, work enjoyment, or earning capacity.
3. Let $U_u(t)=(U_1(t), U_2(t), ...U_u(t))$ be a vector of different aspects of an individual's understanding of the way the physical and human world works.
4. Let $V_v(t)=(V_1(t), V_2(t), ...V_v(t))$ be a vector of different aspects of an individual's values or attitudes toward what he or she understands to be going on in the world.
5. Let $S_s(t)=(S_1(t), S_2(t), ...S_s(t))$ be a vector of different aspects of the social relations that one enters into. That is, just as an individual has characteristics, any group of people have "group characteristics", and depending upon what groups a particular individual is related to, various group characteristics can be associated with an individual.

$U_u(t)$ and $V_v(t)$ together characterize what is often referred to as a person's consciousness, and $S_s(t)$ serves to remind us that the human world is not a world of Robinson Crusoes but a social world.

6. Let $q_q(t)=(q_1(t), q_2(t), ...q_q(t))$ be a vector of all economic goods, or commodities, which for now we assume are purchasable in markets.
7. Let $L_l(t)=(L_1(t), L_2(t), ...L_l(t))$ be a vector of different work activities that can be engaged in that are of any earning or welfare significance to the individual, and again we will assume that there are actually markets for each of these different work activities rather than more general markets for "labor power" only.

$q_q(t)$ and $L_l(t)$ are the "choice" variables in our model, and we assume that each individual is trying to maximize his or her overall well-being through appropriate choices of these variables at all time periods consistent with the individual's wealth constraint. Although we reject the usefulness of the concept of individual utility functions for many purposes, they prove useful in demonstrating the arguments of this appendix about capitalist use and exchange value relations. So here we assume that the individual's overall welfare, W, can be expressed as a weighted sum of his/her utility, or degree of satisfaction, at every point in time.

8. $W = \S_t \&_t u(t)$ where $\S$ is our summation sign, and $\&_t$ is a subjective time discount factor. The fact that the utility, notated $u(t)$, depends on the human characteristics one possesses as well as the economic activities one engages in is indicated by postulating:

9. $u(t) = u(P_p(t), T_z(t), U_u(t), V_v(t), S_s(t); q_q(t), L_l(t))$ where the utility enjoyed in period t is a function of the consumption and work bundles chosen, but the utility gained is influenced by the human characteristics that one possesses at that time. These characteristics may be thought of as parameters. Furthermore, the fact that the human characteristics are in part products of previous economic activities can be expressed by stipulating:

10. $P_p(t) = P_p(q_q(t-1), q_q(t-2), \ldots q_q(0); L_l(t-1), L_l(t-2), \ldots L_l(0))$, and likewise for $T_z(t)$, $U_u(t)$, $V_v(t)$, and $S_s(t)$—each functions of $q_q(t^*)$ and $L_l(t^*)$ where t^* runs over the periods t-1, t-2, ...1, 0. If these human characteristics either came from the sky, or were produced entirely by genetics or by various social and cultural institutions *that were themselves not in any way forged by economic relations and activities,* then there would be no need to specify such relationships over all time periods. But since we have expressed that the human characteristics both influence the degree to which commodity and work bundles are appreciated by the individual, and are influenced themselves by past choices of economic activity, these functions are necessary.

(Since we are not concerned with the borrowing or lending activities of individuals in this discussion, we formulate the individual's budget constraint in such a way that expenditures in each time period must be paid for out of earnings in that time period. This gives rise to the possibility of different marginal utilities of income in different years, but this has no relevance for our demonstration.)

11. Let $g(t) = g(P_p(t), T_z(t), U_u(t), V_v(t), S_s(t); L_l(t))$ represent the earning function for the time period t. Then the budget constraint for period t is given by: $\S_q p_q(t) q_q(t) = g(t)$ where $p_q(t)$ is just the price vector.

USE-VALUE AS A FUNCTION OF EXCHANGE-VALUE

We can treat the individual's welfare maximization problem by using the method of lagrangian multipliers. Throughout the discussion we assume that all functions are continuous and differentiable in the region of concern and that none of the possible inequality constraints on the variables and budget constraints are binding at the solution point. If the later were the case we could easily formulate the problem as a non-linear programming problem instead of a "classical" programming problem and analyze the full set of necessary Kuhn-Tucker conditions. But nothing of relevance to our discussion is sacrificed by making the simplifying assumptions mentioned above. So the lagrangian, $\square$, is given by:

12. $\square = W[q_q(t),\ L_l(t)] - h_t(\S_q p_q(t)q_q(t) - g(P_p(t),\ T_z(t),\ U_u(t),\ V_v(t),\ S_s(t);\ L_l(t))$

and the first order conditions for a welfare maximum can be written:

13. ($d_{q(t)}u(t)$ means the partial derivative of $u(t)$ with respect to $q_q(t)$ and similarly for the other expressions throughout)

$\&_t d_{q(t)}u(t) + \S\ \S_p(\&_i d_{P(i)}u(i) + h_i d_{P(i)}g(i))d_{q(t)}P_p(i)$

$+ \S\ \S_z(\&_i d_{T(i)}u(i) + h_i d_{T(i)}g(i))d_{q(t)}T_z(i)$

$+ \S\ \S_u(\&_i d_{U(i)}u(i) + h_i d_{U(i)}g(i))d_{q(t)}U_u(i)$

$+ \S\ \S_v(\&_i d_{V(i)}u(i) + h_i d_{V(i)}g(i))d_{q(t)}V_v(t)$

$+ \S\ \S_s(\&_i d_{S(i)}u(i) + h_i d_{S(i)}g(i))d_{q(t)}S_s(t) - h_t p_q(t) = 0$ $i=t+1-T$

14. $\&_t d_{L(t)}u(t) + \S\ \S_p(\&_i d_{P(i)}u(i) + h_i d_{P(i)}g(i))d_{L(t)}P_p(i)$

$+ \S\ \S_z(\&_i d_{T(i)}u(i) + h_i d_{T(i)}g(i))d_{L(t)}T_z(i)$

$+ \S\ \S_u(\&_i d_{U(i)}u(i) + h_i d_{U(i)}g(i))d_{L(t)}U_u(i)$

$+ \S\ \S_v(\&_i d_{V(i)}u(i) + h_i d_{V(i)}g(i))d_{L(t)}V_v(i)$

$+ \S\ \S_s(\&_i d_{S(i)}u(i) + h_i d_{S(i)}g(i))d_{L(t)}S_s(i) - h_t d_{L(t)}g(t) = 0$ $i=t+1-T$

15. $\S_q p_q(t)q_q(t) - g(P_p(t),\ T_z(t),\ U_u(t),\ V_v(t),\ S_s(t);\ L_l(t)) = 0$

In "13" there is an equation for every combination of q and t, that is for q=1, 2, ...q, and t=0, 1, ...T. In "14" there is an equation for every combination of l and t, that is for l=1, 2, ...l, and t=0, 1, ...T. In "15" there is an equation for each time period t=0, 1, ...T.

The unusual terms in equations "13" and "14" are those under the double summation signs. The second set of terms under the double summation sign in "13" express the fact that "consumption" choices are in part "investments" in "human capital". In "14" those effects are interpretable as the on the job, "job training" effects of particular work activities. The first set of terms in "13" and "14" express the fact that consumption choices and work choices respectively, through their influences on human characteristics, influence future preferences, or use-values themselves. In order to demonstrate that rational individuals who recognize all these effects will not only adjust to changes in relative prices in a given period by changing the relative amounts of those commodities they consume, but will also change their preferences for those commodities by changing consumption and work activity choices in previous periods to the extent that changes in relative prices are foreseen, we change the relative prices of two commodities and demonstrate that a different set of human characteristics will be developed and therefore a different set of preferences or use-values for various consumption-work bundles will result. In other words, we show that use-value depends upon exchange-value.

We make the demonstration for a change in the relative prices of two goods in the last time period, T, due to greater convenience. The generalization to changes in relative prices in any time period, t, will be indicated.

Suppose there is a change in the relative prices of $p_m(T)$ and $p_n(T)$; specifically letting * indicate new values and ' indicate old values, suppose that:

16. $$p_m(T)^*/p_n(T)^* > p_m(T)'/p_n(T)'$$

Since we are in the last time period all terms under the double summation sign in "13" are zero under either the new or the old price system, so we are led directly to the conclusion that if the individual has maximized his or her welfare in each situation (by choice of the proper coffin?):

17. $$d_{q_m(T)}u(T)^*/d_{q_n(T)}u(T)^* > d_{q_m(T)}u(T)'/d_{q_n(T)}u(T)'$$

If we make the usual assumptions about diminishing marginal utilities of goods, we can conclude that $q_m(T)^*/q_n(T)^* < q_m(T)'/q_n(T)'$. That is, if relative prices were to change in period T our choice of goods would also change in that period. But now consider an agent determining his or her consumption work bundle in some earlier period t, for all periods into the future. The choice will clearly differ depending upon the expected prices in period T. For a change in the relative proportions of commodities m and n to be consumed in period T will change the values of the partial derivatives of u(T) with respect to all the human characteristics that are found under the summation signs in the necessary conditions for all the time periods from the present one, t, up to the final one T, since these partials are still functions of $q_m(T)$ and $q_n(T)$. Letting C_c stand for any of our human characteristics we can conclude that if C_c were a trait that increased the enjoyment of $q_m(T)$ relative to $q_n(T)$, then

18. $$d_{C_c}u(...\ q_m(T)^* ... q_n(T)^* ...) < d_{C_c}u(...\ q_m(T)' ... q_n(T)' ...)$$

Whereas if C_c is a trait that increases the enjoyment of $q_n(T)$ relative to $q_m(T)$, then

19. $$d_{C_c}u(...\ q_m(T)^* ... q_n(T)^* ...) > d_{C_c}u(...q_m(T)' ... q_n(T)' ...)$$

Although it is possible, there is no reason to suppose that the sum total effects of the changes in the values of these partials in any one of the necessary conditions for q=1, 2, ...q and t=t, t+1, ...T-1 would be such as to exactly cancel out at the old values of consumption and work activity choices for those periods. So, in general, we would expect that $q_q(T)^*$ would *not* equal $q_q(t)'$ and $L_l(t)^*$ would not equal $L_l(t)'$ for q=1, 2, ... q and t=t, t+1, ... T-1. That is an expected change in the relative prices of two commodities in the final period, T, yields a change in choice of consumption-work bundle in period t, and in all the intervening periods as well. Moreover, in light of "10" we see there will also be a different set of human characteristics developed under economic choice patterns $[q_q(t)^*;\ L_l(t)^*]$ and $[q_q(t)';\ L_l(t)']$ and therefore also *a different set of preference patterns for various commodity-work bundles.*

This concludes the argument provided it does not rest on our choosing period T as the time when expected prices alter. But the only convenience offered by taking this as our starting time was that a particular change in relative prices could be translated into a shift in the relative amounts of the two commodities consumed whose sign was determinant under the assumption of diminishing marginal utilities. Had we begun with a change in relative prices in any earlier time period, the direction of the shift in the consumption bundle for that time period would not have been determinant due to the many terms of indeterminant sign which would still have been present under the double summation signs. But it should be clear that there is no reason to expect that, in general, there would not be a change required in the values of any $q_m(t)$ and $q_n(t)$, t=1, 2, ...T-1 in order to reestablish the necessary conditions for q=m and q=n and t=t after a change in the relative prices $p_m(t)$ and $p_n(t)$. Then, once $q_m(t)/q_n(t)$ has changed, no matter in what direction, there will be changes required, in general, for all earlier consumption and work activity choices and consequent changes in human characteristics and preference structures exactly as argued before.

BIBLIOGRAPHY

Albert, Michael, *What Is To Be Undone*. Boston: Porter Sargent Publisher, 1974.
Ali, Tariq, *The New Revolutionaries*. New York: William Morrow Inc., 1969.
Allen, Robert, *Black Awakening In Capitalist America*. Garden City: Doubleday 1969.
—————-*Reluctant Reformers*. Garden City: Doubleday, 1975.
Althusser, Louis, *For Marx*. New York: Vintage, 1970.
—————-*Lenin and Philosophy*. New York: Monthly Review Press, (hereafter MR Press), 1971.
Anderson, Perry, *Considerations on Western Marxism*. London: New Left Books, (hereafter NLB), 1975.
Aronowitz, Stanley, *False Promises*. New York: McGraw Hill, 1973.
Arrow, Kenneth J.and Hahn, F.H., *General Competitive Analysis*. San Francisco: Holden Day.
Arrow, Kenneth J., "Political and Economic Evaluation of Social Effects and Externalities", in *Frontiers of Quantitative Economics*. ed. M.D. Intriligator North Holland Publishing Company.
Arshinov, Peter, *History of the Makhnovist Movement*. Detroit: Black and Red, 1974.
Avineri, Sholomo, "Marx and the Intellectuals", *Journal of the History of Ideas*. xxxviii no. 2, April-June 1967.
—————-*Karl Marx: Social and Political Thought*. London: Cambridge University Press, 1968.
Avrich, Paul, *The Russian Anarchists*. Princeton: Princeton University Press, 1967.
—————-*Kronstadt 1921*. Princeton: Princeton University Press, 1970.
Baran, Harold, *The Demand for Black Labor*. Somerville: New England Free Press, 1972.
Baran, Paul, *The Political Economy of Growth*. New York: MR Press, 1957.
Baran, Paul, and Sweezy, Paul, *Monopoly Capital*. New York: MR Press, 1966.
Baxandal, Rosalyn; Gordon, Linda; and Reverby, Susan, *America's Working Women*. New York: Vintage Books, 1976.
Baxandal, Lee, Ed. *Wilhelm Reich: Sex Pol*. New York: Vintage Books, 1972.
de Beauvoir, Simone, *The Second Sex*. New York: Vintage Books, 1974.
Benston, Margaret, "The Political Economy of Women's Liberation", Somerville: New England Free Press. 1970.
Berkman, Alexander, *What Is Communist Anarchism?* New York: Dover,1972
Bettleheim, Charles, *Economic Calculation and Forms of Property*. London: Routlage, Kegan & Paul, 1974.
—————-*Class Struggle in the USSR*. New York: MR Press, 1976.
Blackburn, Robin, Ed. *Ideology and Social Science*. New York: Vintage, 1973.
Boehm-Bawerk, Eugene, *Karl Marx and the Close of his System*. New York: Augustus Kelly, 1949.

Boggs, Carl, *Gramsci's Marxism*. London: Pluto Press, 1975.
Boggs, James, *The American Revolution*. New York: MR Press, 1963.
Boggs, James and Grace Lee, *Revolution and Evolution in the 20th Century*. New York: MR Press, 1974.
Bookchin, Murray, *Post Scarcity Anarchism*. San Francisco: Ramparts Books.
————*The Limits of the City*. New York: Harper Colophon, 1974.
Bottomore, Tom, *Karl Marx*. Englewood: Prentice Hall, 1973.
Bowles, Sam, "Economist as Servant of Power", *American Economic Review*, May, 1974.
Bowles, Sam and Gintis, Herb, *Schooling in Capitalist America*. New York: Basic Books, 1976.
Braverman, Harry, *Labor and Monopoly Capital*. New York: MR Press, 1975.
Brecher, Jeremy, *Strike!*. Boston: South End Press, 1977.
Brinton, Maurice, *The Bolsheviks and Workers' Control 1917-1921*. Montreal: Black Rose Books, 1970.
————*The Irrational in Politics*. Montreal: Black Rose Books, 1974.
Brown, Phil, ed. *Radical Psychology*. New York: Harper Colophon, 1973.
Cabral, Amilcar, *Revolution in Guinea*. New York: MR Press, 1969
————*Return To The Source*. New York: MR Press, 1973.
Calvart, Greg and Neiman, Carole, *The Disrupted History*. New York: Random House, 1971.
Cardan, Paul, *Workers' Councils and the Economics of a Self-Managed Society*. Philadelphia: Philadelphia Solidarity.
————*Crisis of Modern Society*. Philadelphia: Philadelphia Solidarity.
Cammit John, *Antonio Gramsci and the Origins of Italian Communism*. San Francisco: Stanford University Press, 1967.
Carmichael, Stokely, *Stokely Speaks*. New York: Vintage, 1971.
Carmichael, Stokely and Hamilton, Charles, *Black Power*. New York: Vintage, 1969.
Cavalcanti, John and Piccone, Paul, *History, Philosophy, and Culture in the Young Gramsci*. St. Louis: Telos, 1975.
Cesaire, Aime, *A Dying Colonialism*. New York: MR Press, 1972.
Chomsky, Noam, *For Reasons of State*. New York: Pantheon, 1970.
————*American Power and the New Mandarins*. New York: Pantheon.
————*Problems of Knowledge and Freedom*. New York: Pantheon.
————*Reflections On Language*. New York: Pantheon,
Cleaver, Eldridge, *Soul On Ice*. New York: Delta Books, 1968.
Clegg, Ian, *Workers' Self-Management in Algeria*. New York: MR Press, 1971.
Cliff, Tony, *Lenin Vol. 1: Building the Party*. London: Pluto Press, 1975.
————*Lenin Vol. 2: All Power to the Soviets*. London: Pluto Press, 1976.
Cockburn, Alexander and Blackburn, Robin, *Student Power*. London: Penguin Books, 1970.
Cohn-Bendit, Daniel, *Obsolete Communism: A Left Wing Alternative*. New York: McGraw Hill, 1968.
Colletti, Lucio, *From Rousseau to Lenin*. London: NLB, 1972.
————*Marxism and Hegel*. London: NLB, 1973.

Commoner, Barry, *The Closing Circle.* New York: Bantam, 1971.

Cooper, David, ed. *The Dialectics of Liberation.* London: Penguin, 1968.

————————*The Death of the Family.* New York: Vintage, 1971.

Cornforth, Maurice, *Historical Materialism.* New York: International Publishers, 1962.

Dalla-Costa, Mariarosa and James, Selma, *The Power of Women and the Subversion of the Community.* London: Falling Walls Press, 1972.

Debreu, Gerard, *Theory of Value.* New Haven: Yale University Press.

Dellenger, David, *More Power Than We Know.* New York: Doubleday, 1975.

Desai, Meghnad, *Marxian Economic Theory,* London: Gray Mill, 1974.

Dobb, Maurice, *Welfare Economics and the Economics of Socialism.* London: Cambridge University Press (hereafter CUP), 1968.

————————*Theories of Value and Distribution Since Adam Smith: Ideology and Economic Theory.* London: CUP, 1973.

Dolgoff, Sam, *The Anarchist Collectives.* New York: Free Life Editions, 1974.

Dunayeskaya, Raya, *Philosophy and Revolution.* New York: Delta Books, 1973.

Edwards, Richard C. "Alienation and Inequality: Capitalist Relations of Production in a Bureaucratic Enterprise". Unpublished Ph. D. Thesis, Harvard University, July, 1972.

Edwards, Richard C.; Reich, Michael; and Weisskopf, Thomas; eds. *The Capitalist System.* Englewood Cliffs: Prentice Hall, 1972.

Emmanual, Arghiri, *Unequal Exchange,* New York: MR Press, 1972.

Engels, Frederick, *The Origin of the Family, Private Property, and the State. New York: International Publishers.*

Ewen, Stuart, *Captains of Consciousness.* New York: McGraw Hill, 1976.

Fanon, Frantz, *The Wretched of the Earth.* New York: Grove Press, 1968.

————————*Toward An African Revolution.* New York: Grove Press, 1967.

Fleisher, Helmut, *Marxism and History.* New York: Harper Colophon, 1969.

Fiori, Guiseppi, *Antonio Gramsci: Life of a Revolutionary.* London: NLB, 1970.

Firestone, Shulamyth, *The Dialectics of Sex.* New York: William Morrow, 1970.

Freire, Paulo, *Pedagogy of the Oppressed.* New York: Herter and Herter, 1971.

————————*Education for a Critical Consciousness.* New York: Seabury, 1973.

————————*Cultural Action for Freedom.* London: Penguin Books.

Fromm, Erich, *Marx's Concept of Man.* New York: Frederick Unger, 1961.

————————ed. *Socialist Humanism.* Garden City: Doubleday, 1965.

Georgakas, Dan and Surkin, Marvin, *Detroit: I Do Mind Dying.* New York: St. Martin's Press, 1975.

Gershenkron, Alexander, *Continuity in History and other Essays.* Cambridge: Belknap Press, 1968.

Gintis, Herb, "Alienation and Power: Toward A Radical Welfare Economics". Unpublished Ph. D. Thesis, Harvard University, May, 1969.

————————"Welfare Criteria With Endogenous Preferences: The Economics of Education". Harvard Dissertation Paper no. 329, Nov. 1973.

————————"The Nature of the Labor Exchange: Toward A Radical Theory of the Firm". Harvard Disscussion Paper no. 328, Oct. 1973.

Godelier, Maurice, *Rationality and Irrationality in Economics.* New York: MR Press, 1972.

Goldman, Emma, *My Disillusionment in Russia*. New York: Appolo, 1970.

Gombin, Richard, *The Origins of Modern Leftism*. London: Penguin, 1975.

Gorz, Andre, *Strategy for Labor*. Boston: Beacon Press, 1964.

——————*Socialism and Revolution*. Garden City: Anchor, 1971.

Grahl, Bart and Piccone, Paul, eds. *Toward A New Marxism*. St. Louis: Telos, 1973.

Gramsci, Antonio, *Selections From The Prison Notebooks*. New York: International Publishers, 1971.

Guerin, Daniel, *Anarchism*. New York: MR Press, 1970.

Gurley, John G. *Challengers to Capitalism: Marx, Lenin, and Mao*. San Francisco: Stanford University Press, 1975.

Hinton, William, *Fanshen*. New York: MR Press, 1966.

Hobsbawn, E.J. "Karl Marx's Contribution to Historiography" in *Ideology and Social Science*, Robin Blackburn, ed.

Howard, Dick and Klare, Karl, *The Unknown Dimension*. New York: Basic Books, 1972.

Horn, Joshua, *Away With All Pests*. New York: MR Press, 1969.

Horvat, Branko, *Toward a Theory of the Planned Economy*. Belgrade. 1964.

Horowitz, David, *Marx and Modern Economics,* New York: MR Press, 1968.

Howard, Dick, *Selected Political Writings of Rosa Luxemburg*. New York: MR Press, 1971.

Hunnius, Garson, and Case, eds. *Workers' Control*. New York: Vintage, 1973.

Hunt, E.K. and Schwartz, Jesse G. eds. *A Critique of Economic Theory*. London: Penguin, 1973.

Hurwicz, Leonid, "Design of Mechanisms for Resource Allocation", in *Frontiers of Modern Economics*, ed. M D. Intriligator and D.A. Kendrick, North Publishing House.

Ignatin, Noel, "Black Worker, White Worker", in *White Supremacy*. Chicago: Sojourner Truth Organization. 1977.

Jackson, George, *Soledad Brother*. New York: Bantam, 1970.

Jacoby, Russell, *Social Amnesia*. Boston: Beacon, 1975.

——————"The Politics of Crisis Theory", Telos, Spring, 1975.

Jay, Martin, *The Dialectic Imagination*. Boston: Little Brown, 1973.

Johnson, Richard, *The French C.P. Versus the Students*. New Haven: Yale, 1972.

Kalecki, Michael, "The Class Struggle and the Distribution of Income", Kylos, 1971.

——————*Selected Essays on the Dynamics of Capitalist Economy*. London: CUP, 1971.

Karol, K.S. *The Second Chinese Revolution*. New York: Hill and Wang, 1973.

Kenner, Martin and Petras, James, eds. *Fidel Castro Speaks*. New York: Grove Press, 1969

Keynes, J.M. *The General Theory*. New York: Harbinger Books.

Kolakowski, Leszak, *Towards A Marxist Humanism*. New York: Grove Press 1968.

Kollantai, Alexandra, *The Worker's Opposition*. Chicago.

Koopmans, T.C. *Three Essays on the State of Economic Science*. New York, 1957

Korsch, Karl, *Karl Marx*. London: Russell and Russell, 1963.
——————*Marxism and Philosophy*. London: NLB, 1970.
Kovel, Joel, *White Racism: A Psychohistory*. New York: Vintage, 1972.
Kropotkin, Peter, *Kropotkin's Revolutionary Essays*. Cambridge: M.I.T. 1970.
——————*Fields, Factories, and Workshops*. New York: Harper & Row, 1974.
Krupskaya, N.K. *Reminiscences of Lenin*. New York: International Publishers, 1970.
Kuhn, Thomas, *Structure of Scientific Revolutions*. Chicago, 1962.
Laing, R.D. *Politics of the Family and Other Essays*. New York: Vintage, 1969.
——————*The Politics of Experience*. London: London Books, 1970.
Langer, Elinor, "The Women of the Telephone Company". New York Review Of Books, XIV no. 5 and 6, March 12 and 26, 1970.
Lange, Oscar, *Problems of the Political Economy of Socialism*. Calcutta 1962.
Lange, Oscar, "Marxian Economics and Modern Economic Theory," Review of Economic Studies, June, 1935.
Lefebre, Henri, *Dialectical Materialism*. London: Jonathon Cape, 1968.
——————*Everyday Life in the Modern World*. New York: Harper and Row, 1971.
Lenin, Vladimir Illych, *Collected Works*. Moscow: Foreign Language Publishing House.
Lichtheim, George, *From Marx to Hegel*. New York: Seabury, 1974.
Lukacs, Georg, *Lenin*. Cambrige: M.I.T. 1971.
——————*History and Class Consciousness*. Cambridge: M.I.T. 1971.
——————*Tactics and Ethics*. New York: Harper Colophon, 1976.
——————*Marxism and Human Liberation*. New York: Dell, 1972.
Luxemburg, Rosa, *The Russian Revolution*. Ann Arbor: The University of Michigan Press.
——————*The Mass Strike and The Junius Pamphlet*. New York: Harper Torchbooks, 1971.
——————*Reform or Revolution*. New York: Pathfinder, 1970.
Lynd, Staughton and Alperovitz, Gar, *Strategy and Program*. Boston: Beacon Pr₋ss, 1973.
Lynd, Aⁿce and Staughton, *Rank and File*. Boston: Beacon, 1971.
Maletesta, Errico, *Anarchy*. London.
Mandel Ernest, *Marxist Economic Theory*. New York: MR Press, 1971.
Il Manifesto Theses, in Politics and Society, Vol. 1 no. 4, Aug. 1974.
Mao Tse Tung, *Selected Readings From The Works Of Mao Tse Tung*. Peking, 1971.
Marcovic, Mihailo, *From Affluence to Praxis*. Ann Arbor: University of Michigan Books, 1974.
Marcovic, Mihailo and Cohen, Robert S. *The Riṣe and Fall of Socialist Humanism*. London: Spokesman Books, 1975.
Marcuse, Herbert, *One Dimensional Man*. Boston: Beacon Press, 1964.
——————*An Essay on Liberation*. Boston: Beacon Press, 1969.
——————*Counter Revolution and Revolt*. Boston: Beacon Press, 1972.
Marglin, Steve, "What Do Bosses Do?", URPE Vol. 6, No. 2. New York.

Marx, Karl, *Capital.* New York: New World Paperbacks.

Marx, Karl, and Frederick Engels, *Collected Works,* New York, International Publishers.

Maslow, Abraham, *Motivation and Personality.* New York: Harper and Row, 1964.

Mattick, Paul, *Marx and Keynes.* Boston: Porter Sargent Publishers, 1969.

McAfee, Kathy and Wood, Myrna, "Bread and Roses", Somerville: New England Free Press.

McClellan, David, *Karl Marx: His Life and Thought.* New York: Harper and Row, 1973.

Meek, R. L. *Studies in the Labor Theory of Value.* London: Lawrence and Wishart, 1973.

——————*Economics and Ideology and Other Essays.* London: Chapman and Hall, 1967.

Mehring, Franz, *Karl Marx.* London, 1936.

Meisner, Maurice, "Leninism and Maoism: Some Populist Perspectives on Marxism Leninism". China Quarterly, Jan.-March, no.45, 1971.

Memmi Albert, *The Colonizer and the Colonized.* Boston: Beacon Press, 1967.

Mermelstein, David, *The Economic Crisis Reader.* New York: Vintage, 1975.

Meszaros, Istvan, *Marx's Theory of Alienation.* New York: Harper Torchbooks, 1972.

Millett, Kate, *Sexual Politics,* Garden City: Doubleday, 1970.

Miliband, Ralph, *The State in Capitalist Society.* London, 1969.

Mills, C. W. *The Marxists.* New York: Dell, 1972.

Mitchell, Juliet, *Women's Estate.* New York, Pantheon, 1971.

——————*Psychoanalysis and Feminism.* New York: Pantheon, 1974.

Moore, Barrington, *Social Origins of Dictatorship and Democracy.* Boston: Beacon Press, 1966.

Morishima, Michio, *Marx's Economics.* London: CUP, 1973.

Morgan, Robin, *Sisterhood Is Powerful.* New York: Vintage, 1970.

——————*Going Too Far.* New York: Random House, 1977.

Nove, Alex, *An Economic History of the USSR.* London: Penguin, 1969.

O'connor, James, *The Fiscal Crisis of the State.* New York: St. Martin's Press, 1973.

Ogelsby, Carl and Schaull, Richard, *Containment and Change.* New York: Macmillan, 1967.

Ogelsby, Carl, ed. *New Left Reader.* New York: Grove Press, 1972.

Ollman, Bertell, *Alienation.* London: CUP, 1971.

——————*Essays on Marx and Reich.* Forthcoming from South End Press.

Pannekoek, Anton, *Workers' Councils.* Detroit: Root and Branch.

——————*Lenin as Philosopher.* London: Merlin Press, 1975.

Pateman, Carole, *Participation and Democratic Theory.* London: CUP, 1970.

Petrovic, Gajo, *Marx in the Mid-Twentieth Century.* Garden City: Doubleday, 1967.

Poster, Mark, *Existential Marxism in Postwar France.* Princeton: Princeton University Press, 1975.

Poulantzas, Nicos, *Classes in Contemporary Capitalism.* London: NLB, 1974.

Reich, Wilhelm, *Character Analysis*. New York: Farrar, Straus, & Giroux, 1961.
——————*The Mass Psychology of Fascism*. New York: Farrar, Straus, & Giroux, 1967.
——————*The Sexual Revolution*. New York: Farrar, Straus, & Giroux, 1961.
Reiche, Reimut, *Sexuality and the Class Struggle*. London: NLB, 1970.
Ricardo, David, *The Works and Correspndence of David Ricardo*. Piero Sraffa, ed. CUP, 1951.
Richards, Vernon, *Lessons of the Spanish Revolution*. London: Freedom Press, 1972.
Robinson, Joan, *An Essay On Marxian Economics*. London: MacMillan, 1949.
——————*Economic Philosophy*. Garden City: Doubleday, 1964.
——————*Economic Heresies*. New York: Basic Books, 1971.
——————*Freedom and Necessity*. New York: Vintage, 1971.
Robinson, Paul A. *The Freudian Left: Wilhelm Reich, Geza Roheim, Herbert Marcuse*. New York: Harper and Row, 1969.
Rocker, Rudolf, *Anarcho-Syndicalism*. London.
Georgescu-Roegen, *The Entropy Law and the Economic Process*. Cambridge: Harvard University Press, 1971.
Rosenberg, Arthur, *A History of Bolshevism*. Garden City, Doubleday. 1967.
Rowbotham, Sheila. *Women, Resistance, and Revolution*. New York: Vintage, 1972.
——————*Woman's Consciousness, Man's World*. London: Penguin, 1973.
Rubin, I.I. *Essays on Marx's Theory of Value*. Detroit: Black and Red, 1972.
Samuelson, Paul, *Foundations of Welfare Economics*. Cambridge: Harvard University Press.
——————"Understanding the Marxian Notion of Exploitation". Journal of Economic Literature, vol. 9, no. 2, 1971.
——————"Wages and Interest: A Modern Dissection of Marxian Economic Models". American Economic Review, Dec. 1967.
Sartre, Jean-Paul, *Search for a Method*. New York: Vintage, 1968.
——————*Between Existentialism and Marxism*. New York: Morrow Paperbacks, 1974.
Schaff, Adam, *Marxism and the Human Individual*. New York: McGraw Hill, 1970.
Schumpeter, Joseph A. *Capitalism, Socialism, and Democracy*. London: George Allen & Unwin.
Sennet & Cobb, *The Hidden Injuries of Class*. New York: Vintage, 1972.
Serge, Victor, *Memoirs of a Revolutionary*. London: Oxford Paperbacks.
Silverman, Bertram, *ed. Man and Socialism in Cuba*. New York: Athenum, 1976.
Singer, Daniel, *Prelude to Revolution*. New York: Hill and Wang, 1976.
Smith, Adam, *The Wealth of Nations*. New York: Random House, 1937.
Spriano, Paolo, *The Occupation of the Factories*. London: Pluto Press, 1975.
Stone, Kathy, "The Origin of Job Structures in the Steel Industry", URPE Vol. 6, No. 2.
Sraffa, Piero, *The Production of Commodities by Means of Commodities*. London, CUP, 1971.

Stojanovic, Svetozar, *Between Ideas and Reality*. London: Oxford University Press, 1973.

Sweezy, Paul, *The Theory of Capitalist Development*. New York: MR Press, 1942.

Sweezy, Paul and Bettleheim, Charles, *Transition To Socialism,* MR Press, New York, 1971.

Tanzer, Michael, *The Sick Society*. New York: Holt Rhinehart and Winston, 1968.

Tax, Meredith, "Woman and Her Mind: The Story of Daily Life". Somerville: New England Free Press.

Tepperman, Jean, *Not Servants, Not Machines*. Boston: Beacon Press, 1976.

Terkel, Studs, *Working*. New York: Avon, 1972.

Thompson, E. P. *The Making of the English Working Class*. New York: Random House, 1966.

Venable, Vernon, *Human Nature: The Marxian View*. London: Meridan Books, 1946.

Voline, *The Unknown Revolution*. New York: Free Life Editions, 1974.

Walker, Pat; ed. *Between Labor and Capital*. Boston: South End Press, 1978.

Weinstein, James, *The Decline of Socialism in America 1919-1925*. New York: MR Press, 1974.

Williams, William Appleman, *The Contours of American History*. Boston: Beacon Press, 1973.

Williams, Gywn A. *Proletarian Order*. London: Pluto Press, 1975.

Zaretsky, Eli, *Capitalism, the Family, and Personal Life*. New York: Harper Colophon, 1976.

Zinn, Howard, *Disobediance and Democracy*. New York: Vintage, 1968.

INDEX

South End Press wishes to promote communication between readers and authors as well as vice versa. We are eager to pass along any criticisms, suggestions, or other written communiations related to this book. We are also concerned to help our authors reach wider audiences through speaking engagements. Please send comments, requests, or questions c/o South End Press, Box 68, Astor Station, Boston, MA 02123.

MORE TITLES FROM SOUTH END PRESS

Theatre for the 98% by Maxine Klein. A book detailing the past and future, the passion and practice of people's theatre. Includes scenarios for developing a people's theatre of celebration, newstheatre, guerilla theatre.

Ba Ye Zwa by Judy Seidman. Prints and sketches portray the struggle against apartheid in South Africa. Commentaries on day-to-day life, culture, history, and resistence.

Conversations in Maine by Grace Lee and James Boggs and Freddy and Lyman Paine. A five year dialogue seeking to understand personal transformation and the role of community and culture in revolution.

Between Labor and Capital edited by Pat Walker. Essays on class relations in the U.S. Focuses on the interface between professionals, managers, and blue collar workers. Lead article by Barbara and John Ehrenreich.

The Curious Courtship of Women's Liberation and Socialism by Batya Weinbaum. An analysis of the relation between socialist and feminist movements with special emphasis on the importance of kinship categories and the shortcomings of traditional Marxist approaches.

No Nukes! Everyone's Guide to Nuclear Power by Anna Gyorgy and Friends. A comprehensive nuclear power handbook with everything from what it is and how it works, to how to fight it: organizational lessons and strategies.

What's Wrong with the American Economy? by The Institute for Labor Education and Research. A primer for working people which looks at American capitalism in the twentieth century. Based on three years of popular courses for rank and file union members and other workers.

Reprints: **Strike!** by Jeremy Brecher and **Commensense for Hard Times** by Jeremy Brecher and Tim Costello.

Coming Soon: **Crisis in the Working Class** by John McDermott, **Social Revolution and Sexual Revolution** by Bertell Ollman, **Ecology and Freedom** by Andre' Gorz, **Women and Revolution** edited by Lydia Sargent, ...

If you are interested in more information about South End Press and the membership option we offer readers,please write us at:
South End Press, Box 68 Astor Station, Boston, Ma 02123